Filthy Rich Clients

The Java™ Series

Ken Arnold, James Gosling, David Holmes
The Java™ Programming Language, Fourth Edition

Joshua Bloch
Effective Java™ Programming Language Guide

Stephanie Bodoff, Dale Green, Kim Haase, Eric Jendrock
The J2EE™ Tutorial, Second Edition

Mary Campione, Kathy Walrath, Alison Huml
*The Java™ Tutorial, Third Edition: A Short Course on
the Basics*

Mary Campione, Kathy Walrath, Alison Huml, The
Tutorial Team
The Java™ Tutorial Continued: The Rest of the JDK™

Patrick Chan
The Java™ Developers Almanac 1.4, Volume 1

Patrick Chan
The Java™ Developers Almanac 1.4, Volume 2

Patrick Chan, Rosanna Lee
*The Java™ Class Libraries, Second Edition, Volume 2:
java.applet, java.awt, java.beans*

Patrick Chan, Rosanna Lee, Doug Kramer
*The Java™ Class Libraries, Second Edition, Volume 1:
Supplement for the Java™ 2 Platform, Standard Edition,
v1.2*

Kirk Chen, Li Gong
*Programming Open Service Gateways with Java™
Embedded Server*

Zhiqun Chen
*Java Card™ Technology for Smart Cards: Architecture
and Programmer's Guide*

Maydene Fisher, Jon Ellis, Jonathan Bruce
JDBC™ API Tutorial and Reference, Third Edition

Eric Freeman, Susanne Hupfer, Ken Arnold
JavaSpaces™ Principles, Patterns, and Practice

Li Gong, Gary Ellison, Mary Dageforde
*Inside Java™ 2 Platform Security, Second Edition:
Architecture, API Design, and Implementation*

James Gosling, Bill Joy, Guy Steele, Gilad Bracha
The Java™ Language Specification, Third Edition

Mark Hapner, Rich Burridge, Rahul Sharma, Joseph
Fialli, Kim Haase
*Java™ Message Service API Tutorial and Reference:
Messaging for the J2EE™ Platform*

Eric Jendrock, Jennifer Ball
The Java™ EE 5 Tutorial, Third Edition

Jonni Kanerva
The Java™ FAQ

Doug Lea
*Concurrent Programming in Java™, Second Edition:
Design Principles and Patterns*

Rosanna Lee, Scott Seligman
*JNDI API Tutorial and Reference: Building Directory-
Enabled Java™ Applications*

Sheng Liang
*The Java™ Native Interface: Programmer's Guide and
Specification*

Tim Lindholm, Frank Yellin
The Java™ Virtual Machine Specification, Second Edition

Roger Riggs, Antero Taivalsaari, Jim Van Peursem, Jyri
Huopaniemi, Mark Patel, Aleksi Uotila
*Programming Wireless Devices with the Java™ 2
Platform, Micro Edition, Second Edition*

Rahul Sharma, Beth Stearns, Tony Ng
*J2EE™ Connector Architecture and Enterprise
Application Integration*

Inderjeet Singh, Beth Stearns, Mark Johnson, Enterprise
Team
*Designing Enterprise Applications with the J2EE™
Platform, Second Edition*

Inderjeet Singh, Sean Brydon, Greg Murray, Vijay
Ramachandran, Thierry Violleau, Beth Stearns
*Designing Web Services with the J2EE™ 1.4 Platform:
JAX-RPC, SOAP, and XML Technologies*

Kathy Walrath, Mary Campione, Alison Huml, Sharon
Zakhour
*The JFC Swing Tutorial, Second Edition: A Guide to
Constructing GUIs*

Steve Wilson, Jeff Kesselman
Java™ Platform Performance: Strategies and Tactics

Sharon Zakhour, Scott Hommel, Jacob Royal,
Isaac Rabinovitch, Tom Risser, Mark Hoeber
*The Java™ Tutorial, Fourth Edition: A Short Course
on the Basics*

Filthy Rich Clients

Developing Animated and Graphical Effects for Desktop Java™ Applications

Chet Haase
Romain Guy

✦Addison-Wesley

Upper Saddle River, NJ • Boston • Indianapolis • San Francisco

New York • Toronto • Montreal • London • Munich • Paris • Madrid

Capetown • Sydney • Tokyo • Singapore • Mexico City

This Book Is Safari Enabled

The Safari® Enabled icon on the cover of your favorite technology book means the book is available through Safari Bookshelf. When you buy this book, you get free access to the online edition for 45 days.

Safari Bookshelf is an electronic reference library that lets you easily search thousands of technical books, find code samples, download chapters, and access technical information whenever and wherever you need it.

To gain 45-day Safari Enabled access to this book:

• Go to http://www.awprofessional.com/safarienabled
• Complete the brief registration form
• Enter the coupon code XEA8-HSPB-AJP6-RXCY-E29P

If you have difficulty registering on Safari Bookshelf or accessing the online edition, please e-mail customer-service@safaribooksonline.com.

Visit us on the Web: www.awprofessional.com

Library of Congress Cataloging-in-Publication Data

Haase, Chet.
   Filthy rich clients : developing animated and graphical effects for desktop Java applications / Chet Haase, Romain Guy.
      p.   cm.
   Includes index.
   ISBN 978-0-13-241393-0 (pbk. : alk. paper) 1. Object-oriented programming (Computer science) 2. Java (Computer program language) I. Guy, Romain. II. Title.

   QA76.73.C153H33 2007
   005.1'17—dc22   2007019818

Cover Illustration: Nathan Clement

ISBN-13: 978-0-13-241393-0
ISBN-10:   0-13-241393-0
Text printed in the United States on recycled paper at Courier in Stoughton, Massachusetts.
First printing, August 2007

For Kris

*I never quite understood book dedications to spouses/partners/families.
I mean, it always seemed like the polite thing to do, but not really necessary.
Even while I was writing the bulk of my chapters, it just seemed like something
I happened to be doing as part of my work life, completely separate from my
home life. Then came the mad, unending rush at the end and the ensuing
review and editing phase. I basically disappeared from home life
entirely for about three months. Now, I get it.*

*Thank you, Kris, for supporting me in this project; for dealing with the
house, the kids, and everything else when I was nonexistent;
and for still being here when I finally reappeared.*

—Chet

For All of My Friends

*You heard me complain one too many times about this book, but you kept
listening to me. Such a load of work could not have come at a worse time.
Thank you for helping me keep what was left of my sanity.*

For Chet

*Thank you for remaining calm and polite even though you were dying
to see me write my chapters.*

For the Swing Team I Knew

*Thank you for having faith in me and offering me
so many great opportunities.*

—Romain

Contents

Foreword

THIS is a book about creating beautiful applications. Not just blizzards of text boxes and buttons in some nondescript standard look-and-feel, but applications that are truly beautiful.

If you wind the clock back enough years, the world of graphical user interfaces was ruled by standardized look-and-feel specifications. This approach was taken in an effort to centralize all of the GUI coding in applications, make it easy to document the applications (everyone knows what a slider does, therefore it doesn't need to be described), and work around the relatively poor graphics performance of desktop computers.

But the last decade's collision between the computer industry and the consumer has led to a huge increase in the emphasis on aesthetics in user interfaces: for everything from brand awareness to increasing the comprehensibility of sophisticated systems, to eye-catching coolness to draw the customer in, to just plain "Wow!" . . . Aesthetics are *in*.

Combine this with the phenomenal increase in computer power that Moore's Law has brought us, especially as it has been expressed in the performance of commodity graphics rendering hardware, and you've got a huge range of entertaining programming possibilities.

There's a lot of subtlety in this, from "What makes a beautiful interface?" and "How do I make the pixels beautiful?" to "How do I make this fast?" This book covers all of these topics and more. For me, this is the kind of programming task that counts as pure pleasure. I'm sure it will bring you pleasure, too.

—*James Gosling*

Preface

WELCOME to *Filthy Rich Clients*. This book is about building better, more effective, and cooler desktop applications using graphical and animated effects. We started writing this book after our successful session on the topic at the JavaOne conference in 2006. The session explored the use of animation, advanced 2D effects, and even some 3D effects to create richer applications. But it seemed we could have spoken for days on the subject. Understanding why you should develop such applications, how the technologies that enable them work, and how you can properly develop effects that enable Filthy Rich Clients is, well, a rich topic indeed.

Hence, this book. Now we get to spend the next many pages with you, discussing fundamentals of Java, Swing, Java 2D, graphics, graphical user interfaces (GUIs), animation, performance, and advanced effects that build on all of these fundamentals in order to create beautiful applications.

Please join us for the ride. It should be fun.

Organization

The book has a sequential flow from beginning to end, so readers may want to work through it in that order, at least to understand how the material is arranged. There are plenty of code snippets and discussions in the book that are also appropriate for random access, although the technology behind any particular item might relate back to earlier discussions in the book. These relationships are generally noted when they arise so that you can more easily refer back to earlier material as background.

The original intent of the book was to explain the cool effects that we show mostly toward the end of the book. But there is currently no book, to our knowledge, that explains the background of Swing, graphics, Java 2D rendering, and animation that is necessary to understand how the effects work. So we start at the beginning. We develop the fundamentals in these areas early on, building upon them as we go, so that by the time you read the material at the end of the book, everything should make sense.[1]

This book provides not only plenty of snazzy example effects you can use to create Filthy Rich Clients but also the knowledge of how it all works so that you can go further on your own.

Part I: Graphics and GUI Fundamentals

Part I covers the fundamental concepts of Java graphics and user interface programming that we use throughout the rest of the book. A comprehensive description of graphics and user interface development is beyond the scope of this book, but we cover the basic areas that enable Filthy Rich Clients sufficiently to get everyone up to speed with the APIs, techniques, and details necessary to understand the later chapters that build upon these elements.

If you have a solid understanding of AWT, Java 2D, and Swing already, some of the material at the beginning of this section may be old hat for you. However, we build upon these basic concepts as we go. Also, there are plenty of interesting, deep tidbits throughout the book that should be useful to all Desktop Java programmers.

Part II: Advanced Graphics Rendering

Part II covers more advanced topics in Java 2D and Swing that are useful in creating rich interfaces. The first half of Part II covers graphics-specific technologies of composites, gradients, and image processing. The second half of Part II covers more Swing-focused technologies: the glass pane, layered panes, and the repaint manager.

Part III: Animation

A Filthy Rich Client is not static; it is alive. It needs to move. It needs to transition. It needs a heartbeat so that the user knows it is there. Looking good is half the battle. Looking alive is the rest of it.

---

1. Think of it as a `GeneralPath` to enlightenment.

Part III is about the fundamentals of animation that you can use to bring your applications to life. We cover some of the basics of animating graphics and GUIs, discuss the existing facilities in the Java SE core libraries for assisting in developing animations, and cover the Timing Framework library that makes developing animations in Java much easier.

Part IV: Effects

Part IV builds upon everything covered in the earlier parts of the book. Effects are at the core of Filthy Rich Clients, making the difference between a mere rich client and a Filthy Rich Client. The effects are grouped into two categories. The first category is static effects, which use graphics techniques for a richer look in applications. The second category is dynamic, or animated, effects for making GUIs move. We also cover Animated Transitions, another animated effect that is enabled through a utility library available on the book's Web site. The section ends with a chapter that shows how a sample Filthy Rich Client was developed, from initial design diagrams through implementation of the various effects.

Style

We have adopted an informal writing style for the book because we really feel that we are talking to you, the reader. It is not unusual for one of us to use the word "I" in any particular passage in the book. The trick is to figure out which one of us is speaking. It really doesn't matter, of course, and you probably don't care. But in case you do, here's a hint: The pictures and screenshots in Romain's sections are generally more attractive, and there are more footnotes and raw text in Chet's sections. These differences map well to our characters: Romain has a great aesthetic sense and takes beautiful pictures, and Chet talks a lot.

Reader Requirements

Experience with the Java language and Swing is helpful. This book is not a primer on those subjects but rather assumes some familiarity with Java and Swing. However, some of the rendering fundamentals of Swing, which are important to understand in creating Filthy Rich Clients, may not be evident to even advanced Swing programmers, so the first couple of chapters of the book are devoted to explaining how Swing and Java 2D work together to create the kinds of customizable effects that we explore throughout the rest of the book.

External Resources

We have compiled information relevant to the book on the Web site http:// filthyrichclients.org. This site has everything from demos to utility libraries used in the book to other information about the book and related technologies as appropriate. We're positive there are absolutely no miisteakes in this book, but if a miracle occurs and we're wrong about that, expect the errata to show up on this Web site.

Web Site Code

The book is full of demo code.[2] There are snippets of code spread throughout the pages. In most cases, this code is copied from demos that are posted on the book's Web site. Where we refer to an available demo in the text, look for an "Online Demo" icon, like the one next to this paragraph, and the project name to look for on the book's Web site. Each of these demo projects contains the build-able and runnable source code that allows you to see the application in action as well as to use the code as you see fit in your projects. The demos are not just trivial items to ignore. We expect you to go to the Web site and check things out. We specifically developed the demos hand-in-hand with writing the book, and the material in the software on the Web site integrates well with the book material throughout every chapter.

Web Site Libraries

There are also utility libraries used and described in the book. These libraries are useful for some of the demos we developed, but more importantly they are intended to be used as standalone libraries for your projects.

These libraries are available in ongoing development projects on other Web sites, listed below, but versions are provided on the book's Web site, http://

---

2. How full is it? It's so full that our code font got so exhausted it caught mono. It's so full that we edited the book by running lint on it. It's so full that you could probably compile the text in the book if it weren't for all of these annoying footnotes.

filthyrichclients.org, that match the version used in the book. These libraries include:

Timing Framework: This library is described in detail in two chapters in this book (hint: look for the chapters whose names begin with the words "Timing Framework"). The project is being developed at http://timingframework.dev.java.net, but a specific version of the library that matches the one used for the code and descriptions in this book is available on the book's Web site.

Animated Transitions: This library is described toward the end of the book in Chapter 18, cleverly named "Animated Transitions." Again, this project will probably also be available on java.net, although it is not yet posted at the time of this writing. But regardless, a version that matches that described in the book will be available on the book's Web site.

Other Projects

There are many projects out there that would be good to investigate in the pursuit of Filthy Rich Clients, but some in particular are mentioned in the book and used in some of our demos:

SwingLabs: Many of the utilities mentioned in the context of demos and snippets in the book are available on the SwingLabs Web site. Be sure to check out these and other technologies at http://swinglabs.dev.java.net.

JOGL: The Java bindings for OpenGL library provides a way to write 3D applications and effects in Java using the OpenGL API and hardware acceleration across most platforms on which Java runs. You can find JOGL at http://jogl.dev.java.net.

Other Web Resources

We both post irregularly but often to our blogs. When you want to know more about graphics, performance, Java 2D, and Java Desktop Client technologies in general, go visit Chet's technical blog at http://weblogs.java.net/blog/chet/. When you want to see more exciting visuals, go check out the latest Swing demos and discussions on Romain's English-friendly blog at www.curious-creature.org.

You will find invaluable information on those two Web sites that perfectly complements the book. You may even get the chance to read sneak previews of sequels to this book without even knowing it. In fact, we won't know it either when we post the entries, so we'll be even.

If you enjoy reading some of this book's footnotes, please check out Chet's informal humor blog at http://chetchat.blogspot.com. Finally, if you are lucky enough to read French, do not hesitate to visit Romain's French blog at www.progx.org, which is an absurd mix of funny stories and programming advice.

Acknowledgments

THE authors would like to thank everyone they have ever known, but it would take entirely too much time and space. Instead, we limit it to the people who have directly helped influence the technologies, content, style, and fixes to typos in this book.

First of all, we would like to thank the reviewers of the book. These people spent countless hours reading through many pages of manuscript in a valiant attempt to help us make the book as good and as accurate as possible. I wish I had a picture of Scott Violet when he was reading Chapter 3 in the gym, between sets on the bench press. Some of the Sun experts who kicked into this effort include Bob Eckstein, Scott Violet, Chris Campbell, Dmitri Trembovetski, Amy Fowler, Jim Graham, Phil Race, and Hans Muller. Also we want to thank Ken Russell, who helped us with the 3D content in the original JavaOne presentation from which this book was born. It was fantastic (if sometimes painful) to have the creators and implementers of the technologies we describe correcting us where we went astray. The technical lashings, er, reviews of Jim Graham were particularly thorough and helpful. Also, Bob Eckstein's reviews on style were extremely helpful in making the whole book flow better. We also had plenty of assistance from outside of Sun, including help from Jan Haderka, Jeff Kurtz, Guillaume Laforge, Ido Green, Natasha Lloyd, Daniel Klein, Dimitri Baeli, James Lemieux, Bill Snyder, Chris Brown, Jean-Laurent de Morlhon, Jan Bösenberg, and Jean-Baptiste Freymann.

We also thank the people who have helped with brainstorming, testing, design reviewing, and heartily criticizing our technical work in many painful ways. Utilities like the Timing Framework and Animated Transitions would not be the same without their incessant complaints. This long list of people includes many of the people mentioned previously as reviewers in addition to Vincent Hardy, Richard Bair, and Joshua Marinacci from Sun and the following people from outside of Sun: Dieter Krachtus, Stuart Scott, and Stephen Lum. There are many other people who kicked in good suggestions and feedback on our work, but we want to call out these folks in particular who helped out in suggesting and reviewing design changes for various Timing Framework features. We should also mention Chris Campbell specifically, since his work on the `Interpolators` and `Evaluators` in the Timing Framework helped to drastically simplify the way nonlinear interpolation works in the library.

Thanks also to Craig Aspinall, who kindly donated his filthyrichclients.com domain name so that life would be less confusing for people who went looking for the Web site associated with this book. Both filthyrichclients.com and filthyrichclients.org will point to the same site and offer plenty of resources for people who want to make their Swing applications filthy.

We thank all of the people who read our blogs and give us useful feedback. Although these technologies are fun to play with regardless, at the end of the day we want to improve the lives of developers, so hearing from the outside world about the things that developers need is critical. Large portions of this book would not have been possible without our astute readers.

Thanks also go to the java.sun.com and java.net Web sites, both of which have published original articles upon which portions of this book were based. We would like to specifically thank java.net editors Chris Adamson and Daniel Steinberg for their help with our articles for that site and Sun Microsystem's Laureen Hudson, java.sun.com editor extraordinaire and generally funny person. If writing articles for those sites were not so enjoyable, this book probably would not exist right now.

Oh, and thank *you* for purchasing and reading this book. It's fun playing with this stuff and writing about it, but even more fun when people can listen in and play along. Now let us help you to make your applications a bit more Filthy Rich.

About the Authors

Chet Haase is a client architect in the Java SE group at Sun Microsystems. He works with all of the desktop Java technologies, including Swing and Java 2D, and helps figure out how to improve the platform going forward. His passion in software is graphics, and he has spent most of his career (apart from a short stint just after college, when he realized just how dull "network analysis" is) working with graphics technologies of all kinds, from 2D to 3D and from the application down to the driver level. Chet received his B.A. in mathematics from Carleton College and his M.S. in computer and information sciences from the University of Oregon.

Romain Guy wrote this book during his final year at school and should obtain his M.S. in computer science in the Fall of 2007. His passion in software is graphics and graphical user interface development, and he has spent many years working with Java and Swing. Romain cannot stand still and has worked as a freelance journalist for programming magazines for years, as a book translator for O'Reilly, as a Java teacher in a French university, as a videogame developer, as a freelance developer, as a software engineer on the Swing Team at Sun Microsystems, and as a software engineer at Google. His new passion is digital photography.

Introduction

This is not a book on data binding.[1]

Rich Clients

We should describe what we mean by *Filthy Rich Clients*. But first, we need to describe what rich clients are. *Rich clients* is a phrase commonly associated with desktop applications. Rich client applications are usually contrasted with *thin client* or *Web client* applications, which are essentially software applications running on the server with a simple front end that runs in a browser on the user's desktop.

Rich client applications have more of the program logic and functionality local to the user's desktop machine. On one extreme, the application may be all local, such as a word-processing application or photo-editing software. Or the application may run in the client-server world, as do thin client applications. The data may still be provided by the server, and important functionality may still come from a server, a database, the network, or wherever. But the local application is

---

1. We figured we should be honest about this disclaimer. When we described the book and its outline in a blog entry, we received a comment that, in fact, the book should be about data binding. While the interaction of Java Desktop applications with data sources is an interesting and critical area to discuss, it's really not what this book is about. At all. If you opened *Filthy Rich Clients* assuming that it would talk about data binding, you might want to close the book and look on a nearby shelf for other books instead. Or change your mind now and realize that this book will be a lot more fun to read.

1

responsible for much more of the logic, user interface, and interactivity than is a typical Web client.

The distinction between Web and rich clients is an important one because there are trade-offs with each approach that application developers must be aware of in deciding which route to go with their products. The trade-offs vary between different application domains, systems, and technologies but basically boil down to the following:

Web Clients

These applications look like simple Web pages to the user. Their great advantage is their simplicity. They may start up faster than rich clients, taking just the time that it takes for the server to process information and send it over the network to the user's computer. These applications also tend to have a simple, browser-oriented graphical user interface (GUI). This simplicity comes at a cost, however. The application model tends to be very standard: Each page has content, fields for the user to fill in, and buttons to submit information back to the server. The interaction model tends to be batch-oriented: The user sends information, the server processes the information, and the resulting page is sent back to the user. Significant delays in interaction can occur with this complete-send-process-return-display application model.

Rich Clients

These applications have a very "rich" user experience, taking advantage of native facilities of the user's desktop computer, such as graphics hardware acceleration, to provide a more robust and full-featured application experience than is provided by Web clients. Rich client applications can sometimes take longer to start up than a simple Web page because there is more going on in the application, and the GUIs tend to be more involved than Web GUIs because there is more happening in the application than in simple Web-oriented applications. The interaction model is quite different because much of the logic of the application is local, even if the application is talking to a server on the back end.

Lately, a new model has emerged for Web clients, called Asynchronous Java-Script and XML (AJAX), where much of the client-server interaction can be handled in parallel with the user's interacting with each Web page. This transparent client-server interaction can allow for dynamically updated Web pages instead of the more tedious complete-send-process-return-display model of traditional Web client applications. However, this model is still limited by the browser container in which the application lives and by many of the constraints that that browser model places on the application, including the extent to which JavaScript features are supported, the security model of the browser, and the physical GUI of the browser container around the application.

AJAX applications are starting to explore some of the Filthy Rich features described in this book, including some graphical effects in their GUIs. This is obviously great. We believe that these features can make much more useable applications. But given the browser constraints of AJAX, it is still a Web client technology, and we focus our discussion on the rich client model instead.

Filthy Rich Clients

Filthy Rich Clients is a term that we coined to refer to applications that are so graphically rich that they ooze cool. They suck users in from the outset and hang onto them with a death grip of excitement. They make users tell their friends about the applications. In short, they make users actually *enjoy* their application experience. When was the last time you enjoyed using a software application? Maybe you need more Filthy Rich Clients in your life.

The keys to Filthy Rich Clients are graphical and animated effects. These kinds of effects provide ways of enhancing the user experience of the application through more attractive GUIs, dynamic effects that give your application a pulse, and animated transitions that keep your user connected to the logical flow of the application.

We are not just talking about media players here. We are talking about enhancing *all* kinds of software, from typical enterprise form-based applications to the most gratuitously whizzy consumer application. All applications could benefit from thinking about the user experience and how to apply Filthy Rich effects in ways to improve that experience.

As an example of Filthy Rich Client effects and a shameless teaser for content you will see later in the book, let's see some screenshots (Figures I-1 through I-7).

"Effectives": Effects Enabling More Productive Applications

Graphical effects, especially animated ones, can be overdone. The last thing that a user wants is for everything in an application to be blinking, swooping, pulsing, and fading constantly. The techniques we outline in this book can, if misused,

Figure I-1 Chapter 10, "Layered Panes," shows how to support multiple layers of information in your user interface.

Figure I-2 Reflection, discussed in Chapter 11, "Repaint Manager," brings realism and richness to an application.

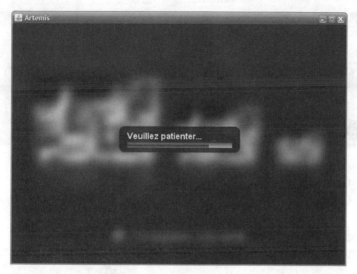

Figure 1-3 The blur effect, discussed in Chapter 16, "Static Effects," can be useful for focusing the user's attention on nonblurred items.

Figure I-4 The Aerith application, available in source and binary form at http://aerith.dev.java.net, demonstrates many of the effects and techniques discussed in this book.

Figure I-5 Aerith's loading screen demonstrates the pulsating effect discussed in Chapter 17, "Dynamic Effects."

Figure I-6 The bloom effect is applied to Aerith's loading screen, as discussed in Chapter 17.

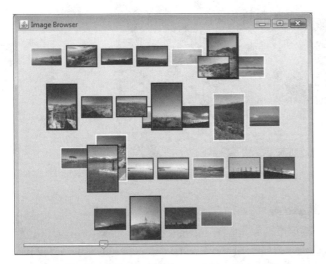

Figure I-7 Chapter 18, "Animated Transitions," discusses automating animations between different states of a GUI. Here, a change in thumbnail sizes causes the pictures to automatically and smoothly animate to their new locations and sizes in the window.

contribute to this horror show. We show how to enrich the graphics and animate anything you want. We also discuss how to do so *effectively*, making sure to enrich applications in sensible ways. It is important that you make the application more effective for the user, not just effect-ridden. Done right, the addition of graphical effects to an application can really draw users in and keep them there.

Note that this book does not attempt to cover the deep topic of interface design. We touch on this topic in the context of particular effects and techniques as we discuss them, but if you wish to know more about designing user interfaces, check out some of the great books out there on the subject. You might start with Chapter 19 of this book, however, which discusses the UI design process used in developing a particular application.

Why Java and Swing for Filthy Rich Clients?

The techniques that we discuss in this book apply to most graphically oriented development toolkits. Anything that allows you to change the appearance of the GUI elements of your application can take advantage of the approaches explored here.

However, we have developed the sample code, the utility frameworks, and most of the techniques around the programming environment of Java and Swing. Swing is the library of classes for developing GUIs for Desktop Java applications. Swing's great advantage over other GUI toolkits is its flexibility and customization. These capabilities are exploited to a great extent in this book as we explore how to use custom rendering and animation to create great-looking effects in applications.

Part I

Graphics and GUI Fundamentals

Desktop Java Graphics APIs: Swing, AWT, and Java 2D

$\mathbf{M}$AYBE it is because I am a graphics geek, but I always find it useful to have a picture in my mind of how the various pieces of libraries fit together. Bear with me while I create and describe such a diagram for the Desktop Java Graphics APIs.

In Figure 1-1, the interesting bit is in the middle: Swing, AWT, and Java 2D interact to provide the graphics and user interface libraries that your application, the piece on top, uses. Swing, Java 2D, and AWT are themselves running on top of the Java Runtime Environment, which includes the Java Virtual Machine as well as other Java libraries. The end result of all of these libraries is that your application can create windows, user interface components, and graphics that are displayed on the user's monitor without that application knowing anything about the window system APIs of the underlying native platform.

Although the layer cake diagram in Figure 1-1 is beautiful in its own right,[1] it is probably worth going into a bit more detail on these desktop libraries.

---

1. Romain would debate this point.

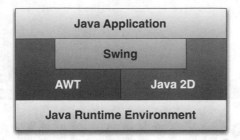

Figure 1-1   Desktop Java Graphics APIs: The layer cake.

Abstract Window Toolkit (AWT)

The AWT library was the first graphical user interface (GUI) toolkit that shipped with Java, available in version 1.0 of the Java Runtime Environment. At that time, AWT was the only core library for user interface programming in Java; any desktop applications that needed user interfaces would use AWT to create and display windows, buttons, and other GUI components. AWT provides this capability by calling upon the native libraries on the user's system to create and display these GUI components. For example, an AWT `java.awt.Window` on the X Windows System is actually an X window[2] underneath. AWT is also responsible for the input event mechanisms of the user interface, such as handling mouse clicks and keyboard events. Events that occur in the native window system are received by the AWT implementation and are then forwarded to Java applications as AWT events.

AWT lives on and can be used now exactly as it was in the beginning (ah, the glories of backwards compatibility!), although it has since taken on more of an infrastructure role for applications that use the Swing GUI toolkit. That is, you can still use AWT to create windows and GUI components, but most current Desktop Java applications use Swing, because Swing provides a more flexible and powerful GUI development environment. However, AWT is still a critical piece of the overall pie; it continues to provide the important platform-specific capabilities that Swing depends on. For example, Swing windows, using Swing's `JFrame` component, use AWT to create the actual window on the screen. AWT also provides certain core functionalities that Swing and desktop applications depend on, such as the event mechanism, cut and paste, drag and drop, keyboard focus management, and input management.

---

2. Not an ex-Window; that's what you get when the application exits.

In Figure 1-1, we can see, from the Java application's standpoint, that AWT may be used both directly, using AWT APIs such as the event mechanism, and indirectly, using Swing APIs that may depend on AWT functionality underneath.

Java 2D

Java 2D, introduced in the JDK 1.2 release, is the graphics library of Java. Whereas AWT included basic drawing APIs in JDK 1.0, Java 2D goes much further and covers a broad set of operations, including basic and advanced drawing operations, image manipulation, text, and printing. We describe these features in more detail later, but for the purposes of this section, Java 2D handles Swing's rendering operations. So, for example, when a Swing button wants to look like a Swing button, it makes calls into Java 2D to draw the background, the border, and the text for that button. In Figure 1-1, we can see that Java 2D methods can be called directly by the application and indirectly through its support of Swing functionality.

Swing

Swing, like Java 2D, was also introduced in JDK 1.2. Swing is the main GUI library used by today's Desktop Java developers. Swing is a *lightweight toolkit*, which means that the Swing components you see in your application, such as buttons, checkboxes, and scrollbars, do not correspond to native components as they do in AWT. This detail is completely irrelevant for the end user; if it looks like a component, clicks like a component, and responds like a component, then it is a component. But the difference is a very important one for Filthy Rich Client applications, as we shall see. The distinction here is that Swing's lightweight components are drawn using Java 2D, and they can have their drawing customized, which leads to applications that look and behave in much more interesting ways.

Swing's relation to AWT for platform-specific GUI functionality, such as the underlying top-level windows, and Java 2D, for drawing the actual Swing components, is illustrated in Figure 1-1. The application may call Swing methods directly, but the functionality of these methods is handled through combinations of AWT and Java 2D calls underneath.

2

Swing Rendering Fundamentals

THIS chapter covers the basics of Swing rendering, by which your Swing application paints the user interface that appears on the display. We cover the following topics:

- *Events:* The way that Swing receives and processes events is key to understanding how threads interact within Swing and how your application threads interact with Swing and AWT events.

- *Painting:* Swing painting is the process by which Swing manages application and system requests to update the display.

- *Rendering:* Swing rendering is the process by which Swing calls its own internal code as well as your application code in order to render components' contents.

- *Double-Buffering:* Swing uses a back buffer to ensure smooth updates to the screen.

- *Threading:* The Event mechanism is explored in more detail, and ways of interacting effectively with the Swing GUI thread are examined.

Note: The sample code in this chapter uses some concepts of Java 2D that we have not yet developed, such as graphics state and drawing primitives. We discuss these topics in depth in Chapter 3, "Graphics Fundamentals," but the basic idea is simple: All rendering operations use a Graphics object, usually supplied to you by Swing; set appropriate attributes on it, such as the color; and draw objects with it, such as a line.

Events

Events in Java can come from the native system, such as a window becoming visible or keyboard input, or from Java itself, such as an application-spawned request. All of these events are put onto a queue of events. The object `java.awt.EventQueue` is responsible for pulling the events off of this queue and dispatching them as appropriate. The dispatch mechanism of `EventQueue` is run on a single thread, called the Event Dispatch Thread (EDT). Figure 2-1 shows the event posting and processing mechanisms.

As we see later in the section "Threading," it is important for applications to interact efficiently and intelligently with this event system. For example, all GUI-related work, such as the painting process we are about to describe, must happen on the EDT. System events related to the GUI are posted onto the event queue and dispatched on the EDT. Any work that an application needs to do that involves modifying the GUI must also be processed on the EDT, which involves wrapping the request in an event and posting it onto the event queue.

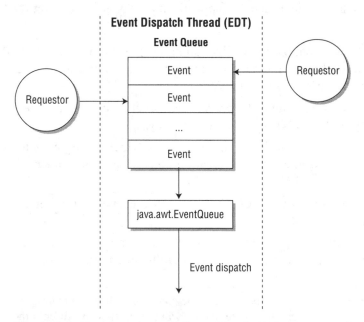

Figure 2-1 Event posting and dispatching in Swing happens via the `EventQueue`, which runs on the Event Dispatch Thread (EDT).

Swing Painting

Painting in Swing is the process by which your application updates the display. This process could involve some of your code, if you have any custom painting behavior, or may involve only Swing internal code that knows how to repaint the standard components. The process consists of a paint request being posted onto the event queue and results in calls to the `paint()` and `paintComponent()` methods on the EDT for each Swing component affected.

Painting requests originate in one of two ways: The Swing or AWT libraries themselves may post a repaint request, or the application code may post such a request. Swing and AWT request a repaint in response to some event in the native system or the GUI components. For example, when an application window first appears on the screen, or when it is resized or exposed on the screen, AWT receives a native expose event and issues a Java event to have the window paint itself. Similarly, when the state of a component changes, such as when a button is pressed, Swing issues a paint request to make sure that the button is displayed in a pressed state. Applications can also issue a paint request to Swing directly; this type of request is done in situations in which the application code may know, on the basis of changes in some internal state, that the display should change.

In general, painting happens automatically; Swing detects when a component's contents have been altered such that the component needs to be repainted. Your application does not normally need to issue paint requests to Swing unless it knows that there has been some change to the display state that would not automatically trigger a repaint. For example, if you change the text in a `JLabel` component, Swing knows to repaint that label with the new text. But if your application has detected a change to some internal variable, such as a variable that affects the translucency of a component, then it might need to tell Swing that a paint should be performed.

There are a handful of methods in components that are used to initiate painting. These methods fall into two main categories: *asynchronous requests* and *synchronous requests*.

Asynchronous Repaint Requests

These requests work by telling Swing what needs to be updated and letting Swing handle the details of scheduling those requests and combining the requests as appropriate.[1] All of the asynchronous requests are variants of the `repaint()` method. There are several of these methods, but they basically come in two flavors: those that request the entire component be updated and those that specify an area that needs to be updated.

Component.repaint()

This variant is the easiest function to deal with; it tells Swing that the entire component, whichever one you specified to be repainted, must be updated. It is important to note that repaint requests get "coalesced," or combined. So, for example, if you request a repaint and there is already one on the queue that has not yet been serviced, then the second request is ignored because your request for a repaint will already be fulfilled by the earlier request. This behavior is particularly helpful in situations where many repaint requests are being generated, perhaps by very different situations and components, and Swing should avoid processing redundant requests and wasting effort.

The downside to `repaint()` is that it tells Swing that the *entire* component area must be updated. If the component is a container, the ensuing call to `paint()` will cause each of the child components to update themselves. This is fine in situations where repaints do not happen often or the GUI is not very complex. But in performance-sensitive cases, you probably want to avoid painting more than is completely necessary, and you may want to use the following variant instead to constrain Swing to repaint only the content that needs to be updated.

Component.repaint(int x, int y, int width, int height)

This method asks Swing to repaint the specified rectangle in the component. This repaint request, like that of the version of `repaint()` with no arguments, also gets coalesced with any other repaint requests. This version is the best method to call when you want only a subregion of the component to be repainted. For example, if you are copying an image from one area of the component to another and nothing else is changing in the display, then you only need to update the old location (to erase it) and the new location (to display the image there). In this case, you can call `repaint()` with a rectangle that spans both locations or call it twice with rectangles for each individual area.

---

1. This information was mentioned just a few short sentences ago, but Swing architect Scott Violet wanted me to be very clear: you typically do *not* need to tell Swing to paint; it usually knows. There are situations in which you might want to schedule a repaint request specifically, but that is not the typical case.

The simpler `repaint()` method is equivalent to calling `repaint(0, 0, getWidth(), getHeight())`.

Synchronous Paint Requests

The synchronous methods of painting must be handled with care. As we see later in the section "Threading," painting of Swing components *must* happen on the EDT. By calling these synchronous paint methods, your code is implying that it is on the correct thread so that the right things will happen at the right time. If the calling code is not on that correct thread, the results could be undefined.[2]

Okay, so we've warned you. Assuming that you know what you're doing, there can be valid reasons for using synchronous painting. For example, you may be in the middle of a method that you know has been called on the EDT, such as handling an input event, and need to repaint as part of that request. Instead of tossing a request onto the `EventQueue` that gets processed later, you could immediately handle the paint and get on with life. That's where the `paintImmediately()` methods come in:

`JComponent.paintImmediately(int x, int y, int w, int h)`
`JComponent.paintImmediately(Rectangle r)`

These methods are equivalent; they both specify the rectangular area that needs to be updated. `paintImmediately()` is the only method that you should need to call to force a synchronous paint of a component's contents. This method tells the component that the specified area must be updated; Swing calls `paint()` internally on all of the appropriate components to make this happen.

The disadvantage of calling `paintImmediately()`, apart from the constraint of having to be on the EDT when you call it, is that it executes the paint call, well, *immediately*. This means that there is no coalescing of paint requests that you would otherwise get through calling the asynchronous repaint mechanisms described earlier.

`Component.paint(Graphics)`

`paint()` should generally *not* be called in the normal course of events in a Swing program. However, we mention it here because there is a specific case in which it is sometimes useful to call paint: when you want to render a Swing

---

2. Undefined is a Bad Thing. Here, it could mean anything from painting being incorrect to exceptions being thrown to deadlocks to plagues to hordes of locusts.

component to an image instead of to its usual place in the Swing window. This is a useful technique in Filthy Rich Clients, as we see later in Chapter 18, "Animated Transitions."

Swing Rendering

The Swing rendering model is straightforward and centers on Swing's single-threaded painting model. First, the paint request is placed onto the event queue, as described previously. Sometime later, on the EDT, the event is dispatched to the Swing `RepaintManager` object, which calls `paint()` on the appropriate component. That paint call results in a component painting first its own content, then its border, and finally any components that it contains (which are called its children). This process is shown in Figure 2-2.

In this way, an entire hierarchy of components, from the `JFrame` down to the lowliest button, gets rendered. Note that this is a back-to-front method of painting, where the backmost content (starting with the `JFrame` itself) gets rendered,

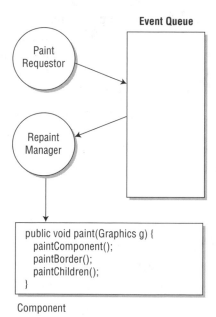

Figure 2-2 Swing painting: Repaint request is handled by the `RepaintManager`, which calls `paint()` on the component, which then renders its content, its border, and its children.

then the items in that component, then the items in that component, and so on, until the frontmost components get displayed.[3]

The trick is figuring out where your application needs to plug into this system in order to get the right stuff painted at the right time. There are three things that your application should be concerned about:

- **JComponent.paintComponent(Graphics):** Applications that have components with any custom rendering, such as Filthy Rich Clients, may need to override this method to perform that custom rendering. This rendering might include drawing graphics inside a canvas, but it also includes doing anything custom to a standard component, such as rendering a gradient for the background of a button. Standard Swing components already handle this functionality for their graphics, so it is only for the case of custom components with specialized rendering that this method must be overridden.

- **Component.paint(Graphics):** For the most part, Swing applications do not override `paint()` directly, unlike older AWT applications. However, there are important situations for Filthy Rich Clients when overriding `paint()` is crucial because by doing so we can set up the graphics state that will be used by a component and its children.

- **JComponent.setOpaque(boolean):** Applications may need to call `setOpaque(false)` on a component depending on whether the component's rectangular bounds are not completely opaque. This action ensures that Swing does the right thing for nonopaque components by rendering contents behind the component appropriately. Note that all Swing components except for `JLabel` are opaque by default.

Let's look at these three items more closely.

paintComponent()

Overriding `paintComponent()` is arguably the most important concept to understand in writing custom Swing components, particularly for applications that are Filthy Rich Clients. It is possible, even typical, to write a Swing application without overriding `paintComponent()`, but doing so assumes that you are using

---

3. In graphics, this method is known as the painter's algorithm, where a scene, like that in an oil painting, is rendered from back to front, with the objects in front covering the objects in the background. Of course, this method doesn't apply to all paintings. Watercolors, for example, do not work well with this algorithm because all of the colors blend together instead of covering (the Swing equivalent would be if all components were translucent). And many modern paintings, such as those by Jackson Pollock, appear to use algorithms that are more reminiscent of rendering artifacts.

the stock Swing components without any modification. Setting label text, setting cell information for tables, creating and using menus, creating buttons—all of these functions work fine with standard Swing components. However, the moment you want to customize anything at all, including rendering any graphics in a drawing area of a component, then you need a mechanism for performing painting. That mechanism is paintComponent(). But sometimes overriding paint() is useful and necessary.

The way that your code performs GUI or graphics operations in cooperation with the Swing threading model is by performing your GUI-related operations on the EDT. This calling mechanism is paintComponent(); whenever your component needs to be updated, your component's paintComponent() method receives a call from Swing on the EDT. Inside this method, you perform whatever operations are necessary to make your component look correct.

Let's look at some examples.

In the first example, the OvalComponent application on the book's Web site, let us assume a simple situation of a custom component that is essentially a blank canvas to fill. On it we will draw a gray oval, as seen in Figure 2-3.

Since Swing does not offer such a standard component, we are going to create a custom component that extends JComponent to handle this rendering for us.

```
public class OvalComponent extends JComponent {
  public void paintComponent(Graphics g) {
    g.setColor(getBackground());
    g.fillRect(0, 0, getWidth(), getHeight());
    g.setColor(Color.GRAY);
    g.fillOval(0, 0, getWidth(), getHeight());
  }
}
```

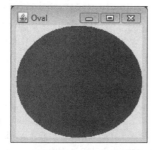

Figure 2-3 Swing rendering into a completely custom component.

In this simple example, we set the color to the component's current background color and fill the area, set the color to gray, fill the oval, and we're done. Note that this code does not call `super.paintComponent()`; our override is completely responsible for drawing the contents of this component. Obviously, real applications would try to draw something more interesting than a gray oval, but the process for drawing in any custom component's drawing area would be very similar.

Another interesting example is one in which we enhance the rendering of an otherwise standard GUI widget. Here, instead of drawing on a blank canvas as we just did, we supplement the standard display of this component's UI.

In this example, the `HighlightedButton` demo on the book's Web site, we rely on Swing to paint a button, but we customize its look slightly (Figures 2-4 and 2-5).

Figure 2-4 Standard and customized `JButtons`.

Figure 2-5 Zoomed-in view of highlight detail from Figure 2-4.

In Figure 2-4, we see two `JButtons`. One button, labeled Standard, is drawn entirely by Swing. The other button, labeled Highlighted, is rendered both by Swing and by our `paintComponent()` method. The second button shows a subtle highlight effect, which was achieved by drawing an image with a radial gradient; the gradient progresses from transparent to opaque white in the middle.

Here is the code for instantiating the two buttons in the `JFrame`:

```
f.add(new JButton("Standard"));
f.add(new HighlightedButton("Highlighted"));
```

And here is the relevant code of HighlightedButton:

```
// Earlier declaration of highlight image
BufferedImage highlight;

public class HighlightedButton extends JButton {
  public void paintComponent(Graphics g) {
    // defer to superclass to paint standard button graphics
    super.paintComponent(g);

    // superimpose highlight on top of standard button
    g.drawImage(highlight, getWidth()/4, getHeight()/4, null);
  }
}
```

This paintComponent() method is all of the code necessary to get this customized behavior; we create a class that extends a standard Swing JButton and then override paintComponent() in that class to perform custom rendering. In this case, we rely on Swing to paint the main button contents with a call to super.paintComponent(g) and then add our own touch with the single call to drawImage(), which paints the highlight image on top.

In fact, the only nontrivial, and hence more interesting, part of this example is how we create the highlight image. We use a RadialGradientPaint, new in Java SE 6, along with a translucent BufferedImage to do this. We discuss these techniques later in the book, so we won't go into that detail here, but check out the example code for this application on the book's Web site if you can't stand the suspense.

paint()

Overriding paint() is not necessary in many Swing applications. In fact, overriding paint() is not really recommended practice in general for Swing applications. This recommendation is in contrast to older AWT applications, where overriding paint() was equivalent to overriding paintComponent() in Swing; this is how applications got custom rendering behavior in some components of their applications. In Swing, however, the paint() method in JComponent, which is the superclass for all Swing components, handles everything that any rendering Swing component would typically want. JComponent's paint() method handles painting the content, borders, and children of any Swing component. Swing's painting model also handles double-buffering, which we read more about shortly.

It is the ability of JComponent to handle all of this functionality for paint() that makes overriding paint() not recommended in general; subclasses may neglect to do something (like drawing borders or painting children) that they should do. It is far better to just let JComponent handle these details instead. But sometimes overriding paint() is useful and necessary.

Tip: There is one important case in which it is useful for custom Swing components to override paint(): when an application wants to alter the graphics state for all of that component's rendering.

A good example of this situation is a translucent component, where the user will see through the component to items that lie behind it in the GUI. If you want a Swing component, including its children and borders, to be completely translucent, then you must change the Composite attribute of the Graphics object passed into the paint() method. You could, of course, change the Graphics object passed into paintComponent(), but that would alter the rendering only for that component's contents. JComponent creates a new Graphics object for each call to paintComponent(), so altering the state of that Graphics object will affect only the contents of that single component. What you should do instead is alter the Graphics object that the contents, the borders, and the children are rendered with. In this case, you should alter the Graphics object passed to the paint() method.

Let's look at an example, the TranslucentButton demo on the book's Web site:

ONLINE
DEMO

```
public class TranslucentButton extends JButton {
  public TranslucentButton(String label) {
    super(label);
    setOpaque(false);
  }

  public void paint(Graphics g) {
    // Create an image for the button graphics if necessary
    if (buttonImage == null ||
      buttonImage.getWidth() != getWidth() ||
      buttonImage.getHeight() != getHeight()) {
      buttonImage = (BufferedImage)createImage(
        getWidth(), getHeight());
    }
    Graphics gButton = buttonImage.getGraphics();
    gButton.setClip(g.getClip());

    // Have the superclass render the button for us
    super.paint(gButton);
```

continued

```
        // Make the graphics object sent to this paint()
        // method translucent
        Graphics2D g2d  = (Graphics2D)g;
        AlphaComposite newComposite =
        AlphaComposite.getInstance(AlphaComposite.SRC_OVER, .5f);
          g2d.setComposite(newComposite);

        // Copy the button's image to the destination
        // graphics, translucently
        g2d.drawImage(buttonImage, 0, 0, null);
    }
  }
```

There are a few things going on here that make the button translucent:

- The button tells Swing that it is not opaque in the constructor. We see more about this issue in the next section.

- The class overrides JButton's paint() method. This is done because we want all of the component's contents, including the border and any children, to be translucent.

- Paint creates an image that we use to hold the result of rendering the button.

- Paint calls super.paint(g) to render the button into the image that we created.

- A translucent Composite is set on the destination graphics. We see much more about Composites later in the book.

- The image is copied into the destination graphics, which has a translucent Composite; thus the button is rendered translucently into the Swing window.

The results can be seen in Figure 2-6.

Figure 2-6 TranslucentButton has the superclass paint the button to an image and then copies the image to the destination with a translucent Composite.

Tip: Note the use of an image in the `TranslucentButton` to get the right result. It is also possible to set the state of the destination `Graphics` object directly and ask the superclass to paint into that `Graphics` object instead of into the image's `Graphics` object. However, this more direct approach can break down in various situations. For example, if the superclass's `paint()` method changes the state of the `Graphics` object and clobbers your setting, then you will not get the result you expected. Also, note that *every* operation using that altered `Graphics` object will use that state, which may not provide the same result as just applying that state to the overall result. For example, if we rendered the `TranslucentButton` by setting the `Composite` on g and then calling `super.paint(g)`, then the text of the button would render translucently over the background of the button. This result is not the same as the text rendering opaquely on top of the button's background and then drawing both translucently to the destination. The difference is subtle but can be quite important in some situations.

It is still useful to take advantage of the facilities of `JComponent`'s `paint()` method for painting the contents, borders, and children, so deferring to the superclass is usually the best way to go for all of the standard rendering of a custom component.

setOpaque()

As we saw in the previous example, we called `setOpaque(false)` for our translucent component. Why? Was it because our component was translucent (and therefore not "opaque")? Yes. And no. Opaque in Swing is different from opaque in Java 2D.

In Java 2D, opacity, or its opposite, translucency, is a rendering concept that is reflected in the combination of an alpha value and a `Composite` mode. The opacity describes the degree to which the pixel colors being drawn should be blended with the pixel values of whatever is already there. So a graphics primitive that is half-translucent should use half of the value of the existing pixel color and half of the value of the primitive's pixel color to determine the new pixel color for every pixel touched by the drawing primitive.

In Swing, opacity refers to whether the contents behind a given component are visible to the user. For example, a normal rectangular button is typically opaque in the Swing sense because it completely obscures whatever happens to be behind the button. A rounded button, on the other hand, is not opaque because there is content behind the button that is visible outside of the rounded corners. Similarly, a component that is translucent in the Java 2D sense, partially see-through, is also nonopaque in Swing because contents behind that component are visible through the component.

The main reason for this distinction between opaque and nonopaque in Swing is performance. Swing takes a shortcut in rendering to optimize performance; it does not render things that do not need to be rendered. In particular, Swing does not render things that cannot be seen behind opaque components. For the case of the rectangular button in our example, Swing knows that the button obscures everything behind it, so repaint requests invoked on the button will not cause Swing to draw the items behind the button, since the user will not be able to see those items anyway.

Swing does not magically know when a component is nonopaque; we have to tell Swing. We do this by setting the opaque property of a component to false.

An opaque component is contractually obligated to paint its background completely. By default, Swing fills the background of an opaque component according to the current color specified by `getBackground()`. If you override `paintComponent()` for a component that is opaque, you must ensure that the entire bounds of the component will be painted completely, since Swing will not do it for the component.

For more information on Swing painting details, please check out this article by Swing engineer Amy Fowler: http://java.sun.com/products/jfc/tsc/articles/painting/index.html.

Double-Buffering

An important concept in Swing rendering is that Swing is *double-buffered*. Double-buffering is typically used in games and other applications in which onscreen content might change rapidly. This technique makes updates to the screen appear smooth to the user.

Tip: Swing's use of double-buffering internally means that you should not need to provide your own double-buffer mechanism. Let Swing take care of it instead.

We have seen some applications that use their own buffering mechanism. These applications render content to their own offscreen image, which is then copied into the Swing back buffer. This situation is known as triple-buffering, since there are three buffers involved: the application back buffer, the Swing back buffer, and the screen itself. The application will not get any smoother with this approach; it's just introducing an extra delay and operation for the additional buffer copy.

Double-buffering uses an offscreen image, called a *back buffer*, as the destination for its rendering operations. At appropriate times, this back buffer is copied to the screen. This process for updating the screen is typically smoother than the individual updates from all of the rendering operations because it happens all at once. We can see the difference between these approaches in Figure 2-7; the picture on the top shows an application drawing directly to the screen. The picture on the bottom shows a double-buffered application drawing to an offscreen image that is then copied onto the screen.

Any application with contents so complex that they flicker when the screen is repainted will immediately benefit from double-buffering. If an application displays an empty window, chances are low that the user would notice if that application was double-buffered. But if the application window has lots of text,

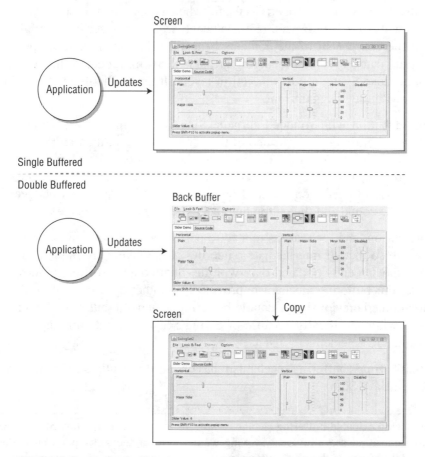

Figure 2-7   Single-buffered compared to double-buffered application.

graphics elements, and GUI widgets, then chances are higher that updates to the window would be noticeable to the user as all of that complex content was updated.

Swing applications, in particular, benefit greatly from double-buffering for two reasons. For one thing, Swing is a general platform upon which any desktop application may be written. So someone might write a game or some other dynamic, graphics-intensive application using Swing; these are exactly the kinds of traditional animation-driven applications that benefit from the smooth updates of double-buffering. Another reason that even simple Swing applications benefit from double-buffering is the layered approach of Swing's painting.

As we saw in the earlier discussion of `setOpaque()`, components may inform Swing that they are nonopaque by calling `setOpaque(false)`. This method tells Swing that it must paint all of the elements behind this component up to the nearest opaque ancestor because the component may or may not paint over those pixels itself. The opacity property is useful when a component is shaped, such as a button with rounded corners, or translucent, where the user can partially see through the component to the contents beneath it. However, setting opacity to false would cause onscreen rendering artifacts if Swing rendered directly to the screen, because Swing renders the UI in layers: It draws the things behind first and ends with the things in front.

Imagine a button with rounded corners. Since this component is nonopaque, Swing would erase the background of the parent panel and then redraw the button. If Swing did this directly to the screen, the user would first see the erasure, then the button, resulting in a flickering artifact during the rendering process. This effect would get even worse if there were other components between the opaque background and the button that had to be redrawn.

For this reason, and for reasons related to performance, Swing uses a buffering mechanism so that all intermediate rendering of the layers are hidden from the user and the screen is updated only with the final contents of the window. Not only does this buffering mechanism provide a smoother update for all of the reasons mentioned previously for double-buffering in general, but it is a better solution for Swing specifically because of Swing's layered rendering approach for nonopaque GUI elements.

Note that Swing's buffering mechanism has changed recently and is much more effective in Java SE 6.

Tip: Swing's double-buffering change in Java SE 6 is probably my favorite feature in that entire release. Previously, Swing would perform necessary painting to the upper-left corner of the back buffer and then copy that content into place on the screen. Therefore, the back buffer was really just a scratch-buffer for each individual update, with no persistence of those contents between repaints, and any future updates to the window required re-rendering to the back buffer. In Java SE 6, Swing changed its model to use true double-buffering, where the back buffer reflects the actual contents of the window and where some re-rendering can occur simply by copying the existing back buffer contents onto the screen, saving time and effort and eliminating the infamous "gray rect" that was a characteristic of Swing's previous double-buffering implementation.[4]

Threading

As we discussed earlier, Swing relies on the older AWT GUI toolkit for top-level window support and event dispatching. Whenever you run a Swing application, three threads are automatically created. The first one is the main thread, which runs your application's main method. A second thread, called the toolkit thread, is in charge of capturing the system events, like keyboard key presses or mouse movements. Although this thread is vital, it is only part of AWT implementation and never runs application code. Capture events are sent over to a third thread, the EDT.

The EDT is very important because it is in charge of dispatching the events captured by the toolkit thread to the appropriate components and calling the painting methods. It is also the thread on which you interact with Swing. For instance, if you press a key in a `JTextField`, the EDT dispatches the key press events to the component's key listener. The component then updates its model and posts a paint request to the event queue. The EDT dequeues the paint request and notifies the component a second time, asking it to repaint itself. In short, everything in AWT and Swing happens on the EDT. Note that if events are received faster than they can be delivered, the EDT queues them until they can be processed.

While easy to understand on the surface, this simple threading model can yield poor performance in Swing applications if the implications of the Swing's single-threaded model are not considered. Indeed, performing a long operation on the EDT, such as reading or writing a file, will block the whole UI. No event can then be dispatched and no update of the screen can be performed while the long operation is underway. The result from the user perspective is that the application appears to be hung or, at least, very slow.

---

4. See the blog postings at http://weblogs.java.net/blog/chet/archive/2005/04/swing_update_no_1.html and http://weblogs.java.net/blog/zixle/archive/2005/04/no_more_gray_re_1.html for more details on this excellent "true double-buffering" feature.

Poorly written applications that block the EDT for long periods of time have contributed to some people thinking that Swing itself is slow. Most Swing application performance issues are actually *perceived* performance issues. The Swing components dispatch their work quite quickly. However, when the application blocks the EDT, it freezes the user interface and the user thinks the application runs slowly. Freezing happens, for instance, when you have long computations or I/O accesses running in a method executed by the EDT.

The following example, available on the book's Web site, exhibits such behavior. Run the application and click the Freeze button. It should remain pressed for a few seconds. Whenever the user clicks on a button, the `actionPerformed()` method of the button's `ActionListener` is called. Since this action is triggered by an event, `actionPerformed()` is invoked on the EDT. In this particular case, the code pauses the current thread for 4 seconds, emulating a long operation that blocks Swing's ability to dispatch events and repaint the GUI.

The following example shows that failure to understand and master Swing's threading can lead to applications that perform poorly.

```
public class FreezeEDT extends JFrame
implements ActionListener {
  public FreezeEDT() {
    super("Freeze");
    JButton freezer = new JButton("Freeze");
    freezer.addActionListener(this);
    add(freezer);
    pack();
  }

  public void actionPerformed(ActionEvent e) {
    // Simulates a long running operation.
    // For instance: reading a large file,
    // performing network operations, etc.
    try {
      Thread.sleep(4000);
    } catch (InterruptedException e) {
    }
  }

  public static void main(String... args) {
    FreezeEDT edt = new FreezeEDT();
    edt.setVisible(true);
  }
}
```

Threading Model

Swing's threading model is based on a single rule: The EDT is responsible for executing any method that modifies a component's state. This includes any component's constructor. According to this rule, and despite what you can read in many books and tutorials about Swing, the main() method in the previous code example is invalid and can cause a deadlock. Because the JFrame is a Swing component, and because it instantiates another Swing component, it should be created on the EDT, not on the main thread.

Swing is not a "thread-safe" API. It should be invoked only on the EDT. The great minds behind Swing made this choice on purpose to guarantee the order and predictability of events. A single-threaded API is also much simpler to understand and debug than a multithreaded one. Incidentally, Swing is not the only single-threaded graphical toolkit: SWT, QT, and .NET WinForms provide a similar threading model.

Now that you know that you must avoid performing any lengthy operations on the EDT, you need to find a solution to this common problem. The first answer that springs to mind is to use another thread, as in the following code example. In this actionPerformed() method, a new thread is spawned to read a large file (of, say, several megabytes) and add the results in a JTextArea:

```
public void actionPerformed(ActionEvent e) {
  new Thread(new Runnable() {
    public void run() {
      String text = readHugeFile();
      // Bad code alert: modifying textArea on this thread
      // violates the EDT rule
      textArea.setText(text);
    }
  }).start();
}
```

At first, this code seems to be the solution to your problem, as it does not block the EDT. Unfortunately, it violates Swing's single-thread rule: it doesn't modify the text component's state on the EDT. Doing so will not necessarily cause any trouble during your tests, but a deadlock can appear anytime, and more often than not, it will happen when one of your customers is using the application.[5]

---

5. Or when you are demonstrating your application onstage in front of a large audience. There is some universal law about such events, as fundamental as the law of gravity and the perpetuation of single socks.

Tracking down and fixing such a bug is very difficult and time consuming, so it is highly recommended to always follow Swing's single-threading rule.

Invoke Later

But don't fret! Swing offers three very useful methods to deal with the EDT in the class javax.swing.SwingUtilities. The first of these methods is called invokeLater(), and it can be used to post a new task on the EDT. Here is how you can rewrite the previous example to be both nonblocking and correct:

```
public void actionPerformed(ActionEvent e) {
  new Thread(new Runnable() {
    public void run() {
      final String text = readHugeFile();
      SwingUtilities.invokeLater(new Runnable() {
        public void run() {
          textArea.setText(text);
        }
      });
    }
  }).start();
}
```

In the new version of the code, the application posts a Runnable task that updates the content of the text area on the EDT. The invokeLater() implementation takes care of creating and queuing a special event that contains the Runnable. This event is processed on the EDT in the order it was received, just like any other event. When its time comes, it is dispatched by running the Runnable's run() method.

Using invokeLater() is as simple as passing a Runnable instance whose sole method, run(), contains the code you wish to execute on the EDT. So what exactly happens in this code? First, the user clicks on a button and the EDT invokes actionPerformed(). Then, the application creates and starts a new thread, which reads the content of a file and stores it in a String. Finally, a new task, the Runnable instance, is created and placed in the queue of the EDT thanks to invokeLater(). Now that you know how to force a block of code to be invoked on the EDT, it is easy to fix the main() method of the first example:

```
public static void main(String... args) {
  SwingUtilities.invokeLater(new Runnable() {
    public void run() {
      FreezeEDT edt = new FreezeEDT();
      edt.setVisible(true);
    }
  });
}
```

Is This the EDT?

The second SwingUtilities method that makes it easier to work with Swing's threading model is called isEventDispatchThread(). When invoked, this method returns true if the calling code is currently being executed on the EDT, false otherwise. You can therefore create methods that can be called from the EDT and any other thread and still obey the rule, as shown in the following example.

```
private void incrementLabel() {
  tickCounter++;
  Runnable code = new Runnable() {
    public void run() {
      counter.setText(String.valueOf(tickCounter));
    }
  };

  if (SwingUtilities.isEventDispatchThread()) {
    code.run();
  } else {
    SwingUtilities.invokeLater(code);
  }
}
```

This method uses an integer, tickCounter, to change the text of a JLabel called counter. When incrementLabel() is called from the EDT, the code executes directly. Otherwise, invokeLater() is used to schedule the task for the EDT. A full working version of this example can be found on the book's Web site under the name SwingThreading.

The third and last SwingUtilities method related to threading, invokeAndWait(), is also the least commonly used (which is probably a good thing, as we will see). Its behavior is similar to invokeLater() in that it allows you to post a Runnable task to be executed on the EDT. The difference is that invokeAndWait() blocks the current thread and waits until the EDT is done executing the task.

Let us imagine an intelligent application that can detect when the time it has spent reading a file has exceeded some threshold. This application reads a file in a separate thread and, after 10 seconds of work, asks the user whether he would like to continue or cancel the operation. To implement such a feature, you would normally initialize a lock to stop the reader thread and then display a dialog box on the EDT.

Writing such a piece of code is possible but dangerous because you can easily introduce a deadlock. The following example shows how you can use invokeAndWait()

ONLINE
DEMO

to do the job safely. The complete, executable version of this example is called SwingThreadingWait and can be found on the book's Web site.

```
try {
  // Holds the answer to the dialog box
  final int[] answer = new int[1];

  // Pauses the current thread until the dialog box
  // is dismissed
  SwingUtilities.invokeAndWait(new Runnable() {
    public void run() {
      answer[0] = JOptionPane.showConfirmDialog(null,
        "Abort long operation?",
        "Abort?",
        JOptionPane.YES_NO_OPTION);
    }
  });

  if (answer[0] == JOptionPane.YES_OPTION) {
    return;
  }
} catch (InterruptedException ie) {
} catch (InvocationTargetException ite) {
}
```

Swing developers should be aware, however, that there is deadlock potential in invokeAndWait(), as there is in any code that creates a thread interdependency. If the calling code holds some lock (explicitly or implicitly) that the code called through invokeAndWait() requires, then the EDT code will wait for the non-EDT code to release the lock, which cannot happen because the non-EDT code is waiting for the EDT code to complete, and the application will hang.

In general, invokeAndWait() may appear simpler to use than invokeLater(), because it executes a Runnable task synchronously, and it would seem as though you don't have to worry about more than one thread executing your code at the same time. But it is risky to use if you are not absolutely sure of the threading and locking dependencies that you are creating, so it should be used only in very clearly risk-free situations.

Besides the three utility methods just covered, every Swing component offers two useful methods that can be called from any thread: repaint() and revalidate(). The latter forces a component to lay out its children, and the former simply refreshes the display. These two methods do their work on the EDT, no matter what thread you invoke them on.

The repaint() method is widely used throughout the Swing API to synchronize components' properties and the screen. For instance, when you change the foreground color of a button by calling JButton.setForeground(Color), Swing stores the new color and calls repaint() to automatically show the new value of the color property. Calling repaint() triggers the execution of several other methods on the EDT, including paint() and paintComponent().

If you place the following component in a JFrame and spawn a new thread called repaint() on the component, you will always see the message "true" in the console output. The complete running example, called SafeRepaint, can be found on this book's Web site.

```java
public class SafeComponent extends JLabel {
  public SafeComponent() {
    super("Safe Repaint");
  }

  public void paintComponent(Graphics g) {
    super.paintComponent(g);
    System.out.println(
      SwingUtilities.isEventDispatchThread());
  }
}
```

Timers and the Event Dispatch Thread

The Java SE API offers two ways to schedule tasks to be executed at regular time intervals: java.util.Timer and javax.swing.Timer. Both classes use a timer thread to offer similar functionalities. Knowing which time class to use for a particular situation can be tricky. Here is how you can use java.util.Timer to change a button's color every 3 seconds:

```java
java.util.Timer clown = new java.util.Timer();
clown.schedule(new TimerTask() {
  public void run() {
    SwingUtilities.invokeLater(new Runnable() {
      public void run() {
        button.setForeground(getRandomColor());
      }
    });
  }
}, 0, 3000); // delay, period
```

A java.util.Timer can schedule several TimerTasks, each with a different execution interval. You can also cancel a TimerTask at any time. The major issue with java.util.Timer is that it does not execute the tasks on the EDT, leaving that responsibility to the developer. Since user interfaces seldom require highly precise timers that can handle hundreds of tasks at once, it is a good idea to use javax.swing.Timer instead.

The Swing Timer class offers a different API that integrates better in a Swing environment. While a single timer supports several tasks, they all have the same repeat period. The following example is a rewrite of the previous one with a Swing timer:

```
javax.swing.Timer clown = new javax.swing.Timer(3000,
  new ActionListener() {
    public void actionPerformed(ActionEvent evt) {
      button.setForeground(getRandomColor());
    }
});
clown.start();
```

Swing's timer makes it trivial to periodically run Actions. This timer also ensures that all the tasks are executed on the EDT rather than in a random thread. Choosing the appropriate timer class will save you a lot of time and debugging efforts when dealing with the Swing threading model. Timers that update the user interface are usually javax.swing.Timer instances; timers that drive background operations, such as polling a Web server, are usually java.util.Timer instances.

Painless Threading through SwingWorker

The SwingUtilities class is a great asset to ensure that your application will run smoothly and flawlessly. Despite its advantages, SwingUtilities often leads to a code base made difficult to read and maintain because of the numerous anonymous Runnable classes you need to create. To remedy this problem, the Swing developers created SwingWorker, a utility class that simplifies the creation of long-running tasks that update the user interface.

This tool has been included in Java SE 6 but remains available for older versions of the JDK, namely J2SE 5.0, on the Web site http://swingworker.dev.java.net. The following code and text assumes that you are using either J2SE 5.0 or Java SE 6.

SwingWorker is a generic class available in the javax.swing package for Java SE 6 and in org.jdesktop.swingworker for J2SE 5.0. This class lets you run a specific task on a background thread, post intermediate results on the EDT, and post the final result on the EDT as well.

Let us imagine a simple use case to better understand the SwingWorker architecture. We want to load a set of images from the hard drive and display those images in the user interface. To avoid blocking the user interface, we want to load the images on a background thread.

At the same time, we want to present progress information to the user by showing the names of the files that have been loaded so far. When the background thread has finished, we want to return a list of the images it has loaded. We also want to show the file name of each loaded image in the user interface.

When you want to implement such a lengthy task for your user interface with SwingWorker, you need to subclass SwingWorker and override doInBackground(). SwingWorker allows you to specify the types of the intermediate and final values with two generic types, called T and V. The first one, T, is the type of result computed by the method doInBackground() in a worker, or background, thread. The other type, V, is the type of intermediate values that you can send to the EDT by calling publish(V...). SwingWorker then invokes process(V...) on the EDT. You should override the process method to display the intermediate results in your GUI. Upon completion, SwingWorker invokes the done() method on the EDT.

The doInBackground() method can publish intermediate results at any time by calling publish(V...), which in turn invokes the process(V...) method in the EDT.

The done() method is also usually overridden to display the final result. Upon completion of doInBackground(), the SwingWorker automatically invokes done() in the EDT. In done(), you can call the get() method to retrieve the value computed by doInBackground().

The relation among doInBackground(), publish(V...), process(V...), and done() is shown in Figure 2-8.

The following code snippet shows a SwingWorker implementation for the use case we defined earlier (loading a set of images from the hard drive and showing the loaded files' names):

```
// Final result is a list of Image
// Intermediate result is a message as a String
public class ImageLoadingWorker extends
    SwingWorker<List<Image>, String> {
  private JTextArea log;
  private JPanel viewer;
  private String[] filenames;
```

continued

```java
  public ImageLoadingWorker(JTextArea log, JPanel viewer,
                            String... filenames) {
    this.log = log;
    this.viewer = viewer;
    this.filenames = filenames;
  }

  // On the EDT
  // Displays the loaded images in the JPanel
  @Override
  protected void done() {
    try {
      for (Image image : get()) {
        viewer.add(new JLabel(new ImageIcon(image)));
        viewer.revalidate();
      }
    } catch (Exception e) { }
  }

  // On the EDT
  // Logs a message in the JTextArea
  @Override
  protected void process(String... messages) {
    for (String message : messages) {
      log.append(message);
      log.append("\n");
    }
  }

  // On a worker (background) thread
  // Loads images from disk and sends a message
  // as a String to the EDT by calling publish(V...)
  @Override
  public List<Image> doInBackground() {
    List<Image> images = new ArrayList<Image>();
    for (String filename : filenames) {
      try {
        images.add(ImageIO.read(new File(filename)));
        publish("Loaded " + filename);
      } catch (IOException ioe) {
        publish("Error loading " + filename);
      }
    }
    return images;
  }
}
```

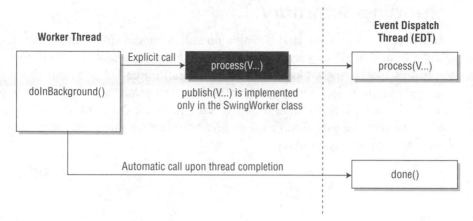

Figure 2-8 The process(V...) and done() methods are automatically invoked in the EDT by the SwingWorker.

In this code, doInBackground() loads a list of Images and logs the success of each operation by publishing a message. Even if only one value is published at a time, the process() method can be called with several values. When the process() method is called on the EDT, the SwingWorker implementation passes along all of the pending values from the publish() calls.

Once doInBackground() has finished, done() fetches the result by calling get() and adds the pictures to the user interface. Since done() executes on the EDT, the single-thread rule is not broken. The final step is to execute the SwingWorker like so:

```
JButton start = new JButton("Start");
start.addActionListener(new ActionListener() {
  public void actionPerformed(ActionEvent e) {
    String[] files = new String[] {
      "Bodie_small.png", "Carmela_small.png",
      "Unknown.png", "Denied.png",
      "Death Valley_small.png", "Lake_small.png"
    };
    new ImageLoadingWorker(log, viewer, files).execute();
  }
});
```

The complete running example, ImageLoader, can be found on the book's Web site.

Threading Summary

Understanding and mastering Swing's threading model does not require much effort and can help you create powerful and snappy applications. With the help of utilities like `SwingWorker`, you can write multithreaded code that is easy to read and maintain. Every time you write a lengthy operation, think of the single-thread rule and check whether or not you might block the EDT. Everyone hates slow, unresponsive user interfaces, so save your users some pain and make your Swing applications responsive.

3

Graphics Fundamentals

ONE of the things that makes Swing such a great platform for Filthy Rich Clients is its ability to have customized rendering for a GUI component, which allows alterations of a component's appearance. Swing's ability to have customized rendering is made richer by its use of Java 2D, the rendering layer of Desktop Java. We explore important elements of Java 2D in this chapter, specifically talking about the most important concepts of Java 2D rendering as they relate to Filthy Rich Clients.

Java 2D

Whenever I give a presentation on Java 2D, I do a quick poll to see how many people use this library. Typically, about 10 to 20 percent of the people raise their hands. Then I ask how many people use Swing, and most of the audience raise their hands.[1] The real answer to the first question is actually the union of both of these. Java 2D users are those who use the 2D APIs directly *and* use Swing, because 2D is the rendering layer of Swing.

Maybe people don't know that they're using the 2D library because there is no "2D" package. Or maybe they don't use 2D APIs directly and do not know that

---

1. It's not clear to me why the remainder of the people are in the room. I suspect that a previous presentation bored them to sleep, and they just haven't woken up yet.

Swing uses 2D. Or maybe they are using simple graphics objects (such as AWT, offered in early releases of Java) and do not understand the difference.

The 2D APIs have many powerful and somewhat niche capabilities, such as intersecting geometrical objects, handling the correct rasterization of a spline, and specifying end caps and joins for polylines. But the 2D APIs also have the plain old capabilities of rendering graphics objects that Swing depends on completely and that Swing developers use either implicitly or explicitly in every application.

In Chapter 2, "Swing Rendering Fundamentals," we saw how a `Graphics` object is sent in as a parameter to `paintComponent()`. Through this object, we set graphics state, such as the current color, and perform rendering operations, such as filling a rectangle or drawing text. In the standard Swing component classes, this is how the basic objects are drawn to the screen. And in Filthy Rich Clients, this is how the custom Swing components are drawn.

Before we get too deep into graphics state, we should note an important distinction in the graphics APIs that may confuse first-timers. A long time ago, Java was released with the GUI toolkit library AWT. This library included a class called `Graphics`, which has exactly the behavior that we just discussed: You set the state of that object and use that object to draw primitives with its current state.

Then along came Java 2D in the J2SE 1.2 release. Because Java is backward-compatible, we could not easily add or change functionality in the `Graphics` class, so we added a subclass of `Graphics` called `Graphics2D`. This class has the same behavior as `Graphics`; you set the state on that object and draw primitives with it that use the state. The main difference is that `Graphics2D` adds capabilities that `Graphics` did not previously have. For example, translucent rendering is now possible via the new `Composite` property in `Graphics2D`, as seen in the `TranslucentButton` demo in Chapter 2.

Some of the graphics state settings and drawing primitives that we use for Filthy Rich Clients are in the `Graphics` object, such as `setColor()`, and some are in `Graphics2D`, such as `setComposite()`.

So which object should you choose, `Graphics` or `Graphics2D`? Actually, this decision is made for you; Swing almost always[2] uses a `Graphics2D` object. Even when a Swing method has `Graphics` as a parameter, it's really a `Graphics2D`

---

2. Printing may use a non-`Graphics2D` object. Also, Swing's `DebugGraphics` object is not a `Graphics2D` subclass. If either of these situations may apply to your code, be careful how you cast. Otherwise, typical Swing usage involves a `Graphics2D` object.

object. The simple answer here is: If you want to call a Graphics method, do it directly in the Graphics object; if you need to call a Graphics2D method, cast the Graphics object and perform the operation in the resulting Graphics2D object.

For simplicity, we refer in this book to the Graphics and Graphics2D objects generically as Graphics objects unless we are talking specifically about operations that require the object to be of type Graphics2D.

Rendering

Rendering: Heating animal remains to extract fat

—MSN Encarta

The process of 2D rendering is as follows:

1. Get a Graphics (or Graphics2D) object.
2. Set attributes on the Graphics object.
3. Draw graphics primitives with the Graphics object.

Let's look at some sample code for a paintComponent() method in a Swing component:

```
// No need to get a Graphics object; it is given to us
protected void paintComponent(Graphics g) {
  // Set Color attribute on g
  g.setColor(Color.RED);
  // Fill this component with red
  g.fillRect(0, 0, getWidth(), getHeight());
}
```

This example does nothing interesting, but it gets the point across. The code gets the Graphics object g as a parameter to paintComponent() method; it sets an attribute on g, the color RED; and it tells g to draw a filled rectangle.

Most of the 2D rendering examples we explore in this book behave similarly. The differences include

- How we get the Graphics object: We may request one from an image or component or be given one, as in the previous example.
- Which attributes we set on the Graphics object.
- Which drawing operations we perform with the Graphics object.

We discuss all of these topics in the sections that follow.

Getting the Graphics Object

For the most part, you will not actually need to get a Graphics object; it will be given to you. Let's say that again:

> Swing usually gives you the Graphics object you need.[3]

Typical cases of rendering in Swing applications happen in the context of a method like paintComponent(), where the Graphics object is given to you as a parameter of the method. You do not usually have to go looking for or creating a Graphics object. However, there are some cases in which it may be handy to know how to best get a Graphics object when you need it. That's what this section is about.

Cloning versus Clobbering

Sometimes you already have a Graphics object and you want to change some of its state temporarily and then return it to its original state. One approach is to create a new Graphics object that is a copy of the original one and to make changes to that copy instead. This technique avoids clobbering the state of the original object. For example, the following code changes the current translation of the Graphics object, which other parts of Swing may then incorrectly depend on:

```
// Wrong: This approach clobbers the state
protected void paintComponent(Graphics g) {
    // Setting state in g sets it for anyone that might
    // use g after this method
    g.translate(x,y);

    // ...render the component contents...

    // return without resetting translation of g
}
```

This cloning-versus-clobbering idea is covered in more detail in the "Graphics State" section of this chapter, but the basic idea is to copy the current Graphics

---

3. I recently gave a talk on this subject and mentioned "Getting the Graphics" as a topic, explaining a couple of slides later that you don't usually need to go to any effort to get a Graphics object. Scott Violet said that I should be more explicit about this point because it didn't sound clear enough. So one more time for Scott (everyone repeat with me): You usually don't have to get the Graphics object explicitly.

object and make changes to that copy rather than directly to the `Graphics` object that Swing gave you. Whether you need to do this depends on your situation: where you got the `Graphics` object, what state you are changing, how you are changing the state, and perhaps most importantly, what other code will do with this same `Graphics` object when you are done.

A reasonable way to get such a copy is to call the `create()` method:

```
// Better: This approach sets the state in a copy instead
protected void paintComponent(Graphics g) {
  // create a copy
  Graphics gTemp = g.create();

  // Set the state in gTemp instead
  gTemp.translate(x,y);

  // ...render the component contents using gTemp...

  gTemp.dispose();
}
```

The `create()` method returns a clone of the object in its current state, so using this copy is just like using the original `Graphics` object except that it maintains its own copy of all of the graphics attributes. An alternative way to achieve this goal is to simply use the original object but then reset the state after you are done.

Rendering into an Image

There are many times, especially in Filthy Rich Clients, when you would like to render graphics into an image. `Image` objects do not have handy `paintComponent()` methods to override, so your application will never be given a `Graphics` object automatically by Swing. However, it is quite easy to get such an object; you can ask an `Image` for a `Graphics` object:

```
// Sample image creation
Image img = createImage(w, h);
// Get the Graphics object for the image
Graphics g = img.getGraphics();
```

The `getGraphics()` method returns a `Graphics` object that is set up for rendering directly to the image. Note that some `Image` objects may be read-only. For example, the images created by loading image data through `Toolkit.getImage()` and `Applet.getImage()` create `Image` objects that can only be displayed, not rendered to. This is one of many great reasons we suggest you use images of type BufferedImage in your applications.[4]

Tip: Speaking of BufferedImage, if you happen to be using one of these wonderful images and need a Graphics2D object, instead of using the getGraphics() call from Image and casting it, you can use the following method to get a Graphics2D object directly:

```
// creation of bImg performed elsewhere
BufferedImage bImg;
// Get the Graphics2D object for the image
Graphics2D g2d = bImg.createGraphics();
```

Getting a Component's Graphics Object

It is also possible to ask a Swing component for a Graphics object directly. However, it is not advisable to do so for rendering purposes. This means of obtaining the Graphics object bypasses and interferes with Swing's buffering and repainting mechanisms. It is far better to handle rendering in the proper context, such as in the paintComponent() method. You may sometimes want a Graphics object for a Component just to query some rendering attributes, but otherwise you will probably have no need to get a Graphics object for a Component. Just leave it to Swing to provide the Graphics object when you need to do the rendering.

Warning: Don't call paint(g) directly. Let Swing call it for you. If you need to have Swing paint a component, call repaint() on the component. Or, if you are on the EDT and must render something immediately, call paintImmediately(). Don't get a Graphics object from the component and call paint() yourself. Bad things will happen.

Graphics State

Graphics objects have several attributes that contribute to what we call the *graphics state*. This state affects all subsequent rendering operations performed with a particular Graphics object. We have already seen one example of graph-

---

4. We discuss the various image types, including the advantages of BufferedImage, in greater detail in Chapter 4, "Images."

ics state: the current color. Just in case you missed it the first time, here is that fascinating example once more:

```
protected void paintComponent(Graphics g) {
    // Set Color attribute on g
    g.setColor(Color.RED);
    // Fill this component with red
    g.fillRect(0, 0, getWidth(), getHeight());
}
```

After the call to g.setColor(Color.RED), all rendering operations on g that use a foreground color will happen in red.

But graphics state can be far more interesting and can affect far more of the rendering results than a simple color change. For example, we can change the position, rotation, or size of the rendering operations by setting the transform property. We can change the translucency of the rendering operations by setting the Composite property. And we can set the graphics to fill or draw with a gradient or image instead of a color.

Now that we have covered the basics of how to set graphics state, let's look at some of the graphics state that we can set. We do not examine all state in the Graphics and Graphics2D classes here but constrain the discussion to those attributes we find most useful in Filthy Rich Clients. It is worth familiarizing yourself with the JavaDocs for the Graphics and Graphics2D classes, however. There are various other interesting attributes not covered here that you may want to use in some situations.

From the Graphics and Graphics2D classes, we examine the following properties:

- *Foreground color:* The color used by drawing primitives.
- *Background color:* The color used when erasing an area.
- *Font:* The font used in text primitives.
- *Stroke:* The attributes used in line-based primitives.
- *Rendering hints:* Information that Java 2D uses to determine the quality and performance of various rendering primitives.
- *Clip:* The region to which drawing is constrained.
- *Composite:* The method of combining color data from drawing primitives with color data in the destination.
- *Paint:* Similar to the color, the Paint property determines how pixels will be colored by drawing primitives.
- *Transform:* The size, position, and orientation of drawing primitives.

public void setColor(Color c)
public Color getColor()

These methods set and get the current foreground color, which controls the current drawing color of the Graphics object. This color is then used in later primitive calls, such as drawLine() and fillRect(). Note that colors may be opaque or translucent.

The setColor() method is closely related to setPaint(), which creates more interesting contents for graphics primitives than a simple solid color. We provide more information on setPaint() later in this chapter.

Usage: The following code draws a red line:

```
public void paintComponent(Graphics g) {
  g.setColor(Color.RED);
  g.drawLine(0, 0, 10, 10);
}
```

public void setBackground(Color c)
public Color getBackground()

These methods set and get the background property, which controls the background color for the Graphics object. This is the color that will be used in calls to clearRect() on the Graphics object.

Usage: The following code clears a component's background to white:

```
public void paintComponent(Graphics g) {
  g.setBackground(Color.WHITE);
  g.clearRect(0, 0, getWidth(), getHeight());
}
```

public void setFont(Font f)
public Font getFont()

The Font property controls the font used by the Graphics object for any future text operations. When drawString() is called on the Graphics object, a text string is rendered using the Font property currently set on that Graphics object. If you want a larger font, a different style (e.g., bold), or a different font type entirely, call the setFont() method to make that change.

Usage: The following code draws a string with a bold, 24-point version of the default font used by the Graphics object:

```
public void paintComponent(Graphics g) {
  Font newFont = g.getFont().deriveFont(Font.BOLD, 24f);
  g.setFont(newFont);
  g.drawString("String with new font", 20, 20);
}
```

public void setStroke(Stroke s)
public Stroke getStroke()

The `Stroke` property controls the line attributes for future line-based drawing primitives, such as `drawLine()`. In particular, a `Stroke` controls the line width, the end caps of the line, and the style of join in multisegment line calls like `drawPolyline()`. End caps and joins are fairly irrelevant with the default line width of 1. They become more important when thick lines are used.

`Stroke` itself is an interface, and the `BasicStroke` class is the standard implementation of this interface. Typical use of `Stroke` is through the `BasicStroke` class.

Usage: The following code draws a wide line with round end caps. Note that the `JOIN_MITER` parameter is not relevant here, since we are simply calling the single-segment `drawLine()` primitive:

```
public void paintComponent(Graphics g) {
  Graphics2D g2d = (Graphics2D)g.create();
  g2d.setStroke(new BasicStroke(10f, BasicStroke.CAP_ROUND,
                                    BasicStroke.JOIN_MITER));
  g2d.drawLine(0, 0, 10, 10);
  g2d.dispose();
}
```

Performance Tip: Java 2D uses 1-pixel-wide lines by default for a good reason: They are *much* faster for Java 2D to render. Once you start asking for wide lines, and the library has to think about the width as well as end caps and joins, then there is a lot more computation involved and things can go much slower. My advice: Use wide lines when you need them, but avoid them when you don't.

Example: Simple State-Setting

Now that we have seen how to set some of the simple `Graphics` attributes, let's look at an example, the demo `SimpleAttributes`, available on the book's Web site.

In the paintComponent() method of this application, we play with various attributes, and the results can be seen in Figure 3-1.

Figure 3-1   SimpleAttributes demo output: Results from simple state-setting.

```
protected void paintComponent(Graphics g) {
  // Create temporary Graphics2D object
  Graphics2D g2d = (Graphics2D)g.create();

  // Set the background color and erase to it
  g2d.setBackground(Color.GRAY);
  g2d.clearRect(0, 0, getWidth(), getHeight());

  // Draw text with default font and Color
  g2d.drawString("Default Font", 10, 20);

  // Draw line with default Color and Stroke
  g2d.drawLine(10, 22, 80, 22);

  // Change the font
  g2d.setFont(g.getFont().
      deriveFont(Font.BOLD | Font.ITALIC, 24f));

  // Change the color
  g2d.setColor(Color.WHITE);

  // Change the Stroke
  g2d.setStroke(new BasicStroke(10f, BasicStroke.CAP_ROUND,
                                BasicStroke.JOIN_MITER));

  // Draw text with new font and Color
  g2d.drawString("New Font", 10, 50);

  // Draw line with new Color and Stroke
  g2d.drawLine(10, 57, 120, 57);

  g2d.dispose();
}
```

The state-setting is happening in the four calls to g2d.set*. The first one sets the background color to Color.GRAY, which results in the gray background in the window. Then we perform our drawString() and drawLine() calls with the default state, which results in the black string and line in the figure. We change the Font to one derived from the current one, but with a different style and size. Then we change the Color to WHITE, and we set the Stroke to a wide line with rounded end caps. Note that the joins are irrelevant in this single-segment example. The final result is seen by the white text and line in the figure.

```
public void setRenderingHint(RenderingHints.Key key, Object value)
public Object getRenderingHint(RenderingHints.Key key)
```

Rendering hints provide information to the Java 2D rendering system about how you would like the rendering performed. The information is provided with key/value pairs that are defined in the RenderingHints class.

Rendering hints are all about controlling the trade-off between quality and performance. In many cases, high-quality rendering is not needed or desired, so a setting that ensures that the operation is fast is more appropriate. In other situations, quality is more important and worth any potential performance trade off. You can make the right call for your situation, but here is the information you need on some of the most common rendering hints.

Hints for Image Scaling

To control image-scaling quality, use the key RenderingHints.KEY_INTERPOLATION with one of the following three values:

RenderingHints.VALUE_INTERPOLATION_NEAREST_NEIGHBOR

This is the default setting and represents the fastest scaling method. When using this approach during an image-scaling operation, the 2D code determines how each destination pixel maps back to the source image and chooses a color from the source pixel nearest that location. This technique has a tendency to lose a lot of information in the original image. Imagine, for example, if you scaled a highly detailed image from 100×100 to 10×10. You would drop 99 out of every 100 pixels of color information and the result would probably be far from the quality of the original image.

However, this approach works adequately in many situations, especially if the image is transient so that you don't see it for long or if the scale factor is small so that this approach does not lose as much color information. The performance can be substantially better for this approach than for some of the others, so it is worthwhile using this default hint if the quality is good enough for your situation.

RenderingHints.VALUE_INTERPOLATION_BILINEAR

This approach determines how each destination pixel maps back to the source image and combines the four source-pixel values closest to that location. This technique provides a much smoother scaling and a much better result than the NEAREST_NEIGHBOR approach. If image quality is important to your application, consider using this hint.

RenderingHints.VALUE_INTERPOLATION_BICUBIC

This approach is like BILINEAR, only instead of using the four pixels nearest the location that the destination pixel maps back to, it uses a 4 × 4 grid of pixels. This hint provides improved quality over BILINEAR but at the cost of increased time due to the increased complexity of the scaling algorithm.

Image-scaling quality and performance is covered in more detail in Chapter 4.

Before we discuss rendering hints for antialiasing shapes and text, we thought that a bit of background in antialiasing might help.

Antialiasing: A Primer

Antialiasing (also called AA) is an approach used to smooth out rendering artifacts known as "jaggies," which are the result of computer screens having a discrete number of visible pixels.

For example, when we draw a diagonal line on a monitor, we turn on and off pixels—it's not just a continuous stream of color. So if you look close, you can see the stair-step effect as we set the color of pixels along the slope of the line. You can see this effect in Figure 3-2, where a diagonal line is shown in the upper right of the figure and a zoomed-in view of some of the pixels that make up that line is shown to the left.

Note that the close-up view of the line in Figure 3-2 does not flow continuously down the screen but just colors individual pixels in the right locations according to the slope of the line. Lines on the screen are exactly the same as the zoomed-in image, only thinner. They look better than the zoomed-in representation because the density of the pixels is such that you do not have to back up or squint to make the line appear smooth. The combination of the small pixel size and your viewing distance

Figure 3-2 Diagonal line, upper right, along with close-up view of some of the pixels that make up that line.

from the screen makes it work. If you scoot forward close enough to the screen, you will see the individual pixels of onscreen lines similar to the example in Figure 3-2.

Although lines and other graphics primitives, such as text, are usually "good enough," there are clear "jaggy" effects that can be improved on. One way to improve things is by using antialiasing, which smoothes the hard edges of rendering primitives to reduce the on-or-off characteristic of the jaggies. In antialiasing, we blend pixels on the edges with the background color to remove the hard-edge effect of non-antialiased primitives.

To see this smoothing effect, imagine the case for just one individual pixel of a larger primitive. The pictures in Figure 3-3 and Figure 3-4 show a single pixel without and with an antialiasing technique applied.

Figure 3-3 Aliased version of a single pixel.

Figure 3-4 Antialiased version of a single pixel.

Note the effect in these figures. We are still drawing the main pixel in the same location as before, but now we have a wider area that is grayed out at the edges, using a color value that is halfway between the black color of the pixel and the white color of the background. The result that the user sees is that the line is smoother and blends in better with the background colors because each of the individual line pixels has a smoother transition from the background color to the line color.

Example: AntiAliasingDemo

We can see the effects of antialiasing on a simple line primitive in the application AntiAliasingDemo, available on the book's Web site. This application draws two lines: The first is drawn with default Graphics attributes, which do not include antialiasing, and the second is drawn after setting the antialiasing rendering hint. Here is the paintComponent() method, where all of the rendering logic is handled:

```java
protected void paintComponent(Graphics g) {
    // We will need a Graphics2D object to set the RenderingHint
    Graphics2D g2d = (Graphics2D)g;

    // Erase to white
    g2d.setBackground(Color.WHITE);
    g2d.clearRect(0, 0, getWidth(), getHeight());

    // Draw line with default (aliased) setting
    g2d.drawLine(0, 0, 50, 50);

    // Enable antialiasing
    g2d.setRenderingHint(RenderingHints.KEY_ANTIALIASING,
                         RenderingHints.VALUE_ANTIALIAS_ON);

    // Draw line with new (anti-aliased) setting
    g2d.drawLine(50, 0, 100, 50);
}
```

The results are shown in Figure 3-5 and Figure 3-6.

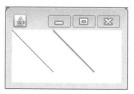

Figure 3-5   Screenshot of AntiAliasingDemo application, showing a default line on the left and a line with antialiasing enabled on the right.

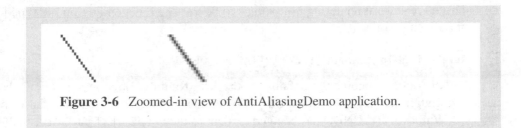

Figure 3-6 Zoomed-in view of AntiAliasingDemo application.

Now that we've seen how the basics of antialiasing work for drawing operations, we are ready to talk about the various rendering hints for controlling antialiasing. Note that there are different hints for drawing primitives and for text. We cover both of these cases.

Hints for Shape Antialiasing

The default for drawing primitives in Java 2D is non-antialiased. If you wish to set the antialiasing attribute for lines and other shapes in your application, you need to set the rendering hint with the key `RenderingHints.KEY_ANTIALIASING` to one of the following values:

```
RenderingHints.VALUE_ANTIALIAS_OFF
RenderingHints.VALUE_ANTIALIAS_ON
```

`VALUE_ANTIALIAS_OFF` is the default value, where antialiased rendering is disabled. `VALUE_ANTIALIAS_ON` enables antialiasing. Note that antialiasing is a more time-intensive rendering operation, so there may be some performance hit for using this value.

Hints for Text Antialiasing

The final rendering hint we cover is text antialiasing, which is controlled by the hint `KEY_TEXT_ANTIALIASING`. The technique behind text antialiasing is the same as that for drawing primitives: Smooth out the jaggies by blending the edges of the text characters with the background color values. In addition, as of Java SE 6, text can take advantage of the newer LCD text antialiasing.

We do not cover LCD antialiasing techniques in depth here, but we cover the rendering hints you need for antialiasing text in general. Check out the article "LCD-Text: Anti-Aliasing on the Fringe" on java.net for more information on this topic.[5]

---

5. The article "LCD Text: Anti-Aliasing on the Fringe" can be found on java.net at http://today. java.net/pub/a/today/2005/07/26/lcdtext.html. If you want to read more about antialiasing, and especially more detailed stuff about how we do antialiasing for LCD displays, check out the article.

There are several rendering hint values to be aware of, depending on the type of antialiasing you want:

RenderingHints.VALUE_TEXT_ANTIALIAS_DEFAULT

This option chooses the default for the Java Runtime Environment (JRE). Up through and including the Java SE 6 release, the default for Sun's platforms (Windows and UNIX) has been equivalent to the VALUE_TEXT_ANTIALIAS_OFF key described next. Note that if *text* antialiasing is set to DEFAULT, then setting the *general* antialiasing hint, KEY_ANTIALIASING, to VALUE_ANTIALIAS_ON will cause text to be antialiased because Java 2D interprets this combination as a hint to enable text antialiasing.

RenderingHints.VALUE_TEXT_ANTIALIAS_OFF

This setting forces antialiasing off, and we get aliased text as a result.

RenderingHints.VALUE_TEXT_ANTIALIAS_ON

This setting forces antialiasing on, and we get smoother text as a result. The algorithm used with this hint is like the results we saw for Figure 3-6, which was the only type of text antialiasing available prior to Java SE 6. It is fine for many situations, but sometimes the quality is noticeably worse. For example, when the characters are quite small, the blurring caused by this approach can make the characters run together because the size of the pixels starts to outweigh the size of the character detail. In Java SE 6, the Java 2D team also enabled LCD text antialiasing, which is described shortly.

RenderingHints.VALUE_TEXT_ANTIALIAS_GASP[6]

This hint specifies that Java 2D should use information that comes from the font itself to determine whether to antialias that font at any given point size.

RenderingHints.VALUE_TEXT_ANTIALIAS_LCD_HRGB
RenderingHints.VALUE_TEXT_ANTIALIAS_LCD_HBGR
RenderingHints.VALUE_TEXT_ANTIALIAS_LCD_VRGB
RenderingHints.VALUE_TEXT_ANTIALIAS_LCD_VBGR

These hints all control the settings for LCD text. For each of the four hints, the antialiasing algorithm assumes a different orientation of the red, green,

---

6. GASP stands for "grid-fitting and scan conversion procedure," which doesn't seem, to me, any more explanatory than the acronym GASP. The term "GASP" at least sounds more dramatic.

and blue stripes in the LCD monitor. The hints with RGB assume that the stripes are in red-green-blue order. The hints with BGR assume blue-green-red order. The HRGB and HBGR hints assume that the striping is in the horizontal direction, where the RGB stripes are vertical. The VRGB and VBGR hints assume that the striping is vertical, with each stripe running horizontally.

The most typical configuration for LCD displays is HRGB, so the most typical setting for this hint is VALUE_TEXT_ANTIALIAS_LCD_HRGB. However, even if you know that the user has an LCD screen and that HRGB is the right setting for that screen, both of which might be difficult to determine at runtime, forcing this rendering hint automatically may be the wrong solution. Instead, you should probably take the approach outlined in the FontHints example that follows.

Setting text antialiasing hints directly can be problematic, especially with all of the new hints added in Java SE 6. A better solution for most situations is for your application to figure out what the user's desktop settings are for fonts and to do something similar for the user's Java application. This, in fact, is what Swing does in some of its look and feels, including: Synth, Metal, Windows, and GTK. Swing queries desktop properties for how text is rendered by native applications and sets RenderingHints appropriately.

Tip: Custom components that perform their own text operations do not get this Swing behavior. The Graphics object received in paintComponent() is set up with defaults that do not know anything about the desktop properties. So if you want text in your custom components to look like Swing's text or to look like native applications' text, for that matter, you need to do something like what Swing is doing. Look at the FontHints demo for tips.

Example: Setting Text Hints from Desktop Properties

The FontHints demo on the book's Web site shows how to accomplish the task of matching the desktop settings for a custom component. The application renders one string with the default Graphics object in paintComponent() for comparison purposes. It then sets `RenderingHints` appropriately to match desktop settings and renders another string with this modified `Graphics` object.

```
public FontHints() {
  Toolkit tk = Toolkit.getDefaultToolkit();
  desktopHints = (Map)(tk.getDesktopProperty(
      "awt.font.desktophints"));
}

protected void paintComponent(Graphics g) {
  Graphics2D g2d = (Graphics2D)g;
  g2d.setColor(Color.WHITE);
  g2d.fillRect(0, 0, getWidth(), getHeight());
  g2d.setColor(Color.BLACK);
  g2d.drawString("Unhinted string", 10, 20);
  if (desktopHints != null) {
    g2d.addRenderingHints(desktopHints);
  }
  g2d.drawString("Desktop-hinted string", 10, 40);
}
```

Figure 3-7 shows the result on my test system (Windows Vista with ClearType enabled).

The screenshot in Figure 3-7 probably looks much better on my display than it does on this page; LCD text rendering is optimized to look good on an LCD screen, not on a piece of paper. But the important thing to note here is not how good it looks on the page but that the two strings are different because the second string was drawn after setting the appropriate desktop property hints on the `Graphics` object.

Figure 3-7   Default and hinted strings rendered in custom component's `paintComponent()` method.

To get the desktop properties in the constructor, we do a query on awt.font.desktophints, which returns a Map of all of the properties.[7] Then we simply add all of those hints through a call to Graphics2D.addRenderingHints(). Now our Graphics object is set up to render text just like native applications.

For more information on desktop properties, check out "AWT Desktop Properties" in the JavaDocs. The document name is DesktopProperties.html, but it might be easier to find it by clicking on the link in the JavaDoc for Toolkit.getDesktopProperty().

```
public void clipRect(int x, int y, int width, int height)
public void clip(Shape s)
public void setClip(int x, int y, int width, int height)
public void setClip(Shape s)
public Shape getClip()
public Rectangle getClipBounds()
```

The clip property controls the shape within which rendering operations are constrained to be visible. That is, the caller passes in parameters that define a bounding area, and future rendering operations to that Graphics object will be visible only within the area defined by those values.

Warning: The setClip() methods set the clip to the specified area, whereas the clipRect() and clip() methods combine the specified area with the clip currently set on that Graphics object. In general, you should use the combined clip approach, not create an entirely new one that ignores the clip previously set on the Graphics object. For example, the Graphics that Swing gives you in paintComponent() has a clip set on it to constrain rendering to the component's area. You probably don't want to clobber that setting by replacing it with your own clip. Use clipRect() and clip().

Swing uses these clip methods internally to limit the visible area to be rendered for any component hierarchy. For example, if an area in the upper left of the Swing back-buffer image needs to be repainted due to some windowing event or a programmatic update request, then a clip will be set on the Graphics for the operation that is bounded by that area.

---

7. Desktop properties could actually change during the course of an application run (although it's pretty unlikely to happen), which this approach of caching the properties would miss. It is possible to listen in on property changes, which is what Swing does; there is more information about this in the "AWT Desktop Properties" document.

There are two good reasons to set the clip during rendering:

1. *Preservation of contents:* The window may have content outside of a particular area that should not change. Constraining the clip ensures that these contents are preserved, since rendering operations will be contained within the clipping area.
2. *Performance:* Why do more than you need to? If only a small area of the window needs to be repainted, it is a waste of time and cycles to paint the rest of the window.

It is this second item that particularly concerns us. If Swing or the application code is going to the trouble of setting a clip to constrain the task, then our painting code should be intelligent enough to check the clip and render accordingly. That is, we should only bother painting those items that lie within the current clip. Your code will probably not need to set the clip. The clip that you get from Swing in the `Graphics` object sent to `paintComponent()` will be sufficient for most of your needs. But you may often need to get the clip by calling `getClip()` and then rendering accordingly. We discuss in detail how to use the clip in Chapter 5, "Performance."

One interesting use of setting the clip is in drawing complex shapes. For example, if you want to draw a rectangular image into some nonrectangular area, you can simply constrain the clip to that `Shape` and then draw the image as usual. The results will be visible only in the area inside that `Shape`.

public void setComposite(Composite c)
public Composite getComposite()

The `Composite` property is used to determine how pixel colors from ensuing graphics operations will be combined or blended with the pixel colors already in the destination. `Composite` is an interface that may be implemented by a custom class. For the most part, we use the `AlphaComposite` class that is part of the core graphics libraries. There is probably little or no need for you to implement your own `Composite` implementation, although Chapter 6, "Composites," describes how to do so.

By default, the rendering rule used by `Graphics2D` is `SrcOver`, which means that the destination pixel colors are obscured by the source colors proportional to the alpha value, or opacity, of the source color. For example, a source color with alpha = 0 has no effect on the destination, whereas a source color with alpha = 1 completely replaces the destination color.

Tip: The Composite property is incredibly important for Filthy Rich Clients, since it enables the translucency effects that we use throughout our applications. We cover this topic in more detail in Chapter 6.

```
public void setPaint(Paint p)
public Paint getPaint()
```

Paint is an interface implemented by various subclasses such as Color, GradientPaint, and TexturePaint. The current Paint on a Graphics object determines how the pixels will be colored when ensuing graphics operations are performed. For example, Color implements Paint and determines what color will be used when rendering graphics primitives. Note that setColor() is really just a special case of setPaint(); every Color is also a Paint.

Paint gets really interesting when you look at some of the other more complex implementations. In particular, GradientPaint is used to define various types of gradients that are used when performing drawing operations. Gradients are so important in achieving great looking Filthy Rich Clients that they are described in their own chapter (Chapter 7).

```
public void rotate(double theta)
public void rotate(double theta, double x, double y)
public void scale(double sx, double sy)
public void translate(int x, int y)
public void translate(double x, double y)
public void transform(AffineTransform xform)
public void setTransform(AffineTransform xform)
public AffineTransform getTransform()
```

There are several related methods that allow you to control the transform on the Graphics object. The sheer number of the methods may seem overwhelming, but they are all just different ways of setting the same object: the AffineTransform of the Graphics object. Transforms can be confusing, so having utility methods to help out is a Good Thing.

The AffineTransform of the Graphics2D object is essentially a matrix (in the linear algebra sense, not the Keanu Reeves sense),[8] which defines the calculations used to figure out the position, size, and orientation of ensuing graphics operations. The process of calculating this new position, size, and orientation for

---

8. It's interesting that the movie *The Matrix* chose the term matrix to mean "the scariest technical thing we can think of." You wonder how much the writers enjoyed their math classes.

objects is called *transformation*, since we are transforming points from their original positions to new positions using the calculations encapsulated by AffineTransform[9].

Some background in matrix math might help in understanding how the underlying operations relate to these methods.

Matrix Math: A Perfectly Painless Primer (Probably)

We can picture the AffineTransform matrix as a series of three rows of three elements each, as follows:

$$\begin{bmatrix} m00 & m01 & m02 \\ m10 & m11 & m12 \\ 0 & 0 & 1 \end{bmatrix}$$

where the last row is always (0, 0, 1). If we picture each (x, y) point of a graphics primitive (such as a line endpoint) as a column vector, like so:

$$\begin{bmatrix} x \\ y \\ 1 \end{bmatrix}$$

where the third element is always 1, then we can see how to transform the point (x, y) to the point (x', y') by simple matrix multiplication:

$$\begin{bmatrix} x' \\ y' \\ 1 \end{bmatrix} = \begin{bmatrix} m00 & m01 & m02 \\ m10 & m11 & m12 \\ 0 & 0 & 1 \end{bmatrix} * \begin{bmatrix} x \\ y \\ 1 \end{bmatrix} = \begin{bmatrix} m00*x + m01*y + m02 \\ m10*x + m11*y + m12 \\ 1 \end{bmatrix}$$

---

9. In the interest of full disclosure, I should point out that my first encounter with linear algebra was pretty awful. I spent the entire term in a misery of confusion and boredom, not understanding a whit about why it was important to have orthonormal bases, or how to derive basis vectors, or why I'd gotten up so early for this class again. It wasn't until three years later that I took my first computer graphics course and it hit me like a ball-peen hammer between the eyes: Matrix math is a *tool*, and a very effective one at that. Matrices are very compact representations of the calculations that we must do to move points from one location to another in space (or, perhaps more correctly, from one space to another), which is what we do a lot of in graphics. Once I understood that, it made a lot more sense why I should care about linear algebra and the ability to transform points using matrices. It did not, however, make morning classes any more enjoyable.

Here, the transformed points (x', y', 1) are the values in the new column vector: ($m00*x + m01*y + m02$, $m10*x + m11*y + m12$, 1), so the new (x', y') point is simply ($m00*x + m01*y + m02$, $m10*x + m11*y + m12$).

As you can see, each element in the matrix affects the outcome of the transform calculation. For example, the elements at the right, $m02$ and $m12$, get added to each respective x or y value. This operation effectively performs a *translation* or move of the original coordinates. So if we wanted to simply shift the original point (x, y) by some distance (dx, dy) to get the new point (x', y'), we could construct a matrix like this:

$$\begin{bmatrix} 1 & 0 & dx \\ 0 & 1 & dy \\ 0 & 0 & 1 \end{bmatrix}$$

and perform the following transform calculation:

$$\begin{bmatrix} x' \\ y' \\ 1 \end{bmatrix} = \begin{bmatrix} 1 & 0 & dx \\ 0 & 1 & dy \\ 0 & 0 & 1 \end{bmatrix} * \begin{bmatrix} x \\ y \\ 1 \end{bmatrix} = \begin{bmatrix} 1*x + 0*y + dx \\ 0*x + 1*y + dy \\ 0*x + 0*y + 1*1 \end{bmatrix} = \begin{bmatrix} x + dx \\ y + dy \\ 1 \end{bmatrix}$$

where the new values (x', y') equal ($x + dx$, $y + dy$).

Similarly, the elements $m00$ and $m11$ multiply the original (x, y) elements to derive new (x', y') values. These elements perform a "scale" operation on the original point. This means that we can perform a scaling operation on a point (x, y) by simply providing the scale factor (sx, sy) in the $m00$ and $m11$ elements, as shown in the following calculation:

$$\begin{bmatrix} x' \\ y' \\ 1 \end{bmatrix} = \begin{bmatrix} sx & 0 & 0 \\ 0 & sy & 0 \\ 0 & 0 & 1 \end{bmatrix} * \begin{bmatrix} x \\ y \\ 1 \end{bmatrix} = \begin{bmatrix} sx*x + 0*y + 0*1 \\ 0*x + sy*y + 0*1 \\ 0*x + 0*y + 1*1 \end{bmatrix} = \begin{bmatrix} sx*x \\ sy*y \\ 1 \end{bmatrix}$$

Rotations are not quite as obvious[10] and involve the upper four elements of the matrix. For example, to rotate an object by θ radians, the rotation matrix would look like this:

$$\begin{bmatrix} \cos\theta & -\sin\theta & 0 \\ \sin\theta & \cos\theta & 0 \\ 0 & 0 & 1 \end{bmatrix}$$

---

10. Don't bother memorizing which elements are sine, cosine, negative, and positive. You'll just forget. Remember that graphics is more fun because you can visually debug it. In my experience, you tend to get the rotation elements wrong, and then you figure out the right elements by trial and error. But the best approach is to simply use the utility functions in `Graphics2D` and `AffineTransform` and make Java 2D construct the rotation matrix for you. Just provide θ and Java 2D will do the rest.

Combining Matrix Operations

Now we can see how these different types of matrices might combine to create matrices of more complexity and utility. A great example is scaling. You do not generally want to scale a set of points around the world origin (at $x = 0$, $y = 0$), as shown in Figure 3-8. Instead, you typically want to scale it around some other center, as shown in Figure 3-9.

The scaling matrix we discussed earlier, using just *sx* and *sy* factors, scales the square around the world origin. We can perform a more complex operation to scale around an arbitrary center by combining matrices. We are still going to scale our points around the world origin, but we are going to *move our arbitrary scaling center to the world origin* prior to scaling (and then move it back afterward). This multistep operation involves three matrices: translating our scaling center to the world origin, scaling, and translating back.

Matrices can be combined by multiplying them together to result in one single matrix that can then be multiplied by the vectors we wish to transform. In this case, we want to combine the translation, scale, and back-translation for our center (dx, dy) as follows:

$$\begin{bmatrix} 1 & 0 & dx \\ 0 & 1 & dy \\ 0 & 0 & 1 \end{bmatrix} * \begin{bmatrix} sx & 0 & 0 \\ 0 & sy & 0 \\ 0 & 0 & 1 \end{bmatrix} * \begin{bmatrix} 1 & 0 & -dx \\ 0 & 1 & -dy \\ 0 & 0 & 1 \end{bmatrix} = \begin{bmatrix} sx & 0 & dx \\ 0 & sy & dy \\ 0 & 0 & 1 \end{bmatrix} * \begin{bmatrix} 1 & 0 & -dx \\ 0 & 1 & -dy \\ 0 & 0 & 1 \end{bmatrix} = \begin{bmatrix} sx & 0 & dx(1 - sx) \\ 0 & sy & dy(1 - sy) \\ 0 & 0 & 1 \end{bmatrix}$$

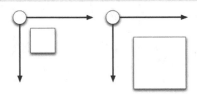

Figure 3-8 Scaling an object (square) around the world origin (circle).

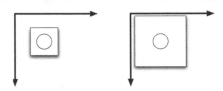

Figure 3-9 Scaling an object (square) around its center (circle).

At first, it might seem counterintuitive that we have the forward translation by (*dx*, *dy*) on the left. After all, we want to back-translate to the origin first and then forward translate after. However, these matrices actually multiply right to left. If you picture the coordinate column vector on the right of all three operations, then you'll see that it actually gets multiplied by the (*–dx*, *–dy*) translation first, then the scale, then the forward translation, just like what we want.

This quick introduction to matrix math is obviously way too light on details to enable a full understanding of the topic, but then, that wasn't really the intent.[11] If you can understand just enough of the basic operations of how translation, scaling, and rotation factors contribute to transforming points, then our discussion of the transform methods in Graphics2D should make more sense.

Utility Transform Methods

Now that we've seen how the various operations of translation, scale, and rotation affect the elements of the transform matrix, the utility functions translate(), scale(), and rotate() in the Graphics2D class should be clear. Instead of complicating your job by adding more methods for you to understand, these methods simplify it by letting you more easily construct the matrix you want. And by implicitly combining the effects of multiple transformations, they allow you to ignore details like the matrix multiplication we just described. You simply ask for the transform operations you need, and the internal AffineTransform constructs the matrix that those operations require.

For example, if you want to perform a translation of (*dx*, *dy*) on graphics primitive calls on the current Graphics object, you can simply call translate(). This method will add the specified translation factor to the current transform used by the Graphics object by combining the matrix created by this translate() call with the current Graphics matrix:

```
translate(dx, dy);
```

Similarly, if you want to scale primitives by (*sx*, *sy*), you can call scale(), which resizes primitives around the world origin, as shown in Figure 3-8.

```
scale(sx, sy);
```

---

11. We're assuming you bought this book to see how to make better, cooler Swing applications, not to bury yourself in math notation. Feel free to pick up a book on linear algebra if you're dying for more details on the math.

If you want to rotate primitives by *theta* radians, you can call `rotate()`, which rotates primitives around the world origin:

```
rotate(theta);
```

There is an additional variant of `rotate()` that is quite useful. This variation performs the translation-to-origin-and-back steps that we discussed earlier for scaling, all in this single method call. This operation effectively rotates future drawing around the specified center (*x*, *y*):

```
rotate(theta, x, y);
```

Example: RotationAboutCenter

You can see the difference between these two rotation operations in this example, taken from the `RotationAboutCenter` demo on the book's Web site. The application calls `fillRect()` three times, each time with a different color and rotation.

```
protected void paintComponent(Graphics g) {
  Graphics2D g2d;
  g2d = (Graphics2D)g.create();

  // Erase background to white
  g2d.setColor(Color.WHITE);
  g2d.fillRect(0, 0, getWidth(), getHeight());

  // base rectangle
  g2d.setColor(Color.GRAY.brighter());
  g2d.fillRect(50, 50, 50, 50);

  // rotated 45 degrees around world origin
  g2d.rotate(Math.toRadians(45));
  g2d.setColor(Color.GRAY.darker());
  g2d.fillRect(50, 50, 50, 50);

  // rotated 45 degrees about center of rect
  g2d = (Graphics2D)g.create();
  g2d.rotate(Math.toRadians(45), 75, 75);
  g2d.setColor(Color.BLACK);
  g2d.fillRect(50, 50, 50, 50);

  // done with g2d, dispose it
  g2d.dispose();
}
```

The first rectangle, in light gray, is drawn at (50, 50). Then the `Graphics2D` object is rotated by 45 degrees and the rectangle is drawn again, this time in dark gray. Then the `Graphics2D` object is reset to the original state to avoid inheriting the intermediate scale property. Finally, the new `Graphics2D` is rotated by 45 degrees, this time around the rectangle's center at (75, 75). You can see the results in Figure 3-10.

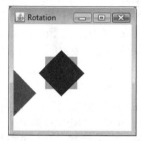

Figure 3-10 `RotationAboutCenter` screenshot. The original, unrotated primitive is in light gray. The dark gray primitive is rotated about the world origin, while the black primitive is rotated about the object center.

You can also specify an arbitrary transform by calling `transform()` with a complete `AffineTransform` object:

```
transform(xform);
```

Note that all of the methods just described combine the requested matrix operation with the matrix that is already in place for the `Graphics` object. These requests effectively multiply the matrix that represents your specified operation, such as `translate(x, y)`, by the current matrix in the `Graphics` object. There is an alternative approach whereby you can request an exact transform to take place:

```
setTransform(xform);
```

This method may look like the `transform()` method, but it has a very different effect. The previous `transform()` method combines the supplied transform with the current transform in the `Graphics` object. `setTransform()`, on the other hand, sets the transform explicitly, effectively replacing the current transform in the `Graphics` object with this new transform.

Warning: In general, you should use the methods that combine transform requests with the current `Graphics` transform. The current transform may have important information embedded in it, such as the correct offset that Swing set up to render to the current lightweight component. Ignoring the current transform may result in incorrect rendering.

It is worth mentioning a few more details about the transform methods. First of all, there is one additional method in `Graphics2D` for setting transforms, `shear()`, which performs a transformation that is important in some graphics operations but not typically in those that we deal with in Filthy Rich Clients. Perhaps more importantly, all of the methods in the `AffineTransform` class itself are available to you. We talked exclusively about the `Graphics2D` methods in our discussion, but an `AffineTransform` can be manipulated directly as well. `AffineTransform` has a host of utility methods for creating, combining, and managing a transform, similar to those we covered for `Graphics2D`. If you are working closely with transforms, you probably want to befriend this class and read the JavaDocs, which go into more detail on transforms than we have done here.

Finally, it is important to note that changing the current transform of a `Graphics` object has implications that are sometimes not obvious and can lead to problems that are difficult to track down. We discuss this topic in more detail later, but the main point is worth emphasizing in the following Tip.

Tip: If you change the `Graphics` object that Swing hands to you, you may mess up other Swing rendering that is using this same `Graphics` object.

When you change the object handed to you in `paintComponent(Graphics)`, for example, you are changing the `Graphics` object that Swing may be using for other purposes, such as rendering your component's borders or children. In general, this is probably not what you want to do, so it is usually good practice to work on a copy of the current `Graphics` object instead, like so:

```
protected void paintComponent(Graphics g) {
  // make a copy to avoid clobbering g
  Graphics2D myG2d = (Graphics2D)g.create();
  // change the transform on the copy
  myG2d.scale(sx, sy); // for example...
  // Now use myG2d for your graphics operations, such as:
  myG2d.fillRect(...);
  // dispose the Graphics object
  myG2d.dispose();
}
```

Final Graphics State-ment[12]: State Is Persistent

One final, important note about graphics state that everyone should remember: *It doesn't go away!* That is, if you set the value of an attribute on a Graphics object, the attribute will retain that value until the object is disposed or until that attribute is set to some other value. This behavior is typically not an issue for temporary Graphics objects or those that are created, used, and disposed in an area of small scope. But it can be an issue for situations in which you are using the Graphics object that Swing gave you, in the paintComponent() method, for example, and that Swing may use elsewhere when you are finished.

> **Tip:** The issue of clobbering graphics state in the paint() method is different from that with the paintComponent() method. If you choose to override paint(),[13] then you have free reign over the changes that you make to the Graphics object because the caller of paint(), at least if it's internal Swing code, will not reuse that object for other purposes. Therefore, changes that you make to the Graphics object within paint() will be irrelevant outside of the context of that paint() method.

There is an inherent trade-off with any powerful tool. You can use the power wisely to create beautiful and functional objects, or you can mess around and cut your hand off. Similarly, the persistent state of the Graphics object can be both powerful and dangerous.

Powerful By setting the state of a Graphics object and then letting Swing go about its usual business with the object, we can automatically control how Swing does otherwise standard rendering. For example, we might use this approach in order to have Swing draw an otherwise normal component with translucency, as in this example of a paintComponent override in a subclass of some Swing component:

```
public void paintComponent(Graphics g) {
  Graphics2D g2d = (Graphics2D)g.create();
  g2d.setComposite(myTranslucencyComposite);
  super.paintComponent(g2d);
  g2d.dispose();
}
```

---

12. In which I meant what I stated.
13. Hopefully, you have a good reason to override paint(); see our discussion in Chapter 2, "Swing Rendering Fundamentals," on overriding paint().

Here, we set the `Composite` attribute of g2d and then defer to the Swing super-class to actually draw the component. Since the `Composite` state in g2d persists in the call to the superclass, the component will be rendered translucently.

Dangerous   The flip side of persistent graphics state is that you should avoid making changes that will cause side effects to the rendering performed in other places that use the same `Graphics` object. The effects from clobbering state can be undefined, since it may be difficult to tell exactly who is doing what with the `Graphics` object once you finish with it. For example, this code alters the current transform of the `Graphics` object:

```
public void paintComponent(Graphics g) {
  g.translate(...);
  g.drawLine(...);
}
```

The side effect of calling `translate()` here is that you will cause all future rendering with this `Graphics` object, even outside of this method, to take place in the location specified by the call to `translate()`, which may not be what you intended.

Avoiding the Clobber

There are two simple workarounds for this situation if you want to alter the state of the `Graphics` object but do not want to cause a side effect to code outside of your method. These examples all use `translate()`, but the same techniques can be applied to any of the state that you might alter on `Graphics` or `Graphics2D` objects.

Create and Use a Copy Instead

```
public void paintComponent(Graphics g) {
  Graphics tmpG = g.create();
  tmpG.translate(...);
  tmpG.drawLine(...);
  tmpG.dispose();
}
```

Here, we create a clone of the original `Graphics` object, which starts out with all of the same state in the original object, and then change and use that copy of g instead. The original `Graphics` was not altered, so any future code relying on the state of that object will not be affected by the `translate()` call made on the copy of g.

Restore Clobbered State

```
public void paintComponent(Graphics g) {
  AffineTransform oldXform = ((Graphics2D)g).getTransform();
  g.translate(...);
  g.drawLine(...);
  ((Graphics2D)g).setTransform(oldXform);
}
```

In this example, we get the original transform state before we alter it, make our translation change, draw our line, and then restore the original transform state when we are finished. Even though we change and use the original Graphics object directly, we restore it to its original condition when we are done so that anyone using the object later will be unaffected by our temporary changes.

Tip: The copy-versus-restore approach that you should use in your code depends on the situation. For example, if you alter many different attributes in the Graphics object, then it might be tedious and error-prone to call the many methods required in order to save and restore the original state. In this case, using a copy of the Graphics object is probably a better choice. On the other hand, if you are changing just one simple property, then the calls to save and restore that property appropriately might be cheaper than creating and using a copy of the original Graphics object for just that one attribute.

In the end, the fact that state is persistent is mostly a powerful tool. We use it quite extensively in Filthy Rich Clients because it allows us to easily alter how core Swing rendering happens through simple overriding, state-setting, and delegating to the superclass. But you need to be aware of the risks involved in changing the state of the Graphics object. That object may be used outside your code, so its state should be treated with care.[14]

Graphics Primitives

Graphics primitives are the objects that we draw, such as lines, rectangles, images, pictures of Duke, ovals, and text. These operations happen, for the most part, through calls to methods in the Graphics and Graphics2D classes. For a

---

14. Your painting code should never assume a particular state set up on the Graphics by another component, be it a sibling or a parent in the component's hierarchy. While this might work on your machine, it is not guaranteed to work across all platforms. For instance, when Romain was working at Sun on a Swing demo for JavaOne 2006, he created a component that relied on the antialiasing state set by another component. It worked fine on Windows. Unfortunately, when he presented this demo on stage in front of 10,000 people, he discovered that Mac OS X was not keeping this state across the components. He nearly had a heart attack on stage, except a coronary, fortunately, was not in the demo script.

simple example, here is how we might draw a diagonal line in the content area of a Swing component:

```
public void paintComponent(Graphics g) {
  g.drawLine(0, 0, 100, 100);
}
```

The code draws a single line from the point (0, 0) to the point (100, 100). There are many details we've skimmed over here, such as the line color (which is defined by the state of the Graphics object we received, as discussed previously under "Graphics State"). But you can see the basic process followed by most graphics primitive operations: We call the method of interest in the Graphics object, passing in the parameters that define the characteristics of the primitive. In the example above, we call the drawLine() method and pass in values that define the start and end points for the line.

Example: DiagonalLineDemo

If we want to make the example slightly more interesting, we can base the line's endpoints on the dimensions of the component into which we are rendering. For example, suppose we want to draw a line from the upper left of the component to the lower right. The following code, which you can see in the DiagonalLineDemo on the book's Web site, is a complete application that does so:

```
public class DiagonalLineDemo extends JComponent {

  public void paintComponent(Graphics g) {
    g.drawLine(0, 0, getWidth() - 1, getHeight() - 1);
  }

  private static void createAndShowGUI() {
    JFrame f = new JFrame("Diagonal Line Demo");
    f.setDefaultCloseOperation(JFrame.EXIT_ON_CLOSE);
    f.setSize(300, 100);
    f.add(new DiagonalLineDemo());
    f.setVisible(true);
  }

  public static void main(String args[]) {
    Runnable doCreateAndShowGUI = new Runnable() {
      public void run() {
        createAndShowGUI();
      }
    };
```

```
        SwingUtilities.invokeLater(doCreateAndShowGUI);
    }
}
```

Figure 3-11 shows the exciting result of this application.

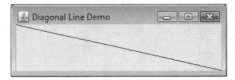

Figure 3-11 Terribly exciting results from the fantastic `DiagonalLineDemo` application.

The only interesting code in this example, beyond the boilerplate of the code used to create and show the `JFrame` and add the custom component that we are defining into that frame, is the code in the `paintComponent()` method:

```
g.drawLine(0, 0, getWidth() - 1, getHeight() - 1);
```

Tip: Note that if a border is set on a component, then the component's insets property will reflect the geometry of that border. These insets should be taken into account when rendering the content for that component to ensure that the border doesn't inadvertently obscure it. For example, the code to fill the non-border area of a component would be:

```
Insets i = getInsets();
g.fillRect(i.left, i.top,
           getWidth() - i.left - i.right,
           getHeight() - i.top - i.bottom);
```

This code is the same as the line-drawing code we saw a page or two ago, except that it uses the width and height of the component to put the endpoints of the line at the upper-left and lower-right corners of the component.

Pretty exciting, no? No. Not really. But simple line drawing is an easy way to see how the basics of all graphics primitives work. Now we can move on to see some more interesting graphics operations.

We look at some of the key primitives used by Swing applications, and Filthy Rich Clients in particular. Our discussion does not cover the full spectrum of primitives available to you in `Graphics` and `Graphics2D`, but, as in our earlier discussion of graphics state, we focus on what we have found to be the most useful graphics primitive operations for Filthy Rich Clients. You should check out the JavaDocs for the `Graphics` and `Graphics 2D` classes for more information on the wealth of other options available.

From the `Graphics` and `Graphics2D` classes, we examine the following primitives:

- **Images**: Copying and scaling images
- **Lines**: Drawing single-segment lines
- **Strings**: Drawing text
- **Rects**: Drawing rectangular borders and interiors
- **Shapes**: Drawing arbitrary shapes
- **CopyArea**: Copying contents from one location to another

public void drawImage(...)

`drawImage()` is one of the most prevalent graphics primitive calls in any Swing application, both in application code and in Swing internally. Its purpose is to copy a Java `Image` object to the destination surface used by the current `Graphics` object. This method may be used for anything from copying a back buffer to the window, to copying icons or other images onto the GUI, to copying contents from one `Image` type to another, to scaling an image from its original size to a new size.

There are several different variants of `drawImage()` in `Graphics` and `Graphics2D`. We discuss those that are most important for Filthy Rich Clients in order to simplify the alternatives.

In the following discussion, it is assumed that there is no scaling transform applied to the `Graphics` object. If there is a transform on the `Graphics` object, that operation will occur in addition to any explicit translation and scaling operations specified by the parameters of the `drawImage()` methods themselves.

> **Note:** For all of the `drawImage()` methods, you will notice that there is an `ImageObserver` argument as the final parameter. This argument is useful for images that may not be fully loaded yet at the time of the `drawImage()` call or that are animating, such as an animated GIF image. But in general, if you are using images that are already loaded, such as any `BufferedImage`, this argument is not needed. You should pass `null` for the final argument in these cases, as follows:
>
> ```
> drawImage(image, x, y, null);
> ```
>
> This is what you will see for the `drawImage()` calls in our demo code, as we generally use `BufferedImage` objects.

drawImage(Image img, int x, int y, ImageObserver observer)

This variant is the simplest version of drawImage(). It just copies the source image to the destination Graphics at the location specified by (*x*, *y*). There is no scaling or other operation performed during the copy apart from any scaling that occurs due to the transform set on the Graphics object.

drawImage(Image img, int x, int y, int width, int height, ImageObserver observer)

This variant is like the previous one except that it performs a scale of the source image, if necessary, to fit the given width and height dimensions. Regardless of the size of the original image, the result will be that the entire source image fits in the width and height dimensions in the destination. Note that any scaling incurred by this operation will use the value of the KEY_INTERPOLATION rendering hint, as discussed previously, to determine the algorithm that should be applied during the scale operation.

drawImage(Image img, int dx1, int dy1, int dx2, int dy2, int sx1, int sy1, int sx2, int sy2, ImageObserver observer)

This variant, the only one to use boundary points for the image area instead of width and height parameters, is a bit more involved, but it is also more flexible. It allows you to specify a subregion of the source image, defined by the s* parameters, that will be copied into the specified region of the destination, defined by the d* parameters. This operation could be a simple copy if the areas are of equal sizes, or it could be a scale if the regions differ in size. Note that any scaling incurred by this operation will use the value of the KEY_INTERPOLATION rendering hint, as discussed previously, to determine the algorithm that should be applied during the scale operation.

There are other variants of drawImage(), but the three we just covered are the most useful for Filthy Rich Client situations. More detail about resizing images with drawImage() is presented in the "Image Scaling" section of Chapter 4.

public void drawLine(int x1, int y1, int x2, int y2)

drawLine() is a simple method that draws a straight line between the two specified points (*x1*, *y1*) and (*x2*, *y2*). Important properties used in conjunction with lines include the current Color, Stroke, and antialiasing rendering hint.

public void drawString(String s, int x, int y)

drawString() is the simplest means of rendering text into a drawing area. You specify the String to draw and the (x, y) position that will be the baseline of the string[15] in the Graphics destination. Important properties associated with this drawing primitive include the current Color and text antialiasing rendering hint.

public void drawRect(int x, int y, int width, int height)
public void fillRect(int x, int y, int width, int height)

These primitives affect the region of pixels specified by the rectangle (x, y, *width*, *height*) with the current Color or Paint. drawRect() draws a border around this area, while fillRect() fills the pixels inside this area. See the section "Fill versus Draw" later for more information about the difference between these results of primitives. Important states associated with these drawing primitives include the current Color and Paint.

Graphics2D.draw(Shape s)
Graphics2D.fill(Shape s)

These methods draw the outline or fill the interior of a Shape, which is an arbitrary piece of geometry described by a series of path objects. There are actually Shape implementations for most of the primitives that you see in the individual draw* and fill* methods. For example, there is a Line2D primitive, an Ellipse2D primitive, and a Rectangle2D primitive.

> **Tip:** For the most part, unless you are looking for some of the added functionality that Shape offers, such as the ability to test a shape for intersection or whether it contains specific points or the use of more precise floating-point instead of integer coordinates, you should use the simpler draw and fill methods in Graphics and Graphics2D when a simpler method exists. That is, you should call drawLine() instead of creating a Line2D and calling draw(Shape). We discuss this topic more in Chapter 5, but the reason is straightforward: Simple primitives are faster for Java 2D to handle because there is simply less to deal with.

---

15. The fact that string origins are at their baseline and origins of other drawing primitives, such as images and rectangles, are at the upper left can be confusing. Correct positioning of text with respect to other graphics objects may involve calculation of various text attributes to correctly determine the baseline. Doug Felt and Phil Race described various details of text positioning in the Advanced Java 2D talk at JavaOne 2005. You can see the slides here: http://developers. sun.com/learning/javaoneonline/2005/desktop/TS-3214.html.

There are more interesting Shapes that you can create and then render with these methods. For example, GeneralPath can be used to construct an arbitrary path from individual line and curve segments. Also, the more sophisticated Area object, which interprets arbitrary Shapes as enclosed regions of 2D space, can perform operations that intersect, combine, and subtract those regions. These shapes are worth investigating if your graphics primitives take you outside the basic shapes provided in the other draw and fill methods.

To whet your appetite, here is a simple method that creates a donut[16] shape by creating two circle shapes and subtracting one from the other:

```
private static Shape generateDonut(double x, double y,
                                   double innerRadius,
                                   double outerRadius) {
  Area a1 = new Area(
      new Ellipse2D.Double(x, y, outerRadius, outerRadius));
  double innerOffset = (outerRadius - innerRadius)/2;
  Area a2 = new Area(
      new Ellipse2D.Double(x + innerOffset, y + innerOffset,
                           innerRadius, innerRadius));
  a1.subtract(a2);
  return a1;
}
```

And here is a routine that constructs a GeneralPath that holds a star of arbitrary size. The inner loop moves around the star, adding to the path with lineTo() calls for each point of the star:

```
private static Shape generateStar(double x, double y,
                                  double innerRadius,
                                  double outerRadius,
                                  int branchesCount) {
  GeneralPath path = new GeneralPath();

  double outerAngleIncrement = 2 * Math.PI / branchesCount;

  double outerAngle = 0.0;
  double innerAngle = outerAngleIncrement / 2.0;

  x += outerRadius;
  y += outerRadius;
```

continued

_____

16. Mmmmmm. Donuts. . .

```
    float x1 = (float) (Math.cos(outerAngle) * outerRadius + x);
    float y1 = (float) (Math.sin(outerAngle) * outerRadius + y);

    float x2 = (float) (Math.cos(innerAngle) * innerRadius + x);
    float y2 = (float) (Math.sin(innerAngle) * innerRadius + y);

    path.moveTo(x1, y1);
    path.lineTo(x2, y2);

    outerAngle += outerAngleIncrement;
    innerAngle += outerAngleIncrement;

    for (int i = 1; i < branchesCount; i++) {
      x1 = (float) (Math.cos(outerAngle) * outerRadius + x);
      y1 = (float) (Math.sin(outerAngle) * outerRadius + y);

      path.lineTo(x1, y1);

      x2 = (float) (Math.cos(innerAngle) * innerRadius + x);
      y2 = (float) (Math.sin(innerAngle) * innerRadius + y);

      path.lineTo(x2, y2);

      outerAngle += outerAngleIncrement;
      innerAngle += outerAngleIncrement;
    }
    path.closePath();
    return path;
  }
```

The donut and star shapes can then be rendered later with a call to draw() or
fill(), as appropriate.

Example: DrawShapes

You can see a sample usage of these shapes in the DrawShapes demo on the
book's Web site. A screenshot of this demo is shown in Figure 3-12, where several donuts and stars have been created by mouse clicks in different regions of
the screen.

In the DrawShapes demo, we alternately create stars and donuts at mouse-click
locations with random sizes inside a MouseListener implementation:

```
private class ClickReceiver extends MouseAdapter {
  public void mouseClicked(MouseEvent me) {
    int centerX = me.getX();
```

```
    int centerY = me.getY();
    double innerSize = 1 + (25 * Math.random());
    double outerSize = innerSize + 10 + (15 * Math.random());
    Shape newShape;
    if (getStar) {
      int numPoints = (int)(8 * Math.random() + 5);
      newShape = generateStar(centerX - outerSize,
                              centerY - outerSize,
                              innerSize, outerSize, numPoints);
    } else {
      newShape = generateDonut(centerX - outerSize/2,
                               centerY - outerSize/2,
                               innerSize, outerSize);
    }
    getStar = !getStar;
    shapes.add(newShape);
    repaint();
  }
}
```

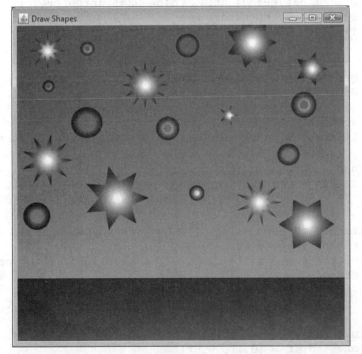

Figure 3-12 DrawShapes demo showing rendering of stars created from mouse-click events.

The shapes data structure is a simple `ArrayList` object:

```
private List<Shape> shapes = new ArrayList();
```

To paint our custom component, we iterate through the list of shapes and fill each one in turn. Note that most of the code in `paintComponent()` is actually related to gradients. We use one `GradientPaint` that goes from the top of the window most of the way down and another `GradientPaint` that goes the rest of the way. These give us a pseudo-night-sky/ground appearance. Finally, we use `RadialGradients` for each shape, white at their centers and black at the outer edges. The actual rendering for the shapes takes place in the simple call to `fill(Shape)` at the end of the loop.

```
protected void paintComponent(Graphics g) {
  Graphics2D g2d = (Graphics2D)g;

  // Paint a gradient for the sky
  GradientPaint background = new GradientPaint(
      0f, 0f, Color.GRAY.darker(),
      0f, (float)getHeight(), Color.GRAY.brighter());
  g2d.setPaint(background);
  g2d.fillRect(0, 0, getWidth(), 4*getHeight()/5);

  // Paint a gradient for the ground
  background = new GradientPaint(
      0f, (float)4*getHeight()/5, Color.BLACK,
      0f, (float)getHeight(), Color.GRAY.darker());
  g2d.setPaint(background);
  g2d.fillRect(0, 4*getHeight()/5, getWidth(), getHeight()/5);

  // Enable anti-aliasing to get smooth outlines
  g2d.setRenderingHint(RenderingHints.KEY_ANTIALIASING,
                       RenderingHints.VALUE_ANTIALIAS_ON);

  // Iterate through all of the current shapes
  for (Shape shape : shapes) {
    // Get the bounds to compute the RadialGradient properties
    Rectangle rect = shape.getBounds();
    Point2D center = new Point2D.Float(
        rect.x + (float)rect.width / 2.0f,
        rect.y + (float)rect.height / 2.0f);
    float radius = (float)rect.width / 2.0f;
    float[] dist = {0.1f, 0.9f};
    Color[] colors = {Color.WHITE, Color.BLACK};
```

```
        // Create and set a RadialGradient centered on the object,
        // going from white at the center to black at the edges
        RadialGradientPaint paint = new RadialGradientPaint(
            center, radius, dist, colors);
        g2d.setPaint(paint);

        // Finally, render our shape
        g2d.fill(shape);
    }
}
```

Note that we set antialiasing to give our shapes nice, smooth edges.

Graphics.copyArea(int x, int y, int width, int height, int dx, int dy)

copyArea() is useful for performing quick copies of content from one area of an image or a window to another area of that same surface. Swing uses this method, for example, when the user drags JInternalFrames around or when the contents of a scroll pane are scrolled up or down. Contents are copied from the area described by (*x, y, width, height*) to an area of the same size that is offset from the original area by (*dx, dy*).

One reason to consider copyArea() for some situations is performance. It may be faster and easier to copy existing contents around than it is to re-render those contents in a different location. This technique is a variant of the performance tip discussed in Chapter 5 under "Intermediate Images."

Example: CopyAreaPerformance

To demonstrate this point about performance, we wrote the CopyAreaPerformance application found on the book's Web site. This application draws lots of smiley faces into the window in varying colors, as seen in Figure 3-13. When the user clicks the arrow keys on the keyboard, the contents scroll 100 pixels in the specified direction.

What's actually happening during rendering is that there is a huge area of smiley-faces, 256×256 of them. This is a much larger area than the application window can fit. The window is just a view into that larger world of happiness. The easiest

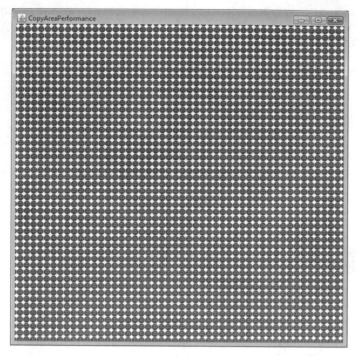

Figure 3-13 A very happy window: output from CopyAreaPerformance.

approach to painting the window is to simply draw all of the smiley faces in the universe, which we can do like this:

```
for (int column = 0; column < 256; ++column) {
  int x = column * (SMILEY_SIZE + PADDING) - viewX;
  for (int row = 0; row < 256; ++row) {
    int y = row * (SMILEY_SIZE + PADDING) - viewY;
    Color faceColor = new Color(column, row, 0);
    drawSmiley(g, faceColor, x, y);
  }
}
```

Here, we iterate through all of the rows and columns of happy faces, altering the face color, which gets redder to the right and greener toward the bottom, and calling our routine that draws each face in the correct location in the window. viewX and viewY are the *x* and *y* coordinates of the left and top of the window, so drawSmiley() may be called with negative *x* and *y* values for faces that are off to the left or top of the window.

The code is instrumented to print out the time that it takes to process the `paintComponent()` method. The simplistic approach presented here has a per-frame rendering time of about 1,200 milliseconds on my test system.

Trick 1: Use the Clip

The first and most obvious performance improvement here would be to not draw objects that do not even show up in the window. This idea is covered more in the earlier discussion of the clip property and in the "Use the Clip" section of Chapter 5. The approach is also illustrated in this demo. The code checks, for any given smiley face, whether it falls within the viewable portion of the field of smileys. If it does, draw it. If not, skip it. Here is the code that performs this logic. It is the same as the above code, with the clip-checking logic, inside the `if (useClip)` blocks, shown in bold:

```
for (int column = 0; column < 256; ++column) {
  int x = column * (SMILEY_SIZE + PADDING) - viewX;
  if (useClip) {
    if (x > clipR || (x + (SMILEY_SIZE + PADDING)) < clipL) {
      // trivial reject; outside to the left or right
      continue;
    }
  }
  for (int row = 0; row < 256; ++row) {
    int y = row * (SMILEY_SIZE + PADDING) - viewY;
    if (useClip) {
      if (y > clipB || (y + (SMILEY_SIZE + PADDING)) < clipT) {
        // trivial reject; outside to the top or bottom
        continue;
      }
    }
    Color faceColor = new Color(column, row, 0);
    drawSmiley(g, faceColor, x, y);
  }
}
```

This logic speeds up the application considerably, dropping the time spent in `paintComponent()` to around 180 ms on my test system, or about 15% of the original rendering time.

Trick 2: Use CopyArea for Existing Contents

Finally, we get to the performance trick that uses `copyArea()`. When scrolling back and forth in the application, most of the contents are the same from frame to frame. We are scrolling by only 100 pixels at a time, which means that only a

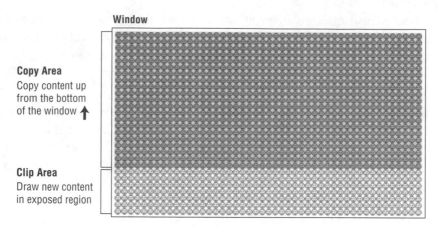

Window

Copy Area
Copy content up
from the bottom
of the window ↑

Clip Area
Draw new content
in exposed region

Figure 3-14   CopyAreaPerformance with copyArea and clipping optimizations. Old content moves up in a down-scroll operation; new content is drawn in the exposed region.

100-pixel-wide swath is new content. The rest is just a copy of smileys that were on the screen previously in a different location. So what happens if we copy that old content around and draw new smileys only for the new content?

We can do this inside our paintComponent() method by first calling copyArea() for copying the old contents and then setting the clip on the Graphics object prior to performing our normal drawing operation. This approach works in conjunction with our earlier performance trick of using the clip area. The basic idea is shown in Figure 3-14.

In this simple demo, we scroll in one direction at a time, either horizontally or vertically, so the copyArea calls are specific to the direction in which we are moving. This behavior could be generalized to movement in both directions at once, although the current demo does not do so. Here is the code for a vertical scroll:

```
g.copyArea(0, copyFromY,
          getWidth(), getHeight() - Math.abs(scrollY),
          0, -scrollY);
g.setClip(0, clipFromY, getWidth(), Math.abs(scrollY));
```

copyFromY and clipFromY are values calculated on the basis of the direction of the scroll (negative or positive). The horizontal scroll operations are similar:

```
g.copyArea(copyFromX, 0,
          getWidth() - Math.abs(scrollX), getHeight(),
          -scrollX, 0);
g.setClip(clipFromX, 0, Math.abs(scrollX), getHeight());
```

This technique yields fantastic results in this application. It reduces the amount of new rendering to a small fraction of what was happening before, dropping the time in `paintComponent()` to around 40 ms in my tests, less than a quarter of our previous rendering time and about 1/30 of the original time!

`copyArea()` is not a general solution for many performance or rendering issues, but it is certainly worth a look when it suits the purpose. In particular, if your application is rendering a complex screen and much of it could be copied instead of rendered from scratch, consider using `copyArea()`.

Fill versus Draw

It's good to understand the rasterization rules that Java2D uses when filling a shape, such as `fillRect()`, as opposed to when it is drawing a shape, such as `drawRect()`.

Tip: The boundaries of fill and draw operations affect different pixels.

A draw operation uses the current `Stroke` setting to determine which pixels to touch. The standard `BasicStroke` draws a line along the boundary like a pen, with half of the pen inside the boundary and half outside. With the default line width of 1, this results in a half pixel inside and half pixel outside the shape all the way around, which cannot be represented using discrete pixels. With these default settings, rounding must be used to determine whether to choose the pixel inside or outside the boundary, and it chooses the pixels that are biased toward the lower right.

The following examples assume that no scaling is taking place: Scaling would introduce other factors in addition to what we are highlighting here.

Example: FillDraw

ONLINE DEMO

To illustrate the differences in fill and draw, suppose we want a 3 × 3 square filled with gray and outlined in black, as illustrated in the `FillDraw` demo on the book's Web site. We might try the following code:

```
g.setColor(Color.LIGHT_GRAY);
g.fillRect(x, y, 3, 3);
g.setColor(Color.BLACK);
g.drawRect(x, y, 3, 3);
```

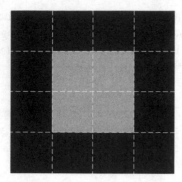

The white dashes show the pixel grid

Figure 3-15 `fillRect(x, y, 3, 3)` followed by `drawRect(x, y, 3, 3)`.

The result looks like Figure 3-15.

It actually looks pretty good, but notice that the border is actually 4×4 instead of 3×3.[17] Let's suppose that that result is okay, though. We got what we wanted: a gray interior and black exterior. Now let's see what happens when we reverse the order of the fill and draw, as in this code:

```
g.setColor(Color.BLACK);
g.drawRect(x, y, 3, 3);
g.setColor(Color.LIGHT_GRAY);
g.fillRect(x, y, 3, 3);
```

This code gives us the result seen in Figure 3-16.

Now we can see that our original border was actually drawing over our fill on the top and left of the square but drawing outside the fill area on the right and bottom. If we wanted to perform the fill only inside the pixels affected by the draw, we would have to change our areas as follows:

```
g.setColor(Color.BLACK);
g.drawRect(x, y, 3, 3);
g.setColor(Color.LIGHT_GRAY);
g.fillRect(x+1, y+1, 2, 2);
```

We can see the results of this approach in Figure 3-17.

---

17. Note that this is a graphics-only example. If this were a Swing component whose bounds were 3×3, Swing would hand you a `Graphics` with a clip set that would constrain rendering to 3×3, which would effectively hide the right and bottom pixels in the figure.

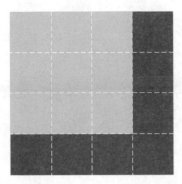

The white dashes show the pixel grid

Figure 3-16 drawRect(x, y, 3, 3) followed by fillRect(x, y, 3, 3).

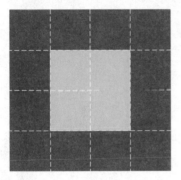

The white dashes show the pixel grid

Figure 3-17 drawRect(x, y, 3, 3) followed by fillRect(x+1, y+1, 2, 2).

The key thing to notice here is that the fill and draw operations both hit the same pixels along the top and left of the rectangle, but the fill covers (width × height) pixels, while the draw affects the pixels that are a boundary around that area. This behavior may not actually matter in many situations. For example, the square in Figure 3-17 looks fine, regardless of whether some pixels were drawn twice. But there may be situations in which you need your draw and fill operations to line up more exactly. For instance, if you are drawing a translucent border where the colors of each operation blend with the colors in the destination, you may not want the border color to be affected by the underlying fill color.

4

Images

IMAGES are just another graphics primitive, as described Chapter 3, "Graphics Fundamentals," in the section "Graphics Primitives." But images are so crucial to most 2D and Swing applications, so important in performance-critical situations, and so fundamental to Filthy Rich Clients, that they are worth discussing in depth. Lucky them: They get their own chapter.

Image objects can be used for many different purposes. They can hold the contents of image files. They can act as back buffers in buffered applications to enable smooth animation, as we saw in the section "Double-Buffering" in Chapter 2, "Swing Rendering Fundamentals." They can provide an easy mechanism for improving application performance through caching intermediate rendering results. And images can provide various means of performing the kinds of interesting graphical effects that we use in Filthy Rich Clients. This chapter explores these and other tasks that can be accomplished with images.

First, we should define some terminology. The term *images*, in the non-Java world, usually refers to image files. While Java Image objects can hold the contents of these files, they are much more than this, as we'll see below. In general, when we say *images* in this book, we are talking about Java Image objects, not image files. Java Image objects are, essentially, rectangular arrays of pixel data in some specified format.

The basics of image usage include the following:

- *Image creation:* Images are created by either loading an image file or creating an image from scratch.
- *Image rendering:* An image that is loaded from a file already has its contents defined by the data in that file. Images that are created from scratch are rendered to by creating a Graphics object for the image, setting the state

of that Graphics object, and using that object to render. This process should seem familiar to you if you read Chapter 3; rendering to an image is the same as rendering to a component, minus the Swing paintComponent() method.

- *Image copying:* Images are copied to other images or to the screen using the drawImage() methods described Chapter 3.

- *Image saving:* Images are saved out to files using the Image I/O APIs. Note that any Image, regardless of whether it was loaded from an image file or created from scratch, can be saved out to an image file.

The details of images are a little more subtle. In particular, there are several kinds of images and various image APIs to choose from; which ones should you use? There are, fortunately, some obvious choices here for Filthy Rich Clients.

Although we focus on specific image types, loading approaches, and copying techniques, it is helpful to see the gamut of possibilities so that we can understand our choices in context. Let's take a look at the various possibilities.

Image Types

There are a few distinct image types, which correspond to specific classes in the JDK:

java.awt.Image

This is the abstract superclass of all images. In general, the images you use are accessible through more capable methods of subclasses of Image, but Image is used as a handy generic class to refer to images of all types. For example, BufferedImage is a subclass of Image but extends the class in various useful ways.

Although we do not instantiate Image directly, we see references in the code to Image because various methods depend on this generic superclass. For example, all of the Graphics.drawImage() methods take Image as a parameter, meaning that they can draw any image type.

java.awt.VolatileImage[1]

This image type was created in J2SE 1.4 as a means of accessing hardware acceleration and video memory storage for images. Video memory, or VRAM,

---

1. There are a couple of older articles on VolatileImage posted on my blog at http://weblogs. java.net/blog/chet. If you're curious about this image type, check out those articles for more information on the VolatileImage API and usage of this image type. Or, better yet, ignore VolatileImage completely and use BufferedImage instead.

is a finicky and constrained resource. On some operating systems, such as Windows, an application may lose its allocation of VRAM without warning, which is known as *surface loss*. This volatility of accelerated memory does not work well with standard Java `Image` objects, which have no way of communicating this loss to the user.

`VolatileImage` was created to work around this issue so that images could be created in VRAM, could communicate memory-loss problems to the application, and could be queried for acceleration characteristics. `VolatileImage` objects may sometimes be used internally by Swing, but Filthy Rich Clients need not use `VolatileImage` directly. Instead, we depend on `BufferedImage`.

`java.awt.image.BufferedImage`[2]

`BufferedImage` objects represent a square region of pixels stored in main memory in any of a variety of formats. `BufferedImage` is the main image type of interest to Filthy Rich Clients because it provides the right combination of flexibility and performance that these applications need. See the section "BufferedImage" later in this chapter for a more thorough discussion on these full-featured image types.

There are also, just to keep things interesting, several other phrases and names associated with images, so it is worthwhile spending some time clarifying the meanings of these other terms. The three base types covered in the preceding list are the true "image" types of Java. Other phrases that refer to images do not refer to specific image types but rather to variations of the base types, used in particular scenarios. Here are some of these other terms:

Toolkit Image

A toolkit image is an image loaded from the original Java APIs, such as `java.awt.Toolkit` and `java.applet.Applet`. For example, we have:

- Image `Toolkit.getImage(String filename)`
- Image `Toolkit.getImage(URL url)`
- Image `Applet.getImage(URL url)`
- Image `Applet.getImage(URL url, String filename)`

---

2. There are a couple of articles on `BufferedImage` posted on my blog at http://weblogs.java.net/blog/chet; check them out for more information.

Objects returned from these APIs tend to be of an internal type whose only public interface is `java.awt.Image`. You can see from our discussion about `java.awt.Image` that this type is not as useful as the image type returned from other loading or creation methods.

Note: One of the biggest limitations of toolkit images is that they are display-only. You cannot get the `Graphics` object for a toolkit image and render to it like you can with other image types, such as `BufferedImage`. Because Filthy Rich Clients use images extensively, often creating them from scratch or modified loaded images, toolkit images are not very useful for our purposes. The Image I/O API provides image-loading mechanisms that integrate better with our preferred image type, `BufferedImage`.

Managed Image

A managed image is an image whose acceleration is being managed automatically by Java 2D. This topic is discussed in Chapter 5, "Performance."

Compatible Image

A compatible image is an image whose pixel data is in a format that best suits the format of the display on which the application is being viewed. For example, if the user has a monitor running in 32-bit mode, a compatible image might be created with type `BufferedImage.TYPE_INT_RGB` with the red, green, and blue bytes aligned the same in the image as they are in the display memory. Typically, compatible images are created with the method `GraphicsConfiguration.createCompatibleImage()`. This method returns an image that is compatible with the given `GraphicsConfiguration`, which is associated with a particular `GraphicsDevice`, or display. Compatible images have certain performance advantages, discussed further in Chapter 5.

Intermediate Image

Intermediate images is an acceleration technique that uses managed images to cache complex rendering operations. We describe this technique in detail in Chapter 5.

Image I/O

This API, in the `javax.imageio` package, was introduced in J2SE 1.4 as a better facility than the older toolkit image approach to reading and writing image files. Images loaded by Image I/O are of type `BufferedImage`.

Image Files

Images stored on disk or on a Web server, or streamed from some other location, are not related to the "Image" objects discussed here except that these files may be loaded into one of the previously mentioned types of Image objects by one of the various mechanisms, including those described under Toolkit Image and Image I/O.

BufferedImage

BufferedImage objects offer a good combination of versatility, functionality, performance, and integration into other APIs. Let's take a look at some of their advantages:

- *Versatility:* BufferedImage objects exist in many different flavors. They vary in how they store their pixels in memory, how many different colors they can support, and whether or not they have an alpha channel. These images can be created by loading files through the Image I/O API, created from scratch using one of several different formats, or created to be compatible with a given GraphicsConfiguration. This variety of ways to create the images makes it easy to use a BufferedImage that is suited to your particular purpose.

- *Functionality:* The data stored in a BufferedImage can be accessed in many different ways. A BufferedImage object can be rendered to and from using the Graphics and Graphics2D operations covered in previous chapters, just as other Image types (aside from toolkit images) can. You can also access the pixels of a BufferedImage directly using the easy getRGB() and setRGB() methods. Finally, this image type offers something that the other image types do not: You can access the pixel data of a BufferedImage directly. Using the Raster and DataBuffer classes, which are part of the internal representation of a BufferedImage, you can get a handle to the pixels of a BufferedImage and manipulate those pixels directly. Note that this more involved technique requires that you know the type of data being accessed, as that array will be exposing the raw data. This is a handy technique for reading the pixels, which was an awkward operation using the original Image type provided in the pre-J2SE 1.2 releases. This technique also provides a fast approach to writing per-pixel information to the image.

> **Performance Tip:** Note that in Java SE releases up through Java SE 6, requesting the `DataBuffer` from a `BufferedImage` will defeat hardware acceleration possibilities for that image. See the section "Managed Images" in Chapter 5 for more information on this detail.

- *Performance:* `BufferedImage` objects cannot be stored in VRAM because of the potential for surface loss, as described earlier in the `VolatileImage` section. `BufferedImage` objects are instead stored in the Java memory heap. This means that you do not have to worry about whether the memory becomes lost, as you do with `VolatileImage`. However, there are also potentially good and bad performance consequences because of this difference.

  First of all, Java 2D cannot hardware-accelerate basic rendering into a `BufferedImage`. Since the image is stored in the Java heap, the 2D library uses software rendering loops to draw to that memory. However, operations *from* these images to an accelerated destination, such as copying a `BufferedImage` to the Swing back buffer, can be accelerated by using the managed images technique discussed in Chapter 5. Finally, direct pixel access and some other advanced rendering techniques require software to get at the pixel data quickly and easily, and the fact that `BufferedImage` objects keep their pixels in main memory makes these operations quicker than if the operations had to access the pixels in VRAM.

- *Integration with other APIs:* Image I/O, the image loading/saving API introduced in J2SE 1.4, works exclusively with `BufferedImages`. So when you load image data through Image I/O, the result is a `BufferedImage`. Or when you want to save an image out to disk, it expects a `BufferedImage`. Also, the method in `GraphicsConfiguration` that creates a compatible image, `createCompatibleImage()`, returns a `BufferedImage`.

We pointed out various mechanisms for creating or loading `BufferedImage` objects, but there are also various older methods in Java for creating images of other types. Should you make the reasonable decision of using `BufferedImages` exclusively, it is a simple matter to copy any other image into a `BufferedImage` instead. The following snippet provides an example of how to convert any image into a `BufferedImage`.

```
public BufferedImage makeBufferedImage(Image oldImage) {
    // Query the old image for its dimensions
```

```
int w = oldImage.getWidth(null);
int h = oldImage.getHeight(null);

// Assume we have a handle to a GraphicsConfig object
// Create a compatible image
BufferedImage bImg =
    graphicsConfig.createCompatibleImage(w, h);

// Get the image Graphics
Graphics g = bImg.getGraphics();

// Copy the contents from the old image into the new one
g.drawImage(oldImage, 0, 0, null);
// dispose the temporary Graphics object we used
g.dispose();

// Return the BufferedImage
return bImg;
}
```

Note that the details are a bit different for transparent and translucent images. A translucent or transparent image would require a translucent or transparent `BufferedImage` instead of the opaque `BufferedImage` created in our code example. A transparent image is one in which each pixel is either fully transparent or fully opaque. Such an image can be created like this:

```
BufferedImage bImg = graphicsConfig.
    createCompatibleImage(w, h, Transparency.BITMASK);
```

A translucent image is one in which each pixel can have a varying level of opacity, ranging from fully transparent to fully opaque or anything in between. A translucent image can be created like this:

```
BufferedImage bImg = graphicsConfig.
    createCompatibleImage(w, h, Transparency.TRANSLUCENT);
```

Some of the advantages of `BufferedImage`, and of images in general, will become clear in Chapter 5. The general idea is that *many* graphical objects can be represented very cheaply as images, and operations on those images can be much cheaper, faster, and easier than other approaches.

Image Scaling³

Let's talk about one particular image operation that has bugged me for years: scaling. Scaling tends to be a problem area for 2D programmers because of the many options available for scaling images and the accompanying variety of differences in terms of quality and performance.

Tip: One of the most important items to mention here is that you should avoid performing a scaling operation repeatedly for any particular image that you need to display at the same scaled size. If you find that you are constantly re-rendering the same image with the same scaling factor, it may make sense to cache another prescaled version of the image and simply copy from that prescaled image instead of scaling from the original image. This idea is discussed further in Chapter 5 under "Intermediate Images." The idea of caching intermediate results goes beyond scaling images, but scaling is a great example of why this technique is useful.

There are so many ways to scale an image. For any scaling operation that you need to perform, which method should you use? Here are some of the most obvious ways that you might consider, although this is only a partial list:

Method 1:

```
g.drawImage(img, x, y, width, height, null);
```

Method 2:

```
g.drawImage(img, dx1, dy1, dx2, dy2,
            sx1, sy1, sx2, sy2, null);
```

Method 3:

```
g.translate(x, y);
((Graphics2D)g).scale(sx, sy);
g.drawImage(img, 0, 0, null);
```

---

3. I have been planning to write an article on this topic for years. I even started the article a couple of years back but deadlocked when I realized that I needed some nice code and screenshots to go along with it. So it sat on the back burner until I found myself in the middle of writing this book and wanted to discuss the topic in the chapter on images. I wrote up a draft of this section, complete with a demo application and screenshots, sent it to Chris Campbell to review . . . and he replied that he'd just written his own article on the subject. Clearly, the topic scales quite well. For more details on this topic, check out Chris's excellent article, "The Perils of Image.getScaledInstance()" at http://today.java.net/pub/a/today/2007/04/03/perils-of-image-getscaledinstance.html.

Method 4:

```
AffineTransform at = new AffineTransform();
at.translate(x, y);
at.scale(sx, sy);
((Graphics2D)g).drawImage(img, at, null);
```

Method 5:

```
Image scaledImg = img.getScaledInstance(w, h, hints);
g.drawImage(scaledImg, x, y, null);
```

You can see these different approaches in action in the ScalingMethods application on the book's Web site (see Figure 4-1).

The first four of these methods are all actually quite similar, at least under the hood. Java 2D sets up scaling calculations internally that match the requirements in all four methods. The only real functional difference in the first four approaches is that the second alternative, with all of the d* and s* parameters, allows the flexibility of specifying source and destination subrectangles, instead of scaling the entire source image into place. All of these options are affected by the RenderingHints.KEY_INTERPOLATION hint, as discussed later in this chapter and in the "Graphics State" section of Chapter 3.

The getScaledInstance() method is really a different kind of beast, which we discuss later in this chapter. Just know that there are good reasons for you to consider the other alternatives that we cover.

Let's discuss these approaches in more detail.

g.drawImage(img, x, y, width, height, null);

This approach is by far the simplest. The source image (img) is resized into an area of size (width × height) and drawn at the location (x, y). It is a great choice

Figure 4-1 The ScalingMethods application scales the same image using the five scaling methods described here.

for scaling operations that fit this simple model in which the source image is resized in its entirety into the destination area.

Tip: If you have no overriding reason to use one of the other options, `drawImage(img, x, y, w, h, null)` is the scaling method you should use.

`g.drawImage(img, dx1, dy1, dx2, dy2, sx1, sy1, sx2, sy2, null);`

This version is more flexible than the previous version and allows a subregion of the source image, defined by (`sx1, sy1, sx2, sy2`), to be scaled to fit into the area in the destination defined by the rectangle (`dx1, dy1, dx2, dy2`). Note that this variant uses the actual boundary points of the regions instead of the width and height parameters of some of the other approaches. This difference can make the method slightly more complicated to use than the other methods, but also more flexible. Otherwise, it has similar performance characteristics to the first option. In fact, the simpler `drawImage()` option can be seen as a degenerate example of this more flexible method. But if you do not need the extra flexibility, why bother with all of the dx/dy/sx/sy parameters?

```
g.translate(x, y);
((Graphics2D)g).scale(sx, sy);
g.drawImage(img, 0, 0, null);
```

and

```
AffineTransform at = new AffineTransform();
at.translate(x, y);
at.scale(sx, sy);
Graphics2D)g).drawImage(img, at, null);
```

These two options are listed together because they are functionally equivalent, differing only in the extra step of creating and composing the `AffineTransform` object in the latter approach. These options change the state of the transform used by the `Graphics` object and translate and scale the source image according to that transform.[4] It is a more tedious way to scale an image than the previous options and may, in the `at.scale(sx, sy)` case, cause you to create an unnecessary temporary `AffineTransform` object. But if you happen to be doing other transforms or just have a hankering for working with matrices, feel free to use these alternatives.

---

4. Note the necessary translation to or from some origin to perform the scaling operation around that origin. This technique is explained in the section on transforms in Chapter 3.

```
Image scaledImg = img.getScaledInstance(w, h, hints);
g.drawImage(scaledImg, x, y, null);
```

This method is quite different from the other four options. `getScaledInstance()` does not render the image directly but instead creates a new image of the specified size, which you can then use as your source image in a `drawImage()` operation. The `hints` parameter controls the trade-off between quality and performance for the scaling operation and can take on one of the following five values:

```
Image.SCALE_AREA_AVERAGING
Image.SCALE_DEFAULT
Image.SCALE_FAST
Image.SCALE_REPLICATE
Image.SCALE_SMOOTH
```

In Sun's current implementation, `REPLICATE` is basically equivalent to the `NEAREST_NEIGHBOR` algorithm discussed in Chapter 3 under "`RenderingHints`." `FAST` and `DEFAULT` are both set to use `REPLICATE`.

`AREA_AVERAGING` averages all of the pixel values that contribute to a destination pixel value. This approach tends to give the highest quality during downscale operations, especially when scaling by large factors, at the cost of *much slower* performance. `SMOOTH` is, in Sun's current implementation,[5] set to be equivalent to `AREA_AVERAGING` and thus has the same quality and performance.

Quality versus Performance

The whole reason for launching into the topic of image scaling is to discuss the performance of the different scaling algorithms available to you. Like many situations in graphics rendering, there is a trade-off between quality and performance. If you want better quality from your image-scaling operation, you may have to take a hit in performance. However, there are some hidden "gotchas" in the various techniques of scaling images that may trip you up unnecessarily. You can, in fact, get excellent image-scaling quality without taking a huge performance hit. You just have to know how to avoid the pitfalls.

---

5. Rumor has it that Sun may try to change how `SCALE_SMOOTH` is implemented in a future version of Java SE to make it perform much better than the current implementation. It is apparently difficult to change `AREA_AVERAGING` while remaining compatible with the API specification, but the same is not true for `SMOOTH`. Read on for the discussion of progressive bilinear scaling, which is what Sun is currently investigating to gain much better performance from `SMOOTH`.

Let's start the discussion with a subtle tip:

Tip: Do not use `getScaledInstance()`.
Let me repeat that sentiment in a nicer way:
Please don't use `getScaledInstance()`. Or else . . .
It's just, well, slow. And there are much better alternatives available.

You may be wondering why this method is an issue. In a word: *quality*. The quality of an image-scaling operation is controlled by two mechanisms:

1. The method invoked to scale the image.
2. The scaling hint used to control the quality.

Method

Methods 1 through 4, discussed earlier, all use the internal implementation of `Graphics`, whereas Method 5 uses `getScaledInstance()`. To simplify the discussion, let's assume that if you're not using `getScaledInstance()`, you're using the `drawImage(img, x, y, w, h, null)` method of `java.awt.Graphics` shown earlier.

Scaling Hints

Each of the two approaches, `drawImage()` and `getScaledInstance()`, uses a different set of hints. The hints for scaling with `drawImage()` are set by a call to `setRenderingHint()`, which we introduced in the "Graphics State" section of Chapter 3, with the key `RenderingHints.KEY_INTERPOLATION`. Recall that that key takes one of the following three values:

```
RenderingHints.VALUE_INTERPOLATION_NEAREST_NEIGHBOR
RenderingHints.VALUE_INTERPOLATION_BILINEAR
RenderingHints.VALUE_INTERPOLATION_BICUBIC
```

The default hint for scaling with `drawImage()` is `NEAREST_NEIGHBOR`. This algorithm is the simplest to compute and, as you would expect, the fastest. `BILINEAR` is slower, but provides better quality. `BICUBIC` is better still, but comes at an even higher performance cost.

The hints for `getScaledInstance()`, on the other hand, are provided during the call to that function and come from the `java.awt.Image` class:

```
Image.SCALE_DEFAULT
Image.SCALE_REPLICATE
Image.SCALE_FAST
```

```
Image.SCALE_SMOOTH
Image.SCALE_AREA_AVERAGING
```

These hints break down into two categories: DEFAULT, REPLICATE, and FAST are all equivalent on Sun's Java implementation and use the same approach as the NEAREST_NEIGHBOR hint for drawImage(). The AREA_AVERAGING and SMOOTH approaches are equivalent on Sun's Java implementation, producing a higher quality result in general than either the other hints for getScaledInstance() or the BILINEAR and BICUBIC results for drawImage(), especially when scaling down an image by a large factor.

Downscaling Quality Results

With the bilinear technique, the scaling algorithm samples the four pixels closest to the source pixel that each pixel in the scaled image maps back to, averaging those colors to get the final result. This approach provides a reasonable result when these surrounding pixels represent most of the color information that should go into that final pixel. However, if the image is downscaled by a large factor from the original, each pixel in the resulting image must represent a far greater number of pixels from the original image, so sampling only the four nearest pixels is not enough. Important information from the original image is lost in the process.

Bicubic is similar to bilinear except that it uses a 4 × 4 grid of pixels surrounding the source pixel. This increased amount of data means that downscales retain more information from the original image than is the case for bilinear downscales. But downscaling by a large factor will still lose a lot of pixel data, resulting in a loss of quality.

Area averaging, on the other hand, samples *all* of the pixels that contribute to the scaled pixel value, no matter what the scaling factor. This approach provides a far more accurate value for each of the pixels in the final image. Consequently, using getScaledInstance() with the Image.SCALE_AREA_AVERAGING hint provides much higher quality for large downscales than drawImage() using either BILINEAR or BICUBIC.

Let's look at the quality of the various algorithms from lowest to highest:

- **NEAREST_NEIGHBOR:** This algorithm is used when you call drawImage() with no hint, as well as when you call getScaledInstance() with either SCALE_REPLICATE, SCALE_FAST, or SCALE_DEFAULT. This algorithm is the fastest but results in the worst quality, with artifacts that are more noticeable as the scale magnitude increases.

- **BILINEAR:** drawImage() with the hint RenderingHints.VALUE_
  INTERPOLATION_BILINEAR provides reasonable quality for small downscales in which the scaled image is greater than half the size of the original.
  However, as with NEAREST_NEIGHBOR, artifacts are more noticeable as the
  scale magnitude increases. This approach does, however, tend to provide
  the best results for upscales.

- **BICUBIC:** drawImage() with the hint RenderingHints.VALUE_
  INTERPOLATION_BICUBIC provides good quality for small downscales.
  However, artifacts are more noticeable as the scale magnitude increases.

- **AREA_AVERAGING:** getScaledInstance() in conjunction with Image.SCALE_
  AREA_AVERAGING provides the best filtering quality of these options for
  large downscales. For downscales in which the result is more than half
  the size of the original image, this approach is roughly equivalent to
  BILINEAR, but as the downscale factor increases, this approach looks better
  than BILINEAR and BICUBIC. Upscaling, in which the result is larger than the
  original image, tends to have worse quality than the BILINEAR approach.

If the quality comparison is that clear, why are we even discussing it? If you
need a quality downscale, shouldn't you use getScaledInstance() with
Image.SCALE_AREA_AVERAGING, regardless of the performance implications?

No. With the performance differences involved, which can easily be *orders of
magnitude* between getScaledInstance() and any of the other approaches, it is
worth seeing if there is a better alternative that provides both the quality and performance that you need. We don't want to sacrifice too much performance for
the sake of quality, but we would like our images to look good. Let's consider an
alternate approach instead: progressive bilinear scaling.

Progressive Bilinear Scaling

We know that a significant problem with the quality of the bilinear approach
occurs when the downscale is by more than 50 percent. So what if we compen-
sated for that problem by scaling iteratively toward the final size, scaling down
by exactly 50 percent each time until the final iteration, when we scale by 50
percent or less? Then we would account for all of the pixels along the way that
should figure into the final image. And, believe it or not, we can do this in a fraction of the time required by the area-averaging technique.

We show the code for this approach, but first let's see some pictures to motivate
the quality and performance angles of this discussion.

Example: ScaleTest

The ScaleTest demo on the book's Web site shows how an image looks when it is scaled down by progressively larger factors. The original image is a collage of four different images, shown in Figure 4-2, representing four different types of graphics situations:

- *RGB stripes:* The upper-left quadrant is simply repeating stripes of red, green, and blue. This is probably not something you would see in a typical application, but it's great for demonstrating some of the artifacts in these scaling operations.
- *Photograph:* The upper-right quadrant is a thumbnail of a photograph, which represents pictures that a typical application might show in its UI.
- *Vector drawing:* The beautiful smiley face in the lower-left quadrant is a simple line drawing, black on white.
- *Grid:* The lower-right quadrant is a simple black-and-white line grid, which shows some of the rendering artifacts of scaling nicely.

The ScaleTest demo scales the image down several times from the original image, increasing the amount of the scale each time. It does this for five different

Figure 4-2 ScaleTest: Source image with RGB stripes, a photograph, vector art, and a black and white grid.

approaches to scaling, timing the results for each approach and displaying the rendering times in the window.

You can see the results of a sample run of ScaleTest in Figure 4-3. The columns in the figure show the different scaled sizes, with the original image on the left. The rows represent the different ways of scaling the images, from NEAREST_ NEIGHBOR to BILINEAR to BICUBIC to getScaledInstance() with the AREA_

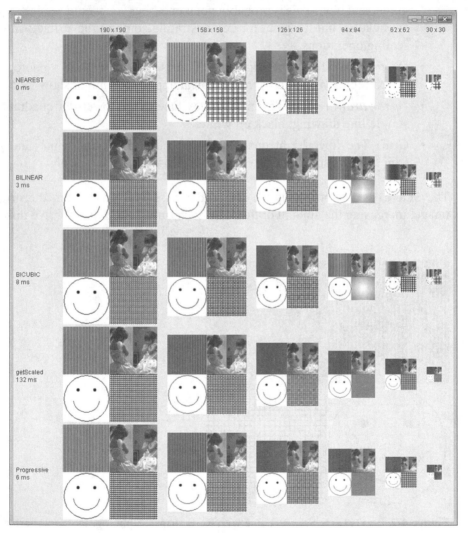

Figure 4-3 ScaleTest results for various alternative approaches to scaling. Times are in milliseconds for the total time taken to render each row of scaled images.

AVERAGING hint and finally to our new progressive bilinear approach. The time that each row took to produce the series of scaled images is displayed on the left of each row.

What you should notice about the figure is that the artifacts of scaling increase as the scaled images get smaller and that the artifacts are more noticeable in the first three rows (NEAREST, BILINEAR, and BICUBIC). You should also notice the performance times for each of the rows. Rendering all of the NEAREST images took the least time ("0" here means that the real time was within the resolution of the timer being used, or about 1 to 2 milliseconds). BILINEAR took a bit more at 3 milliseconds. BICUBIC took 8 milliseconds. getScaledInstance() took the most at a whopping 132 milliseconds. And finally, the progressive bilinear approach took 6 milliseconds.

Tip: Some people have reported fast performance from getScaledInstance(), but beware: getScaledInstance() is asynchronous and may not actually have completed the scaling operation when it returns to the caller. It will complete the scaling when the image data is requested (which it is in the ensuing drawImage() call in this demo). So if you just time getScaledInstance() without a following operation that requires the data, you may get misleadingly fast results. Don't buy it; getScaledInstance() is a slow way to scale images.

It might help to see a larger version of the smallest image on the right from the ScaleTest application, where the artifacts are most pronounced because more information from the original image is lost in deriving the final image. We can see these close-up results for the five rows in Figures 4-4 through 4-8.

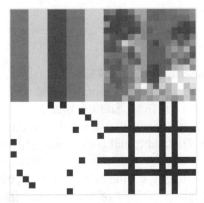

Figure 4-4 NEAREST results for smallest scaled image.

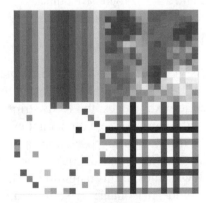

Figure 4-5 BILINEAR results for smallest scaled image.

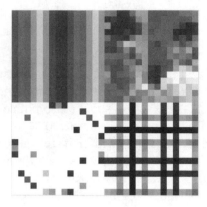

Figure 4-6 BICUBIC results for smallest scaled image.

Figure 4-7 getScaledInstance results for smallest scaled image.

Figure 4-8 Progressive bilinear results for smallest scaled image.

As you can see in the close-up pictures, the errors for NEAREST, BILINEAR, and BICUBIC are fairly large, especially for the parts of the original image with discrete pixel values: the RGB stripes, the vector drawing, and the black and white grid. For example, you cannot even tell in these first two snapshots that the vector drawing is supposed to be a smiley face. The additional computation involved in BILINEAR and BICUBIC compared to NEAREST_NEIGHBOR seems wasted for downscales of this magnitude. The last two images, on the other hand, appear to provide reasonable, if slightly different, approximations of the original image. Even the smiley face is clearly discernible at this extreme size reduction with the getScaledInstance() and progressive bilinear approaches.

Finally, you should notice that even though the quality of the progressive bilinear approach nearly matches that of getScaledInstance(), it does so in a small fraction of the time that getScaledInstance() took. This improved performance for similar quality is the big takeaway from this section.

Tip: You can get high-quality scaling without resorting to the performance hit of getScaledInstance() by using the progressive bilinear approach.

It is worth making some final points about getScaledInstance(), just in case you are still, for unknown reasons, thinking that it's a pretty great way to scale images on the fly. First, as we noted earlier, the call to getScaledInstance() is asynchronous. The getScaledInstance() method will return immediately and will not actually perform the scaling operation until the image data is requested at some later time. This means that there could be hidden side effects from changing the original image after you have supposedly received your scaled image; those changes to the original image may show up in the scaled version, depending on when the scaling operation actually occurs. The other point is that getScaledInstance() accesses the pixel array for the image directly, which, as we see in Chapter 5, means that managed image acceleration is not possible for the image. So, all things considered, you should just avoid this method.

Example: PictureScaler

We can see what happens to a higher resolution picture as we put it through the various scaling approaches just discussed. Figure 4-9 shows a snapshot from the PictureScaler demo on the book's Web site. This application scales an original high-resolution picture on the fly through the same mechanisms used in the

Figure 4-9 PictureScaler: High-resolution photo scaled on the fly using the same five approaches as before.

ScaleTest application. We can see the quality results in the thumbnails and the performance results listed below each picture.

The three images on the left, using drawImage() with the NEAREST_NEIGHBOR, BILINEAR, and BICUBIC approaches, show clear scaling artifacts. For example, look at the straight and diagonal lines in the pictures and notice that the jaggies are very prominent. Figure 4-10 shows a close-up view of these three images, where you can see some of these artifacts quite clearly.

The two images on the right, using the getScaledInstance() and progressive bilinear approaches, show much smoother lines and transitions between areas of high contrast, as shown in the close-up view of Figure 4-11.

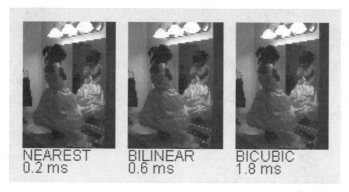

Figure 4-10 Close-up of the NEAREST, BILINEAR, and BICUBIC scaling results. All have similar artifacts for this large downscale.

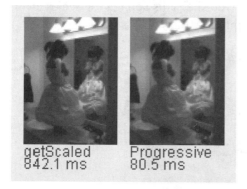

Figure 4-11 Close-up of the getScaledInstance() and progressive bilinear scaling results. Note the smoother lines with these approaches compared to those in Figure 4-10.

Note, once again, that the performance of getScaledInstance() is completely out of sync with the performance of the other approaches. The quality of that approach comes at a substantial cost. But note more importantly that the performance of the progressive bilinear approach is substantially better, providing a good-quality alternative at a fraction of the time that getScaledInstance() takes.

getFasterScaledInstance(): Utility for Faster, Better Scaled Images

I have taken the liberty of borrowing and modifying a utility from Chris Campbell and Jim Graham, which also exists in some form in the SwingLabs project on http://swinglabs.dev.java.net. You can use this method to create a scaled version of an image with various approaches. This is an easy way to use the progressive bilinear approach for your own images, since you simply pass it a flag to tell it to choose this approach. This method is used in the PictureScaler demo, and is therefore also available online in that demo code.

```java
public BufferedImage getFasterScaledInstance(BufferedImage img,
        int targetWidth, int targetHeight, Object hint,
        boolean progressiveBilinear)
{
    int type = (img.getTransparency() == Transparency.OPAQUE) ?
        BufferedImage.TYPE_INT_RGB : BufferedImage.TYPE_INT_ARGB;
    BufferedImage ret = (BufferedImage)img;
    BufferedImage scratchImage = null;
    Graphics2D g2 = null;
    int w, h;
    int prevW = ret.getWidth();
    int prevH = ret.getHeight();
    if (progressiveBilinear) {
        // Use multistep technique: start with original size,
        // then scale down in multiple passes with drawImage()
        // until the target size is reached
        w = img.getWidth();
        h = img.getHeight();
    } else {
        // Use one-step technique: scale directly from original
        // size to target size with a single drawImage() call
        w = targetWidth;
        h = targetHeight;
    }
```

continued

```
      do {
        if (progressiveBilinear && w > targetWidth) {
          w /= 2;
          if (w < targetWidth) {
            w = targetWidth;
          }
        }

        if (progressiveBilinear && h > targetHeight) {
          h /= 2;
          if (h < targetHeight) {
            h = targetHeight;
          }
        }

        if (scratchImage == null) {
          // Use a single scratch buffer for all iterations
          // and then copy to the final, correctly sized image
          // before returning
          scratchImage = new BufferedImage(w, h, type);
          g2 = scratchImage.createGraphics();
        }
        g2.setRenderingHint(RenderingHints.KEY_INTERPOLATION,
                            hint);
        g2.drawImage(ret, 0, 0, w, h, 0, 0, prevW, prevH, null);
        prevW = w;
        prevH = h;

        ret = scratchImage;
      } while (w != targetWidth || h != targetHeight);

      if (g2 != null) {
        g2.dispose();
      }

      // If we used a scratch buffer that is larger than our
      // target size, create an image of the right size and copy
      // the results into it
      if (targetWidth != ret.getWidth() ||
          targetHeight != ret.getHeight()) {
        scratchImage = new BufferedImage(targetWidth,
                                         targetHeight, type);
        g2 = scratchImage.createGraphics();
        g2.drawImage(ret, 0, 0, null);
        g2.dispose();
        ret = scratchImage;
      }

      return ret;
    }
```

The method is not too complex, so we leave most of the details to curious readers. The basic idea is that a caller requests a scaled image, specifying whether progressive bilinear filtering is desired with the cleverly named `progressiveBilinear` flag. If this flag is true, and if `targetWidth` or `targetHeight` is less than half of the original image width or height, then the image will be progressively scaled by halves using the `BILINEAR` rendering hint until the target size is reached.

Note the use of the `scratchImage` variable; we create a single image the first time through that is used for future iterations through the loop, finally creating an image of the correct size and copying to it before returning. This approach avoids having to create a new `BufferedImage` for every new intermediate scaling size.

Let's leave this chapter with one final performance tip about image scaling.

Tip: No matter which approach you decide to use for your quality-versus-performance needs, consider the approach of using intermediate images. The fastest operation is the one that you don't have to perform. If you need to constantly scale the same image to the same size, consider creating a cached version of the scaled image and simply copying that version around instead. Java 2D can copy the prescaled version of the image much faster than it can scale the original image.

5

Performance

A<small>N</small> application that looks great but performs like a dog[1] is a sad thing. Users may like the look, but they'll hate the feel, and they'll probably avoid running the application again. Java, Swing, and Java 2D work just fine and perform great as-is, and you generally do not need to care about performance. But it is always good to know about things that may cause performance problems and to know techniques you can use to speed up your application.

We have not been shy about sprinkling performance information throughout the book where applicable. This chapter goes much deeper in detail into some particular techniques and information about performance that are useful to know in order to write great, fast Filthy Rich Clients.

Use the Clip

Tip: The most important optimization rule of graphics-oriented applications is to never draw anything unnecessarily. Swing offers an internal mechanism to help with this optimization: the clip.

We've mentioned a few times that you should call `repaint(x, y, width, height)` to refresh only the areas of the screen that need to be refreshed. What

---

1. It's not clear to me where this saying came from; I've known some very fast dogs. In fact, most dogs tend to be a lot faster than me. Perhaps the saying should be changed to "performs like a Chet."

was not necessarily obvious, however, is that calling this method can vastly improve the rendering speed. We also glossed over the fact that calling `repaint(x, y, width, height)` alone is not sufficient to get good performance when your own painting code is involved in the rendering process.

In earlier chapters, we saw two methods that belong to the `Graphics` class:

```
Graphics.setClip(int x, int y, int width, int height)
Graphics.setClip(Shape s)
```

The clip defines the shape within which drawing operations are constrained to be visible. For instance, if the clip is a 100×100 rectangle starting at (50, 50) in a drawing surface of 640×480 pixels, a 10×10 square drawn at (200, 200) will not appear on screen. Note that changing the clip does not affect existing pixels; it only affects future rendering with that `Graphics` object (just as all state affects only future rendering with that `Graphics` object). Figure 5-1 shows a screen with four colored circles that were drawn before the clip was set. The white area shows the clip where future drawing operations are permitted. Drawing operations performed in the space outside this clip area, shown in gray, will be ignored.

The clip does not need to be a rectangle; you can use an arbitrary shape. For instance, you can pass a circle to the `setClip()` method to constrain drawing operations to be within a circular area of the drawing surface.

No matter what clip shape you use, Swing honors your settings, so you can safely draw outside the bounds of a component when you override the `paintComponent` method. When Swing calls the painting methods of a compo-

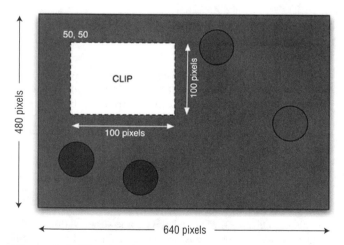

Figure 5-1 The drawing operation works only in the area defined by the clip.

nent, it sets up a clip rectangle that encapsulates that component's bounds beforehand. Therefore, any drawing operation attempted outside of the component's bounds is ignored.

Swing also sets the clip for you whenever you call repaint(x, y, width, height). There is no real magic behind this code that would explain the performance gain. The API simply sets a clip rectangle on the drawing surface according to the parameters you specify.

Unfortunately, setting a clip is only valuable when the painting code honors it. Let's take the example of a very simple component that fills its background with a solid color:

```
@Override
protected void paintComponent(Graphics g) {
    g.setColor(Color.BLACK);
    g.fillRect(0, 0, getWidth(), getHeight());
}
```

This code attempts to fill the entire component in black every time paintComponent() is invoked. Java2D improves the performance by not painting the pixels lying outside of the clip. Nevertheless, you give Java2D extra work by asking it to figure out what to paint and what to ignore. To avoid this situation, you must honor the clip.

Honoring the clip refers to the task of checking the clip boundaries and preventing unnecessary drawing operations from being issued to Java2D. The previous example can, for example, be rewritten to honor the clip as follows:

```
@Override
protected void paintComponent(Graphics g) {
    Rectangle clip = g.getClipBounds();
    g.setColor(Color.BLACK);
    g.fillRect(clip.x, clip.y, clip.width, clip.height);
}
```

This new version fills only the pixels belonging to the clip area, making sure that Java2D does not have to do any extra work before putting your beautiful artwork on screen.

Honoring the clip usually results in one of two possible outcomes: Either you don't issue a drawing operation[2] or you manually constrain that operation to the

---

2. In graphics terminology, skipping such an operation is referred to as a *trivial reject*; you check to see whether your primitive overlaps the clip area at all. If it does not, then you don't bother trying to draw it.

clip area. The previous code snippet was an example of the latter. Ignoring a drawing operation is usually easier because you always know[3] the boundaries of the primitive that you want to draw on the screen. The following example shows how to ignore the drawing of a logo in a custom component.

```
@Override
protected void paintComponent(Graphics g) {
    // paint the logo at location logoX, logoY
    Rectangle clip = g.getClipBounds();
    Rectangle logo = new Rectangle(logoX, logoY,
                                   logoWidth, logoHeight);

    // if the logo is outside the clip, ignore it
    if (clip.intersects(logo)) {
      g.drawImage(logoImage, logo.x, logo.y, null);
    }

    // paint the rest
}
```

You can also combine both techniques by first checking that your primitive intersects with the clip and then constraining the primitive to the clip area. The following code snippet comes from the JXGraph component that I wrote for the SwingLabs project.[4] This method is responsible for the painting of the main axes (vertical and horizontal), as seen in Figure 5-2.

```
private void drawAxis(Graphics2D g2) {
    if (!isAxisPainted()) {
      return;
    }

    double axisH = yPositionToPixel(originY);
    double axisV = xPositionToPixel(originX);

    Rectangle clip = g2.getClipBounds();

    g2.setColor(getAxisColor());
    Stroke stroke = g2.getStroke();
    g2.setStroke(new BasicStroke(STROKE_AXIS));
```

---

3. Or Java2D can at least compute them for you. You should refer to the java.awt.geom.Shape documentation and read about its getBounds() and getBounds2D() methods.

4. www.swinglabs.org

```
    if (axisH >= clip.y && axisH < clip.y + clip.height) {
      g2.drawLine(clip.x, (int) axisH,
                  clip.x + clip.width, (int) axisH);
    }
    if (axisV >= clip.x && axisV < clip.x + clip.width) {
      g2.drawLine((int) axisV, clip.y,
                  (int) axisV, clip.y + clip.height);
    }

    g2.setStroke(stroke);
}
```

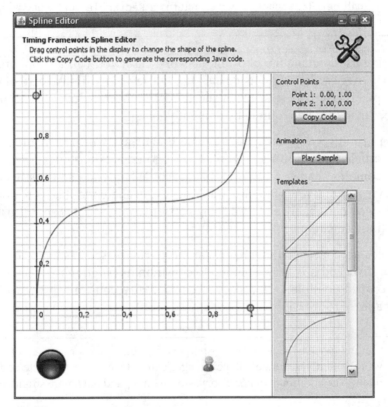

Figure 5-2 The JXGraph component honors the clip for every line drawn.

As you can see, the component first checks that the lines to be drawn intersect with the clip area. When they do, it constrains them to this area, thus avoiding unnecessary guesswork for Java2D.

Tip: Although you should always try to honor the clip, there are some cases in which it would be either too hard or too costly to do so. Honoring nonrectangular clip areas and honoring clips against nonrectangular primitives are good examples of these cases.

For instance, how would you honor a circular clip? You could call `Graphics.getClip()` to retrieve a `Shape` instance defining the circular area very precisely, but it would then be difficult to know how to constrain the primitives to this area.

Tip: Always call `getClipBounds()`, which returns a `Rectangle`, and work with rectangular clip areas only.

Besides, Swing uses rectangular clips. In the worst case, you will attempt drawing operations over areas lying outside the clip, but Java2D will take care of the superfluous pixels. Nonetheless, the induced cost of having Java 2D do it is much cheaper than the one required by doing it yourself.

Constraining primitives to the clip area is also not always worth it. While horizontal and vertical lines[5] and rectangles are easy to constrain, things get much harder with complex shapes, like polygons or text. When you can't easily constrain a drawing primitive to the clip, don't do it. All the code that you would have to write would probably end up hurting performance. Java2D can be trusted to optimize these situations.

Finally, images need a special treatment. An image can be seen as a rectangular drawing primitive, and it is very tempting to constrain its painting to a rectangular clip area when possible. After all, you could easily constrain it by calling `BufferedImage.getSubimage(x, y, width, height)`.

Warning: Calling `getSubimage()` for this purpose is a bad idea for two reasons. First, you will implicitly generate another image, which takes time to create and copy the content. The additional image also wastes memory and puts more strain on

---

5. Even simple diagonal lines are probably more trouble than they are worth; you would have to compute the intersection of the line with the clip area and pick a new endpoint at the place where the line exits the clip area, and you would have to be sure that your endpoint is in the same position as the one that Java 2D might otherwise draw for you. Rasterization algorithms can vary slightly from each other, so this is not necessarily a simple task. Diagonal lines therefore also fall clearly into the "don't bother" category.

the garbage collector. Second, this approach might, in some situations, defeat optimizations performed under the hood by Java2D.

You could also use the various `Graphics.drawImage()` methods that let you paint only a subregion of an image, but you are better off leaving this work to Java2D, thus making sure you do not interfere with any optimization that the rendering pipeline could perform.

Tip: Images and Clipping. When it comes to images, make sure they at least intersect with the clip area, and then simply draw them entirely. Java 2D does the necessary work to constrain the operation to the visible region so that no rendering cycles are wasted.

The clip is a very powerful and efficient tool to make your applications fast. Just remember that setting the clip or calling `repaint(x, y, width, height)` is only half of what you must do. Always honor the clip. For an example of how respecting the clip can improve performance, check out the `CopyAreaPerformance` demo in the "`GraphicsState`" section of Chapter 3, "Graphics Fundamentals." It shows how simply not drawing objects outside the clip made the application perform significantly faster.

Compatible Images

We have mentioned *compatible images* in several places so far in the book:

- They are created with `GraphicsConfiguration.createCompatibleImage()`.
- They are of type `BufferedImage`.
- They are in the suitable format for the display device associated with the `GraphicsConfiguration` with which they were created.
- They have certain performance advantages.

But why? Why should you use them? Why are they faster? Why do we keep talking about them?

The answer is simple: Compatible images require less of Java 2D when copying them to the display hardware. And when Java 2D has less to do, your application can go faster.

Why You Should Care

Imagine a display device with a typical display format of 32 bits holding the color values in the format xRGB (where the x byte is essentially ignored).[6] Now imagine an image whose pixels are stored in a different way, say a 16-bit format such as 565: 5 bits of red, 6 bits of green, and 5 bits of blue. Finally, imagine what happens when that image gets copied to the screen or to the Swing back buffer, which is in the same format as the screen. *Every single pixel* of the image will have to be modified along the way to suit the new format.

In this example, each pixel will undergo the transformation similar to that depicted in Figure 5-3, where src refers to a pixel in the image and dest refers to a pixel in the display:[7]

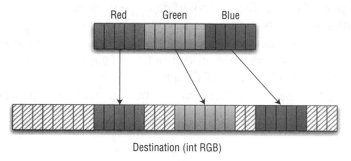

Figure 5-3   Pixel in 565 format being copied to destination in Int RGB format.

---

6. In typical current (especially older) graphics hardware, the red, green, and blue channels of color are represented by, at most, 8 bits. So even when the display is running in 32-bit color, there are actually only 24 bits of color information, and the remaining byte is ignored. Of course, if the display is going to ignore a quarter of the information in every integer, it might as well have a 24-bit display, right?

    Actually, there were (and may still be) video boards with a 24-bit display depth. The last one I saw was one of the Intel integrated graphics chips that was current about 4 years ago. But this type of display device is not typical—and it's a serious hassle. You end up having to detect this special device-specific color format and making sure your images are in a format compatible to it, which is not usually the case. Integers are just so easy to work with. Addressing subintegers is a pain. So even though one of the bytes in a 32-bit xRGB format is ignored, that situation is much better than having to address subintegers in a 24-bit RGB format device.

7. The actual computations are slightly more complex in Java 2D; we end up OR-ing the src bits into the low-order bits of the destination bytes as well, instead of just leaving empty bits as seen in the figure. But the idea is the same. The computation is simplified here to make the figure and idea easier to understand.

As seen in Figure 5-3, the color bits from the source pixel would become the most significant bits of the colors in the destination pixel. Internally, the code would be something like this:

```
int red = (src & 0xF8) >> 8;
int green = (src & 0x7C) >> 2;
int blue = (src & 0x1F) << 3;
int dest = (red << 16 | green << 8 | blue);
```

Each color component in the source pixel is singled out through the AND operation and then shifted into the right location for an 8-bit color representation. Then these colors are combined into the final pixel value. Altogether, there are three AND operations, two ORs, and five shifts. We could optimize this code slightly to shift the components directly into place, like this:

```
dest = ((src & 0xF8) << 8) | ((src & 0x7C) << 6) | ((src & 0x1F) << 3);
```

This optimized version still has three ANDs and two ORs, but only three shifts. None of these are expensive operations, but when you have to perform all of them per-pixel in a large image, they add up.

Compare this process to one in which the source image is in the same format as the destination, 32-bit xRGB. In this case, we simply call a single memory-copy routine to operate on all of the pixels at once. Copy routines are highly optimized in the operating system for transferring large amounts of data very quickly. In this case, instead of performing several operations per-pixel as we did before, we perform one simple and fast copy operation on the entire image.

What about Managed Images?

To some extent, Java 2D takes care of the issue of compatible images automatically. As explained later in the section "Managed Images," Java 2D usually makes an internal copy of any image that is copied to the display device. That copy is in the device's format and thus has all of the advantages of a compatible image. So once an image is being managed by Java 2D, compatibility needn't be a concern.

However, it should still be a concern for those first couple of copies or for whatever operations you are doing for which Java 2D is not managing the image. For example, suppose you have an extremely large image in a format different from that of the screen. This image would have to undergo a large per-pixel transformation when it is copied to the Swing back buffer. Even if Java 2D will eventually manage this image, the first couple of copies before image management begins will be horrendously expensive.

Make Mine Compatible

The mechanism that you use to load an image may result in an image that is not compatible with the display device. For example, the Image I/O library in current Java SE releases loads some JPEG images in a format that does not match most display formats. So while PNG and BMP images may be loaded through Image I/O in fairly reasonable formats, device-compatible image formats is not something that you should assume in general. Also, Toolkit images, loaded through the older JDK 1.0 APIs, are probably not in an optimal format when loaded. It might be easier and better to simply copy the result of a loaded image into an image type that you *know* is a compatible image.

Sometimes you cannot help the format an image is in, or you may not care about performance in a particular situation. But in general, if there is a way that you can use a compatible image instead of some suboptimal format, then it is probably worthwhile doing so.

Tip: Converting an image from its current format into a better one is as easy as creating a compatible image and copying the old suboptimal image into it:[8]

```
// Assume that we are in the component to which we will
// copy the image; its GraphicsConfiguration is the one that
// we want to use to create the compatible image
GraphicsConfiguration gc = getGraphicsConfiguration();
BufferedImage compatibleImage = gc.createCompatibleImage(
    suboptimalImage.getWidth(),
    suboptimalImage.getHeight());
Graphics g = compatibleImage.getGraphics();
g.drawImage(suboptimalImage, 0, 0, null);
```

It is worth extending this idea further and having a utility class that just does the right thing for you. Here is a sample class that has several useful methods you can use to create and load compatible images:[9]

```
public class MakeMineCompatible {

    // This method returns an image that is compatible with the
    // primary display device.  If a user has multiple displays
    // with different depths, this may be suboptimal, but it
```

---

8. Note that this code snippet is specific to an opaque image. The utility class MakeMineCompatible covers the other cases.

9. If you want to use this class but don't want to transcribe from this page, check out the online version in the GraphicsUtilities class in the SwingLabs project at http://swingx.dev.java.net.

```
// should work in the general case.
private static GraphicsConfiguration getConfiguration() {
   return GraphicsEnvironment.getLocalGraphicsEnvironment().
      getDefaultScreenDevice().getDefaultConfiguration();
}

// Creates a compatible image of the same dimension and
// transparency as the given image
public static BufferedImage createCompatibleImage(
    BufferedImage image) {
   return createCompatibleImage(image, image.getWidth(),
                                 image.getHeight());
}

// Creates a compatible image with the given width and
// height that has the same transparency as the given image
public static BufferedImage createCompatibleImage(
    BufferedImage image, int width, int height) {
   return getConfiguration().createCompatibleImage(width,
      height, image.getTransparency());
}

// Creates an opaque compatible image with the given
// width and height
public static BufferedImage createCompatibleImage(
    int width, int height) {
   return getConfiguration().createCompatibleImage(width,
                                 height);
}

// Creates a translucent compatible image with the given
// width and height
public static BufferedImage createCompatibleTranslucentImage(
    int width, int height) {
   return getConfiguration().createCompatibleImage(width,
      height, Transparency.TRANSLUCENT);
}

// Creates a compatible image from the content specified
// by the resource
public static BufferedImage loadCompatibleImage(URL resource)
    throws IOException {
   BufferedImage image = ImageIO.read(resource);
   return toCompatibleImage(image);
}

// Creates and returns a new compatible image into which
// the source image is copied
```

continued

```
// If the source image is already compatible, then the
// source image is returned
// This version takes a BufferedImage, but it could be
// extended to take an Image instead
public static BufferedImage toCompatibleImage(
    BufferedImage image) {
  GraphicsConfiguration gc = getConfiguration();
  if (image.getColorModel().equals(gc.getColorModel())) {
    return image;
  }

  BufferedImage compatibleImage = gc.createCompatibleImage(
      image.getWidth(), image.getHeight(),
      image.getTransparency());
  Graphics g = compatibleImage.getGraphics();
  g.drawImage(image, 0, 0, null);
  g.dispose();

  return compatibleImage;
  }
}
```

Now you have all of the code that you need to use compatible images always. No more excuses!

Managed Images

The phrase *managed images* does not refer to image types but rather to a mechanism of accelerating rendering operations for any types of images. The phrase came from the idea that a developer should have to worry only about creating and using an image and that Java 2D should "manage" the performance opportunities for the developer automatically.[10]

---

10. The first phrase we used to denote this acceleration mechanism was "acceleration under the hood," which was a bit of a mouthful and thankfully didn't gain any recognition or reuse. The more concise "automatic images" then arose, which meant the same thing in a much quicker and more pronounceable manner. This second attempt gained some reuse in the developer community . . . and made no sense to me whatsoever. I have to admit I was never comfortable with "automatic images" because there's nothing automatic about the images themselves. The phrase just didn't quite parse correctly in my brain. Finally, we started talking about "managed images," which seemed to gain more traction, since it is pretty clear what it refers to: Java 2D is managing the images and their acceleration for you. It is concise and pronounceable, and it maps well onto similar mechanisms in other toolkits. This time the name stuck.

The idea behind managed images is that an image is created by whatever mechanism is appropriate: loading it from disk, creating a `BufferedImage` from scratch, or creating a compatible image. Meanwhile, Java 2D caches the image contents in a location that is most suitable from a performance standpoint.

For example, suppose an application on Windows creates a compatible image and that the image's contents are created once and not changed thereafter. This image's contents exist in system memory. The image's contents cannot be stored in video memory on Windows because that memory may be lost and the contents destroyed at any time (read about `VolatileImage` under "Image Types" in Chapter 4, "Images"). Now suppose that that image is copied several times to the Swing back buffer, which may exist in VRAM.

Java 2D will notice that it is being asked repeatedly to copy the same image contents from system memory to the back buffer in VRAM. This is not a horribly slow operation, but there are certainly better ways of spending the computer's time than having it move images pixel-by-pixel over the bus from main memory to video memory. At this point, Java 2D may choose to create a second, cached version of this image in VRAM, closer to the Swing back buffer. The next time that the application requests a copy from the image to the Swing back buffer, or to any other image in VRAM, Java 2D will notice that this image has a cached version in VRAM. Java 2D will then perform the copy operation from that VRAM-cached version instead.

Some pictures might help to illustrate how the system works (Figures 5-4 and 5-5). After all, this is a graphics book.

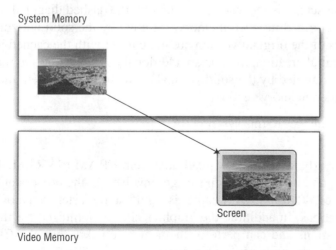

Figure 5-4 Unmanaged images copy from system memory to video memory.

System Memory

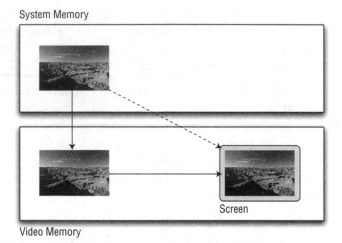

Video Memory

Figure 5-5 Managed images copy from a cached video memory version of the image to other locations in video memory.

We can see in Figure 5-4 the process of copying images to the computer screen without managed images. The image is stored in system memory and the copy operation simply copies the contents of the image from system memory, over the system bus, onto to the screen that resides in video memory.

In Figure 5-5, we can see how this process works with managed images. The original image is still stored in system memory, as before. But in this figure, there is also an accelerated version of the image stored in video memory. When a copy operation to the screen is requested, signified by the dashed diagonal line, the actual copy is performed in video memory, signified by the solid horizontal arrow. If the contents of the original version are not current with the cached version, such as upon initial creation, there is an additional copy operation to make the contents current, signified by the solid vertical arrow from the system memory version of the video memory version.

There are several advantages to this system:

- *Speed:* It is clearly faster to copy pixel data from VRAM to VRAM. The CPU, the bus, and main memory never get involved in the process at all, and the speed of VRAM–VRAM copies is significantly faster than moving traffic over the bus. In addition, the graphics chip is optimized for these types of operations and can perform them more quickly than the CPU, even discounting the memory and bus issues.

- *Parallel processing:* The managed image copy takes advantage of multi-processing capabilities of the computer. The graphics chip is a separate processor, so asking that chip to handle a VRAM–VRAM copy is like spawning a thread on this other processor. This leaves the CPU free to perform other tasks. This advantage can be seen clearly in some tests in which an approach using unmanaged images may peg the CPU, whereas the same application using managed images shows a negligible amount of work being done by the CPU. Freeing up the CPU to do other work has real advantages outside of mere benchmarks. There is usually other work that an application can think of to keep the CPU busy, and not having to waste its time on simple pixel operations enables applications and the operating system overall to run faster.

- *Ease of development:* These advantages are as true for `VolatileImage` operations as they are for managed images. The big win for the managed-image approach is that the developer need not worry about the management aspects of acceleration. Java 2D handles the content loss issues associated with VRAM, as well as decisions about when, how, and whether to accelerate particular images and image operations.

It is worth noting some of the hidden details of managed images. Images are not always accelerated, and it may be a mystery to developers why that is the case in any particular situation. In general, the system makes good decisions based on the information it has about the images and operations, and the developer may be better off with the choices made by the system. But if the system is not accelerating something that would benefit from acceleration, it is good to know what might be contributing to the cause.

Tip: There are two factors in working with an image that will cause Java 2D to avoid accelerating it: grabbing the pixel array and frequent rendering to the image.

Grabbing the DataBuffer

Recall the discussion about the original image contents being stored in system memory and the cached version being stored in VRAM. The key that makes this work is that Java 2D knows when the contents of the original image have been altered. When the original image contents have been updated, the new contents can be copied to the accelerated version. There is one usage of `BufferedImage` objects that causes a problem, however: accessing the `DataBuffer` from a `BufferedImage`'s `Raster` object.

If you get a handle to the DataBuffer, you can change pixel data in a BufferedImage without Java 2D knowing. From a DataBuffer, you can request an array of the raw pixel data and then access the pixels the same as you would any other array of data. Since Java 2D cannot tell when the array data changes, it cannot appropriately update any accelerated version of the image. So Java 2D does the only thing it can when the DataBuffer is accessed: It gives up.[11] Once this happens on an image, Java 2D can no longer manage it, and there will be no more acceleration for it via the managed-image approach.

Let's look at an example, DataBufferGrabber, which can be found on the book's Web site. This example copies an image to the Swing back buffer several times, timing how long the copies take. Then the image is modified through the image's DataBuffer, and the timing test is performed once more.

Here is the method used to copy the image:

```
private long copyImage(Graphics g, BufferedImage image,
                       int x, int y) {
  long startTime = System.nanoTime();
  for (int i = 0; i < 100; ++i) {
    g.drawImage(image, x, y, null);
  }
  long endTime = System.nanoTime();
  return (endTime - startTime) / 1000000;
}
```

The method performs the same copy operation 100 times and returns the number of milliseconds that those 100 copies took.

Note: Notice that we do this operation 100 times. We do so in order to make the benchmarking times larger and more significant. This is a common approach in most of our timing-related tests, especially for quick operations in which test anomalies or the resolution of timing utilities could otherwise be quite significant compared to the actual time that an operation takes.

11. The 2D team is currently working on changes for future releases that may reduce the cases that cause this acceleration punting. For example, up through Java SE 6, simply requesting the DataBuffer would cause Java 2D to give up on accelerating a BufferedImage. Future changes may make it possible to use a DataBuffer and still have Java 2D accelerate the image, although requesting the actual pixel array itself may still force 2D to give up on accelerating for the reasons explained here.

Here is the paintComponent() method in which we create and fill the image and benchmark managed and unmanaged copy operations.

```
protected void paintComponent(Graphics g) {

    // Create the image and fill it with white
    BufferedImage bImg = new BufferedImage(SWATCH_SIZE,
        SWATCH_SIZE, BufferedImage.TYPE_INT_RGB);
    Graphics gImage = bImg.getGraphics();
    gImage.setColor(Color.WHITE);
    gImage.fillRect(0, 0, SWATCH_SIZE, SWATCH_SIZE);

    // Time how long it takes to copy the managed version
    long managedTime = copyImage(g, bImg, 0, 0);
    System.out.println("Managed: " + managedTime + " ms");

    // Now grab the pixel array, change the colors, rerun the test
    Raster raster = bImg.getRaster();
    DataBufferInt dataBuffer =
        (DataBufferInt)raster.getDataBuffer();
    int pixels[] = dataBuffer.getData();
    for (int i = 0; i < pixels.length; ++i) {
      // Make all pixels black
      pixels[i] = 0;
    }

    // Time this unmanaged copy
    long unmanagedTime = copyImage(g, bImg, SWATCH_SIZE, 0);
    System.out.println("Unmanaged: " + unmanagedTime + " ms");
}
```

Note that the code to get the data array is hard-coded to use a DataBufferInt because we know that the DataBuffer would be in integer format, since we created the BufferedImage to be of type INT_RGB. A more flexible version of this approach would check the DataBuffer type before casting. Nevertheless, this code shows how we can grab the pixel array from the DataBuffer and what effect that has on the performance of the system.

The results of this test depend greatly on the platform on which it is run and the extent to which Java 2D can accelerate managed images. On one test system, I got a time of 24 milliseconds for the managed version and 225 milliseconds for the unmanaged one. Note that the managed version includes the time it takes for Java 2D's image management to kick in, which typically occurs on the second copy operation. Also, note that the variable bImg in the code is in an optimal format for my test, since the screen of the test system is in INT_RGB format. This means that software copies are as fast as possible since no pixel format translation is necessary. A different version of this test used INT_BGR as the image type, and the unmanaged results took twice as long as before, while the managed results stayed the same. After all, the original format of the image does not matter after Java 2D starts managing it.

The reason that Java 2D cannot manage an image that has had its pixel array accessed is that Java 2D can no longer track changes made to the image. If the image contents are altered through a regular API call, then Java 2D notices that operation and knows to update the accelerated version of the image before copying from it. But if the image contents are altered directly through an array, Java 2D has no way of knowing that it happened. Because Java 2D cannot guarantee that the original image and the cached copy will remain in sync in this situation, it disables acceleration for this image entirely and the image will not be managed or accelerated. Since there is no way to "return" an array to the DataBuffer or to otherwise disable access to the pixel data through the array, the only way to for the developer to re-enable acceleration for the image is to create a new image and copy the old contents into it.

There may be valid reasons for accessing the array directly. After all, the ability to have direct pixel access is one of BufferedImage's strengths. But you should be aware of the consequences of that decision so that you can make the appropriate trade-off in your code between the speed of pixel access and the performance of managed images.[12]

Frequent Rendering to the Image

Rendering frequently to an image, unlike accessing the DataBuffer object, will not permanently disable image management. But frequent rendering may effectively disable acceleration for the period during which the image is being constantly re-rendered.

It only makes sense for Java 2D to manage an image if it can copy from an accelerated version more often than it has to update that accelerated version from the original image. Suppose an application changed an image's contents every time it was about to copy the image to the Swing back buffer. In this case, the changes would happen once for every copy of the image to the back buffer. Here, image

---

12. The flag that controls this de-acceleration behavior is my favorite variable in the Java 2D code. The variable is named rasterStolen, meaning that someone snuck into the image and ran off with the Raster object. A more correct name might be something like pixelArrayAccessed or userCodeHasDirectAccessToDataBufferArray, but I like rasterStolen much better. It sounds so sneaky and subversive.

management would actually introduce extra operations and adversely affect performance in a fruitless attempt to keep the cached copy of the image in sync. Let's look at the operations that would occur for every update of the back buffer in this suboptimal situation:

1. Application renders new contents to image.
2. Application requests image to be copied to Swing back buffer.
   a. Java 2D notices that the image has changed since the last time it used the accelerated version of the image. Java 2D copies the new contents from the image to the accelerated version.
   b. Java 2D copies the accelerated version of the image to the Swing back buffer.

If this is how managed images worked, it would mean that step 2b is just an extra step above what would normally occur if the image were not managed at all. Let's look at the unmanaged case for this situation:

1. Application renders new contents to image.
2. Application requests image to be copied to Swing back buffer.
   a. Java 2D copies the image to the Swing back buffer.

Steps 1, 2, and 2a are the same as steps 1, 2, and 2b in the first list, but we've skipped the superfluous step of the accelerated copy. The operation to put the image contents into the accelerated version of the image is equivalent to getting the contents into the Swing back buffer directly.

Because Java 2D does not actually want to introduce performance delays into your application, it notices when this situation happens and acts accordingly. An image must be copied to accelerated destinations more than it is written to in order for Java 2D to bother accelerating it. This heuristic kicks in at any time. If you start out with a static image that is not re-rendered, Java 2D will quickly[13] decide to manage it, and future copy-from operations will go through the accelerated version. If the application then modifies the image, Java 2D will stop using the accelerated version and instead use the image itself as the source for its copy operations. If the application stops modifying the image contents again, Java 2D will again notice and go back to using the accelerated version after updating it.

---

13. Typically, Java 2D manages an image on the second copy *from* that image to an accelerated destination since the last rendering *to* the image.

Intermediate Images

In a previous life, I worked in the 3D graphics arena writing applications, APIs, and drivers for real-time 3D graphics visualization. At that time, there was an idea kicking around the 3D graphics world of *image-based rendering*. This approach played tricks with images in order to simulate real-time 3D viewing. So, for example, instead of rendering the 3D model associated with a building on every frame as the viewer walks around that world, you might render that model once from a single viewpoint, cache that result in an image, and use that image thereafter. As the viewer moves around, this image warps to appear as though it is being re-rendered from different viewpoints on every frame, but it is actually just neat image-rendering tricks to make it look "good enough."

This is indeed a neat trick. You can get great performance because you avoid complex model re-rendering and do simple image operations instead. Of course, you must re-render models into images occasionally when the errors get bad enough. You can't walk around to the other side of a building model and not expect to re-render that building a few times in the process. For one thing, the original rendering of that model didn't include any details about the side facing away from the original view location, so looking at it from the other side would result in some pretty awful rendering artifacts.[14]

Some example uses of this approach to rendering include the following:

- Apple's Quicktime VR,[15] which uses several surrounding 3D views of a scene, allowing you to smoothly animate around that scene by interpolating between the various pre-rendered images
- Proposals for hardware that could use this approach. For example, Microsoft proposed the Talisman[16] graphics hardware architecture
- Various academic papers at graphics conferences

Sadly, graphics hardware moved on, 3D rendering performance got orders of magnitude faster, and the need for using image-based tricks instead of re-rendering 3D geometry became less important. After all, with current graphics hardware using

---

14. The effect might be similar to what you would see in a Hollywood set if you walked around a building that only had a front.
15. www.apple.com/quicktime/technologies/qtvr/
16. http://research.microsoft.com/research/pubs/view.aspx?pubid=222

fast, programmable pixel shaders, why should anyone have to play image tricks and deal with associated rendering artifacts?

I love neat performance tricks, so part of me is sad to see it go away. Fortunately, image-based rendering still has a place in the world, at least in my current world of 2D graphics. While not as complex or fascinating as the 3D image-based rendering techniques, the technique discussed here does have similar performance advantages in the 2D realm. We call this approach *intermediate images*.

The Big Idea

The motivation for the intermediate images technique is this:

> **Note:** It is a lot faster to copy an image than to perform a complex rendering operation.

In general, a simple image copy (`Graphics.drawImage(img, x, y, null)`) operation is at least as fast as an optimized memory copy operation and may even end up being accelerated in the graphics hardware and video memory in the best case. On the other hand, operations such as transforms, complex `GeneralPath` drawing, and even drawing text may involve lots of operations per-pixel and end up being a bottleneck for what could otherwise be simple and fast code.

That's the "why" of the idea. Image copies are simply faster. Now let's look at the "how."

How It's Done

The basic approach with intermediate images is to create an image of the type and size that you need, perform your expensive rendering operations to that image, and thereafter copy from that image to your destination instead of performing your rendering operations directly.

For example, suppose that you have an image of some size and you want to display it in your component at some different size (`scaleW` × `scaleH`). You could do this in your `paintComponent()` method like so:

```
protected void paintComponent(Graphics g) {
    g.drawImage(img, 0, 0, scaleW, scaleH, null);
}
```

This code causes Java2D to scale the image every time `paintComponent()` is called. You could, instead, use the intermediate image approach, where you create an image of the target size (scaleW × scaleH), scale the original image to that new image, and then do a simple copy from that image instead:

```
// Earlier declaration of intermediate image
Image intermediateImage = null;

protected void paintComponent(Graphics g) {
    // Check for situations that should cause re-creation
    // of intermediate image
    if (intermediateImage == null ||
        intermediateImage.getWidth() != scaleW ||
        intermediateImage.getHeight() != scaleH) {
      intermediateImage = createImage(scaleW, scaleH);
      Graphics gImg = intermediateImage.getGraphics();
      gImg.drawImage(img, 0, 0, scaleW, scaleH, null);
      gImg.dispose();
    }
    g.drawImage(intermediateImage, 0, 0, null);
}
```

Note that, in this code, the intermediateImage object is cached between calls to paintComponent() and will only be re-created or re-rendered when either the image is null, which is the case the first time through that method, or the scaling size has changed. Otherwise, all scaling operations from that original image have been reduced to a simple copy operation from the intermediate image.

This approach is not limited to scaling transforms. You can use the same approach for arbitrary transformations. Note, however, that some transforms of an image may produce nonrectangular results; thus, you may need an image with a transparent background so that the intermediate image background does not show up during the copy operation. See the drawSmiley() code example later for an example using a transparent-background image.

But wait: There's more!

We've shown that you can use this technique for pre-transforming images, saving on the cost of scaling, rotating, or whatever you want to do with an image. But intermediate images are not limited to image rendering operations.

Note: Intermediate images is a technique that can be used for any arbitrary rendering operations, including imaging operations, complex shapes, and even text. Any rendering that will be performed repeatedly in the same manner, such as scaling to the same sized image or drawing the same complex geometry, is a candidate for acceleration via intermediate images.

The idea is to create an image of the appropriate size and type, render your graphics operations into it once, or whenever they change, and thereafter just call drawImage() from that intermediate image instead of doing the actual rendering. Note that, depending on the type of graphics rendering you are doing, you may need a transparent-background image, like we use in the drawSmiley() example, or a translucent-background image.

Example: IntermediateImages

Let's look at some example code and results to see how this technique works in practice. Check out the IntermediateImages example on the book's Web site to play with this code. This application creates intermediate images for an image-scaling operation and a complex rendering operation. It times how long it takes to perform the rendering directly to the Swing back buffer versus using an intermediate image and then reports the results in the application window.

Prescaled Images

The IntermediateImages example uses the prescaling approach to cache a thumbnail of a picture at a given size. Without an intermediate image, the operation looks like this:

```
g.drawImage(picture, SCALE_X, DIRECT_Y, scaleW, scaleH, null);
```

The operation simply scales picture into place at the location (SCALE_X, DIRECT_Y) with the final size (scaleW, scaleH).

Using an intermediate image instead, the operation looks like this:

```
private BufferedImage scaledImage = null;

private void drawScaled(Graphics g) {
  // Recreate image if null or if scale size changed
  if (scaledImage == null ||
      scaledImage.getWidth() != scaleW ||
      scaledImage.getHeight() != scaleH) {

    GraphicsConfiguration gc = getGraphicsConfiguration();

    // Opaque image is fine here; our cached operation
    // is opaque
```

continued

```
    scaledImage = gc.createCompatibleImage(scaleW, scaleH);
    Graphics gImg = scaledImage.getGraphics();

    // Set BILINEAR to get better scaling quality
    ((Graphics2D)gImg).setRenderingHint(
        RenderingHints.KEY_INTERPOLATION,
        RenderingHints.VALUE_INTERPOLATION_BILINEAR);

    // Scale picture into our intermediate image
    gImg.drawImage(picture, 0, 0, scaleW, scaleH, null);

    gImg.dispose();
}

// Now our scaling operation becomes a simple copy
g.drawImage(scaledImage, SCALE_X, INTERMEDIATE_Y, null);
}
```

Here, the actual operation to scale into the Swing back buffer is nearly the same, only without the scaling parameters:

```
    g.drawImage(scaledImage, SCALE_X, INTERMEDIATE_Y, null);
```

The rest of the code in drawScaled() is concerned with creating the image and scaling picture into it. Note that these operations happen only once, the first time our intermediate image is created.

Complex Shapes

The IntermediateImages example also draws some complex geometry using intermediate images, using the happy shape seen in Figure 5-6.

Figure 5-6   Insipid smiley face.

We can render this shape with the following graphics operations:

```
private void renderSmiley(Graphics g, int x, int y) {
  Graphics2D g2d = (Graphics2D)g.create();

  // Yellow face
  g2d.setColor(Color.yellow);
  g2d.fillOval(x, y, SMILEY_SIZE, SMILEY_SIZE);

  // Black eyes
  g2d.setColor(Color.black);
  g2d.fillOval(x + 30, y + 30, 8, 8);
  g2d.fillOval(x + 62, y + 30, 8, 8);

  // Black outline
  g2d.drawOval(x, y, SMILEY_SIZE, SMILEY_SIZE);

  // Black smile
  g2d.setStroke(new BasicStroke(3.0f));
  g2d.drawArc(x + 20, y + 20, 60, 60, 190, 160);

  g2d.dispose();
}
```

To draw the smiley into the back buffer, we simply call

```
renderSmiley(g, SMILEY_X, DIRECT_Y);
```

Rendering this graphic once is not a problem. But suppose your application had to render this same graphic several times every time you painted the component.[17] At some point, it just doesn't make sense to keep redoing all of the same rendering. You may as well cache the rendering results in an intermediate image and perform simple image copies instead.

Note that in this case, the graphics you are rendering are nonrectangular. When you cache the graphics as an image, you must make the background of the image transparent so that copying that image will result in copying only the colors from the graphics, not the colors from the background of the image. You can make this work by creating a BITMASK transparent image, and then rendering your graphics.

––––––––––––

17. Maybe it's a graphical chat room application with many happy people in it.

Here is code that caches this shape as an image and copies from that image:

```
private BufferedImage smileyImage = null;

private void drawSmiley(Graphics g) {
  if (smileyImage == null) {
    GraphicsConfiguration gc = getGraphicsConfiguration();
    smileyImage = gc.createCompatibleImage(
        SMILEY_SIZE + 1, SMILEY_SIZE + 1,
        Transparency.BITMASK);
    Graphics2D gImg = (Graphics2D)smileyImage.getGraphics();
    renderSmiley(gImg, 0, 0);
    gImg.dispose();
  }
  g.drawImage(smileyImage, SMILEY_X, INTERMEDIATE_Y, null);
}
```

The smiley face is now rendered with this single `drawImage()` call:

```
g.drawImage(smileyImage, SMILEY_X, INTERMEDIATE_Y, null);
```

The rest of the code in `drawSmiley()` is responsible for creating the intermediate image and rendering the smiley into it the first time.

By inserting some timing code in our application, we can compare the performance of each alternative. The results from a sample run are seen in Figure 5-7.

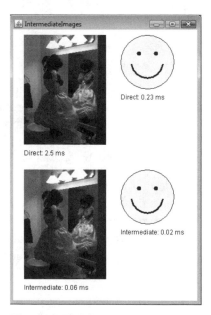

Figure 5-7 Direct rendering compared to intermediate images for scaling and complex rendering. Times are in milliseconds.

You can see that using intermediate images for prescaling in this example took less than 3 percent of the time of the direct approach. And using intermediate images for the relatively simple operations in the smiley face took less than 9 percent of the time of the direct rendering approach.

> **Note:** In general, the time you save by using the intermediate images technique is relative to the complexity of the rendering in the image compared to the cost of copying the image. Simple operations, such as drawLine() or fillRect(), do not generally benefit from this technique. But more complex rendering operations, such as those shown in our example, stand to gain substantially from this approach.

The examples presented here are meant merely to illustrate the concept. You can earn extra credit by figuring out how to apply the technique to your particular situations. Keep an eye out for examples of this technique throughout the book. Intermediate images are flexible, are easy to implement, and are much faster than the alternative for many rendering situations.

Notes

There are some important things to note about the intermediate images technique.

Cache Cow

In creating intermediate images, you are necessarily taking up more space on the memory heap. For example, if you are using a 500 × 500 intermediate image with a color depth of 32 bits, then you would allocate about 1 megabyte of memory on the heap for that single image (500 pixels × 500 pixels × 4 bytes/pixel = 1,000,000 bytes). While intermediate images can be quite beneficial if used correctly, you may not want to create large intermediate images willy-nilly because your application will suddenly be using a much bigger runtime memory footprint than it would otherwise. Be aware of the trade-off between size and speed for this approach and choose appropriately.

> **Tip:** If you do use a lot of intermediate images and are concerned about memory footprint, you might want to investigate SoftReferences, which are a useful way of letting Java manage the memory issues for you. SoftReferences will hold onto your object as long as they can, but will allow it to be collected when the heap is under pressure. Swing uses this approach for managing various image resources internally.

Image Type

The examples we presented used an opaque image for the scaling example and a transparent image for the smiley. It is also possible that you would need a translucent image instead, depending on the type of rendering you need to cache in the image. For example, antialiased text or geometry requires translucency in the destination, so our intermediate image would need to be translucent in order to represent the rendering faithfully. The general rule is to use whatever image type makes sense for your situation. If you require translucency, use a translucent image. If an opaque image works for you, as in the earlier scaling example, then use an opaque image.

Translucent Image Performance

Java2D does not currently benefit from hardware acceleration for translucent image copies by default on any platform. So if your main goal is to get hardware acceleration for some rendering operations (prescaled images, text, whatever), be aware that if you convert your graphics operations to translucent image copies, you may not get what you came for.[18] Java 2D does offer hardware acceleration for this type of operation through its OpenGL and Direct3D rendering pipelines, but these pipelines are not enabled by default as of the Java SE 6 release. The OpenGL pipeline is available on releases since J2SE 5.0 on all Sun platforms and is enabled by the command-line flag -Dsun.java2d.opengl=true. The Direct3D pipeline is available on all Windows releases since J2SE 1.4.2 and is enabled by the command-line flag -Dsun.java2d.d3d=true.[19] The Java 2D team is working on enabling hardware acceleration by default for this feature, and many others, in a future release. Read more about the OpenGL and DirectX pipelines in the section "Command-Line Flags" at the end of this chapter.

On the other hand, there is much to be gained from intermediate images, regardless of whether any particular image is accelerated, so don't let the lack of acceleration for a particular operation deter you. Test it out and see if it works in your situation.

Summary

Intermediate images are not very difficult to understand or to program, as the simple examples in this chapter hopefully demonstrate. The only tricks here are getting the image type correct to account for transparent and translucent back-

---

18. This is why the non-antialiased examples use transparent (BITMASK) images instead; this type of image does benefit from hardware acceleration by default on some platforms (e.g., Windows XP).
19. Prior to Java SE 6, translucent image acceleration required a different flag: -Dsun.java2d.translaccel=true. As of Java SE 6, as long as you enable Direct3D, you will get translucent image acceleration automatically.

ground situations and getting the cached image sized and positioned correctly to match the size and position of the original rendering.

You can apply this technique across all of your graphics operations. *Anything that you draw repeatedly in the same way is a candidate for intermediate image rendering. It may not be quite as graphics-geeky-cool as the 3D image-based rendering algorithms we talked about earlier, but I figure anything that makes an application perform better is pretty cool in its own right.

Optimal Primitive Rendering

This tip is a simple one. When rendering objects, *tell Java 2D exactly what you want it to do*. To put it a different way: *Simpler is faster.*

Java 2D is not magic. It cannot tell exactly what you mean. And for several reasons, it cannot afford to do serious amounts of analysis on your data to figure out what you really meant to do:

- It would take time for the 2D team to implement that depth of analysis—time that the team could be spending on problems of more general need, like making everything go faster to begin with.
- The problem is unsolvable in many cases. For example, if you hand Java 2D a Shape, it's going to be nearly impossible for the library to figure out that you are really trying to draw text.
- Perhaps most importantly, runtime analysis to determine optimal rendering paths for simple operations would take time during execution and would thus cause a performance hit to callers that did not need it.

For example, you could do, and people have done, something like this:

```
Shape line = new Line2D.Double(x1, y1, x2, y2);
graphics.draw(line);
```

But it would make a lot more sense to do this instead:

```
graphics.drawLine(x1, y1, x2, y2);
```

Similarly, you could fill a rectangle like this:

```
Shape rect = new Rectangle(x, y, w, h);
graphics.fill(rect);
```

But it would make a lot more sense to do this instead:

```
graphics.fillRect(x, y, w, h);
```

These examples are encapsulated in the `OptimalPrimitives` demo on the book's Web site. The application shows the previous code in action and times how long each operation takes. Figure 5-8 is a screenshot of the application running on my test system.

Figure 5-8   Rendering and performance results for different approaches to `line` and `rect` operations.

As you can see, the result of each operation is the same, but the rendering time is significantly faster for the "good" primitives, which in this case are the more sensible `drawLine()` and `fillRect()` calls.

As the preceding descriptions, code, and example make clear, telling Java 2D exactly what you want to do instead of issuing more generic primitives can benefit both your code simplicity and your application performance.

Benchmark

Here is a very quick performance tip, but one that comes up frequently in our conversations with developers. It can be combined with any of the performance approaches we discuss in the book.

Tip: When you want to figure out the best performance approach for a given situation, benchmark the alternatives.

Use existing application code if you have it, or write a prototype if not. Instrument the code with timing facilities, as we do with various demos on the book's Web site. See how the different alternatives perform. Use a profiler, like the one that comes with NetBeans. Test it under conditions and platforms that you think your users are likely to have. Try out different approaches and see how they trade off in terms of complexity versus performance.

All of the tips that we discuss in this chapter and this book are just that: tips. It's impossible to know what would work best as a general solution, so you'll have to apply these techniques to your code and benchmark them to see what works for you.

Command-Line Flags

Before we get into the details in this section, please note the following disclaimer:

Note: Most Swing developers will not need to use or know about these flags. Feel free to skip this section. We don't mind.

This disclaimer is actually fairly important. When you see some of the various command-line flags that are available, it's easy to get the impression that you have to understand them all in order to write decent Java applications. That is not the case. Everything in this book works well regardless of any command-line flags you do or do not use. So feel free to ignore the flags and just get down to the business of writing Filthy Rich Clients.

However, there are some situations in which it may be useful to know about some of the flags, in case you are running into performance issues, debugging issues, or issues related to interaction with other libraries. In these cases, you might want to play around with some of the flags to see if they can help.

We provide a brief glimpse into some of the more relevant flags for creating and running Filthy Rich Clients. We do not go into great depth on the flags, nor do we cover the entire spectrum of flags available to you. For more information on these and other graphics-related flags, please check out the latest document on system properties, *System Properties for Java 2D Technology*, currently at http://java.sun.com/javase/6/docs/technotes/guides/2d/flags.html. For a more general site on 2D information overall, go to the Java 2D FAQ at http://java.sun.com/products/java-media/2D/reference/faqs/index.html.

The flags discussed here are mostly about Java 2D, because Java 2D is the rendering layer of Swing and these flags affect how that rendering happens. There are also flags for Swing, AWT, and Java SE overall, but we focus specifically on flags that relate to graphics-rich Filthy Rich Clients here, so we stick to graphics-related 2D flags in particular. Feel free to spend the rest of your lives chasing down other flags that you might use (but again, you really won't need flags in most situations, so don't panic).

Command-line flags are runtime parameters that are used when you first launch a Java application. If you launch your application from the command line, you simply type these flags inline with the launch command, like so:

```
java –D<flag>=<value> MyClass
```

where `<flag>` and `<value>` are one of the flag/value pairs described for each flag in this section.

You can also specify these flags at the top of your `main()` method in an application. The trick is to make sure that these flags are passed into the Java VM before the graphics system is initialized, because the state of these flags is checked when the Java graphics system starts up. For example, this code sets a flag value as the first line of its main method:

```
public static void main(String args[]) {
   System.setProperty("flag", "value");
   // rest of main method
}
```

where `"flag"` and `"value"` are one of the flag/value pairs described for each flag in this section.

Applets and Java Web Start applications can also use command-line flags, specified through the Java Control Panel. In Java SE 6, they are specified through the Java tab in the appropriate Runtime Settings section. Note that setting the runtime flags in code, as in the earlier `main()` example, will not work for applets in general because the Java VM and the 2D graphics system are already running by the time any of your applet code is executed.

You can also specify flags in your JNLP file for applications that use Java Web Start. JNLP and Java Web Start are beyond the scope of this book. Please check out information on those technologies at http://java.sun.com.

We can break down the relevant flags into two main categories: rendering and debugging performance issues.

Rendering

There are numerous flags for controlling different aspects of 2D rendering. We focus on just a couple of the more important ones that relate to Filthy Rich Clients. If you want to see the full spectrum of 2D flags available, we encourage you to check out the *System Properties for Java 2D Technology* site referenced earlier.

OpenGL

The OpenGL pipeline is one of the mechanisms by which Java 2D can choose to issue rendering commands to the display. This pipeline is not enabled by default. To use this pipeline for Java 2D rendering, you need to run with this command-line flag:

```
sun.java2d.opengl=true
```

The OpenGL rendering pipeline for Java 2D has had a tumultuous history because of the availability and robustness of OpenGL drivers on the various platforms that Java SE supports combined with the features from OpenGL that Java 2D requires. This pipeline, when enabled, is actually the best overall platform for support and acceleration of nearly everything that Java 2D can manage to throw at it. Gradients, transforms, image copies, shapes, buffering—all of these things run blindingly fast in Java 2D when they are rendered through the OpenGL pipeline. However, general robustness issues across the wide spectrum of platforms that Java must support mean that this pipeline cannot yet be enabled by default. Drivers and hardware support are improving for OpenGL, so this situation may change in the future, and the pipeline could be more widely available.

In the meantime, the OpenGL pipeline is available via the command-line flag on all Sun-developed JDK platforms since J2SE 5.0: Linux, Solaris, and Windows.

There are two important uses for this flag, depending on your situation:

- *Java 2D performance:* If you happen to be on a platform that has a good hardware and driver combination to benefit from the pipeline, and if your application is using some of the advanced drawing primitives and operations that could do with some serious acceleration, then enabling this flag could result in significant performance improvements.
- *JOGL:* If you are using the Java Bindings for OpenGL (JOGL) API, which enables high-performance 3D applications written in Java, then you may want to enable Java 2D's use of OpenGL so that Swing rendering can cohabitate in a better and faster way with JOGL rendering. This capability was enhanced in Java SE 6, as Chris Campbell discusses in his blog at http://weblogs.java.net/blog/campbell/archive/2005/09/java2djogl_inte_1.html.

DirectX on Windows

DirectX is the default rendering pipeline for Java 2D on Windows. Its introduction in J2SE 1.4 enabled Swing to start taking advantage of hardware-accelerated graphics for key operations such as storing the Swing back buffer in VRAM and copying that buffer to the screen using the GPU. While the operations originally enabled in DirectX, such as rectangular fills and copies and horizontal and vertical lines, were fairly basic to begin with, they actually make up a majority of the GUI operations that Swing does in a typical application.

Work has continued on the DirectX pipeline, although by default it still accelerates only the basic operations described previously. A future release of Java SE should bring the DirectX pipeline up to the functionality and performance level of the OpenGL pipeline, but hopefully with a guarantee of driver robustness on Windows that would enable this acceleration pipeline to be enabled by default.

There are two reasons you might want to tweak flags for DirectX in some situations:

1. *Enabling more acceleration:* By turning on Direct3D capabilities, you might get acceleration for more advanced primitives and operations, such as translucent images.
2. *Disabling:* Some situations, including use of other libraries such as JOGL, may come up that might benefit from turning off the DirectX pipeline.

To enable 3D acceleration, which accelerates such things as diagonal lines, transforms, and translucent images, use the d3d flag:

```
sun.java2d.d3d=true
```

To disable Java 2D's use of DirectX completely, use the noddraw flag:

```
sun.java2d.noddraw=true
```

Debugging Performance

Sometimes you may notice that your application is getting much poorer rendering performance than you think it should. Many of the tips explained in this book should help in general, but you may just want to know what is going on under that big 2D hood. That is why Java 2D introduced the trace flag. It outputs information about who is drawing what so that you can see if there is anything unexpected happening.

This flag is more flexible than the other flags we covered. You do not simply enable this flag, you tell it how you want it to work. The usage is as follows:

```
-Dsun.java2d.trace=[log],[count],[help],[out:filename]
```

where:

- **log** prints out a list of the drawing primitives as they occur.
- **count** tracks the unique drawing primitives and outputs the totals of each one when the application quits.
- **out** prints the output in a specified file instead of on the command line.
- **help** prints out a more detailed explanation of the usage of `trace` than has been done here.

The information printed by the `trace` command is not in the user-friendliest format. It outputs the names of the raw internal drawing operations that are called. However, it can sometimes help to understand what Java 2D is doing and whether it seems like the library is doing a lot more work through obtuse drawing primitives than, say, the simple `drawLine()` operations you thought it would execute. Please see the *System Properties for Java 2D Technology* document mentioned earlier for more information on using this flag.

Part II

Advanced Graphics Rendering

6

Composites

Cₒₘₚₒₛᵢₜₑₛ are very important tools for programmers of Filthy Rich Clients. A composite can be thought of as a rule that determines how to store or combine the colors of a drawing primitive into the destination. A composite could, for instance, state that only the red components of the drawing primitive can be copied onto the graphics area. Composites are also known as blending modes in graphics editing applications like Adobe Photoshop or The GIMP, in which they are often used to create complex lighting effects. In Java, a Composite is an instance of the interface java.awt.Composite and can be set on a Graphics2D by calling setComposite().

AlphaComposite

The Java platform comes with only one implementation of Composite, called java.awt.AlphaComposite. This particular composite implements the basic alpha compositing rules for achieving translucency effects. AlphaComposite implements a set of 12 rules as described by T. Porter and T. Duff in a paper[1] entitled "Compositing Digital Images." All of the rules are based on mathematical equations defining the value of the color and alpha components of the resulting pixels given a source (the primitive you are drawing) and a destination (the graphics area). The Java implementation introduces one additional parameter, an alpha value that is used to modify the opacity of the source prior to blending.

---

1. Porter, Thomas, and Duff, Tom, "Compositing Digital Images." *Computer Graphics*, 18:253–259, July 1984.

Note: Components and Channels. Colors are encoded with three values, also called components or channels. The most common encoding in software is called RGB, which uses the red, green, and blue components. Yuv is another encoding, which uses a luminance channel (Y) and two chrominance channels (u and v).

The alpha channel, or the alpha component, is a fourth component, independent from the color encoding, which defines the level of translucency or opacity of the color. For instance, a color with an alpha channel value of 50 percent will be semitransparent.

To decide what rule to use and when, it is important to understand the Porter-Duff equations presented in the documentation of `java.awt.AlphaComposite`. To avoid boring you to death with mathematical descriptions (and also because my head hurts at the thought of going through 12 equations), let's focus on one of the most useful rules, Source Over, which composites the source over the destination, as if the source were a translucent painting on a piece of glass being held over the destination. The equation describing this rule is the following:

$$A_r = A_s + A_d * (1 - A_s)$$
$$C_r = C_s + C_d * (1 - A_s)$$

Factor A stands for the alpha channel of the pixel and C for each color component of the pixel. The subscripts r, s, and d stand for result, source, and destination respectively. Putting these together means that A_s stands for the alpha channel of the source, the primitive being drawn on the graphics area, and A_d for the alpha channel of the pixels already on the graphics area. Those two values are used to compute the resulting alpha channel, A_r. All of the values in these equations are floats between 0.0 and 1.0, and the results are clamped to lie in this range.

In your code, these values are converted to the ranges of the Java data types. For instance, when colors are stored with unsigned byte components, each component is a value between 0 and 255 instead of 0.0 and 1.0.

Note: Premultiplied Components. It is important to note that the Porter-Duff equations are all defined to operate on color components that are premultiplied by their corresponding alpha component.

What would happen if we drew a semi-opaque red rectangle on top of a blue rectangle? Let's start by writing down the equations as Java code, with each color component fully represented:

```
int srcA = 127; // semi-opaque source
int srcR = 255; // full red
int srcG =   0; // no green
int srcB =   0; // no blue

int dstA = 255; // fully opaque destination
int dstR =   0; // no red
int dstG =   0; // no green
int dstB = 255; // full blue

srcR = (srcR * srcA) / 255; // premultiply srcR
srcG = (srcG * srcA) / 255; // premultiply srcG
srcB = (srcB * srcA) / 255; // premultiply srcB

dstR = (dstR * dstA) / 255; // premultiply dstR
dstG = (dstG * dstA) / 255; // premultiply dstG
dstB = (dstB * dstA) / 255; // premultiply dstB

int resultA = srcA + (dstA * (255 - srcA)) / 255;
int resultR = srcR + (dstR * (255 - srcR)) / 255;
int resultG = srcG + (dstG * (255 - srcR)) / 255;
int resultB = srcB + (dstB * (255 - srcR)) / 255;

System.out.printf("(%d, %d, %d, %d)",
    resultA, resultR, resultG, resultB);
```

Running this program produces the following result:

```
(255, 127, 0, 128)
```

The resulting color is a fully opaque magenta, which is what you would expect when placing a translucent red sheet over a blue background.[2] While we highly encourage you to follow the same process to understand each rule, nothing beats screenshots.

AlphaComposite: The 12 Rules

Following is a list of Porter and Duff's 12 rules with a short description of each and a picture of a red oval drawn on top of a blue rectangle. Behind the scenes, the actual rendering is as follows: An opaque blue rectangle is drawn onto a transparent image, so we have a destination image with transparent pixels (alpha = 0)

---

2. Why you would do that, however, remains a mystery.

outside of the blue rectangle and opaque pixels (alpha = 1) inside the blue rectangle. Then the red oval is drawn on top with the rule and extra alpha, as shown in the application window of Figure 6-1. Finally, the image is copied to the Swing component and results in the views of the window seen in the figure.

Each rule was set up with an extra opacity of 50 percent. You can try each composite on your own by running the application `AlphaComposites` that you will find on this book's Web site. You can also compare the result produced by each rule to the graphics shown in Figure 6-1, which shows the scene with the default rule set on the `Graphics2D`, `AlphaComposite.SrcOver` with an alpha value of 100 percent.

The following rules are shown with the actual equations used to compute the result. As in the Source Over description, *A* stands for the alpha channel of the pixel and *C* for a color component of the pixel. The subscripts *r*, *s*, and *d* stand for result, source, and destination respectively.

Note: Terminology. When we refer to a *source* pixel, we mean those areas of the source that are not transparent. Similarly, a *destination* pixel refers to those areas of the destination that are not transparent. So, for example, the phrase "area of the source inside the destination" means those nontransparent source pixels being drawn to nontransparent areas of the destination.

Besides reading the descriptions (and seeing how they compare to the screenshots, which might be more illuminating), you might want to check out the Java-Doc for `AlphaComposite`, which goes into more detail on how these rules work.

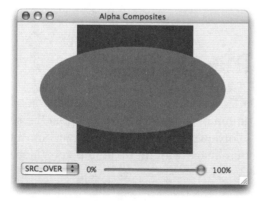

Figure 6-1 `AlphaComposites` demo with `SRC_OVER` rule and extra alpha of 100 percent.

Clear

$$A_r = 0$$
$$C_r = 0$$

Both the color and the alpha of the destination are cleared. Whatever color or shape you paint with, every pixel of the destination covered by the source will disappear, as in Figure 6-2.

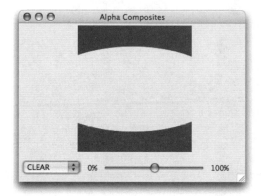

Figure 6-2 `AlphaComposites` demo with `Clear` rule.

Dst

$$A_r = A_d$$
$$C_r = C_d$$

The destination is left untouched. Whatever you draw on the destination will be discarded, as in Figure 6-3.

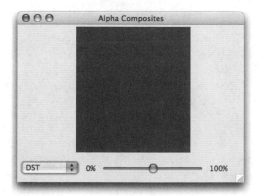

Figure 6-3 `AlphaComposites` demo with `Dst` rule.

DstAtop

$$A_r = A_s * (1 - A_d) + A_d * A_s = A_s$$
$$C_r = C_s * (1 - A_d) + C_d * A_s$$

The part of the destination lying inside of the source is composed with the source and replaces the destination. This results in the destination appearing to be drawn on top of the source (Figure 6-4) instead of the other way around.

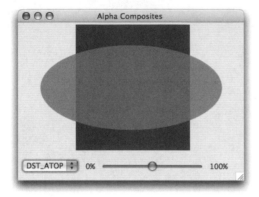

Figure 6-4 `AlphaComposites` demo with `DstAtop` rule.

DstIn

$$A_r = A_d * A_s$$
$$C_r = C_d * A_s$$

The part of the destination lying inside of the source replaces the destination. It is the opposite of `DstOut`, but with an alpha value of 50 percent, both operations look the same (Figure 6-5).

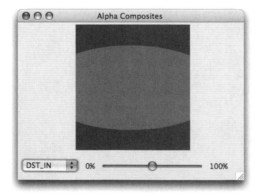

Figure 6-5 `AlphaComposites` demo with `DstIn` rule.

DstOut

$$A_r = A_d * (1 - A_s)$$
$$C_r = C_d * (1 - A_s)$$

The part of the destination lying outside of the source replaces the destination. It is the opposite of `DstIn`, but with an alpha value of 50 percent, both operations look the same (Figure 6-6).

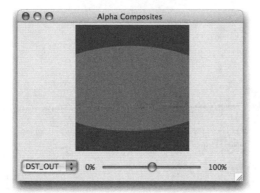

Figure 6-6 `AlphaComposites` demo with `DstOut` rule.

DstOver

$$A_r = A_s * (1 - A_d) + A_d$$
$$C_r = C_s * (1 - A_d) + C_d$$

The destination is composed with the source, and the result replaces the destination. The parts of the source outside of the destination are drawn normally, with the added opacity of the composite, as in Figure 6-7.

Figure 6-7 `AlphaComposites` demo with `DstOver` rule.

Src

$$A_r = A_s$$
$$C_r = C_s$$

The source is copied to the destination. The destination is replaced by the source. In Figure 6-8, the blue rectangle (the destination) does not appear underneath the red oval because the red oval (the source) replaces it.

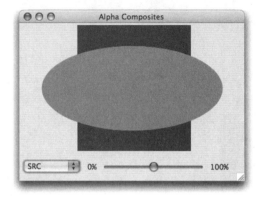

Figure 6-8 `AlphaComposites` demo with `Src` rule.

SrcAtop

$$A_r = A_s * A_d + A_d * (1 - A_s) = A_d$$
$$C_r = C_s * A_d + C_d * (1 - A_s)$$

The part of the source lying inside of the destination is composed with the destination. The part of the source lying outside of the destination is discarded (Figure 6-9).

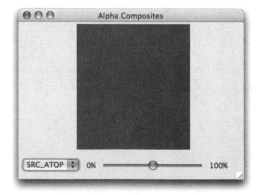

Figure 6-9 `AlphaComposites` demo with `SrcAtop` rule.

SrcIn

$$A_r = A_s * A_d$$
$$C_r = C_s * A_d$$

The part of the source lying inside of the destination replaces the destination. The part of the source lying outside of the destination is discarded (Figure 6-10).

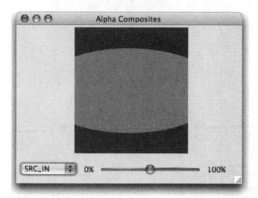

Figure 6-10 AlphaComposites demo with SrcIn rule.

SrcOut

$$A_r = A_s * (1 - A_d)$$
$$C_r = C_s * (1 - A_d)$$

The part of the source lying outside of the destination replaces the destination. The part of the source inside the destination gets discarded (Figure 6-11).

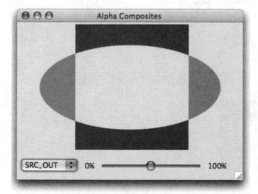

Figure 6-11 AlphaComposites demo with SrcOut rule.

SrcOver

$$A_r = A_s + A_d * (1 - A_s)$$
$$C_r = C_s + C_d * (1 - A_s)$$

The source is composed or blended with the destination (Figure 6-12). SrcOver is the default rule set on a Graphics2D surface.

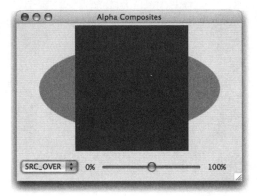

Figure 6-12 AlphaComposites demo with SrcOver rule.

Xor

$$A_r = A_s * (1 - A_d) + A_d * (1 - A_s)$$
$$C_r = C_s * (1 - A_d) + C_d * (1 - A_s)$$

The part of the source that lies outside of the destination is combined with the part of the destination that lies outside of the source (Figure 6-13).

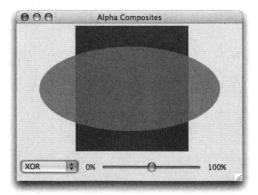

Figure 6-13 AlphaComposites demo with Xor rule.

Creating and Setting Up an AlphaComposite

An AlphaComposite can be set on a Graphics2D object at any time by calling the method setComposite(). This method affects the operations of all future graphics primitives, so it is important to restore the initial composite after you are done with your drawing.

Tip: You can also use Graphics.create() to make a copy of the drawing surface and throw it away when you're done.

To get an instance of AlphaComposite, you have two choices. The first choice is also the simplest and uses the instances predefined by the AlphaComposite class. All of those instances are exposed as public, static fields whose names follow the naming conventions of the classes. For instance, the Source Over instance can be accessed with the expression AlphaComposite.SrcOver. Here is an example of how to use this rule:

```
@Override
protected void paintComponent(Graphics g) {
  Graphics2D g2 = (Graphics2D) g;
  Composite oldComposite = g2.getComposite();

  g2.setComposite(AlphaComposite.SrcOver);
  g2.setColor(Color.RED);
  g2.fillOval(0, 0, 80, 40);

  g2.setComposite(oldComposite);
}
```

The predefined instances of AlphaComposite use an additional alpha value of 100 percent.

Another way to create an instance with an alpha of 100 percent is to use the getInstance(int) method. The previous code would be the same, save for the following line:

```
g2.setComposite(AlphaComposite.getInstance(
    AlphaComposite.SRC_OVER));
```

When you need to use an AlphaComposite with an alpha value lower than 100 percent, you must call getInstance(int, float). The second parameter is the opacity, in the range 0.0f to 1.0f. The following line creates a Source Over instance with an alpha value of 50 percent:

```
g2.setComposite(AlphaComposite.getInstance(
    AlphaComposite.SRC_OVER, 0.5f));
```

Create an AlphaComposite More Easily

One of my favorite features in Java SE 6[3] is the addition of two new methods in the `AlphaComposite` class: `derive(int)` and `derive(float)`. You can use them to get a copy of an existing `AlphaComposite` instance with new settings. Here is an example of converting a Source In composite to a Source Over:

```
AlphaComposite composite = AlphaComposite.SrcIn;
composite = composite.derive(AlphaComposite.SRC_OVER);
```

Calling `derive()` to change the rule retains the current alpha value and applies it to the new rule. You can, instead, change the opacity of an existing alpha composite but retain the rule. Instead of calling `getInstance(int, float)`, write the following:

```
g2.setComposite(AlphaComposite.SrcOver.derive(0.5f));
```

Calls to `derive()` can be chained to change the alpha value and the rule at the same time, as an alternative to `getInstance()`:

```
g2.setComposite(composite.derive(0.5f).derive(
    AlphaComposite.DST_OUT));
```

This code is easier to read and easier to maintain than the more verbose `getInstance()` approach necessary prior to Java SE 6.

Common Uses of AlphaComposite

`AlphaComposite`s are a versatile and powerful tool when used properly. While we can't tell you when and where you will use the 12 rules, we can present you the four most useful ones: `Clear`, `Src`, `SrcOver`, and `SrcIn`.

---

3. In fact, it is my favorite. Try to use `AlphaComposite` every day and you will soon rather swallow your desk than call `getInstance(int, float)` one more time.*

   * Yes, it is that bad.

Using Clear

Clear can be used when you want to reuse a transparent or translucent image. It is an easy way to erase a background so that the image is totally transparent. Remember the equation for Clear:

$$A_r = 0$$
$$C_r = 0$$

As you can see, the result does not depend on the source or the destination. Hence, you can draw anything you want to erase the picture. This also means that the opacity of the composite does not matter. The net effect is that an operation with this rule will simply cut a hole in it in the shape of the primitives you draw. In this case, Clear can be seen as the eraser tool from Adobe Photoshop or any popular alternative. The following code shows how to erase the content of a translucent image:

```
// The picture has an alpha channel
BufferedImage image = new BufferedImage(200, 200,
  BufferedImage.TYPE_INT_ARGB);
Graphics2D g2 = image.createGraphics();
// Draw stuff
// ...
// Erase the content of the image
g2.setComposite(AlphaComposite.Clear);
// The Color, the Paint, etc. do not matter
g2.fillRect(0, 0, image.getWidth(), image.getHeight());
```

The Clear rule lets you erase areas of arbitrary shape.

Using SrcOver

SrcOver is the default composite set on the Graphics2D context. This composite ensures that the source is drawn entirely, without any modification, on the destination. You can use it to ensure that the graphics area is correctly set up and that the rendering will not suffer from any mischief done on your Graphics object by another component of your application.

You can also use SrcOver to draw translucent objects without affecting the destination. Take a look at the application in Figure 6-14.

In this screen, you may notice several places where SrcOver was used to achieve translucency effects. The dialog box in the middle and the palettes on the edges are all translucent.

Figure 6-14   The result of the Source Over alpha composite.

You can control the opacity of the source by changing the alpha value associated with the instance of `AlphaComposite`, as we saw in the section "Creating and Setting Up an `AlphaComposite`."

Remember that composites work with all drawing primitives, most notably with pictures. You can also animate the alpha value of the `SrcOver` instance to create interesting apparition and fading effects.

Using SrcIn

`SrcIn` is a useful and amazingly underutilized composite. It can be used whenever you want to replace the content of an existing drawing. Figure 6-15 shows an application that paints a simple shield on the screen and fills it with a blue gradient.

What if you wanted to draw a similar shield, but with a photo inside instead of the gradient? This is easily achieved by setting the `SrcIn` alpha composite on the graphics area:

```
// Draws the blue shield
g2.drawImage(image, x, y, null);
// Replaces the content of the shield with Grand Canyon
g2.setComposite(AlphaComposite.SrcIn);
g2.drawImage(landscape, x, y, null);
```

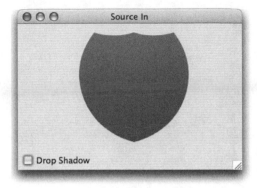

Figure 6-15 A simple gradient-filled shape.

Following the SrcIn rule, Java 2D replaces the destination with the pixels of the source that lie within the destination, as shown in Figure 6-16.

You can use this technique to create frames for pictures, to cut out drawings or images, or even to produce drop shadows. If you fill a black rectangle over the original drawing, you will obtain a shadow. Paint the original drawing again, on top and at an offset to the shadow, and you'll get the desired effect, as seen in Figure 6-17.

Note that you can change the opacity of the shadow by changing the opacity of the SrcIn instance.

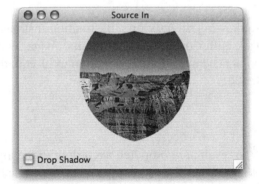

Figure 6-16 The photo is clipped by the shape of the shield.

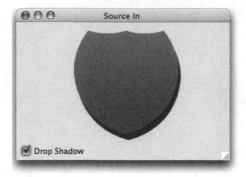

Figure 6-17   A simple drop shadow.

The complete source code of these examples can be found in the project SourceIn on this book's Web site.

> **Note: Soft-Clipping.** This example shows that the SrcIn rule can be used to perform soft-clipping, or antialiased clipping, with arbitrary shapes.

Issues with AlphaComposite

Some of the AlphaComposite rules might yield strange results when you use them to draw on a Swing component. You know this has happened when you see a large black hole in places meant to be empty or of a different color on your drawing, as shown in Figure 6-18.

This problem occurs when you are drawing directly on a destination that has no alpha value, such as the Swing back buffer or another non-alpha image, with a rule that requires the value of the alpha channel of the destination in its equation. This is the case, for instance, of SrcOut,

$$A_r = A_s * (1 - A_d)$$
$$C_r = C_s * (1 - A_d)$$

The color and the alpha values of the result are computed according to the alpha value of the destination. When you draw on a Swing component, the destination is the Swing back buffer, an image with no alpha channel. In this situation, all destination pixels are treated as being opaque, and the alpha value (A_d) is always 1.0. This is rather unnatural because, as developers, we think of user interfaces as layered documents. When you look at the screenshot in Figure 6-18, you

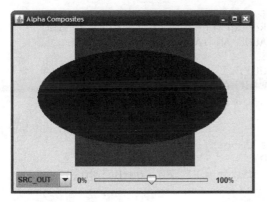

Figure 6-18 The black oval was supposed to be red in this composition with SrcOut.

probably see one layer of gray (the background), one layer of blue (the rectangle), one layer of black (the oval), and so on. You may therefore think it obvious that the blue rectangle is surrounded by transparent pixels. In reality, a Swing window is flat, not layered. Each time you draw something on a Swing component, the Swing back buffer represents a unique, opaque picture.

So why is the oval still black?

If we solve the previous equations and replace A_d by its value 1.0, we obtain the following results:

$$A_r = A_s * (1 - 1) = 0$$
$$C_r = C_s * (1 - 1) = 0$$

A color with all of its components set to 0 is black. Even though the resulting alpha channel is 0, or completely transparent, it does not matter because the Swing back buffer does not take alpha into account. Every time you draw on a Swing component, or on another opaque destination, with a composite rule that reads the alpha value of the destination, you will get a wrong result.

The solution to this problem is thankfully simple to implement. Instead of drawing directly onto a Swing component, you must first draw into an image with an alpha channel and then copy the resulting image onto the screen:

```
@Override
protected void paintComponent(Graphics g) {
  // Creates a picture with an alpha channel
  // This image could be cached for better performance
  BufferedImage image = new BufferedImage(getWidth(),
      getHeight(), BufferedImage.TYPE_INT_ARGB);
```

continued

```
        Graphics2D g2 = image.createGraphics();
        g2.setRenderingHint(RenderingHints.KEY_ANTIALIASING,
            RenderingHints.VALUE_ANTIALIAS_ON);

        g2.setColor(Color.BLUE);
        g2.fillRect(4 + (getWidth() / 4), 4,
            getWidth() / 2, getHeight() - 8);

        // Sets the composite
        g2.setComposite(AlphaComposite.SrcOut);
        g2.setColor(Color.RED);
        g2.fillOval(40, 40, getWidth() - 80, getHeight() - 80);
        g2.dispose();

        // Draws the image onto the screen
        g.drawImage(image, 0, 0, null);
    }
```

A picture with an alpha channel is completely empty after its creation; every pixel is transparent by default. Thus, the equations work as promised.

Tip: Temporary Offscreen Images. Creating a temporary offscreen image is an extra step that can be costly if you do it every time the component is painted, so you probably want to reuse the picture. You can either cache the finished drawing, caching the results of your rendering, or just cache the `BufferedImage` object and paint onto it every time `paintComponent()` is called. If you choose the latter, do not forget to clear the picture beforehand.

Whenever you see unexpected black pixels on the screen, make sure that the destination has an alpha channel. Failing that, use an offscreen image to solve the problem.

Create Your Own Composite

As of Java SE 6, `AlphaComposite` is the only implementation of `Composite` available in the core platform. For most applications, this is more than sufficient, as most of the other rules are rarely used. Nevertheless, it can be useful to have other kinds of composites available, particularly when you must implement a mockup created by a visual or graphics designer.

We developers live in a world made of IDEs and compilers, but visual designers are surrounded by powerful graphics editing tools like Adobe Photoshop. Such tools let the user apply various blending modes, or composites, to the layers making up the artwork, and most designers do not hesitate to put those blending modes to good use.

Implementing visual designs built with those blending modes can become a daunting task if you stick to the core composites offered by the JDK. But do not despair; you can write your very own composite!

The Add Composite

Writing a composite does not require a lot of work. In fact, the most difficult part is coming up with an interesting compositing rule, not coding it.

This book's Web site offers a project called BlendComposites, which contains 31 new composites, all inspired by the blending modes found in graphics editing tools like Adobe Photoshop. We show you how to implement one of them here: Add. You can refer to the project to see how the others are implemented.

The Add blending mode, as its name suggests, simply adds the value of both the source and the destination:

$$A_r = A_s + A_d$$
$$C_r = C_s + C_d$$

Figure 6-19, Figure 6-20, and Figure 6-21 illustrate the effect of this composite.

Figure 6-19 The destination of the composite.

Figure 6-20 The source of the composite.

Figure 6-21 The result of the composition: Dark pixels in the source have less effect on the result.

Here is the first step is to create a new class that implements the interface `java.awt.Composite`:

```
public class AddComposite implements Composite {
   private static boolean checkComponentsOrder(ColorModel cm) {
      if (cm instanceof DirectColorModel &&
         cm.getTransferType() == DataBuffer.TYPE_INT) {
       DirectColorModel directCM = (DirectColorModel) cm;
```

```
        return directCM.getRedMask() == 0x00FF0000 &&
              directCM.getGreenMask() == 0x0000FF00 &&
              directCM.getBlueMask() == 0x000000FF &&
              (directCM.getNumComponents() == 3 ||
                directCM.getAlphaMask() == 0xFF000000);
    }

    return false;
}

public CompositeContext createContext(
    ColorModel srcColorModel, ColorModel dstColorModel,
    RenderingHints hints) {
  if (!checkComponentsOrder(srcColorModel) ||
      !checkComponentsOrder(dstColorModel)) {
    throw new RasterFormatException(
      "Incompatible color models");
  }

    return new BlendingContext(this);
  }
}
```

A composite is actually a very simple class because only one method, `createContext()`, needs to be implemented. The `checkComponentsOrder()` method is used by `createContext()` to guarantee that the source and the destination are in the expected format. The code checks the color model and ensures the pixels are stored as integers. It also makes sure that the color components are in the following order within an integer: alpha (if present), red, green and blue.

Besides this, the documentation urges developers to make their composites immutable.

Note: Why Is Immutability Important? When you are given an instance of an immutable composite class, it is not possible for you to change its internal values. Try to imagine what would happen if a background thread changed the settings of a composite while this composite is used to paint a primitive on the screen. With immutable composites, you can guarantee the result of a drawing operation.

You can see how immutability was achieved in `AlphaComposite` by looking at its documentation. The only methods that let you modify the values of the composite actually return a new instance: `getInstance()` and `derive()`. There is absolutely no way to get the composite currently set on the graphics area and to modify its settings.

The AddComposite class shown previously respects this rule, since no setter is publicly available. The AddContext instance returned by the createContext() method is part of the implementation and is shown next.

Implementing the CompositeContext

All of the work of a composite is performed by its CompositeContext, returned by createContext(). Once again, the documentation warns against multi-threaded environments and explains that several contexts can be used at the same time. This is why the method as implemented in AddComposite returns a new instance of AddContext. If your composite contains parameters, for instance, an alpha value as in AlphaComposite, you can pass them to the constructor of your context. The method createContext() is the place where you can save the context you need to perform the compositing operation.

Here are the two methods that a class that implements the CompositeContext interface needs to implement:

```
void compose(Raster src, Raster dstIn, WritableRaster dstOut);
void dispose();
```

The first method, compose(), is where the actual composition is performed. The second method is called when the composition has finished and can be used to clear any resources you might have cached in the constructor or in compose().

Implementing compose() requires a good understanding of its three parameters. A Raster is a Java representation of a rectangular array of pixels. The src Raster, therefore, is the array of pixels representing the source, which is the drawing primitive to compose onto the graphics area. The dstIn Raster represents the array of pixels of the destination, or the pixels that are already in the graphics area. Finally, dstOut is the array of pixels where the result of the composition will be stored. Both src and dstIn are read-only, and new data will be stored in dstOut. A Raster holds quite a lot of information, including the size of the array and its storage type.

For simplicity's sake, AddContext works only with Rasters storing pixels as integers. For example, if you try to draw a picture of type BufferedImage. TYPE_3BYTE_BGR with this composite, an exception will be thrown.

To implement the Add composite, there is no need to cache values, so the dispose() method will be empty. Before writing any code in compose(), you need two utility methods called fromRGBArray() and toRGBArray(). Since this composite works on pixels stored as integers, all four components (alpha, red, green, and blue) are represented as a single integer. To apply our equation defined earlier, it is essential to break up the pixel integer into four integers, each representing one component. The methods fromRGBArray() and toRGBArray() are simple helpers that turn pixels into color components and color components into pixels. The incomplete implementation of AddContext looks like this:

```
private class AddContext implements CompositeContext {
  public void dispose() {
  }

  public void compose(Raster src, Raster dstIn,
                      WritableRaster dstOut) {
    // More code to come
  }

  private static void toRGBArray(int pixel, int[] argb) {
    argb[0] = (pixel >> 24) & 0xFF;
    argb[1] = (pixel >> 16) & 0xFF;
    argb[2] = (pixel >>  8) & 0xFF;
    argb[3] = (pixel      ) & 0xFF;
  }

  private static int fromRGBArray(int[] argb) {
    return (argb[0] & 0xFF) << 24 |
           (argb[1] & 0xFF) << 16 |
           (argb[2] & 0xFF) <<  8 |
           (argb[3] & 0xFF);
  }
}
```

Composing the Pixels

The first step in implementing compose() is to define the area on which the composite must be applied. You can query the dimensions of the input Rasters, but they are not necessarily the same. For instance, the source can be smaller than the destination. To avoid reading or writing beyond the bounds of a Raster, you must find the dimensions common to both Rasters:

```
int width = Math.min(src.getWidth(), dstIn.getWidth());
int height = Math.min(src.getHeight(), dstIn.getHeight());
```

Because of the equations defined earlier, the composite must go through all the pixels of the source and the destination in the area you just defined and blend them together. To achieve this task, you could simply write two loops, one for each row and one for each column, read the pixels by calling `src.getPixel()` and `dstIn.getPixel()`, and perform the composition.

This approach works flawlessly but requires you to call `Raster.getPixel()` two times for every pixel in the composition area, which easily amounts to several hundreds of thousands of method invocations. You can reduce this number and improve performance by using `Raster.getDataElements()` instead. This method lets you grab an entire rectangular area of pixels at once.

Imagine we are blending a 640×400 picture onto a 640×400 graphics area: We can either call `getPixel()` 512,000 times or read the Rasters line by line and call `getDataElements()` only 800 times. Calling methods in an inner loop should be avoided when possible, and `getDataElements()` offers a very efficient way to avoid those numerous method calls. The size of the area you read with `getDataElements()` is up to you. The larger the area is, the fewer calls are necessary, but more memory will be required for each addition in the loop.

In this case, we read the Rasters line by line, a good trade-off between speed and memory use. Now that the strategy to read the Rasters has been defined, you can declare the data structures in which the composite will store the pixels:

```
// Temporary storage for the blending operation
// Stores the color components of one source pixel
int[] srcPixel = new int[4];
// Stores the color components of one destination pixel
int[] dstPixel = new int[4];
// Stores one row of the source raster
int[] srcPixelsArray = new int[width];
// Stores one row of the destination raster
int[] dstPixelsArray = new int[width];
// Stores the result of the blending
int[] result = new int[4];
```

The most important part of the composite is yet to be implemented. An outer loop goes through all the rows of the composition area and stores them in `srcPixels` and `dstPixels`. The role of the inner loop is to read all of the pixels stored in a row and to perform the composition. The results are stored in `dstPixelsArray` and written in the `dstOut` Raster:

```
// For each row in the graphics area
for (int y = 0; y < height; y++) {
  // Reads one scanline from the input rasters
  src.getDataElements(0, y, width, 1, srcPixelsArray);
  dstIn.getDataElements(0, y, width, 1, dstPixelsArray);
```

```
  // For every pixel in a row
  for (int x = 0; x < width; x++) {
    // Extracts the color components
    toRGBArray(srcPixelsArray[x], srcPixel);
    toRGBArray(dstPixelsArray[x], dstPixel);

    // Performs the blending
    result[0] = Math.min(255, srcPixel[0] + dstPixel[0]);
    result[1] = Math.min(255, srcPixel[1] + dstPixel[1]);
    result[2] = Math.min(255, srcPixel[2] + dstPixel[2]);
    result[3] = Math.min(255, srcPixel[3] + dstPixel[3]);

    // Retains the result
    dstPixelsArray[x] = fromRGBArray(result);
  }
  // Writes one row in the destination raster
  dstOut.setDataElements(0, y, width, 1, dstPixelsArray);
}
```

Implementing a composite requires a lot of boilerplate code. If you look closely at AddComposite and AddContext, you will notice that only four lines are really tied to the equations that define the composite. The project BlendComposites implements 32 composites in less than 600 lines of code by creating generic Composite and Context classes and by defining each blending mode with the four lines of code required to do the actual work.

Summary

Composites are difficult to understand at first but soon prove to be useful in many situations. By creating your own composites, you can even go further than what the teams behind the JDK imagined possible with Java 2D and easily duplicate some of the most common features of graphics editing applications such as Adobe Photoshop.

7

Gradients

GRAPHICS design follows trends, and a current trend is to use gradients everywhere. Beyond the fashion, gradients are easy and versatile tools that can be used to create advanced effects like reflections and fade-out. Because of their versatility and ease of use, they are the most widely used Paint state of the Graphics objcct.

Up to J2SE 5.0, drawing a gradient was as simple as creating a new instance of java.awt.GradientPaint and setting it on a Graphics object. This class is very useful but sports some limitations. For example, you can draw only linear gradients, and you can specify only two colors. If you work with graphic designers, who use advanced tools like those found in Adobe Photoshop, you might find yourself in a difficult situation where you need to decompose a multistops gradient into several Java 2D two-color gradients.

Note: A multistops gradient is a gradient made of more than two colors.

Java SE 6 addresses these issues with two brand new Paint implementations, called LinearGradientPaint and RadialGradientPaint. These new gradients open the door to a host of rendering techniques and effects and can even simplify some of your existing code.

Two-Stops Linear Gradient

A two-stops linear gradient, or regular gradient, is an instance of java.awt. GradientPaint, the only gradient you can safely use with J2SE 1.2 up to J2SE 5.0.

Regular gradients are normally used to mimic volumes. With carefully chosen colors, you can easily lower a component or, on the contrary, raise it. To achieve these effects, gradients are often designed to simulate a particular lighting condition. Mac OS X scrollbars are a good example of how to use gradients to simulate depth.

If you take a close look at Figure 7-1, you will notice a dark gray-to-white gradient in the scrollbar track. The dark gray at the top simulates a shadow cast by the border of the component, creating an impression of depth.

Figure 7-1   Mac OS X scrollbars simulate depth with gradients.

Note: Lighting from Above. Shading such as that shown in the scrollbar track in Figure 7-1 falls under the guideline that people typically presume a light (like the sun) always shines from above them, not below them.

You can also create a gradient from a light color to a dark one to make a component stand out of the window, as in Figure 7-2.

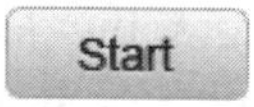

Start

Figure 7-2   Button with simulated depth.

The following code example shows how to use a `GradientPaint` to achieve an effect similar to Figure 7-2.

```
public class DepthButton extends JButton {
  public DepthButton(String text) {
    super(text);
    // Prevents Swing from painting the background
    setContentAreaFilled(false);
  }

  @Override
  protected void paintComponent(Graphics g) {
    Graphics2D g2 = (Graphics2D) g;
```

```
// Creates a two-stops gradient
GradientPaint p;
p = new GradientPaint(0, 0, new Color(0xFFFFFF),
    0, getHeight(), new Color(0xC8D2DE));

// Saves the state
Paint oldPaint = g2.getPaint();

// Paints the background
g2.setPaint(p);
g2.fillRect(0, 0, getWidth(), getHeight());

// Restores the state
g2.setPaint(oldPaint);

// Paints borders, text...
super.paintComponent(g);
    }
}
```

DepthButton extends JButton and overrides paintComponent() to change the background of the component. Figure 7-3 shows what the result looks like.

When you create a new GradientPaint, you must specify the coordinates and the color at which the gradient both starts and ends. For a vertical gradient that fills the button entirely, as in Figure 7-3, the coordinates (0, 0) and (0, button height) are specified. A diagonal gradient can be created by using (width, height) as the second coordinates, and you can also choose coordinates that are outside or inside the bounds of the component. In this figure, white is the start color and light blue is the end color.

The complete example, TwoStopsGradient, can be found on the book's Web site.

Two-stops linear gradients can be used for purposes other than regular painting. You can use advanced rendering techniques that rely on gradients to add beautiful effects to your application.

Figure 7-3 Swing buttons painted with a regular gradient.

Special Effects with Regular Gradients

Filthy Rich Clients need more than your average components; they need details and special effects. Reflections are one of the most widely popular effects in Filthy Rich Clients and are, surprisingly, one of the easiest to implement. The idea behind reflections is to enhance the realism of the user interface by mimicking reflective materials such as shiny plastic and polished metals.

Aerith, an example of a Filthy Rich Client whose source code can be found at http://aerith.dev.java.net, uses reflections in several places to give a more modern and realistic look to the user interface. These reflections can be seen in Figure 7-4.

To achieve the same effect, you need a `GradientPaint`, an `AlphaComposite`, and a bit of theory. Creating a reflection is a three-step process:

1. Render the subject as you normally would.
2. Render an upside-down clone of the subject, as if it were seen in a mirror on the ground.
3. Mask portions of the clone to make it fade out as it gets farther from the original subject.

In effect, you want to paint a gradient not with colors but with an arbitrary object. Although it is not possible to perform such an operation directly, you can cheat with an alpha mask and the appropriate `AlphaComposite`, as shown in Figure 7-5.

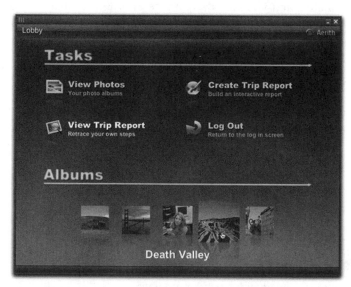

Figure 7-4   Aerith paints reflections to enhance realism.

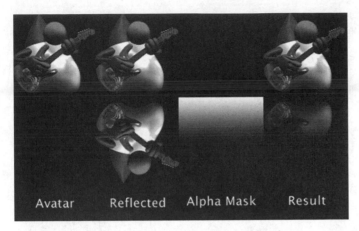

Figure 7-5 The three steps required for a reflection.

An `AlphaComposite` can be used to blend the pixel values of a source, in this case the alpha mask, with the pixel values of a destination, the mirrored clone of the subject. The idea is to blend the subject with a gradient that goes from a fully opaque color to a fully transparent color. Therefore, we need a compositing rule that mixes the alpha value of the source and the destination. Luckily, `AlphaComposite.DstIn` matches exactly our needs. Its equation is the following:

$$A_r = A_d * A_s$$

As in our discussion of composites in Chapter 6, "Composites," A_r represents the resulting alpha value, A_d the alpha value of the destination, and A_s the alpha value of the source. Imagine blending an alpha mask with a fully opaque destination. Following this rule, painting an opaque pixel from the alpha mask ($A_s = 1$) onto the destination results in a fully opaque pixel ($A_r = 1 * 1 = 1$). By contrast, painting a transparent pixel from the alpha mask ($A_s = 0$) onto the destination results in a fully transparent pixel ($A_r = 1 * 0 = 0$). Thus, each pixel of the destination gets an alpha value from the mask, creating the desired effect. Since the alpha channels are multiplied together, it also works with translucent destinations, as in Figure 7-5. Once you know which `AlphaComposite` to use, writing the code becomes quite easy:

```
private BufferedImage createReflection(BufferedImage image) {
    int height = image.getHeight();

    BufferedImage result = new BufferedImage(image.getWidth(),
        height * 2, BufferedImage.TYPE_INT_ARGB);
    Graphics2D g2 = result.createGraphics();
```

continued

```
      // Paints original image
      g2.drawImage(image, 0, 0, null);

      // Paints mirrored image
      g2.scale(1.0, -1.0);
      g2.drawImage(image, 0, -height - height, null);
      g2.scale(1.0, -1.0);

      // Move to the origin of the clone
      g2.translate(0, height);

      // Creates the alpha mask
      GradientPaint mask;
      mask = new GradientPaint(0, 0, new Color(1.0f, 1.0f,
                                               1.0f, 0.5f),
        0, height / 2, new Color(1.0f, 1.0f, 1.0f, 0.0f));
      g2.setPaint(mask);

      // Sets the alpha composite
      g2.setComposite(AlphaComposite.DstIn);

      // Paints the mask
      g2.fillRect(0, 0, image.getWidth(), height);

      g2.dispose();
      return result;
  }
```

This method takes a `BufferedImage` as input and returns another `BufferedImage` containing the original one and its reflection. In this code, we first create a new, empty, translucent `BufferedImage` with twice the height of the original picture so that the reflection will fit below the original.

After copying the original picture onto the new image, we paint the mirrored subject. This operation is a simple matter of using a negative scale transform on the y-axis (see Chapter 3, "Graphics Fundamentals," for more on transforms). By setting this transform on the `Graphics` context, every pixel drawn at the top will appear at the bottom, and so on down the picture as each pixel is inverted vertically. Be aware that the coordinates are also inverted, as you can see in the values used by the `drawImage()` call.

To paint the clone below the original subject, you must paint it at the y-coordinate of value (−height − height). To facilitate the next steps, we reset the scale transform and translate the origin to the position of the clone.

Applying the alpha mask is a simple matter of setting the appropriate `AlphaComposite` on the `Graphics` context and painting a gradient on top of the clone. The gradient is a regular two-stops gradient, which starts from the origin and goes to half of the height of the clone. You can play with the gradient's coordinates to change the distance of the reflection. The most important thing is to choose a transparent final color with an alpha channel value of 0. The alpha channel of the starting color is arbitray; just avoid choosing a fully opaque color because it would simulate a perfect mirror, something we don't find very often in the real world. Also note that the actual color of the gradient does not matter.

Last but not least, we fill a rectangle over the clone, with the `DstIn` composite and the alpha mask set on the `Graphics` context. Be sure to cover the entire clone, or you will get artifacts, since any part of the clone lying outside the gradient will remain unaffected. You can test the result of this method by running the example entitled `Reflection`, found on the book's Web site. You should see a window similar to Figure 7-6.

Figure 7-6 Example of a reflection created with `AlphaComposite.DstIn`.

The final effect seen Figure 7-6 is achieved with the following code:

```
BufferedImage image = null;

@Override
protected void paintComponent(Graphics g) {
  if (image == null) {
    try {
```

continued

```
        image = ImageIO.read(getClass().getResource(
                            "Mirror Lake.jpg"));
        image = createReflection(image);
    } catch (IOException ex) {
    }
}

    g.drawImage(image, 0, 0, null);
}
```

After loading the picture, the application calls `createReflection()`, which returns the original picture and its reflection in a single `BufferedImage`.

Tip: The `DstIn` composite can be used for any situation in which you want to fade out an object. Reflection is probably the best-known case of fade-out, but it is not the only one.

Figure 7-7 shows the same technique used to fade out the content of a list, indicating the user that there are other items on both sides (note the fade effect on the extreme right and left of the picture).

Tip: Work on Offscreen Images. The technique just described works only with translucent destinations. Therefore, you should not attempt to perform the same operations directly on a Swing component, because Swing's back buffer is opaque. Doing so would lead to unpredictable results, dependent on the underlying implementation of the Java platform. This restriction is related to the `AlphaComposite` rules' reliance on having alpha in the destination surface, as discussed in Chapter 3.

`Gradient` and `AlphaComposite` can be used together to create very interesting effects that will help you build your own Filthy Rich Clients. Take the time to learn how to use both of these classes and you will soon get excellent feedback from your users.

Figure 7-7   The fade-out on the sides uses `AlphaComposite.DstIn`.

Multistops Linear Gradient

The GradientPaint supplied in Java releases J2SE 1.2 through J2SE 5.0 is useful but lacks a very convenient feature: the ability to specify more than two colors at once. A current trend among graphics designers is the use of *dual gradients*. Such effects can be seen in some Windows XP themes, in Windows Vista, on Mac OS X, and on most Web 2.0 Web sites. Figure 7-8 shows an example of a dual gradient.

Dual gradients are used for their ability to mimic shiny, highlighted materials. Multistops linear gradients can also be used to draw better-looking gradients. Graphic designers often use them because they are extremely easy to create in applications like Adobe Photoshop. This means that whenever you have to implement a visual design, you may need to write the Java code to reproduce a multistops gradient. Although it is possible prior to Java SE 6, it is quite a pain.

Let's try to implement the example of Figure 7-8 with J2SE 5.0. To do so, we use the java.awt.GradientPaint class whose constructor is defined as follows:

```
public GradientPaint(float x1, float y1, Color color1,
                     float x2, float y2, Color color2)
```

As shown by this constructor, a gradient is made of two locations and two colors. The gradient is the interpolation of color1 and color2 between the start point and the end point. Here is the code that creates the effect seen in Figure 7-8.

```
GradientPaint p;

p = new GradientPaint(0, 0, new Color(0x63a5f7),
  0, 10, new Color(0x3799f4));
g2.setPaint(p);
g2.fillRect(0, 0, getWidth(), getHeight() / 2);

p = new GradientPaint(0, 10, new Color(0x2d7eeb),
  0, 20, new Color(0x30a5f9));
g2.setPaint(p);
g2.fillRect(0, getHeight() / 2, getWidth(),getHeight() / 2);
```

Gradient 2 — Multi-stops Gradient Gradients — Gradient 1

Figure 7-8 Dual-gradient effects are common among modern applications and Web sites.

The component has an overall height of 20 pixels. An initial gradient is painted from the top to the middle of the component: from (0, 0) to (0, 10). Then a second gradient is painted from the middle of the component to the bottom: from (0, 10) to (0, 20). Drawing these two gradients makes the code more difficult to read and, worse, harder to maintain. If you wanted to change the length of both gradients, you would have to change four lines of code. Using constants to define those lengths would not help much, since you would likely end up with many similar constants.

Java SE 6 offers a better solution with the class java.awt.LinearGradientPaint. It works in a very similar way to GradientPaint; you define the coordinates of the start and end points of the gradient. The difference lies in the number of colors you can specify and how you define their positions. The constructor of LinearGradientPaint takes two arrays, one of floats and one of colors:

```
public LinearGradientPaint(float startX, float startY,
                           float endX, float endY,
                           float[] fractions,
                           Color[] colors)
```

The first one contains the position, in percentage of the total length, of each color used in the gradient. Each position/color couple is called a *stop*. This makes it easier to write the previous example:

```
LinearGradientPaint p;

p = new LinearGradientPaint(0.0f, 0.0f, 0.0f, getHeight(),
    new float[] { 0.0f, 0.499f, 0.5f, 1.0f },
    new Color[] { new Color(0x63a5f7),
                  new Color(0x3799f4),
                  new Color(0x2d7eeb),
                  new Color(0x30a5f9) });
g2.setPaint(p);
g2.fillRect(0, 0, getWidth(), getHeight());
```

The gradient still spans from (0, 0) to (0, 20) but only one rectangle is filled this time. The first color used in the dual gradient is positioned at the top, at 0 percent of the overall length; two others are put in the middle, at 49.9 percent and 50 percent; and the last one is at the bottom, at 100 percent. Note that you cannot put two colors at the exact same position; we therefore use the values 49.9% and 50% for the middle colors. This code not only is clearer than the previous one but also runs faster, since it avoids changing the state of the Graphics context twice when calling setPaint().

The full example is available on the book's Web site in the project `MultiStopsGradient`.

> **Tip: Multistops Gradients for J2SE 5.0.** If you desperately need a multistops linear gradient in a project targeted at J2SE 5.0 or earlier, one alternative is to download Batik, an Apache SVG toolkit. You can achieve the same results with this toolkit because it also contains a class called `LinearGradientPaint`, which works exactly as its equivalent in Java SE 6.

Radial Gradient

Until Java SE 6, Java did not offer any way to create radial, or circular, gradients. This kind of gradient is especially useful for drawing specular highlights (bright spots of light that appear on shiny objects when illuminated).

Specular highlights are important because they provide a strong visual clue for the shape of an object. They are most often used to create images of spheres. Illuminated spheres are yet another popular trend in current graphic design. Mac OS X and Vista provide many examples of this effect. Figure 7-9 shows how specular highlights can be used to paint spheres.

Try as you might, you will never be able to easily achieve the same result with any JDK prior to Java SE 6. To implement this drawing, you have to use a new class in Java SE 6 called `java.awt.RadialGradientPaint`. Just like the other new class, `LinearGradientPaint`, `RadialGradientPaint` is a multistops gradient. The example in Figure 7-9 is actually composed of three different radial gradients, as shown in Figure 7-10.

A radial gradient is a bit harder to manipulate than a linear gradient because it provides more control over the drawing. Besides the color stops, which are

Figure 7-9 Specular highlights can be used to draw spheres.

Figure 7-10 The sphere in Figure 7-9 are drawn with these three successive radial gradients.

defined in the same manner as those in `LinearGradientPaint`, you need to define at least a center point and a radius:

```
public RadialGradientPaint(Point2D center,
                           float radius,
                           float[] fractions,
                           Color[] colors)
```

To draw the sphere, the first step is to fill a circle with a radial gradient:

```
// The gradient is centered in the sphere
p = new RadialGradientPaint(new Point2D.Double(
  getWidth() / 2.0,
  getHeight() / 2.0), getWidth() / 2.0f,
  new float[] { 0.0f, 1.0f },
  new Color[] { new Color(6, 76, 160, 127),
                new Color(0, 0, 0, 204) });
g2.setPaint(p);
g2.fillOval(0, 0, getWidth(), getHeight());
```

The center and the radius of the circle are the same as the center of the gradient in this example. As defined here, the radial gradient goes from blue in the center to black on the edges.

The second radial gradient of the sphere is used to paint a slight highlight at the bottom. This step is interesting because the gradient is not circular, but elliptic. Since `RadialGradientPaint` lets you define only a center and a radius, the only way to create an ellipse, rather than a circle, is to use an `AffineTransform` with the following constructor:

```
public RadialGradientPaint(Point2D center,
    float radius,
    Point2D focus,
    float[] fractions,
    Color[] colors,
    MultipleGradientPaint.CycleMethod cycleMethod,
    MultipleGradientPaint.ColorSpaceType colorSpace,
    AffineTransform gradientTransform)
```

This gradient is much more complicated than the previous one. In addition to the center, the radius and the color stops, you must define the focus point, the cycle mode, the color space, and an AffineTransform.

The focus point defines the position at which the gradient actually starts. When the focus is not defined, as was the case in the first gradient, it is set at a default of the center point. The RadialGradientPaint interpolates the colors in a circle. The color of each pixel depends on its distance from the focus point. Figure 7-11 shows an oval filled with a radial gradient whose focus point is different from its center.

The cycle mode allows you to repeat (RadialGradientPaint.CycleMethod. REPEAT) or reflect (RadialGradientPaint.CycleMethod.REFLECT) the colors when the area covered by the gradient is larger than the radius. The default cycle mode is RadialGradientPaint.CycleMethod.NO_CYCLE, which does nothing.

The color space defines how the colors are interpolated between the stops. You can choose between a linear space and the sRGB space. The latter is the default and should be used most of the time.

The last parameter of the constructor is an AffineTransform that can be used to alter the shape of the circular gradient. It lets you, for instance, scale or rotate the gradient.

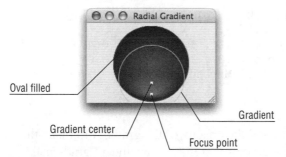

Figure 7-11 Anatomy of a radial gradient.

The following code shows how to use these parameters to create the gradient detailed in Figure 7-11.

```
// The gradient is horizontally centered, located toward
// the bottom.  The focus point is set lower than the
// center of the gradient
p = new RadialGradientPaint(
  new Point2D.Double(getWidth() / 2.0,
                        getHeight() * 1.5),
  getWidth() / 2.3f,
  new Point2D.Double(getWidth() / 2.0,
                        getHeight() * 1.75 + 6),
  new float[] { 0.0f, 0.8f },
  new Color[] { new Color(64, 142, 203, 255),
              new Color(64, 142, 203, 0) },
  RadialGradientPaint.CycleMethod.NO_CYCLE,
  RadialGradientPaint.ColorSpaceType.SRGB,
  AffineTransform.getScaleInstance(1.0, 0.5));
g2.setPaint(p);
g2.fillOval(0, 0, getWidth(), getHeight());
```

In this example, the focus is set at the bottom of the sphere to simulate lighting from below. The scaling AffineTransform is defined to squeeze the gradient vertically and make it looks like an ellipse. By dividing the height by 2, using a scale factor of 0.5 on the y-axis, the ellipse becomes two times wider than it is tall.

The third and last gradient composing the sphere is set up to simulate a specular highlight to emphasize the 3D appearance of the drawing. To do this, we define a focus point located in the upper-left region of the sphere:

```
p = new RadialGradientPaint(
  new Point2D.Double(getWidth() / 2.0,
                        getHeight() / 2.0),
  getWidth() / 1.4f,
  new Point2D.Double(45.0, 25.0),
  new float[] { 0.0f, 0.5f },
  new Color[] { new Color(1.0f, 1.0f, 1.0f, 0.4f),
              new Color(1.0f, 1.0f, 1.0f, 0.0f) },
  RadialGradientPaint.CycleMethod.NO_CYCLE);
g2.setPaint(p);
g2.fillOval(0, 0, getWidth(), getHeight());
```

You can play with the distance and the opacity of the gradient to make the sphere look more like plastic (opaque gradient) or glass (translucent gradient).

ONLINE DEMO   This demo is available on the Web site in the project called RadialGradient.

Optimizing Gradients

In most situations, Java 2D paints gradients very quickly—so quickly, in fact, that you needn't bother optimizing your drawing code.[1] There are some cases, however, in which gradient performance will haunt you. Drawing a gradient is an expensive operation when you are filling a large area. Actually, any large drawing is expensive, but gradients require some involved calculations to compute the colors, and gradients can become a source of problems if your application needs a lot of processing power to draw other interesting things, like animations.

Aerith, the first application christened as a Filthy Rich Client, is a great example of why gradients might need to be optimized. Indeed, its background is a huge, full-frame gradient, as show in Figure 7-12.

When developing this application, our team ran into some minor performance issues whose root cause was soon identified as being the background gradient. Aerith is a window of about 700×500 pixels, and drawing a gradient on such a large area requires many CPU cycles to compute and draw all of the different colors.

Caching the Gradient

The solution used to work around this problem was to turn the gradient into an image and paint only that image.[2] Caching a gradient that way is very easy and

Figure 7-12   Aerith draws a huge gradient on its backdrop.

---

1. Life is sweet when smart people at nice companies do all the work for you.
2. This is a great example of the intermediate image performance tip, which is covered in Chapter 3.

can help when you need to squeeze out as much performance as you can from your code:

```
private BufferedImage gradientImage = null;
@Override
protected void paintComponent(Graphics g) {
  if (gradientImage == null ||
      gradientImage.getWidth() != getWidth() ||
      gradientImage.getHeight() != getHeight()) {
    gradientImage = new BufferedImage(getWidth(), getHeight(),
        BufferedImage.TYPE_INT_RGB);
    Graphics2D g2d = (Graphics2D) gradientImage.getGraphics();
    g2d.setPaint(backgroundGradient);
    g2d.fillRect(0, 0, getWidth(), getHeight());
    g2d.dispose();
  }

  g.drawImage(gradientImage, 0, 0, null);
}
```

The first time the `paintComponent()` method is called, this code creates a new `BufferedImage` the size of the enclosing frame and draws the gradient in it. Every successive painting of the background will copy this image, which is a very fast operation even at that size. Whenever the frame is resized, the current cached image is discarded and recreated with the appropriate dimension.

Caching a gradient in a picture outperforms a direct gradient drawing by a factor of more than 3,200 on Windows. The only caveat is the large memory consumption. The gradient shown in the screenshot in Figure 7-12 takes about 500kb in memory. Depending on the number of gradients you plan draw and the amount of memory you are willing to spend, this memory consumption may or may not suit you.[3] But there is another solution, which is both fast and memory friendly, although it works for only two kinds of gradients.

Smarter Caching

When you draw a vertical (or horizontal) gradient, every column (or row) is the same as the previous one. Given this fact, is it really necessary to store all the duplicates in memory in a big fat image? It is not, and the solution is quite sim-

---

3. Although filthy, it does not mean your rich clients can forget about good behavior and pleasing manners. Save the memory!

ple. Whenever you draw an image on a `Graphics` surface, you can ask Java 2D to stretch it at the same time by supplying its new dimensions. This means we can optimize our gradient by painting it in a single-column (or row) image and then stretching that image to cover the whole target area:

```
private BufferedImage gradientImage = null;

protected void paintComponent(Graphics g) {
  if (gradientImage == null ||
      gradientImage.getHeight() != getHeight()) {
    gradientImage = GraphicsUtil.
        createCompatibleImage(1, getHeight());
    Graphics2D g2d = (Graphics2D) gradientImage.getGraphics();
    g2d.setPaint(backgroundGradient);
    g2d.fillRect(0, 0, 1, getHeight());
    g2d.dispose();
  }

  g.drawImage(gradientImage, 0, 0, getWidth(),
          getHeight(), null);
}
```

This example is very similar to the previous one except it creates an image only one pixel wide. The appropriate width is set in the call to `drawImage()`. Instead of using 500kb of RAM, the application now uses only 700 bytes! Best of all, the speed is 800 times faster than the regular gradient on Windows.

Tip: Profile before Optimizing. These optimization techniques are very tempting but must be handled with care. The speed improvement numbers given to illustrate our purpose are true only for Swing applications running on Windows XP with the default rendering pipeline (DirectDraw, as of Java SE 6).

On Mac OS X, using images gives a speed increase of only four times faster. On Windows, with the OpenGL pipeline enabled (with the command-line flag `-Dsun.java2d.opengl=true`), there is no speed difference at all between the three techniques.

Optimization with Cyclic Gradients

If you want to draw a nonhorizontal, nonvertical gradient and can't afford the memory consumption induced by the caching of a large gradient, there is one last trick you can use. Java 2D always creates acyclic gradients by default. This feature is very important when you fill a primitive larger than the area covered by the gradient paint. Take a look at the following example:

```
@Override
protected void paintComponent(Graphics g) {
  Graphics2D g2 = (Graphics2D) g.createGraphics();
  g2.setPaint(new GradientPaint(0.0f, 0.0f, Color.WHITE,
    0.0f, getHeight() / 2.0f, Color.DARK_GRAY);
  g2.fillRect(0, 0, getWidth(), getHeight());
}
```

In this painting code, a rectangle covering the whole graphics area is filled with a gradient with a height only half the total height of the component. If you execute this code, you will see that Java 2D paints the gradient from (0, 0) up to (0, height/2) and fills the remaining pixels with the last color of the gradient, a dark gray. To do so, Java 2D must constantly check whether the current pixel lies outside of the gradient area. This is a simple test, but performed against thousands of pixels, it can take significant time.

Instead of repeating the last color, a cyclic gradient would be repeated until the whole area is filled. In our example, you would see the same gradients twice: one between (0, 0) and (0, height/2) and the other between (0, height/2) and (0, height).

Painting a cyclic gradient is much faster because Java 2D does not have to check whether the current pixel is outside the gradient area. Because the gradient is constantly cycling, the GradientPaint implementation has some clever code to generate the correct color that never needs tests to deal with boundary conditions. Since conditional tests in an inner rendering loop cause performance problems, the cyclic code can run much faster by avoiding these tests.

This means you can improve performance by using cyclic gradients in your applications. Be aware, though, that cyclic gradients can replace acyclic gradients only when the gradient area coincides with the bounds of the primitive you are drawing. Finally, creating a cyclic gradient is very easy, no matter what kind of gradient you are using:

```
// Cyclic gradient paint
new GradientPaint(new Point(0, 0), Color.WHITE,
 new Point(0, getHeight()), Color.DARK_GRAY, true);

// Cyclic linear gradient paint
new LinearGradientPaint(new Point(0, 0),
                        new Point(0, getHeight()),
  new float[] { 0.0f, 1.0f }, new Color[] {
      Color.WHITE, Color.DARK_GRAY },
  MultipleGradientPaint.CycleMethod.REPEAT);
```

The boolean parameter of `GradientPaint` constructors must be set to true to define a cyclic gradient, false otherwise. `LinearGradientPaint` and `RadialGradientPaint` offer more control over this behavior; you can choose from among three options: acyclic, repeated cyclic, and reflected cyclic. These behaviors are defined by the enumeration called `MultipleGradientPaint.CycleMethod`. `CycleMethod.REFLECT` is similar to a cyclic `GradientPaint`, whereas `CycleMethod.REPEAT` starts the gradient over each time it gets repeated. No matter which one you choose, the result will be faster than regular acyclic gradients.

Performance Tip: Donald Knuth is famous for, among other things, a very important statement: "Premature optimization is the root of all evil." Keep this in mind when trying to optimize your gradients. Are your gradients big enough to justify the added complexity to your code? Does your application repaint those gradients often enough to merit the effort? Will the user notice the speed difference?

The more you optimize your code, the messier it gets, and the messier it gets, the more expensive it is to maintain.

The gradients offered by the Java platform are very powerful tools to create both modern and good-looking user interfaces. The new gradient classes introduced in Java SE 6 not only make your code easier to read and maintain but also bring you new capabilities with which you can create even more impressive graphical effects.

8

Image Processing

IMAGE-PROCESSING tools such as Adobe Photoshop and The GIMP offer a wide variety of filters you can apply on your pictures to create various special effects (see Figure 8-1). When you are designing a user interface, it is very tempting to use those effects. For instance, you could use a filter to blur an out-of-focus element in the UI. You could also increase the brightness of an image as the user moves the mouse over a component.

Figure 8-1 Applications like Adobe Photoshop have advanced image-processing capabilities.

Image Filters

Despite the impressive-looking results, image processing is not a difficult task to implement. Processing an image, or applying a filter, is just a matter of calculating a new color for each pixel of a source image. The information required to compute the new pixels varies greatly from one filter to another. Some filters, a grayscale filter for instance, need only the current color of a pixel; other filters, such as a sharpening filter, may also need the color of the surrounding pixels; still other filters, such as a rotation filter, may need additional parameters.

Since the introduction of Java 2D in J2SE 1.2, Java programmers have access to a straightforward image-processing model. You might have learned or read about the old producer-consumer model of Java 1.1. If you did, forget everything you know about it because the new model is much easier and more versatile. Java 2D's image-processing model revolves around the `java.awt.image.BufferedImage` class and the `java.awt.image.BufferedImageOp` interface.

A `BufferedImageOp` implementation takes a `BufferedImage` as input, called the source, and outputs another `BufferedImage`, called the destination, which is altered according to specific rules. Figure 8-2 shows how a blur filter produces the final image.

While the JDK does not offer concrete image filters, it does provide the foundations for you to create your own. If you need a sharpening or blurring filter, for example, you must know how to provide parameters to a `ConvolveOp` filter. We teach you such techniques in this chapter. Before we delve further into image-processing theory, let's see how we can use a `BufferedImageOp` to process an image.

BufferedImage   BufferedImageOp   BufferedImage
The source   The filter   The destination

Figure 8-2   Filtering an image with Java 2D.

Processing an Image with BufferedImageOp

Filtering a `BufferedImage` can be done onscreen at painting time or offscreen. In both cases, you need a source image and an operation, an instance of `BufferedImageOp`. Processing the image at painting time is the easiest approach; here is how you might do it:

```
// createImageOp returns a useful image filter
BufferedImageOp op = createImageOp();
// loadSourceImage returns a valid image
BufferedImage sourceImage = loadSourceImage();

@Override
protected void paintComponent(Graphics g) {
  Graphics2D g2 = (Graphics2D) g;
  // Filter the image with a BufferedImageOp, then draw it
  g2.drawImage(sourceImage, op, 0, 0);
}
```

You can filter an image at painting time by invoking the `drawImage(BufferedImage, BufferedImageOp, int, int)` method in `Graphics2D` that filters the source image and draws it at the specified location.

> **Warning: Use Image Filters with Care.** The `drawImage(BufferedImage, BufferedImageOp, int, int)` method is very convenient but often has poor runtime performance. An image filter is likely to perform at least a few operations for every pixel in the source image, which easily results in hundreds of thousands, or even millions, of operations on medium or large images. Besides, this method might have to create a temporary image, which takes time and memory. For every filter you want to use, you will have to see whether the runtime performance is acceptable or not.

Here is an example of how to preprocess an image by doing all the operations offscreen:

```
BufferedImageOp op = createImageOp();
BufferedImage sourceImage = loadSourceImage();
BufferedImage destination;

destination = op.filter(sourceImage, null);
```

Calling the filter() method on a BufferedImageOp triggers the processing of the source image and the generation of the destination image. The second parameter, set to null here, is actually the destination image, which, when set to null, tells the filter() method to create a new image of the appropriate size. You can, instead, pass a non-null BufferedImage object as this parameter to avoid creating a new one on each invocation. Doing so can save performance by reducing costly image creations.

The following code example shows how you can optimize a routine applying the same filter on several images of the same size:

```
BufferedImageOp op = createImageOp();
BufferedImage[] sourceImagesArray = loadImages();
BufferedImage destination = null;

for (BufferedImage sourceImage : sourceImagesArray) {
  // on the first pass, destination is null
  // so we need to retrieve the reference to
  // the newly created BufferedImage
  destination = op.filter(sourceImage, destination);
  saveImage(destination);
}
```

After the first pass in the loop, the destination will be non-null and filter() will not create a new BufferedImage when invoked. By doing so, we also make sure that the destination is in a format optimized for the filter, as it is created by the filter itself.

Processing an image with Java 2D is an easy task. No matter which method you choose, you will need to write only one line of code. But we haven't seen any concrete BufferedImageOp yet and have just used an imaginary createImageOp() method that was supposedly returning a useful filter. As of Java SE 6, the JDK contains five implementations of BufferedImageOp we can rely on to write our own filters: AffineTransformOp, ColorConvertOp, ConvolveOp, LookupOp, and RescaleOp.

You can also write your own implementation of BufferedImageOp from scratch if the JDK does not fulfill your needs. Before learning how to write your own, let's take a closer look at what the JDK has to offer. Each filter we investigate will be applied to the sample picture shown in Figure 8-3 to give you a better idea of the result.

 The complete source code for all the examples can be found on this book's Web site in the project named ImageOps.

Figure 8-3 The image used in our filter examples.

AffineTransformOp

An `AffineTransformOp` is a geometry filter. It does not work on the actual color of the pixels but on the shape of the picture. As its name suggests, however, it is not meant to perform any kind of geometry transformation. Instead, it is limited to linear mapping from 2D coordinates in the source image to 2D coordinates in the destination image.

This kind of filter is created with an `AffineTransform` instance, which you should be familiar with if you have worked with the `Graphics2D` class (this class is also discussed in Chapter 3, "Graphics Fundamentals"). An `AffineTransform` can be used to rotate, scale, translate, and shear objects in a 2D space.

The following code illustrates how to divide the size of an image by two using an `AffineTransformOp`:

```
BufferedImage dstImage = null;
AffineTransform transform =
    AffineTransform.getScaleInstance(0.5, 0.5);
AffineTransformOp op = new AffineTransformOp(transform,
    AffineTransformOp.TYPE_BILINEAR);
dstImage = op.filter(sourceImage, null);
```

The `AffineTransformOp` constructor used in this example takes two parameters: an `AffineTransform`, in this case a scale operation of 50 percent on both axes,

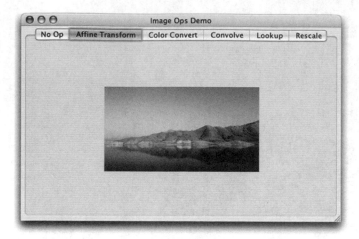

Figure 8-4 The size of the original image is reduced by 50 percent with an `AffineTransformOp`.

and an interpolation type, which is equivalent to the interpolation rendering hint you can find in the `RenderingHints` class (see Chapter 3). You can also pass a `RenderingHints` instance instead of the interpolation type, in which case the interpolation rendering hint will be used.

Figure 8-4 shows the result of our scaling operation.

ColorConvertOp

This `BufferedImageOp` implementation performs a pixel-by-pixel color conversion of the source image into the destination image. This particular image-processing operation has an interesting feature: It transforms a given pixel from one color model to another. To do this, the filter needs the color value of only this single pixel, which means that it is possible to use the same image as both the source and the destination.

Converting an image from one color model to another has little practical use if you are not building an advanced imaging tool. And it is definitely useless if terms like "CMYK," "sRGB," and "Adobe RGB 1998 color profile" mean nothing to you. Color spaces are very useful, but describing them and their applications goes way beyond the scope of this book. Even so, we can use a `ColorConvertOp` to create something more basic and potentially useful to us: a grayscale version of a source image.

You first need to create a `ColorSpace` instance that represents the color model to which you want to convert your image. A `ColorSpace` can be instantiated by invoking `ColorSpace.getInstance(int)` and passing one of the five following constants:

```
ColorSpace.CS_CIEXYZ
ColorSpace.CS_GRAY
ColorSpace.CS_LINEAR_RGB
ColorSpace.CS_PYCC
ColorSpace.CS_sRGB
```

You might have already guessed which one is best suited to our purpose of performing a grayscale conversion:

```
BufferedImage dstImage = null;
ColorSpace colorSpace = ColorSpace.getInstance(
    ColorSpace.CS_GRAY);
ColorConvertOp op = new ColorConvertOp(colorSpace, null);
dstImage = op.filter(sourceImage, null);
```

Similar to `AffineTransformOp`, `ColorConvertOp` can use a set of `RenderingHints` to control the quality of the color conversion and the dithering. Figure 8-5 shows the result of the our color conversion.

Last but not least, it is important to know that performing such a conversion on an image may make it incompatible with your graphics display hardware, thus hurting the performance if you need to paint the filtered image to the Swing window.

Figure 8-5 `ColorConvertOp` can be used to create a grayscale version of an image.

You may want to convert the image to be a compatible image instead for general usage. See Chapter 3 for more information.

ConvolveOp

The ConvolveOp is the most complicated BufferedImageOp but also the most versatile. It is the only BufferedImageOp you should master and know by heart. A ConvolveOp is used to perform a convolution from the source image to the destination. If you never took any math courses, or more likely, if you forgot everything about what you learned during those classes, a convolution is a spatial operation that computes the destination pixel by multiplying the source pixel and its neighbors by a convolution kernel.[1] Don't be frightened: You will soon understand what this gobbledygook means.

Any convolution operation relies on a convolution kernel, which is just a matrix of numbers. Here is an example:

$$kernel = \begin{bmatrix} 1/9 & 1/9 & 1/9 \\ 1/9 & 1/9 & 1/9 \\ 1/9 & 1/9 & 1/9 \end{bmatrix}$$

The kernel defined here represents a 3×3 matrix of floating-point numbers. When you perform a convolution operation, this matrix is used as a sliding mask over the pixels of the source image. For instance, to compute the result of the convolution for a pixel located at the coordinates (x, y) in the source image, the center of the kernel is positioned at these coordinates. In the case of a 3×3 kernel, here are the coordinates, in the source image, of the pixels that each corresponding kernel value is applied to:

$$kernel\ coordinates = \begin{bmatrix} x-1, y-1 & x, y-1 & x+1, y-1 \\ x-1, y & x, y & x+1, y \\ x-1, y+1 & x, y+1 & x+1, y+1 \end{bmatrix}$$

---

1. And if this does not make sense to you, consider the mathematical definition from the Wikipedia: "Convolution is a mathematical operator which takes two functions, f and g, and produces a third function that in a sense represents the amount of overlap between f and a reversed and translated version of g." At least my version talks about pixels.

To compute the value of the destination pixel at (x, y), Java 2D multiplies the kernel values with their corresponding color values in the source image. Imagine a 3×3 white image with a single black pixel in its center, as suggested in Figure 8-6.

To convolve the black pixel with our 3×3 kernel, we must start by placing the matrix over the pixels, as shown in Figure 8-7.

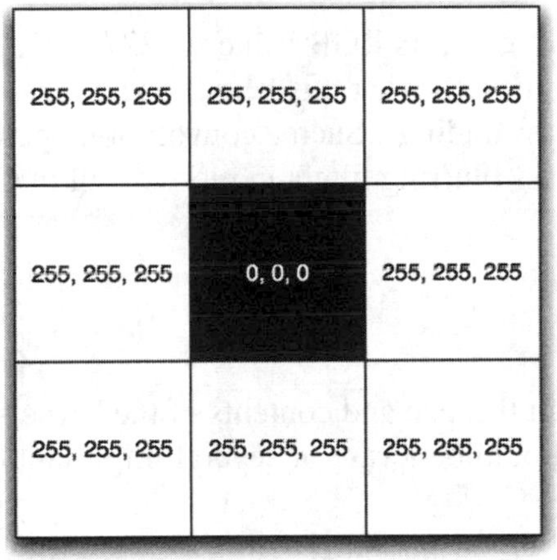

Figure 8-6 A black pixel surrounded by white pixels. The numbers show the RGB value of each pixel.

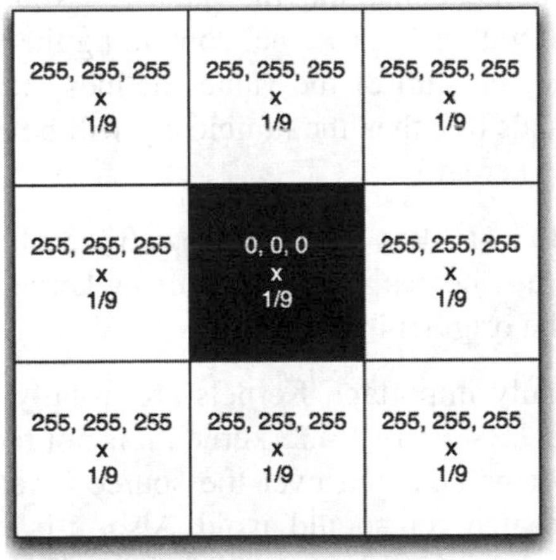

Figure 8-7 Each color value is multiplied by the corresponding value of the kernel.

Now we can compute all the multiplications, add up the results, and get the color value of the destination pixel:

$$R = 255 \cdot \frac{1}{9} + 255 \cdot \frac{1}{9} + 255 \cdot \frac{1}{9} + 255 \cdot \frac{1}{9} + 0 \cdot \frac{1}{9} + 255 \cdot \frac{1}{9} + 255 \cdot \frac{1}{9} + 255 \cdot \frac{1}{9} + 255 \cdot \frac{1}{9} + 255 \cdot \frac{8}{9}$$

$$B = 255 \cdot \frac{1}{9} + 255 \cdot \frac{1}{9} + 255 \cdot \frac{1}{9} + 255 \cdot \frac{1}{9} + 0 \cdot \frac{1}{9} + 255 \cdot \frac{1}{9} + 255 \cdot \frac{1}{9} + 255 \cdot \frac{1}{9} + 255 \cdot \frac{1}{9} + 255 \cdot \frac{8}{9}$$

$$G = 255 \cdot \frac{1}{9} + 255 \cdot \frac{1}{9} + 255 \cdot \frac{1}{9} + 255 \cdot \frac{1}{9} + 0 \cdot \frac{1}{9} + 255 \cdot \frac{1}{9} + 255 \cdot \frac{1}{9} + 255 \cdot \frac{1}{9} + 255 \cdot \frac{1}{9} + 255 \cdot \frac{8}{9}$$

The destination pixel is therefore a light gray; its RGB value is (227, 227, 227), or #E3E3E3. By now, you might have guessed what this kernel does: It replaces each pixel by the average color of its surroundings. Such a convolution operation is commonly known as a blur. We discuss blurring filters in more detail in Chapter 16, "Static Effects."

Constructing a Kernel

There are no particular restrictions about the size and contents of the kernels you can use with Java 2D. However, you should be aware of several important characteristics of kernels.

First, the values of a kernel should add up to 1.0 in the typical case, as in the previous example where all nine entries have the value 1/9. If these values do not add up to 1.0, the luminosity of the picture will not be preserved. This can, however, be turned to your advantage. For instance, you can increase the luminosity of a picture by 10 percent with a 1×1 kernel containing the value 1.1. Similarly, you can darken a picture by 10 percent with a 1×1 kernel containing the value 0.9. When dealing with larger kernels, the sum of the values defines the new luminosity. For instance, if the sum equals 0.5, then the luminosity will be cut in half. Keep that in mind when creating a kernel.

The size of a kernel defines the strength of a filter. For instance, a 3×3 blurring kernel produces a slightly blurry picture, whereas a 40×40 blurring kernel produces an indistinguishable blob from the original image.

The dimensions of the kernel are equally important. Kernels are usually odd-sided. While it is perfectly safe to use a 4×4 or a 12×12 kernel, it is not recommended. An even-sided kernel will not be centered over the source pixel and might give unbalanced visual results, which you should avoid. Also, it is easier for code readers to understand how an odd-sided kernel will behave. The Java 2D documentation defines the value of the matrix used as the center of the kernel as being the one at the coordinates $(w − 1)/2$, $(h − 1)/2$. This definition makes it harder to know which value is used as the center.

Your kernels do not have to be square shaped. Vertical kernels, for example with a 1×5 matrix, and horizontal kernels, for example with a 5×1 matrix, can be used to apply effects that work in only one direction. Chapter 16 presents examples of such kernels.

Last but not least, avoid using large kernels. When convolving a picture with a 3×3 kernel, Java 2D performs at least 17 operations (9 multiplications and 8 additions) per color component per pixel. Convolving a 640×480 picture requires at least $640 \times 480 \times 3 \times 17 = 15,667,200$ operations! That's quite a lot.[2] And this number does not even include the operations of reading and writing the actual pixel values from and to the source and destination pictures. We therefore strongly advise you not to perform convolve operations at painting time. Instead perform the operations once prior to painting and cache the results instead.

No matter what kernel you create, writing the code to perform the convolution is simple:

```
BufferedImage dstImage = null;
float[] sharpen = new float[] {
     0.0f, -1.0f,  0.0f,
    -1.0f,  5.0f, -1.0f,
     0.0f, -1.0f,  0.0f
};
Kernel kernel = new Kernel(3, 3, sharpen);
ConvolveOp op = new ConvolveOp(kernel);
dstImage = op.filter(sourceImage, null);
```

In Java 2D, a kernel is an array of floats and two dimensions. In this case, we use a 3×3 sharpening kernel to create an array of nine floats and tell the `Kernel` class that we want this array to be treated as a 3×3 matrix.

Figure 8-8 shows the result of the convolution with the 3×3 sharpening kernel shown in the previous code example.

Working on the Edge

Everything is not perfect yet. Take a close look at the generated result: You should see a black border surrounding the picture. During the convolve operation, Java

---

2. Even with today's CPU, it's still a lot. Really. And we are talking about convolving a small picture with a small kernel.

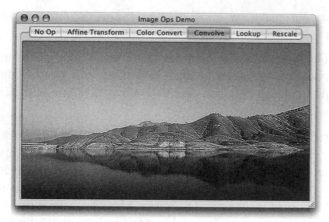

Figure 8-8   The sharpened picture shows enhanced details.

2D always matches the center of the kernel with one pixel of the source image. This works well for every pixel except the ones on the edges of the picture. Try to line up a 3×3 kernel with any pixel on the edge of an image and you will see that some parts of the kernel lie outside of the image. To work around this problem, Java 2D replaces the pixels it cannot compute with black pixels, which results in darkened edges because of the extra black introduced into the convolve operations for these edge pixels. To avoid this result, you can instruct Java 2D to do nothing and to keep the original color:

```
// the default is ConvolveOp.EDGE_ZERO_FILL
// the last parameter is the RenderingHints set
ConvolveOp op = new ConvolveOp(kernel,
    ConvolveOp.EDGE_NO_OP, null);
```

Unfortunately, neither of these solutions generates good-looking results. To get rid of any problem on the edges, you can simply increase the size of the original picture, as follows:

```
int kernelWidth = 3;
int kernelHeight = 3;

int xOffset = (kernelWidth - 1) / 2;
int yOffset = (kernelHeight - 1) / 2;

BufferedImage newSource = new BufferedImage(
  sourceImage.getWidth() + kernelWidth - 1,
  sourceImage.getHeight() + kernelHeight - 1,
  BufferedImage.TYPE_INT_ARGB);
Graphics2D g2 = newSource.createGraphics();
```

```
g2.drawImage(sourceImage, xOffset, yOffset, null);
g2.dispose();

ConvolveOp op = new ConvolveOp(kernel,
    ConvolveOp.EDGE_NO_OP, null);
dstImage = op.filter(newSource, null);
```

The original image is drawn centered into a new, larger, transparent image. Because we added enough transparent pixels on each side of the original image, the convolution operation will not affect the pixels of the original image. It is important to use the `ConvolveOp.EDGE_NO_OP` edge condition so you will keep the pixels transparent around the image. This technique of adding transparent pixels on the sides provides better-looking results, but you have to take the extraneous pixels into account.

LookupOp

A `LookupOp` maps the color values of the source to new color values in the destination. This operation is achieved with a lookup table that contains the destination values for each possible source value.

Lookup operations can be used to generate several common filters, such as negative filters, posterizing filters, and thresholding filters. Negative filters are interesting because they help illustrate how lookup tables work. Pixel colors are usually represented using three components (red, green, and blue) stored in 8 bits each. As a result, the color values of a negative image are the 8 bits' complements of the source image color values:

```
dstR = 255 - srcR;
dstG = 255 - srcG;
dstB = 255 - srcB;
```

To apply such a conversion to the source image, you must create a lookup table that associates all the values in the 8 bits range (from 0 to 255) to their complements:

```
short[] data = new short[256];
for (short i = 0; i < 256; i++) {
    data[i] = 255 - i;
}

BufferedImage dstImage = null;
LookupTable lookupTable = new ShortLookupTable(0, data);
LookupOp op = new LookupOp(lookupTable, null);
dstImage = op.filter(sourceImage, null);
```

Figure 8-9 shows the result of this negative filter.

The LookupTable from this example contains only one lookup array, used for all of the color components of the source image, resulting in the same conversion of all of the color components.

To perform a different conversion for each component, you simply need to create one lookup array per color component in the source image. Since the example relies on an RGB picture, we can create a filter that inverts only the red component by defining three lookup arrays:

```
short[] red = new short[256];
short[] green = new short[256];
short[] blue = new short[256];

for (short i = 0; i < 256; i++) {
    red[i] = 255 - i;
    green[i] = blue[i] = i;
}

short[][] data = new short[][] {
    red, green, blue
};

BufferedImage dstImage;
LookupTable lookupTable = new ShortLookupTable(0, data);
dstImage = op.filter(sourceImage, null);
LookupOp op = new LookupOp(lookupTable, null);
```

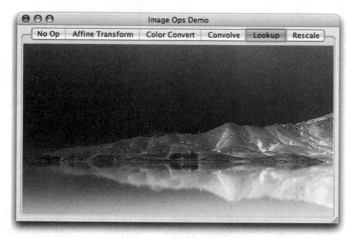

Figure 8-9 A simple lookup operation can be used to produce a negative image.

You do not need to provide a lookup array for the alpha channel of your picture, if present. In this case, Java 2D will simply preserve the original alpha values. Whenever you create a new LookupOp, ensure that the number and size of your lookup arrays match the source image structure.

RescaleOp

RescaleOp does not scale the size of an image as you would expect it to. Instead, RescaleOp performs a rescaling operation by multiplying the color value of each pixel in the source image by a scale factor and then adding an offset. Here is the formula applied to each color component of the source pixels:

```
dstR = (srcR * scaleFactor) + offset
dstG = (srcG * scaleFactor) + offset
dstB = (srcB * scaleFactor) + offset
```

Rescaling operations can be used to brighten, darken, or tint images. The following code example increases the overall brightness of the picture by 10 percent:

```
BufferedImage dstImage = null;
RescaleOp op = new RescaleOp(1.1f, 0.0f, null);
dstImage = op.filter(sourceImage, null);
```

The first two parameters of the RescaleOp constructor are respectively the scale factor and the offset. Note that a RescaleOp with an offset of 0 is no different from a ConvolveOp with a 1 × 1 kernel. You can also adjust each color component independently:

```
BufferedImage dstImage = null;
float[] factors = new float[] {
    1.4f, 1.4f, 1.4f
};
float[] offsets = new float[] {
    0.0f, 0.0f, 30.0f
};
RescaleOp op = new RescaleOp(factors, offsets, null);
dstImage = op.filter(sourceImage, null);
```

In this case, the overall brightness is increased by 40 percent, and all of the pixel colors are shifted toward the blue color. The offset of 30 increases the blue component of each pixel by 12 percent (30/256). Remember, the offset is added to the color value and must therefore be a value between 0 and 255, as opposed to the scale factor, which acts as a percentage.

Figure 8-10   The image is brighter and the blues are bluer after processing.

Figure 8-10 shows the result produced by a RescaleOp with a scale factor of 1.4 for each component and an offset of 30 for the blue component.

Just as in LookupOp, the number of values used in the scale factors and offset arrays depend on the number of components in the source image. Working on TYPE_INT_RGB or TYPE_INT_ARGB pictures is therefore easier than working on other types of BufferedImage. When the source image contains an alpha channel, you do not need to specify a factor and an offset for the alpha component. Java 2D automatically preserves the original values.

These five BufferedImageOps will probably be all you need for most situations. Nevertheless, you might want to create your own specialized BufferedImageOp to create advanced graphical effects.

Custom BufferedImageOp

Creating a new filter from scratch is not a very complicated task. To prove it, we show you how to implement a color tint filter. This kind of filter can be used to mimic the effect of the colored filters photographers screw in front of their lenses. For instance, an orange color tint filter gives a sunset mood to a scene, while a blue filter cools down the tones in the picture.

You first need to create a new class that implements the BufferedImageOp interface and its five methods. To make the creation of several filters easier, we first define a new abstract class entitled AbstractFilter. As you will soon discover, all filters based on this class are nonspatial, linear color filters. That means that they will not affect the geometry of the source image and that they assume the destination image has the same size as the source image.

The complete source code of our custom BufferedImage is available on this book's Web site in the project entitled CustomImageOp.

Base Filter Class

AbstractFilter implements all the methods from BufferedImageOp except for filter(), which actually processes the source image into the destination and hence belongs in the subclasses:

```java
public abstract class AbstractFilter
    implements BufferedImageOp {
  public abstract BufferedImage filter(
    BufferedImage src, BufferedImage dest);

  public Rectangle2D getBounds2D(BufferedImage src) {
    return new Rectangle(0, 0, src.getWidth(),
                            src.getHeight());
  }

  public BufferedImage createCompatibleDestImage(
    BufferedImage src, ColorModel destCM) {
    if (destCM == null) {
        destCM = src.getColorModel();
    }

    return new BufferedImage(destCM,
        destCM.createCompatibleWritableRaster(
          src.getWidth(), src.getHeight()),
        destCM.isAlphaPremultiplied(), null);
  }

  public Point2D getPoint2D(Point2D srcPt,
                              Point2D dstPt) {
    return (Point2D) srcPt.clone();
  }

  public RenderingHints getRenderingHints() {
    return null;
  }
}
```

The getRenderingHints() method must return a set of RenderingHints when the image filter relies on rendering hints. Since this will probably not be the case for our custom filters, the abstract class simply returns null.

The two methods getBounds2D() and getPoint2D() are very important for spatial filters, such as AffineTransformOp. The first method, getBounds2D(), returns the bounding box of the filtered image. If your custom filter modifies the dimension of the source image, you must implement this method accordingly. The implementation proposed here makes the assumption that the filtered image will have the same size as the source image.

The other method, getPoint2D(), returns the corresponding destination point given a location in the source image. As for getBounds2D(), AbstractFilter makes the assumption that no geometry transformation will be applied to the image, and the returned location is therefore the source location.

AbstractFilter also assumes that the only data needed to compute the pixel for (x, y) in the destination is the pixel for (x, y) in the source.

The last implemented method is createCompatibleDestImage(). Its role is to produce an image with the correct size and number of color components to contain the filtered image. The implementation shown in the previous source code creates an empty clone of the source image; it has the same size and the same color model regardless of the source image type.

Color Tint Filter

The color tint filter, cleverly named ColorTintFilter, extends AbstractFilter and implements filter(), the only method left from the BufferedImageOp interface. Before we delve into the source code, we must first define the operation that the filter will perform on the source image. A color tint filter mixes every pixel from the source image with a given color. The strength of the mix is defined by a mix value. A mix value of 0 means that all of the pixels remain the same, whereas a mix value of 1 means that all of the source pixels are replaced by the tinting color. Given those two parameters, a color and a mix percentage, we can compute the color value of the destination pixels:

```
dstR = srcR * (1 - mixValue) + mixR * mixValue
dstG = srcG * (1 - mixValue) + mixG * mixValue
dstB = srcB * (1 - mixValue) + mixB * mixValue
```

If you tint a picture with 40 percent white, the filter will retain 60 percent (1 or 1 – mixValue) of the source pixel color values to preserve the overall luminosity of the picture.

The following source code shows the skeleton of `ColorTintFilter`, an immutable class.

> **Note: Immutability.** It is very important to ensure that your filters are immutable to avoid any problem during the processing of the source images. Imagine what havoc a thread could cause by modifying one of the parameters of the filter while another thread is filtering an image. Rather than synchronizing code blocks or spending hours in a debugger, go the easy route and make your `BufferedImageOp` implementations immutable.

```java
public class ColorTintFilter extends AbstractFilter {
  private final Color mixColor;
  private final float mixValue;

  public ColorTintFilter(Color mixColor, float mixValue) {
    if (mixColor == null) {
      throw new IllegalArgumentException(
          "mixColor cannot be null");
    }

    this.mixColor = mixColor;
    if (mixValue < 0.0f) {
      mixValue = 0.0f;
    } else if (mixValue > 1.0f) {
      mixValue = 1.0f;
    }
    this.mixValue = mixValue;
  }

  public float getMixValue() {
    return mixValue;
  }

  public Color getMixColor() {
    return mixColor;
  }

  @Override
  public BufferedImage filter(BufferedImage src,
                              BufferedImage dst) {
    // filters src into dst
  }
}
```

The most interesting part of this class is the implementation of the `filter()` method:

```java
@Override
public BufferedImage filter(BufferedImage src,
                           BufferedImage dst) {
  if (dst == null) {
    dst = createCompatibleDestImage(src, null);
  }

  int width = src.getWidth();
  int height = src.getHeight();

  int[] pixels = new int[width * height];
  GraphicsUtilities.getPixels(src, 0, 0, width,
                              height, pixels);
  mixColor(pixels);
  GraphicsUtilities.setPixels(dst, 0, 0, width,
                              height, pixels);

  return dst;
}
```

The first few lines of this method create an acceptable destination image when the caller provides none. The javadoc of the `BufferedImageOp` interface dictates this behavior: "If the destination image is null, a `BufferedImage` with an appropriate `ColorModel` is created."

Instead of working directly on the source and destination images, the color tint filter reads all the pixels of the source image into an array of integers. The implications are threefold. First, all of the color values are stored on four ARGB 8-bit components packed as an integer. Then, the source and the destination can be the same, since all work will be performed on the array of integers. Finally, despite the increased memory usage, it is faster to perform one read and one write operation on the images rather than reading and writing pixel by pixel. Before we take a closer look at `mixColor()`, where the bulk of the work is done, here is the code used to read all the pixels at once into a single array of integers:

```java
public static int[] getPixels(BufferedImage img,
                              int x, int y,
                              int w, int h,
                              int[] pixels) {
  if (w == 0 || h == 0) {
    return new int[0];
  }
}
```

```
    if (pixels == null) {
      pixels = new int[w * h];
    } else if (pixels.length < w * h) {
      throw new IllegalArgumentException(
          "pixels array must have a length >= w*h");
    }

    int imageType = img.getType();
    if (imageType == BufferedImage.TYPE_INT_ARGB ||
        imageType == BufferedImage.TYPE_INT_RGB) {
        Raster raster = img.getRaster();
        return (int[]) raster.getDataElements(x, y, w, h, pixels);
    }

    return img.getRGB(x, y, w, h, pixels, 0, w);
}
```

There are two different code paths, depending on the nature of the image from which the pixels are read. When the image is of type INT_ARGB or INT_RGB, we know for sure that the data elements composing the image are integers. We can therefore call Raster.getDataElements() and cast the result to an array of integers. This solution is not only fast but preserves all the optimizations of managed images performed by Java 2D.

When the image is of another type, for instance TYPE_3BYTE_BGR, as is often the case with JPEG pictures loaded from disk, the pixels are read by calling the BufferedImage.getRGB(int, int, int, int, int[], int, int) method. This invocation has two major problems. First, it needs to convert all the data elements into integers, which can take quite some time for large images. Second, it throws away all the optimizations made by Java 2D, resulting in slower painting operations, for instance. The picture is then said to be unmanaged. To learn more details about managed images, please refer to the Chapter 5, "Performance."

Note: Performance and getRGB(). The class BufferedImage offers two variants of the getRGB() method. The one discussed previously has the following signature:

```
int[] getRGB(int startX, int startY, int w, int h,
              int[] rgbArray, int offset, int scansize)
```

This method is used to retrieve an array of pixels at once, and invoking it will punt the optimizations made by Java 2D. Consider the second variant of getRGB():

```
int getRGB(int x, int y)
```

This method is used to retrieve a single pixel and does not throw away the optimizations made by Java 2D. Be very careful about which one of these methods you decide to use.

The setPixels() method is very similar to getPixels():

```
public static void setPixels(BufferedImage img,
                             int x, int y,
                             int w, int h,
                             int[] pixels) {
if (pixels == null || w == 0 || h == 0) {
   return;
} else if (pixels.length < w * h) {
  throw new IllegalArgumentException(
      "pixels array must have a length >= w*h");
}

int imageType = img.getType();
if (imageType == BufferedImage.TYPE_INT_ARGB ||
    imageType == BufferedImage.TYPE_INT_RGB) {
    WritableRaster raster = img.getRaster();
    raster.setDataElements(x, y, w, h, pixels);
} else {
    img.setRGB(x, y, w, h, pixels, 0, w);
}
}
```

Performance Tip: Working on a TYPE_INT_RGB or TYPE_INT_ARGB results in better performance, since no type conversion is required to store the processed pixels into the destination image.

Reading and writing pixels from and to images would be completely useless if we did not process them in between operations. The implementation of the color tint equations is straightforward:

```
private void mixColor(int[] inPixels) {
   int mix_a = mixColor.getAlpha();
   int mix_r = mixColor.getRed();
   int mix_b = mixColor.getBlue();
   int mix_g = mixColor.getGreen();

   for (int i = 0; i < inPixels.length; i++) {
       int argb = inPixels[i];

       int a = argb & 0xFF000000;
       int r = (argb >> 16) & 0xFF;
       int g = (argb >>  8) & 0xFF;
       int b = (argb      ) & 0xFF;
```

```
        r = (int) (r * (1.0f - mixValue) + mix_r * mixValue);
        g = (int) (g * (1.0f - mixValue) + mix_g * mixValue);
        b = (int) (b * (1.0f - mixValue) + mix_b * mixValue);

        inPixels[i] = a << 24 | r << 16 | g << 8 | b;
    }
}
```

Before applying the equations, we must split the pixels into their four color components. Some bit shifting and masking is all you need in this situation. Once each color component has been filtered, the destination pixel is computed by packing the four modified color components into a single integer. Figure 8-11 shows a picture tinted with 50 percent red.

The above implementation works well but can be vastly improved performance-wise. The `ColorTintFilter` class in the `CustomImageOp` project on this book's Web site offers a better implementation that uses a few tricks to avoid doing all of the computations in the loop.

Note: As an exercise, you can try to improve this implementation on your own before looking at the final version. (Hint: You can use lookup arrays.)

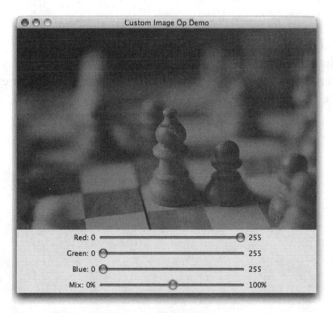

Figure 8-11 A red-tinted picture.

A Note about Filters Performance

Image filters perform a lot of operations on images, and performance can easily degrade if you do not pay attention to a few details. Whenever you write a filter assuming the source image will be of type `INT_RGB` or `INT_ARGB`, make sure the source image is actually of that type.

Usually, compatible images (images created with `GraphicsConfiguration.createCompatibleImage()`), which are designed to be in the same format as the screen, are stored as integers. It is often the case that the user's display is in 32-bit format and not the older 8-, 16-, and 24-bit formats. Therefore, it is a good idea to always load your images as compatible images.

The `CustomImageOp` demo loads a JPEG picture, which would normally be of type `3BYTE_BGR`, and turns it into a compatible image of type `INT_RGB`. You can look for the call to `GraphicsUtilities.loadCompatibleImage()` in the source code of the demo and replace it with `ImageIO.read()` to see the difference when moving the sliders of the user interface. As a rule of thumb, do not hesitate to use the various methods from the `GraphicsUtilities` class to always use compatible images.

Summary

Java 2D offers several powerful facilities to perform image processing on your pictures. The built-in `BufferedImageOp` implementations let you write your own custom filters very quickly. And if you need more flexibility, you can even create a new `BufferedImageOp` implementation from scratch.

9

Glass Pane

THE glass pane is one of the most marvelous features of Swing. Despite a misleading name, the glass pane has proven over the years to be a unique asset to any Swing developer who wants to create advanced effects in user interfaces. To understand the qualities of the glass pane and why it is so important to Filthy Rich Clients, you first need to understand the layout of Swing's frames and dialogs.

Despite their appearance, `JFrame`, `JDialog`, `JWindow`, and `JInternalFrame` are not flat containers. Swing windows always contain a single child, an instance of `JRootPane`. A root pane is a unique container, made of a glass pane and of a `JLayeredPane`. We explore `JLayeredPane` in more detail later, but you need to know that the root pane's layered pane contains, among other things, the content pane and the menu bar of Swing windows.

The glass pane sits on top of everything in the `JRootPane` and fills the entire view. This particular position allows two distinct capabilities:

- Intercepting mouse and keyboard events
- Drawing over the entire user interface

It is the second item that is particularly interesting for Filthy Rich Clients. Drawing over the existing UI becomes essential in producing some of the effects seen in this book. Component painting is always limited within the boundaries of the components themselves, thus preventing drawing across several widgets. For example, a button can draw only within the confines of the button area, not over other content outside of the button. With a glass pane, however, this constraint disappears, and the application is free, for example, to draw pictures that overlap several components in the UI.

Figure 9-1 and Figure 9-2 show the visual hierarchy of a JFrame and how the various containers relate to each other. The actual GUI of your Java applications is contained in the layered pane, just beneath the glass pane, as shown in Figure 9-1.

As shown in Figure 9-2 a glass pane is a simple java.awt.Component. As such, you can install any Swing component of your choice as the glass pane. Most, if not all, of the time, though, you will use a custom component, for there is not much benefit in installing a JLabel or a JTable as the glass pane.

Remember that the glass pane sits on top of the whole user interface of a JFrame. Therefore, it is wise to set up a translucent glass pane to let the user see the com-

Figure 9-1   The glass pane sits on top of every other component in a Swing UI.

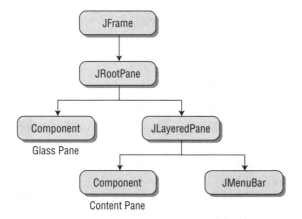

Figure 9-2   Component hierarchy of a JFrame.

ponents beneath. Common glass pane implementations rely on a JComponent or a nonopaque JPanel.

Installing a glass pane on a frame is as easy as calling one method:

```
JFrame frame = new JFrame();
frame.setGlassPane(new CustomGlassPane());
```

However, most developers are bewildered by the ensuing result: Nothing happens. The confusion comes from the expected behavior of Swing that ensures that your components are visible when you add them into a frame. The glass pane is treated in a very different manner because it is made *nonvisible* by default. As a result, you need to call setVisible(true) on your glass pane:

```
JFrame frame = new JFrame();
frame.setGlassPane(new CustomGlassPane());
// ...
frame.getGlassPane().setVisible(true);
```

This behavior is actually very sensible because glass panes are mostly used for temporary operations. Hence, the glass pane is usually installed beforehand and made visible only when necessary, as we will see in several examples. Keeping the glass pane visible when it is not needed might also cause a performance penalty.

Tip: Glass Pane Visibility. When you install a glass pane, its visibility is changed to match that of the current glass pane. If you call getGlassPane().setVisible(true) and then call setGlassPane(), the new glass pane will be visible.

Painting on the Glass Pane

The glass pane is a great place to put custom paintings. Its position in the frame hierarchy lets you create visual effects not typically seen. Actually, it lets you create visual effects that are just not possible in any other way.

To paint on a glass pane, you first need to create a custom component. Most of the time, you will want to use the glass pane as a large drawing canvas rather than a full-fledged component. Since the glass pane sits on top of the whole UI, it is generally a good idea to let the user see through to the rest of the UI. That means you need a nonopaque component to paint on, which is easily achieved in two different ways:

```
// First technique: JComponent
public class CustomGlassPane extends JComponent {
  @Override
  protected void paintComponent(Graphics g) {
    // do some painting
  }
}

// Second technique: JPanel
public class CustomGlassPane extends JPanel {
  public CustomGlassPane() {
    setOpaque(false);
  }

  @Override
  protected void paintComponent(Graphics g) {
    // do some painting
  }
}
```

Unless you have a perfectly valid reason to use a JPanel as the parent class, you are better off with a JComponent. You can use it as a regular panel by setting a layout and adding child components, but it has the advantage of being nonopaque by default. And don't tell me you're not happy with saving only one line of code!

On the contrary, if you know that your glass pane will be fully opaque, it is a good idea to choose JPanel over JComponent. The only important difference between a JComponent and a JPanel is that the latter is opaque and will be decorated by the appropriate look and feel UI delegate.[1]

Whatever your decision, all that is left is to override paintComponent(), as in the following example:

```
public class CustomGlassPane extends JComponent {
  @Override
  protected void paintComponent(Graphics g) {
    Rectangle clip = g.getClipBounds();
    Color alphaWhite = new Color(1.0f, 1.0f, 1.0f, 0.65f);
    g.setColor(alphaWhite);
    g.fillRect(clip.x, clip.y, clip.width, clip.height);
  }
}
```

---

1. A JPanel is opaque in most look and feels, but it is not a requirement.

This particular glass pane draws a translucent white area on top of the frame, a simple technique to visually disable a user interface. A similar effect can be achieved with the help of an `AlphaComposite`, especially when you want to draw more complex primitives, like pictures or text.

Custom glass panes are easy to implement but can result in surprisingly awful performance once you get it running. Remember that the glass pane covers the whole frame. Therefore, if you have created a nonopaque glass pane, Swing will repaint all of the components when you call `repaint()` on your glass pane. You will probably never notice any problem in small projects, but as soon as you install a glass pane on a frame containing dozens of complex components, all hell breaks loose.[2]

Tip: Repaint Performance. To prevent performance problems, repaint only what is necessary. The first thing to do is to make sure you honor the clipping rectangle set on the graphics context. This is exactly what the previous code example does. It fills the only part of the frame that has been damaged and needs to be repainted.

You also must avoid calling `repaint()` when you know the area that needs updating; call `repaint(x, y, width, height)` instead.

Optimized Glass Pane Painting

This book's Web site hosts a project entitled `GlassPanePainting`. This application shows a simple user interface with a Start Download button at the bottom right. When the button is pressed, a glass pane shows up with an animated progress bar that fakes the progress of a file download task. The screenshot in Figure 9-3 shows what the glass pane looks like.

The animation is driven by a simple thread that repetitively calls the method `setProgress(int)` on the glass pane. A first, naïve implementation of this method might look like this:

```
public void setProgress(int progress) {
  this.progress = progress;
  repaint();
}
```

---

2. Okay, I might have exaggerated a bit. I promise you won't see headless minions come out of your closet when you call `repaint()`. But just in case, try `repaint(x, y, w, h)`. After all, if flying bloodthirsty imps did come out of your closet, you would have a hard time explaining the resulting delay in the project to your client. In the end, it's your call: a fast and responsive application or a legion of doomed souls and an angry client.

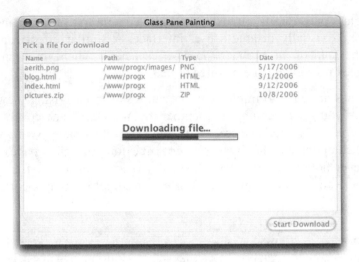

Figure 9-3 The glass pane simulates a download task.

This code simply saves the progress value in an instance field and then calls repaint() to refresh the progress bar. Assuming the parameter progress is a positive number between 0 and 100, the painting code would look like this:

```java
@Override
protected void paintComponent(Graphics g) {
  // gets the current clipping area
  Rectangle clip = g.getClipBounds();

  // sets a 65% translucent composite
  AlphaComposite alpha = AlphaComposite.SrcOver.derive(0.65f);
  g2.setComposite(alpha);

  // fills the background
  g2.setColor(getBackground());
  g2.fillRect(clip.x, clip.y, clip.width, clip.height);

  // computes x and y, draws the text
  // [...] snipped [...]

  // computes the size of the progress indicator
  int w = (int) (BAR_WIDTH * ((float) progress / 100.0f));
  int h = BAR_HEIGHT;

  // draws the content of the progress bar
  Paint gradient = new LinearGradientPaint(x, y, x, y + h,
          GRADIENT_FRACTIONS, GRADIENT_COLORS);
```

```
    g2.setPaint(gradient);
    g2.fillRect(x, y, w, h);

    // cleans up stuff
}
```

The painting code first fills the clipping rectangle with a white color and then draws the progress bar with a gradient. Notice how the length of the bar, denoted by w in the code, is computed from the field progress previously set in the method setProgress(int). Even though this piece of code takes into account the clipping rectangle to avoid unnecessary and expensive operations, all of our efforts are ruined by the aforementioned call to repaint() in setProgress(int) because it sets a clipping rectangle as large as the glass pane itself. By repainting the glass pane every time, we trigger the repaint of the underlying frame, thus dragging performance down.

As you may have guessed, the solution to our problem is to replace the call to repaint() with a call to repaint(x, y, width, height). This fix involves just a simple rewrite of setProgress(int):

```
public void setProgress(int progress) {
    int oldProgress = this.progress;
    this.progress = progress;

    // computes the damaged area
    // always assume that progress > oldPogress
    int w = (int) (BAR_WIDTH * ((float) oldProgress / 100.0f));
    int x = w + /* centers the bar on screen */;
    int y = /* centers the bar on screen */;

    w = (int) (BAR_WIDTH * ((float) progress / 100.0f)) - w;
    int h = BAR_HEIGHT;

    repaint(x, y, w, h);
}
```

The method now looks a bit more complicated, but it does a much more decent job at repainting the progress bar. The first computation of the variable w computes the current width of the progress bar as seen on the screen. Then the value x is computed to match the end of the current progress bar. Finally, w is computed again, this time containing the length difference between the new progress bar and the old one. By using these values in our call to repaint(x, y, w, h), we can now tell Swing to repaint only the few pixels of the screen that have changed since the last invocation of setProgress(int). All the computations assume that the new progress value is greater than the current progress value because the progress bar can only fill up in this particular application.

Previously, the application was repainting an area of 553×394 pixels, whereas now it repaints only a rectangle of about 4×10 pixels. This difference can amount to a huge savings in performance, and the more complicated the underlying GUI, the more time it will save.

Glass pane painting can bring a lot of fun to your development and can tremendously improve the quality and richness of your applications.

Blocking Input Events

While the previous example looks fine, it contains a very serious flaw. If you try to click on the table, you will be able to select one of the rows. Likewise, you can click the Start Download button and watch the application go wild. The problem is that, while the glass pane looks like it has taken over the user interface, the events are still going directly through the glass pane to the UI objects underneath.

To avoid these issues, you can set up the glass pane to intercept all mouse and keyboard events and prevent them from being dispatched to the other components. To intercept events on the glass pane, you need to add mouse and key listeners. To consume these events and prevent them from reaching the underlying components, you can use empty listeners, as in the following example:

```
public NullEventsGlassPane() {
  addMouseListener(new MouseAdapter() { });
  addMouseMotionListener(new MouseMotionAdapter() { });
  addKeyListener(new KeyAdapter() { });
}
```

In this new example, all of the events are caught by the glass pane and ignored. But something is still not quite right. While mouse events are handled correctly, keyboard events are still going through because Swing sends the keyboard event to the currently focused component. If a component already has the focus, which in this case is the table, it will still be able to receive key events. Even worse, you can press Tab and Ctrl-Tab to navigate focus between the various controls.

Giving the focus to the glass pane is the only remedy to this problem. The solution seems easy at first; you simply need to call `requestFocusInWindow()` to grab the focus. Unfortunately, this approach works only when the component requesting the focus is visible. Here is the code you need to put in the constructor of your glass pane:

```
addComponentListener(new ComponentAdapter() {
  public void componentShown(ComponentEvent evt) {
    requestFocusInWindow();
  }
});
```

This `ComponentListener` is invoked as soon as the glass pane is made visible, providing a great mechanism to grab the focus. If you run your application with this code, you will be pleased to see that the keyboard events are indeed trapped in the glass pane. But it's not over yet because the user can still press the Tab key to give the focus back to one of the components lying beneath the glass pane. Once again, the solution is easy and requires only one more line of code in the constructor of the glass pane:

```
setFocusTraversalKeysEnabled(false);
```

This method call disables the focus traversal keys (usually the Tab key), effectively preventing the user from moving the focus away from the glass pane.

 The full source code of this example can be found on this book's Web site in the project `InterceptEvents`.

Mouse Events Issues

Despite what you must do to block all input events in the glass pane, there is a situation in which the glass pane will block some events by itself. Create a new frame and put some components in it, making sure you have at least a couple of text components. The resulting UI might look like the one in Figure 9-4.

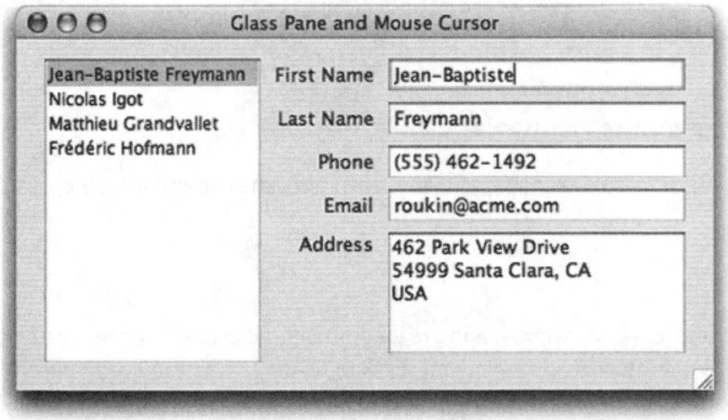

Figure 9-4 The mouse cursor changes when it moves over a text component.

When you run the application, you can see the mouse cursor change to a text caret when you move it over a text field or a text area. This behavior is expected, but it does not happen when a glass pane is set, even if the glass pane is transparent (Figure 9-5).

In Figure 9-5, the glass pane simply paints a picture in the lower right corner of the frame. Implemented as a JComponent, the glass pane is nonopaque and lets the user see through it to the components underneath. But if you move the mouse over one of the text components, the cursor will remain the same, as shown in the screenshot; it will not react to being over the text area. This is rather surprising, since we have not installed any mouse listener on the glass pane, or any event listener for that matter.

The problem here is that Swing shows the mouse cursor of the topmost visible component. Even though the glass pane looks transparent, it remains visible and is therefore seen by Swing as the topmost element.

To fix this issue, all you need to do is to make the glass pane transparent to mouse events by overriding the method called contains(x, y). This method returns true when the mouse cursor is within the component's bounds, and false otherwise.[3] To

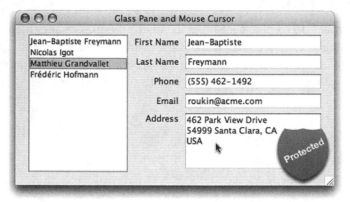

Figure 9-5 A glass pane, even a transparent one, prevents mouse cursor changes.

---

3. Even though we do not discuss this approach in great depth here, it can be used to create nonrectangular components. For instance, to implement a triangle-shaped button, you could override contains() and return true only when the mouse cursor is actually in the triangle.

allow the mouse cursor to change appropriately, here is how you should implement this method:

```
@Override
public boolean contains(int x, int y) {
  return false;
}
```

This code ensures that your glass pane will receive no more mouse events. Therefore, you might need a more robust implementation of contains():

```
@Override
public boolean contains(int x, int y) {
  if (getMouseListeners().length == 0 &&
      getMouseMotionListeners().length == 0 &&
      getMouseWheelListeners().length == 0 &&
      getCursor() == Cursor.getPredefinedCursor(
                        Cursor.DEFAULT_CURSOR)) {
    return false;
  }
  return super.contains(x, y);
}
```

In this case, adding a mouse listener or changing the default cursor of the glass pane will prevent contains() from rejecting the mouse events. Unfortunately, this behavior would lead back to the original problem.

The definitive solution is to ignore mouse events in transparent areas of the glass pane, even when mouse listeners have been added or the mouse cursor has been changed. In our example, we simply need to check whether the cursor is over the bottom-left picture instead of simply returning false:

```
if (image == null) {
  return false;
} else {
  int imageX = getWidth() - image.getWidth();
  int imageY = getHeight() - image.getHeight();

  return x > imageX && x < getWidth() &&
         y > imageY && y < getHeight();
}
```

You can further refine this approach by ignoring mouse events only when the mouse is over the opaque pixels of the picture. If you look at Figure 9-5, you can see that the picture of the shield contains transparent areas. With the implementation above, the mouse cursor will not change even when the mouse cursor is over these areas.

To remedy this problem, you must check the value of the alpha channel of the pixel under the mouse cursor. The previous code example becomes the following:

```
if (image == null) {
    return false;
} else {
    int imageX = getWidth() - image.getWidth();
    int imageY = getHeight() - image.getHeight();

    // if the mouse cursor is on a nonopaque pixel,
    // mouse events are allowed
    int inImageX = x - imageX;
    int inImageY = y - imageY;

    if (inImageX >= 0 && inImageY >= 0 &&
        inImageX < image.getWidth() &&
        inImageY < image.getHeight()) {

        int color = image.getRGB(inImageX, inImageY);
        return (color >> 24 & 0xFF) > 0;
    }

    return x > imageX && x < getWidth() &&
            y > imageY && y < getHeight();
}
```

The code computes the location of the mouse cursor within the image's bounds and retrieves the color of the corresponding pixel by calling getRGB(). Finally, the code returns true and accepts mouse events if the alpha channel of the pixel is greater than 0, which means that the pixel is not transparent.

The complete source code for this example can be found on this book's Web site in the project called MouseCursor.

You can also look at the project entitled GlassDragAndDrop, which shows how to combine glass pane painting and mouse event handling to display thumbnails of pictures dragged from the file explorer onto the application's window, as shown in Figure 9-6.

Using a glass pane in your application is surprisingly easy and relies mostly on custom painting code. The overlay capabilities offered by a glass pane let you create impressive effects.

Figure 9-6 The application displays thumbnails that follow the mouse when a picture file is dragged onto the frame.

10

Layered Panes

THE glass pane offers numerous possibilities when it comes to creating advanced user interfaces. However, it suffers from two annoying limitations:

1. You can set up only one glass pane at a time on a given frame. While one is enough in most cases, you might encounter situations in which you need two or more glass panes to paint several effects on the user interface. Things get even worse when the glass pane is set up by code you have no control over, like an external Java library.

2. A glass pane must also cover the entire frame, which makes it difficult to write custom glass panes that paint on top of a particular component or set of components.

Fortunately, Swing offers a solution to this problem with the JLayeredPane. You can refer to the Chapter 9, "Glass Pane," to get a better understanding of the relationship between a glass pane and a layered pane in a frame. The advantage of the layered pane over a glass pane is that you can use one wherever you want to in the component hierarchy. Even though every Swing frame contains at least one layered pane, you are free to create a new instance of JLayeredPane and add it to any other container. This is the main difference between the layered pane and the glass pane. There may be several layered panes, whereas there is only ever one unique glass pane.

Using layered panes is fairly easy, especially when you are already familiar with glass panes, but you must be aware of some issues that might arise when using them.

Using Layered Pane Layers

As its name suggests, the JLayeredPane component is a Swing container, a panel that holds several layers of children. Swing frames rely on a layered pane to display specific components that must span across other components. For instance, a button's tooltip might appear over both the button and a text field next to it. Frame menus and popup menus are also common examples of components drawn over the frame's other widgets.

Each layer of a layered pane is identified by an integer defining the depth in the layer's stack. The highest values denote the highest layers in the stack or the layers that sit on top of the others; lower values refer to bottommost layers. The lowest layer has a depth of 0. For convenience, the JLayeredPane offers several layer identifiers to ease the insertion of components into the right layer. Those identifiers are the following, from the lowest layer to the highest one:

- **JLayeredPane.DEFAULT_LAYER:** This is the bottommost layer where all regular components, like buttons and tables, should be placed. Its identifier is 0.

- **JLayeredPane.PALETTE_LAYER:** This layer is meant for palettes and floating toolbars. Its identifier is 100.

- **JLayeredPane.MODAL_LAYER:** This layer is used for modal dialogs. Its identifier is 200.

- **JLayeredPane.POPUP_LAYER:** This layer is meant to display popup windows, including tooltips, combo-box drop-down lists, the frame's menus, and contextual menus. Its identifier is 300.

- **JLayeredPane.DRAG_LAYER:** This layer is used to display items during drag-and-drop operations. You could use it to show components being dragged in an IDE's GUI builder, for example. Its identifier is 400.

As you can see, Swing sets these layers with identifiers 100 units apart so that you can easily insert your own layers in between without causing problems.

 This book's Web site offers a project entitled Layers, which shows how to add a component into a layered pane. The application consists of a single frame containing various input fields. When the user types in a value and navigates to another field, the program performs a validation process. The user interface indicates invalid values, like a phone number containing letters, with a small icon in the bottom left of the input fields, as shown in Figure 10-1.

The component responsible for drawing the warning signs is called Validator. It extends JComponent and overrides the paintComponent() method to draw a

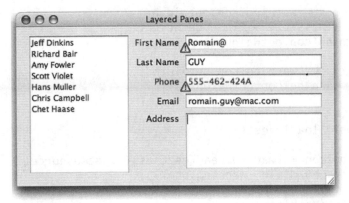

Figure 10-1   The layered pane is used to paint the warning signs on top of the components.

BufferedImage over each invalid component. The complete source code of this component is simple and quite short:

```
public class Validator extends JComponent {
  private Set<JComponent>
      invalidFields = new HashSet<JComponent>();
  private BufferedImage warningIcon;

  public Validator() {
    loadImages();
  }

  public void removeWarning(JComponent field) {
    if (invalidFields.contains(field)) {
      invalidFields.remove(field);
      repaintBadge(field);
    }
  }

  public void addWarning(JComponent field) {
    invalidFields.add(field);
    repaintBadge(field);
  }

  private void repaintBadge(JComponent field) {
    Point p = field.getLocationOnScreen();
    SwingUtilities.convertPointFromScreen(p, this);
```

continued

```java
    int x = p.x - warningIcon.getWidth() / 2;
    int y = (int) (p.y + field.getHeight() -
        warningIcon.getHeight() / 1.5);

    repaint(x, y, warningIcon.getWidth(),
            warningIcon.getHeight());
  }

  private void loadImages() {
    try {
      warningIcon = ImageIO.read(getClass().getResource(
          "images/dialog-warning.png"));
    } catch (IOException ex) {
      ex.printStackTrace();
    }
  }

  @Override
  protected void paintComponent(Graphics g) {
    for (JComponent invalid : invalidFields) {
      if (invalid.getParent() instanceof JViewport) {
        JViewport viewport = (JViewport) invalid.getParent();
        // the parent of the viewport is a JScrollPane
        invalid = (JComponent) viewport.getParent();
      }

      Point p = invalid.getLocationOnScreen();
      SwingUtilities.convertPointFromScreen(p, this);

      int x = p.x - warningIcon.getWidth() / 2;
      int y = (int) (p.y + invalid.getHeight() -
          warningIcon.getHeight() / 1.5);

      if (g.getClipBounds().intersects(x, y,
          warningIcon.getWidth(), warningIcon.getHeight())) {
        g.drawImage(warningIcon, x, y, null);
      }
    }
  }
}
```

Calling removeWarning() and addWarning() respectively hides and shows the
warning sign. As you can see, Validator simply retains the list of invalid input
fields and draws an image over their lower-left corners in paintComponent().
To do this properly, the location of each component is first converted into the
Validator's coordinate space.

To use this component, we need to set it up on top of regular Swing components. Therefore, we want to use a layer whose identifier is greater than `JLayeredPane.DEFAULT_LAYER`. In this case, we choose `DEFAULT_LAYER + 50` as the identifier, since there is room for 99 layers between `DEFAULT_LAYER` and the next layer, `PALETTE_LAYER`. By referring to the documentation, we learn that we must add a `Validator` instance to the layered pane by passing an `Integer` instance during the `add()` call:

```
// calls add(Component, Object)
aLayeredPane.add(aComponent, new Integer(50));
```

Adding a `Validator` instance is extremely easy when you specify an absolute value as the layer identifier, but things are much harder when you need a relative value, as in our example.

J2SE 5.0 Subtlety

Prior to J2SE 5.0, the only way to use a relative identifier was to create a new `Integer`:

```
int value = JLayeredPane.DEFAULT_LAYER.intValue() + 50;
aLayeredPane.add(aComponent, new Integer(value));
```

As of J2SE 5.0, we can take advantage of the autoboxing feature of the language to make the code easier to write and read:

```
aLayeredPane.add(aComponent, JLayeredPane.DEFAULT_LAYER + 50);
```

Does this code work? If you think it does not, can you guess why?

Unfortunately, it does not work. The `javac` compiler will automatically unbox the `DEFAULT_LAYER` `Integer` instance into an `int` primitive and add another `int` primitive of value 50. As a result, the call will be `add(Component, int)`, not `add(Component, Object)`, which has a totally different meaning. To prevent this problem, you can use the following idiom:

```
aLayeredPane.add(aComponent,
    (Integer) (JLayeredPane.DEFAULT_LAYER + 50));
```

In this new version, we force the compiler to box the computed `int` primitive into a new `Integer` instance. Autoboxing is a very powerful feature, but you must sometimes be careful of the results.

Finally, we can add the Validator to the frame's layered pane:

```
validator = new Validator();

JLayeredPane layeredPane = getRootPane().getLayeredPane();
layeredPane.add(validator,
    (Integer) (JLayeredPane.DEFAULT_LAYER + 50));
```

When this code is executed, however, you will soon notice another problem: The Validator is apparently invisible. Unlike the glass pane, JLayeredPane's children are visible by default, so the problem lies elsewhere. In fact, layered panes do not have any layout by default, which means the Validator has no dimension. This problem can be fixed easily by calling setBounds():

```
validator.setBounds(0, 0, getWidth(), getHeight());
```

Setting the bounds directly in this way works only when the frame already has a size. Also, the component does not expand accordingly when the user resizes the frame. To solve this problem, you need to set up a layout manager on the layered pane. Unfortunately, this task proves to be more complicated than with regular Swing containers. Before we delve any further into this topic, there is another feature of JLayeredPane that you should be aware of.

Ordering Components within a Single Layer

We have seen how to add a single component into a specific layer of a layered pane. We have not yet addressed a very common use case: What happens when you add several components into the same layer? You can control the order of the components within a layer by setting another property, called position. The position, akin to the layer identifier, is an integer (but not an instance of the Integer class!) whose value defines the depth of component within the layer. To make things more complicated, the numbering scheme is different from the layer identifiers. For instance, the layer 0 is the bottommost layer, whereas the position 0 indicates the topmost component in the layer. The higher the position value, the lower the depth is. Here is a small code example that shows how to set the position of a component:

```
layeredPane.add(blue, new Integer(10), 15);
layeredPane.add(green, new Integer(10), 42);
layeredPane.add(red, new Integer(5));
```

With this configuration, the red component is at the bottom of the frame, and then we have both blue and green components on the same layer. Because the blue component has a lower position value than the green one, it sits on top. Therefore, the component stack is the following:

```
Blue (topmost)
Green
Red (bottommost)
```

The position property is very important when you expect other parts of your application to use the same JLayeredPane as your own code. Instead of relying on the layer identifiers, pick one layer and stack all your components inside using the position properties.

Layered Panes and Layouts

Layered panes, like any other Swing or AWT container, can use a layout manager to compute their children's locations and dimensions. Traditional layout managers do not work very well with layered panes because they work in a 2D space, whereas layered panes work in a 3D space. Therefore, traditional layout managers, when used with a JLayeredPane, arrange the components as if they all had the same depth—as if they were all on the same layer.

The book's Web site offers a small application showing the effect of a FlowLayout set up on a layered pane. In Figure 10-2, you can see several photos next to one another and a loupe (magnifier) overlapping some of the photos. In reality, each

Figure 10-2 Traditional layout managers do not bother checking the depth of layered pane children.

photo and the loupe belong to a different layer in the layered pane. Nevertheless, because the application uses a FlowLayout, the components are simply laid out side by side. You can change the layer of the loupe to clearly see that every photo is on its very own layer. The source code for this application can be found in the project called LayeredPaneLayout.

The only efficient ways to use a layout with a layered pane are to write your own or to use the least-known layout of all time, java.awt.OverlayLayout. This very simple layout stacks the components on top of each other and we can use this layout to fix the previous application (the project called Layers). The following code snippet shows how to set up the Validator component on the frame without experiencing frame resizing issues:

```
validator = new Validator();

JLayeredPane layeredPane = getRootPane().getLayeredPane();
layeredPane.setLayout(new OverlayLayout(layeredPane));
layeredPane.add(validator,
    (Integer) (JLayeredPane.DEFAULT_LAYER + 50));
```

To write a custom layout that takes the depth into account, you must read a specific property in each component to be laid out. The following code snippet reads the layer identifier of a component:

```
Integer layered = (Integer)
    aComponent.getClientProperty("layeredContainerLayer");
```

You can also ask the layered pane for the layer identifier of a given component. This technique is much cleaner, but it implies that you know that the component belongs to a layered pane:

```
int layeredId = layeredPane.getLayer(aComponent);
```

Layers can be used to add depth support to Swing component hierarchies. Another way to achieve the effect of depth is through the use of layouts, as we see in the next section.

Alternative to JLayeredPane with Layouts

There may be situations in which you need layered components without the hassle of using a JLayeredPane. This might happen when you are working on an existing, complicated code base or when you simply do not want to deal with the API of JLayeredPane. Starting with J2SE 5.0, there is an easy way to add depth support to regular Swing containers through two new methods that were added to java.awt.Container: setComponentZOrder() and getComponentZOrder().

The z-order defines the position of a component along the z-axis, which you can think of as an axis perpendicular to the Swing window itself. In simpler terms, it defines the depth of a component. The lower the number is, the higher the component is in the stack. For instance, a component with a z-order of 10 will be painted on top of a component of z-order 0.

You will find a project called StackLayout on this book's Web site. This project contains a sample application that relies on a custom layout manager named StackLayout. When you add a component to a container using StackLayout, you can choose to add it at the top or at the bottom of the display stack. The demo application, as seen in Figure 10-3, is a photo chooser with three different layers: a background gradient, the photos, and the animated white curves.

Figure 10-3 Any container can support depth with the appropriate layout manager.

The StackLayout API is a simpler approach to achieving depth than using JLayeredPane, but you can add components only at the top or at the bottom of the stack, as seen in the following code:

```
JPanel pane = new JPanel();
pane.setLayout(new StackLayout());
```

continued

```
// gradient background
GradientPanel gradient = new GradientPanel();
// pictures selector
AvatarChooser chooser = new AvatarChooser();
// animated curves
CurvesPanel curves = new CurvesPanel();

pane.add(gradient, StackLayout.TOP);
pane.add(chooser, StackLayout.TOP);
pane.add(curves, StackLayout.TOP);
```

For this application, each component is added on top of the previous one, effectively creating the visual stack I was looking for. Whenever a component is added to a container with a StackLayout, it is added to a list, depending on its position in the stack:

```
public class StackLayout implements LayoutManager2 {
    public static final String BOTTOM = "bottom";
    public static final String TOP = "top";

    private List<Component> components =
        new LinkedList<Component>();

    public void addLayoutComponent(Component comp,
                                   Object constraints) {
      synchronized (comp.getTreeLock()) {
        if (BOTTOM.equals(constraints)) {
          components.add(0, comp);
        } else {
          components.add(comp);
        }
      }
    }

    // ...
}
```

Thanks to this implementation, the components list always contains the component in the appropriate order. The layout then needs to set the z-order of the components according to their position in the list:

```
public void layoutContainer(Container parent) {
    synchronized (parent.getTreeLock()) {
      int width = parent.getWidth();
      int height = parent.getHeight();
```

```
        Rectangle bounds = new Rectangle(0, 0, width, height);

        int componentsCount = components.size();

        for (int i = 0; i < componentsCount; i++) {
            Component comp = components.get(i);
            comp.setBounds(bounds);
            parent.setComponentZOrder(comp, componentsCount - i - 1);
        }
    }
}
```

Akin to a `BorderLayout`, a `StackLayout` expands each component so it fills up all the available space. Finally, the layout manager calls `setComponentZOrder()` on the parent container to give each component its appropriate depth. Since the lower values designate the topmost components, the z-order value of a component is the opposite of the component's index in the list. The complete source code of the layout manager can be found in the `StackLayout` project on the book's Web site.

Layers are extremely useful, no matter how you decide to create them, with a `JLayeredPane`, a custom layout manager, or a combination of both. They can solve many headaches when you want your application to support several glass panes, but they are unfortunately very often overlooked.

Tip: Remember the Layered Pane. As a rule of thumb, consider switching to a layered pane whenever you are about to use the glass pane. This is especially important in complex applications in which the glass pane may be overused or layered panes may offer the additional flexibility that you need.

Small or very simple applications may not justify the burden of using a layered pane instead of a glass pane.

11

Repaint Manager

SWING is a powerful and flexible toolkit. Most of the time, Swing does the right thing. However, there are situations when you need to outsmart Swing and change its default behavior. The RepaintManager is a special class that lets you hook into Swing's internals and that will prove to be very useful in this chapter to create advanced visual effects.

When Swing Gets Too Smart

Swing's painting mechanism always attempts to repaint only what's necessary. It paints *only the regions* of those components that need to be repainted. This is very useful from a performance perspective but can hinder some particular visual effects.

To highlight the problem that might arise with Swing, let's examine the example of the project called TranslucentPanel that you can find on the book's Web site. The following TranslucentPanel class extends JPanel and makes all its children translucent:

```
public class TranslucentPanel extends JPanel {
  BufferedImage image = null;

  @Override
  public void paint(Graphics g) {
    if (image == null ||
        image.getWidth() != getWidth() ||
        image.getHeight() != getHeight()) {
```

continued

```
        image = (BufferedImage) createImage(getWidth(),
                                             getHeight());
    }

    Graphics2D g2 = image.createGraphics();
    g2.setClip(g.getClip());
    super.paint(g2);
    g2.dispose();

    g2 = (Graphics2D) g.create();
    g2.setComposite(AlphaComposite.SrcOver.derive(0.2f));
    g2.drawImage(image, 0, 0, null);
  }
}
```

On painting, this component creates a temporary offscreen image, draws its content inside with a translucency of 20 percent, and displays the image on screen. Figure 11-1 shows what the result looks like when you add a JTable and a few JButtons inside a TranslucentPanel.

At first glance, the TranslucentPanel seems to work perfectly. Unfortunately, the truth is not so pretty. If you run the application and click on the table or on one of the buttons, the component will suddenly become opaque, as shown in Figure 11-2. There is no need to double-check the code in TranslucentPanel; there is no error.

The problem comes from Swing's painting mechanism: Swing tries to repaint only the components and regions that need to be repainted. When you click a JButton, for instance, Swing calls the paint() method of the JButton but not

Figure 11-1 A JTable and three JButtons painted by the TranslucentPanel.

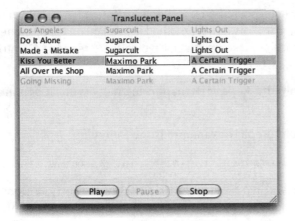

Figure 11-2 When a child gets repainted, the translucency is lost.

that of its parent. So the paint() method in TranslucentPanel, which is responsible for enabling the translucency, is not invoked.

> **Note: Nonopaque Components.** Swing may actually call the paint() method of the parent when the component that needs to be repainted is nonopaque. Unfortunately, we cannot ask the users of our TranslucentPanel to make sure that every component it contains is nonopaque.

The only solution to this problem is to change the way that Swing decides which components need to be repainted and force it to repaint TranslucentPanel instead of its children. The RepaintManager is the key to this solution.

Meet the RepaintManager

The role of the RepaintManager is to optimize the repaint processing of Swing components. It does so by intercepting all repaint requests on Swing components and by keeping track of what needs to be repainted. The regions of components that need to be updated are called *dirty regions*.

After intercepting a repaint request, the RepaintManager uses SwingUtilities. invokeLater() to post the request on the event dispatch thread. The EDT then processes the request and dispatches it to the components that need to be updated.

As a result a repaint request is posted to the RepaintManager whenever the repaint(), or repaint(int, int, int, int), method is invoked on a JComponent. The RepaintManager manages coalescing successive calls to repaint() into as few requests as possible to the EDT.

Figure 11-3 summarizes how the RepaintManager interacts with JComponent and the EDT.

The most interesting method in RepaintManager is the following:

```
void addDirtyRegion(JComponent c, int x, int y, int w, int h)
```

The addDirtyRegion() method is responsible for tracking the dirty regions of the components that need to be repainted. This method is always invoked after a call to repaint() and thus can be used to catch all of the repaint requests. More interestingly, addDirtyRegion() can be used to *extend* the dirty region. We see later why this feature is useful.

Managing the RepaintManager

In Sun's Swing implementation, there is only one global RepaintManager. You can get the current RepaintManager by calling either one of the following methods in the RepaintManager class:

```
static RepaintManager currentManager(Component c)
static RepaintManager currentManager(JComponent c)
```

The parameters are currently unused since the same RepaintManager will always be returned. You can also replace the current RepaintManager with your own:

```
void setCurrentManager(RepaintManager aRepaintManager)
```

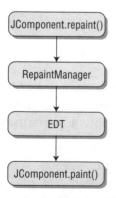

Figure 11-3 The RepaintManager intercepts all repaint events.

A Reflection on RepaintManager

To explain how to use the `RepaintManager`, we use the project called `RepaintManager` on the book's Web site. This project contains an extension of `JPanel` called `ReflectionPanel`. This class paints a reflection for every child it contains. You can use it, for instance, to add a nice reflection effect to a movie, as shown in Figure 11-4. If you run the application, you will see the reflection being updated in real time.

> **Warning: Playing Movies with the Demo.** To run the example application with a movie, you must have QuickTime installed on your system. If QuickTime is not present, on Linux for instance, the application will automatically display regular Swing components instead, as shown in Figure 11-5. In this case, the reflection will react to any change on the Swing components. For instance, when you press a button, the reflection will also appear pressed.

Making Room for the Reflection

By default, a `JPanel` has a preferred size that is just large enough to display all of its children. Therefore, there is no empty space in the panel where the `ReflectionPanel` can paint the children's reflections.

Figure 11-4 `ReflectionPanel` paints a real-time reflection effect for any child it contains.

Figure 11-5 The reflection reacts to all component updates thanks to a special RepaintManager.

To be able to paint the reflection, we must enlarge the size of the ReflectionPanel, as shown in Figure 11-6. The ReflectionPanel is actually made up of a content pane, an embedded JPanel where the components will be added, and empty space.

The height of the empty space, and thus of the ReflectionPanel, depends on the height of the content pane and the length of the reflection. The reflection's length is a number between 0.0 and 1.0. For instance, a reflection length of 0.5 will produce a reflection length equal to half of the height of the content pane.

The ReflectionPanel uses the GridBagLayout layout to anchor the content pane at the top of the component. The bottom part of the ReflectionPanel is filled with a vertical glue, created by the Box class. A glue is an empty component that takes as much space as possible in one direction.

It is possible to override the getPreferredSize() method and extend the height of the ReflectionPanel. The following code shows how ReflectionPanel is built:

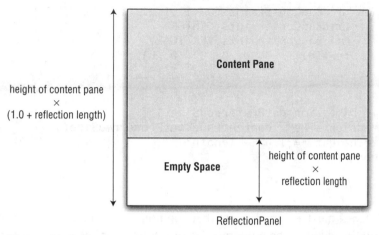

Figure 11-6 Empty space is added to the panel to make room for the reflection.

```java
public class ReflectionPanel extends JPanel {
  private JPanel contentPane;
  private boolean initialized = false;
  private float length = 0.65f;

  public ReflectionPanel() {
    super(new GridBagLayout());
    setOpaque(false);

    buildContentPane();
    buildFiller();

    initialized = true;
  }

  private void buildContentPane() {
    contentPane = new JPanel(new BorderLayout());
    contentPane.setOpaque(false);

    add(contentPane,
      new GridBagConstraints(0, 0, 1, 1, 1.0, 0.0,
        GridBagConstraints.CENTER,
        GridBagConstraints.BOTH,
        new Insets(0, 0, 0, 0), 0, 0));
  }

  private void buildFiller() {
    add(Box.createVerticalGlue(),
```

continued

```
          new GridBagConstraints(0, 1, 1, 1, 1.0, 1.0,
             GridBagConstraints.CENTER,
             GridBagConstraints.VERTICAL,
             new Insets(0, 0, 0, 0), 0, 0));
   }

   @Override
   public Dimension getPreferredSize() {
     Dimension size = contentPane.getPreferredSize();
     size.height *= 1.0f + length;
     return size;
   }
}
```

ReflectionPanel must also make sure that components added by the user of the
class are actually added to the content pane, not to the ReflectionPanel itself.
The boolean variable initialized plays an important role in delegating the
calls to add(), remove(), and setLayout() to the content pane:

```
   @Override
   protected void addImpl(Component comp,
                         Object constraints, int index) {
     if (initialized) {
        contentPane.add(comp, constraints, index);
     } else {
        super.addImpl(comp, constraints, index);
     }
   }

   @Override
   public void remove(int index) {
      contentPane.remove(index);
   }

   @Override
   public void remove(Component comp) {
      contentPane.remove(comp);
   }

   @Override
   public void removeAll() {
      contentPane.removeAll();
   }

   @Override
   public void setLayout(LayoutManager mgr) {
     if (initialized) {
        contentPane.setLayout(mgr);
```

```
    } else {
        super.setLayout(mgr);
    }
}
```

After the `ReflectionPanel` is initialized, all of the calls are delegated to the content pane.

Painting the Reflection

The next step is to paint the reflection:

1. Paint the content of the panel in an offscreen image (the content buffer).
2. Paint the content buffer onscreen.
3. Create the reflection of the content buffer in another image (the reflection buffer).
4. Paint the reflection buffer onscreen.

The `paint()` method of `ReflectionPanel` requests the painting first of the content, then of the reflection:

```
@Override
public void paint(Graphics g) {
    paintContent(g);
    paintReflection(g);
}
```

The `paintContent()` method processes the first two operations at the same time: it creates the content buffer and paints it on screen. The implementation is as follows:

```
private BufferedImage contentBuffer = null;
private Graphics contentGraphics = null;

private void paintContent(Graphics g) {
  if (contentBuffer == null ||
     contentBuffer.getWidth() != contentPane.getWidth() ||
     contentBuffer.getHeight() != contentPane.getHeight()) {
    if (contentBuffer != null) {
      contentBuffer.flush();
      contentGraphics.dispose();
    }
```

continued

```
        contentBuffer = new BufferedImage(contentPane.getWidth(),
            contentPane.getHeight(), BufferedImage.TYPE_INT_ARGB);
        contentGraphics = contentBuffer.createGraphics();
    }

    Graphics2D g2 = contentGraphics;
    g2.clipRect(contentPane.getX(), contentPane.getY(),
            contentPane.getWidth(), contentPane.getHeight());

    // because the content buffer is reused, the image
    // must be cleared
    g2.setComposite(AlphaComposite.Clear);
    Rectangle clip = g.getClipBounds();
    g2.fillRect(clip.x, clip.y, clip.width, clip.height);

    g2.setComposite(AlphaComposite.SrcOver);
    g2.setColor(g.getColor());
    g2.setFont(g.getFont());

    super.paint(g2);

    g.drawImage(contentBuffer, 0, 0, null);
}
```

This code contains a few optimizations. For instance, the same content buffer is used over and over unless the size of the panel has changed. This behavior saves a lot of time when repaints occur often, as is the case with video. Also, note that the clip is intersected with the content pane's bounds, which is necessary when the repaint() request covers part of the ReflectionPanel's empty area.

Painting the reflection is a bit more complicated. First, the reflection itself must be generated in the reflection buffer, and then the reflection buffer must be painted in the ReflectionPanel's empty space:

```
private void paintReflection(Graphics g) {
    int width = contentPane.getWidth();
    int height = (int) (contentPane.getHeight() * length);
    createReflection(g, width, height);

    Graphics2D g2 = (Graphics2D) g.create();
    g2.scale(1.0, -1.0);
    g2.drawImage(reflectionBuffer, 0, -contentPane.getHeight()
                - height, null);
    g2.dispose();
}
```

The call to scale(1.0, -1.0) should not be a surprise if you read Chapter 7, "Gradients," in which we explained how to create a reflection effect. Please refer to the section called "Special Effects with Regular Gradients" in Chapter 7 to see how the createReflection() method invoked in our current code example was created.

The painting code is now complete. However, if you try to run the application, you will run into the same issue that was exposed with the example of the TranslucentPanel. As shown in Figure 11-7, the reflection is not updated when the movie plays. Indeed, when the movie component asks to be repainted, the default RepaintManager figures there is no need to ask its parent, the ReflectionPanel, to update itself. The reflection therefore remains stuck on the first frame of the movie.

To solve this issue, all we need is a custom RepaintManager that will tell the ReflectionPanel to update itself.

A Dumber, Therefore Smarter, RepaintManager

To make our reflection work, we must install our own RepaintManager. This new RepaintManager will be dumber in that it will repaint components that

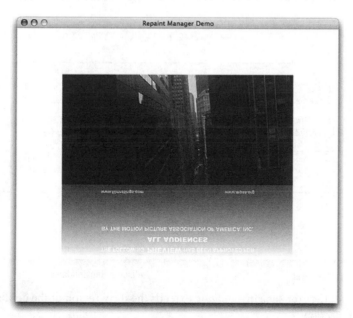

Figure 11-7 Without a special RepaintManager, the reflection does not update when it should.

Swing deems unnecessary to update. Installing the `RepaintManager` is quite easy:

```
private void installRepaintManager() {
    ReflectionRepaintManager manager =
        new ReflectionRepaintManager();
    RepaintManager.setCurrentManager(manager);
}
```

The `ReflectionRepaintManager` overrides only the `addDirtyRegion()` method. Remember that this method is invoked whenever a repaint request is issued to a component.

For every component that needs to be repainted, our `addDirtyRegion()` implementation traverses the parents of the component to find an instance of `ReflectionPanel`. When such an instance can be found, the dirty region is extended to cover both the old dirty region and the corresponding area in the reflection. Figure 11-8 shows the dirty regions used by the default `RepaintManager` and the `ReflectionRepaintManager`.

With the `ReflectionRepaintManager`, the dirty region expands over the reflection. Therefore, when `paint()` is invoked in `ReflectionPanel`, the clip bounds of the `Graphics` will also cover the reflection, allowing updates to that area.

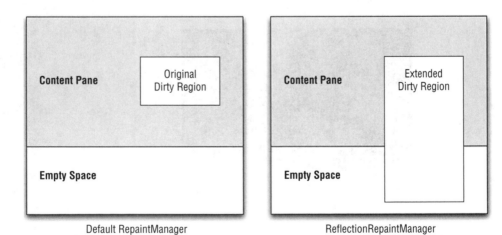

Default RepaintManager   ReflectionRepaintManager

Figure 11-8 The `ReflectionRepaintManager` extends the dirty region of the content pane to cover the reflection.

The complete source code of the `ReflectionRepaintManager` is as follows:

```
private class ReflectionRepaintManager extends RepaintManager {
  public void addDirtyRegion(JComponent c,
      int x, int y, int w, int h) {
    Rectangle dirtyRegion = getDirtyRegion(c);

    int lastDeltaX = c.getX();
    int lastDeltaY = c.getY();

    Container parent = c.getParent();
    // as long as we can find a parent
    while (parent instanceof JComponent) {
      // if the parent is not visible,
      // neither is the component
      if (!parent.isVisible()) {
        return;
      }

      if (parent instanceof ReflectionPanel) {
        x += lastDeltaX;
        y += lastDeltaY;

        // extends the dirty region to cover the
        // corresponding area in the reflection
        int gap = contentPane.getHeight() - h - y;
        h += 2 * gap + h;

        lastDeltaX = lastDeltaY = 0;

        // the component that needs to be repainted
        // is now the ReflectionPanel
        c = (JComponent) parent;
      }

      // calculates the location delta between
      // the parent and the dirty component
      lastDeltaX += parent.getX();
      lastDeltaY += parent.getY();

      parent = parent.getParent();
    }

    // posts the repaint request in the EDT
    super.addDirtyRegion(c, x, y, w, h);
  }
}
```

This code simply retrieves the parent of the "dirty" component and checks whether it is an instance of ReflectionPanel. If not, it continues with the parent's parent, and so on.

When a ReflectionPanel is found, the height of the dirty region is modified to include the area of the reflection corresponding to the area of the original dirty region. The component to be updated, called c in the code, is finally replaced by the ReflectionPanel.

At the end of the loop, the code invokes super.addDirtyRegion() and passes the ReflectionPanel and the extended dirty region. The super class's method takes care of posting the repaint request in the EDT for us.

Note: Fixing the TranslucentPanel. Given the previous example, try to implement a RepaintManager that can fix the issues of the TranslucentPanel. The translucent repaint manager does not need to extend the dirty region but only change which component needs to be updated.

Summary

The RepaintManager lets you hook into Swing's repainting mechanism. It can be used to catch repaint requests as well as to create visual effects that are otherwise very difficult to implement correctly. Be aware, however, that only one RepaintManager can exist at a time. You should create your own RepaintManager only when necessary.

Part III

Animation

12

Animation Fundamentals

It's About Time

Animation is one of the key concepts and techniques behind Filthy Rich Clients, giving our applications a more dynamic feel as the interface moves smoothly in response to user actions. Animation is a large and diverse topic, covering operations as simple as copying an image around on the screen or as complex as the latest 3D shooter game or animated movie. For our purposes, we focus on a specific use of the term and technique: *Animation* is the time-based alteration of graphical objects through different states, locations, sizes, and orientations. There are two important concepts to grasp from this simple definition: *time-based* and *alteration*.

Alteration is easy to explain. It simply means that we need to change the way we are drawing objects. We learned how to do this for Swing applications in earlier chapters; we change the graphics state and re-render GUI and graphics objects appropriately.

Time-based is perhaps less obvious and is at the heart of the next few pages. The basic idea is that we define how objects are supposed to change over time and then render the objects accordingly as time ticks on.

Fundamental Concepts

Frame-Based Animation

In the real world, the world outside my computer of which I've heard occasional rumors, we see an animation by watching the continuous changes occur in front of our eyes. The fly buzzes past, my hand swats it, the fly hits the wall, and the fly drops down to the ground.[1] In computer animation, as in movies, we see the changes of an animation as a series of still pictures, which our mind puts together as a smooth flow. See Figure 12-1 and Figure 12-2.

In Figure 12-1 and Figure 12-2 we see the before and after positions of a fly, along with the path that the fly takes in getting from the before to the after position. In Figure 12-3, we see individual pictures taken during the fly's journey, which, if shown in rapid sequence, could approximate the actual flight closely enough to convince our minds that we saw the fly moving and not just a series of pictures of the fly standing still in different locations.[2]

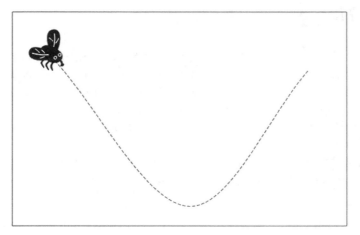

Figure 12-1　Before.

---

1. No animals were harmed in the making of this book. At least none that people care about.
2. I considered doing a flip-book animation in the book, in the lower corner of the pages, like I remember from the *Mad* magazines of my youth. While this is a great demonstration of the frame-based animation technique, it's also a great way to get a lot of dog-eared copies of our books on the store shelves. So I've opted for the more boring and theoretical figures in this discussion. I leave it as an exercise for you to cut out the pictures in Figure 12-3 and make a flip-book animation for yourself. Besides being a nifty demonstration of the technique, it will make the time fly. Or the fly timed. But please wait to perform this experiment until after you've purchased the book.

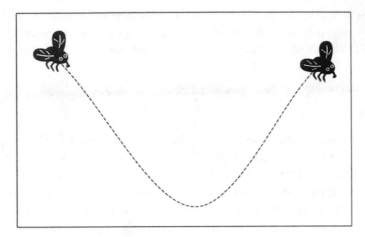

Figure 12-2 After.

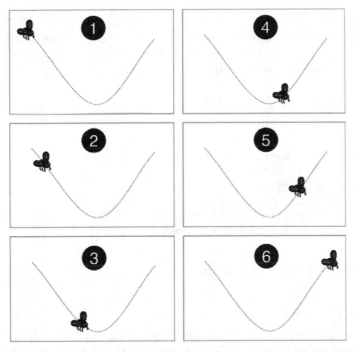

Figure 12-3 Flies timed while you're having fun: individual animation frames for the fly's movement.

This picture-based, or *frame*-based, animation approach works fine in most situations. As long as we show the frames fast enough, the mind construes the series as fluid motion. There are other tricks that can help fool our minds,[3] and they are covered in Chapter 13, "Smooth Moves."

Frame Rate

One of the terms we should mention up front, since we use it often, is *frame rate*. Each separate view of an animation is called a *frame*, and an animation is a succession of these frames. The rate at which these frames are displayed is called, not surprisingly, the frame rate. This rate is determined by a combination of the rate required to achieve smooth motion and the rate that is possible to achieve given the performance of your system and the complexity of what you are trying to render in each frame.

Time-Based Motion

The simplest approach to animated rendering is to change a scene in steps and draw the new versions sequentially. For example, assume that you want to animate movement of an image from the left of the window to the right. You could accomplish this task by drawing the object on the left and then on the right, like this:

```
public void paintComponent(Graphics g) {
   int imgW = img.getWidth();
   int imgH = img.getHeight();
   // Draw image in first location
   g.drawImage(img, 0, 0, null);
   // Erase first location
   g.setColor(bgColor);
   g.fillRect(0, 0, imgW, imgH);
   // Draw image in final location
   g.drawImage(img, windowWidth - imgW, 0, null);
}
```

There are several of problems with this approach:

Teleportation != Animation

This example is really not much of an "animation" if the object just appears in the start and then the end locations. The desirable effect for any animation is

---

3. Without resorting to chemicals.

for the object to gradually move from one location to the other, not to simply appear in the final location.

Tip: In fact, getting applications to smoothly animate graphics is one of the goals of this entire book. Filthy Rich Clients are trying to get away from the traditional model of applications in which objects, GUI elements, text, and application state simply change immediately. There should be movement and transition in the application, not abrupt and discontinuous change.

Too Fast

By drawing the start and end versions directly after one another, we are effectively showing the user only the end location. In Swing, as we discuss later, the user would see only the end version, not the initial drawing at (0, 0). But even in toolkits in which both of the versions would be drawn onscreen, it would all happen so fast that it would end up being just a blip of the object in the initial location, and then the object would appear in the final location. This kind of animation is not so much a flick as a flicker.

Swing Buffering

Because of the rendering model of Swing, discussed in Chapter 2, "Swing Rendering Fundamentals," the user sees only the final result. The user won't even see a glimpse of the initial rendering because all Swing rendering happens offscreen on a back buffer. The result of Swing's double-buffering is that all commands in the `paintComponent()` method draw to the back buffer, at the completion of which the buffer is copied to the screen. The previous code draws the first location, erases it, and then draws the final version. The user sees only the final version, not the intermediate drawing and erasure. So there are no disturbing flicker artifacts—but there is actually no animation at all, only a single rendering of the image in its final location.

Motion Should Be Time-Based

There is nothing governing how fast the object gets from the left to the right apart from the speed of the system on which the code is run. If we want realistic animations that the user accepts, we must use some time-based algorithm to control the motion of an object.

Let's see what we can do to address all of these issues.

Movement, Not Teleportation

The first issue is easy. We add intermediate steps to the animation to make it more gradual. In the extreme case, we could try to make the animation as smooth as possible by moving the image only one pixel between each rendering, as in the following code:

```
public void paintComponent(Graphics g) {
  int imgW = img.getWidth();
  int imgH = img.getHeight();
  for (int i = imgW; i <= windowWidth; ++i) {
    // Erase old location
    g.setColor(bgColor);
    g.fillRect(i - imgW - 1, 0, imgW, imgH);
    // Draw image in next location
    g.drawImage(img, i - imgW, 0, null);
  }
}
```

This new approach renders the image many times, each time erasing the old image and then drawing it again one pixel to the right. Instead of teleporting the image from the left to the right, we are moving it incrementally through all of the intervening pixels.

The other problems we identified, however, are still present. For one thing, the animation happens entirely too quickly, even when we shift it one pixel at a time.

Slow It Down

When we draw one frame right after the other, whether using the original tele-portation approach or the improved pixel-by-pixel version, we're still updating the frames at the speed of the system, which is too fast for our purposes. Users need to see movement that is gradual, not as fast as the machine can perform it. What we need, then, is a mechanism to pause between each frame of the animation to give the user time to soak in the new image position or at least to see what is happening. Such code might look something like this:

```
int imgX, imgY;
int prevImgX, prevImgY;
```

```
public void paintImage(Graphics g) {
  g.setColor(bgColor);
  g.fillRect(prevX, prevY, img.getWidth(),img.getHeight());
  g.drawImage(img, imgX, imgY, null);
  prevX = imgX;
  prevY = imgY;
}

public void paintComponent(Graphics g) {
  imgX = prevX = imgY = prevY = 0;
  imgW = img.getWidth();
  for (int i = imgW; i <= windowWidth; ++i) {
    paintImage(g);
    // ... some time passes
    imgX = i - imgW;
  }
}
```

This second attempt is slightly more intelligent about how it draws the two versions. It refactors the painting code into the paintImage() method and uses the variables imgX and imgY to determine where the image will be drawn when the method is executed.

There is a big unknown in this version in the comment line that says "// ... some time passes." How much time? How do we pass that time? Do we spin in a loop waiting for time to pass? Spinning in a tight loop is a bad idea. Occupying the CPU just to let time pass is considered a breach of application etiquette. Other applications and that are running, as well as the operating system itself, have enough to contend with without some application pegging the CPU for this purpose. As we see in the next section, there are convenient mechanisms in the Java class libraries, as in other GUI toolkits, for providing this time-passing functionality in a system-friendly way.

Swing Buffering

We still have the problem of the Swing window not showing anything in these examples except the final frame. As we saw in our discussion of double buffering in Chapter 2, the contents of a Swing window are copied to the screen only after the window is completely finished with being updated. In the previous examples, the component is not done with rendering in its paintComponent() method until the animation has ended. So although the entire animation will be rendered to the back buffer, and the image will be drawn and erased in all of its positions as a part of that process, the only result that the user will see on the screen is the final one with the image at the endpoint of the animation.

The fix for this issue is that we must work within the Swing painting model, which means completing a component's painting after each frame of the animation, as opposed to our previous model in which we rendered all frames of the animation in one tight loop inside paintComponent(). This task is actually quite simple. Instead of performing our animation inside the paintComponent() method, we perform the animation elsewhere and then call repaint() on the component for each frame. Swing then calls our component to render the animation for that particular frame. Making this change to the example looks like this:

```
int imgX, imgY;
int prevImgX, prevImgY;

public void paintComponent(Graphics g) {
  g.setColor(bgColor);
  g.fillRect(prevX, prevY, img.getWidth(),img.getHeight());
  g.drawImage(img, imgX, imgY, null);
  prevX = imgX;
  prevY = imgY;
}

public void someMethod() {
  imgX = prevX = imgY = prevY = 0;
  imgW = img.getWidth();
  for (int i = imgW; i <= windowWidth; ++i) {
    repaint();
    // ... some time passes
    imgX = i - imgW;
  }
}
```

Of course, this code is still academic; we glibly wave our hands with that vague "// ... some time passes" comment. We obviously need to fill in some details there; how do we effectively pass some time for the application?

Most GUI toolkits, and many system-level libraries, provide various timing mechanisms intended exactly for this sort of purpose. We learn more about them in a few pages, but first we have to solve the last problem: motion should be time-based.

Realistic Motion

The final problem with our example is that the movement of the image is completely unrealistic. No matter how much time passes between each step of the object, we are still moving it one pixel at a time. One problem with this approach is that the behavior of the animation will vary widely between systems. Maybe it looks good on your fast development system but takes twice as long on some other user's system.[4] Surely there is a better way to move an object than to just bump its position by some hard-coded increment.

Indeed, there is a better way: we need *time-based* movement. In fact, for all animations that we want to do in GUIs, be they moves or fades or whatever, we should base the animations on time. That is, we should define how much to alter some property, like the position of the image in this example, over some period of time. Then, during the animation, we can calculate the correct value for that property according to how much time has passed. With this approach, it doesn't matter how fast or slow a system is or whether there were any hiccups during the animation. The object being animated will always be in the right place at the right time.

The simplest approach to time-based animation is to use a linear interpolation of values based on their starting value, their end value, and the fraction of time that has elapsed during the animation.

The equation for linear interpolation of any value x is the parametric equation:

$$x = x0 + t * (x1 - x0)$$

where:

- x = the value we want to calculate during the animation.
- $x0$ = the starting value.
- $x1$ = the ending value.
- t = the elapsed fraction of the animation duration, from 0 to 1.

We can see how this approach changes our example:

```
int imgX, imgY;
int prevImgX, prevImgY;
```

continued

---

4. There was a demo I saw years ago advertising a cool, new graphics card. This hardware was pretty fast at drawing lines and the demo did a really nice job of showing this off. The application showed a wireframe piano as the camera zoomed around it in 3D. The piano was playing a tune and you could see the keys moving, the hammers striking, and the strings vibrating, all synchronized with a soundtrack. It was a great piece of work.

I happened to see the demo years later on a different system with even faster graphics hardware ... and it looked silly. All of the frames of the animation were displayed in about a tenth of the time that the demo author had planned, so the piano was done playing the piece while the music was still wafting out of the speakers.

In this case, the positions of the objects were not calculated according to the time that had elapsed, but rather to some hard-coded formula that broke down once the demo was run on a platform with different speed characteristics.

```
public void paintComponent(Graphics g) {
    g.setColor(bgColor);
    g.fillRect(prevX, prevY, img.getWidth(),img.getHeight());
    g.drawImage(img, imgX, imgY, null);
    prevX = imgX;
    prevY = imgY;
}

public void someMethod() {
    int imgW = img.getWidth();
    int startX = 0;
    int endX = windowWidth - imgX;
    imgX = prevX = imgY = prevY = 0;
    // Note: getTime() is pseudo-code, not a real method
    long currentTime = getTime();
    long startTime = currentTime;
    long endTime = currentTime + animationDuration;
    while (currentTime < endTime) {
        long elapsedTime = currentTime - startTime;
        float f = (float)(elapsedTime / animationDuration);
        imgX = startX + f * (endX - startX);
        repaint();
        // ... some time passes
        currentTime = getTime();
    }
}
```

There are several new elements in this version of the example. The getTime() function is a placeholder for a real function to get the current time. We discuss this topic in depth in the next few pages. For now, just assume that there is such a function. Given the time we start, startTime, and the time during any iteration through the loop, currentTime, we can calculate the elapsedTime. With elapsedTime and some animationDuration, we can calculate the fraction elapsed (f) of animationDuration. And given f, we can calculate the position of the image at any point between its starting (startX) and ending (endX) positions:

```
imgX = startX + f * (endX - startX);
```

This calculation should look a lot like the linear interpolation function that we discussed earlier.

This time-based approach gives us much more flexibility in our animations. We can start to specify animations in terms of what we want to do during the animation, such as move an object from x0 to x1 or fade a button between alpha values a0 and a1, and how long we want the animation to take. The calculations of the interim values during the animation handle the details of changing object properties accordingly.

This approach also addresses the need for the animation to run similarly across a wide spectrum of user platforms, which Java has been known to do. Just because a simple pixel-by-pixel animation might look good on your development system does not mean it will look good on someone else's computer. But since different computers still measure time the same,[5] calculations of animations based on elapsed time would get the same results even on wildly different platforms. Moving to a time-based animation approach smooths out these issues and helps animations look the same wherever they happen to run.

We glossed over a lot of details here, from the "// ...some time passes" comment to the fake "getTime()" function. The next few pages resolve these issues and show how to make the fake functionality work for real in Java.

Timing (and Platform Timing Utilities)

There are various situations in which we need to use time in applications, and there are different utilities provided by any runtime platform for those purposes. We see the various categories of timing functionality in this section, along with how these facilities are provided by Java.

"What Time Is It?"

One of the most fundamental time queries that an application needs is simply finding out the current time. This functionality may be required because the application needs to know the actual time, say, for time-stamping a transaction, but for our purposes applications usually need the information more for relative-time purposes. That is, an application does not necessarily care what time it is as an absolute but rather how much time has passed since some other event.

For example, maybe an application would like to measure the performance of certain operations. Or maybe it would like to do a particular action, like render the next frame of an animation, at some predetermined interval. In such situations, we need to know how much time has passed since some previous operation.

---

5. This premise assumes, of course, that the computers are in the same time continuum. Development of multidimensional Filthy Rich Client applications is beyond the scope of this book. We'll have to see if we can cover that topic in a sequel.

Modern runtime platforms generally provide one or more mechanisms for querying the current time. The format in which the times are reported can vary, but it is straightforward to compare with other times of similar format so that applications can calculate the difference.

Java provides a couple of methods for this purpose: `System.currentTimeMillis()` and `System.nanoTime()`.

Java Time: currentTimeMillis() and nanoTime()

System.currentTimeMillis()

`System.currentTimeMillis()` has existed since Java's original 1.0 release. This simple function returns the number of milliseconds since January 1, 1970, a date known as the UNIX Epoch. It seems unlikely that anyone would want to know how many milliseconds have passed since this arbitrary date in the past, but for the purpose of determining relative times, this result is fine. For example, suppose we want to know our animation frame rate, or how many frames per second (fps) are currently being drawn. We can determine the fps by measuring the time that has passed since the last frame in our `paintComponent()` method:

```
private long previousTime = 0;
private float fps = 0.0f;
public void paint(Graphics g) {
  long currentTime = System.currentTimeMillis();
  long delta = (currentTime - previousTime);
  if (delta > 0) {
    // only calculate fps for positive delta times
    fps = 1000.0f / (float)delta;
  }
  previousTime = currentTime;
  // ... actual rendering operations
}
```

This example tracks the exact fps for every frame we render by dividing 1 second—1,000 ms—by the number of milliseconds elapsed since the last time we were in this method. There are some quirks to this measurement that are worth noting:

First Frame Rate Wrong

Because we set `previousTime` from the old `currentTime`, the first time we calculate delta, the `previousTime` is incorrect, leading to an incorrect delta. In practice, we would either ignore this initial value or start calculating fps some time after the first frame.

High Volatility

The time between frames may be quite different, like 15 ms for one frame and then 60 ms for the next. Rather than see our frame rate jump wildly between these different values, it is probably more useful to track the fps over a longer time period to smooth out the volatility and measure an average frame rate instead.

Resolution

One of the factors that contribute to interframe volatility is the resolution of the timing mechanism, which is discussed further under "Resolution" later in this chapter. Again, we get better results by calculating an average frame rate, eliminating the per-frame volatility.

Let's see another example that addresses these issues:

```
private long startTime = 0;
private int numFrames = 0;
private float fps = 0.0f;
private float getFPS() {
  ++numFrames;
  if (startTime == 0) {
    startTime = System.currentTimeMillis();
  } else {
    long currentTime = System.currentTimeMillis();
    long delta = (currentTime - startTime);
    // Average the fps over each second
    if (delta > 1000) {
      fps = numFrames / delta * 1000;
      numFrames = 0;
      startTime = currentTime;
    }
  }
  return fps;
}
public void paintComponent(Graphics g) {
  float fps = getFPS();
  // ... actual rendering operations
}
```

In this version, we calculate fps over periods of about a second. That is, we calculate fps only when the delta, which measures the time between now and the last time we calculated fps, is greater than 1000 ms. For intermediate values, we simply return the previous fps value. Note that our initial fps values are bogus, since fps equals 0 until we have passed our first second of measurements, so there are no real fps results until after this warm-up period.

This is just a simple example. Other methods of measuring and calculating the fps could be used that better account for initial values, calculate the frame rate over longer or shorter periods, or account for particular application situations. But this example at least shows the basics of how you might do this in your application, using Java's simple System.currentTimeMillis() timer.

System.nanoTime()

System.nanoTime() was introduced in J2SE 5.0 as a means of getting a higher-resolution time value. Resolution is further discussed later, but it is important to note that nanoTime() offers better resolution in two senses: It offers time values in nanoseconds, or billionths of a second, and the times may be measured by a higher-resolution timer in the operating system than is the case with current-TimeMillis().

I have found that I rarely have the need for sub-millisecond timings. But the resolution issue is huge, as we'll see later, and the improved resolution of nanoTime() makes it a very attractive alternative to currentTimeMillis(). For example, on some systems, currentTimeMillis() cannot time anything accurately at less than 16 ms, whereas nanoTime() can time accurately down to the millisecond range. This degree of accuracy can make nanoTime() critical for situations in which you need to need to know how much time has passed and the coarser resolution of currentTimeMillis() is just not enough. In practice, you use this function exactly like currentTimeMillis(), adjusting the values according to the time increments you need. In the previous example, the only change apart from the method name is that we multiply delta by 1,000,000,000 instead of 1,000 to get the right answer for fps:

```
if (startTime == 0) {
  startTime = System.nanoTime();
} else {
  long currentTime = System.nanoTime();
  long delta = (currentTime - startTime);
  if (delta > 1000) {
    fps = numFrames / delta * 1000000000;
    numFrames = 0;
    startTime = currentTime;
  }
}
```

"Can I Get a Wake-up Call?"

Another common usage for time utilities is to ask for a wake-up call, just like at a hotel.[6] A wake-up call is exactly the need we have in our simple animation examples in which the program wanted to "pass some time" without simply spinning in a tight loop. In this situation, the application would like to hand control back to the system, with the agreement that the application will get woken up at some specified time.

This process is called *sleeping*, because the thread that requests this wake-up call is put to sleep by the system. Most GUI and system libraries have some kind of mechanism for putting a thread to sleep, like a function called something catchy, say sleep(). Typically, a sleep() function is called with a number denoting the duration that the thread would like to remain asleep. The system puts the thread to sleep, hands control over to other running threads and processes, and eventually awakens that initial thread after the sleep duration has passed.

Thread.sleep()

> **Tip:** Another mechanism that has some characteristics in common with Thread.sleep() is Object.wait(). We can also call wait() to specify a timeout period after which we wish to be woken up. However, wait() is actually more suited to other situations (where other threads can force our waiting thread to wake up), so we skip it here, since it is not something we would typically use in this situation. We will come back to wait() later on in our discussion on resolution, since it is used under the covers by our use of the Swing timer.

In Java, the wake-up functionality is handled by the method Thread.sleep(ms), where ms is the number of milliseconds that the thread would like to remain asleep. The method may throw an exception if the system causes the thread to be interrupted during its sleep cycle, so the full procedure for calling sleep() is as follows:

```
try {
  // sleep for 100 milliseconds
  Thread.sleep(100);
} catch (InterruptedException e) {
  // handle exception appropriately
}
```

---

6. Except that this wake-up call saves you the price of the hotel room.

Now let's return to our previous animation example and substitute this sleep functionality for our hand-wavy "some time passes" as follows:

```
int imgX, imgY;
int prevImgX, prevImgY;

public void paint(Graphics g) {
  g.setColor(bgColor);
  g.fillRect(prevX, prevY, img.getWidth(),img.getHeight());
  g.drawImage(img, imgX, imgY, null);
  prevX = imgX;
  prevY = imgY;
}

public void someMethod() {
  imgX = prevX = imgY = prevY = 0;
  for (int i = 0; i <= windowWidth; ++i) {
    repaint();
    try {
      Thread.sleep(30);
    } catch (InterruptedException e) {
      // handle exception
    }
    imgX = window - img.getWidth();
  }
}
```

This code should look better than it did before. It even looks like you might actually be able to compile and use it. In its current form, it now pauses for 30 ms, which would make the animation run at about 33 fps, and then renders the next frame of the animation.

But this approach to the problem doesn't scale beyond this tiny example. An application that sleeps for long periods of time just to get a reasonable frame rate doesn't seem very workable. What about the rest of the work that an application might want to do besides calculating object positions and sleeping? We can do better than this; let's check out the timers.

"Call Me Again. And Again. And Again."

sleep() is useful for getting a single wake-up call. But what if you want to perform an operation repeatedly with similar time increments? You could keep performing individual sleep() calls, which works adequately in some situations, but there is a more convenient mechanism in most libraries for this situation. It's called a *timer*. In addition to the convenience of not having to manually call sleep() every time, you have the powerful capability to continue doing whatever you need to do, knowing that you will get a call when you need it.

Let's overload our previous hotel wake-up call metaphor a bit more to illustrate the advantages here. First, let's look at the repetitive nature of wake-up calls. Suppose you are staying at the hotel all week, and every day you want to wake up at the same time to get yourself to work. You could call the front desk every night and ask for a wake-up call some number of hours and minutes in the future and then fall immediately asleep. This approach is the equivalent to our sleep() method. But wouldn't it be more convenient to call the front desk once when you arrive and ask for a regular wake-up call at some specified time every morning that week?

But here's an even better reason for using timers instead of sleep(): parallel processing. In the original hotel wake-up call scenario, we asked for a wake-up call and then went straight to sleep. How often does this really happen? Isn't it more likely that we would make this request during the evening, and then we would watch some TV, work a little, toss and turn, read the phone book, make crank calls, and generally do whatever it is we do when we can't sleep in our awful little hotel room?

The sleep() approach does not work as a general solution. We cannot necessarily go to sleep right after we schedule our wake-up call. There's just too much to do in life. What we really need is a pending wake-up call request while we go about our regular business, hopefully falling asleep sometime between when we made the request and when the phone rings. This is what timers are for. We put in the request and the system logs that request. Then we go ahead and do whatever else we need to do, knowing that the wake-up call will occur at the right time, regardless of what we do in the meantime.

Timers exist to help you perform repetitive operations at regular time intervals in a way that allows other work to happen asynchronously. Imagine a text-insertion caret that wants to blink once per second. Now imagine if the GUI thread tried to implement this through the sleep() call. It could do so—but it could not do anything else because it would be sleeping in between the last blink and the next one. Instead, it should use a timer to request a callback once per second. It can then do whatever else it needs to do to service the overall user interface, such as processing user events and drawing other GUI components. Every second, the GUI thread will receive a call to its timer callback method that tells it that a second has elapsed, and it can make the cursor flash as appropriate.

Timers are fairly simple objects with just a few parameters driving them, the most important of which are the frequency with which the wake-up call will occur and the method that will be called with the wake-up message.

Let's see how timers are implemented in the Java platform.

java.util.Timer

java.util.Timer creates a separate Thread that schedules TimerTasks that you schedule with Timer. Each TimerTask is a Runnable object whose run() method is called by Timer according to the frequency you specify when you schedule the task. You can schedule tasks to occur either at fixed-rate or fixed-delay intervals. Fixed-rate tasks occur at an overall rate that is consistent, say 30 times per second, although the delay between any particular occurrences may vary from that average. For example, if one task takes longer to complete than the delay requested, subsequent delays may be shorter than the requested delay until the timer catches up. Fixed-delay tasks occur with regular frequency, and each task occurs close to the specified delay after the previous begins. If any particular task takes longer to complete than the delay requested, all subsequent events are shifted by that delay, because the system tries to issue callbacks only at fixed delays from previous requests and does not compensate for any hiccups during processing.

Example: UtilTimerDemo

Let's look at an example to see how this timer works. This example is found on the book's Web site in the project UtilTimerDemo. In this demo, we run an animation that calls back into our code every 100 ms (DELAY) for a total duration of a half second (DURATION). Just to make the example slightly more interesting, we add a PROCESSING_TIME constant that is incurred while processing each callback to see how it affects the timings. Also, we add an INITIAL_PROCESSING_TIME of twice the normal timer delay, which is incurred only the first time we are called.

```
private static final long DELAY = 100;
private static final long DURATION = 5 * DELAY;
private static final long PROCESSING_TIME = 30;
private static final long INITIAL_PROCESSING_TIME = 2 * DELAY;
```

We set up the Timer to schedule a TimerTask, an abstract class that is extended by our class. We want to compare the fixed-delay to the fixed-rate approach, so we create and run two different timers in our main() method, one at a time. First, we create and start the fixed delay timer:

```
timer = new Timer();
startTime = prevTime = System.currentTimeMillis();
timer.schedule(new UtilTimerDemo(), DELAY, DELAY);
```

The timer is scheduled with an instance of UtilTimerDemo, which extends TimerTask and overrides the run() method, and with DELAY for both the initial delay before the first event and for subsequent delays between events.

Next, we sleep for some amount of time to allow the first timer to complete:

```
try {
  Thread.sleep(DURATION * 2);
} catch (Exception e) {}
```

Next, we create our fixed-rate timer. This is exactly like the other timer, except that we call the scheduleAtFixedRate() method instead of schedule().

```
timer = new Timer();
startTime = prevTime = System.currentTimeMillis();
timer.scheduleAtFixedRate(new UtilTimerDemo(),
                          DELAY, DELAY);
```

Finally, we implement the run() method of our class, which is abstract in TimerTask. This method receives the timing events. In this method, we calculate the elapsed time since the last call to run() and the total time since this timer began. We stop the animation if totalTime exceeds the DURATION. We then sleep for either INITIAL_PROCESSING_TIME, the first time through, or PROCESSING_TIME milliseconds to simulate performing real work in this routine:

```
public void run() {
  long nowTime = System.currentTimeMillis();
  long elapsedTime = nowTime - prevTime;
  long totalTime = nowTime - startTime;
  if (totalTime > DURATION) {
    timer.cancel();
  }
  prevTime = nowTime;
  try {
    if (firstTime) {
      Thread.sleep(INITIAL_PROCESSING_TIME);
      firstTime = false;
    } else {
      Thread.sleep(PROCESSING_TIME);
    }
  } catch (Exception e) {}
}
```

The results from a sample run of this program are shown here:

```
Fixed Delay Times
Elapsed time = 101
Elapsed time = 200
Elapsed time = 100
Elapsed time = 100

Fixed Rate Times
Elapsed time = 102
Elapsed time = 200
Elapsed time = 36
Elapsed time = 63
Elapsed time = 100
```

These results show how much time passed since the previous call into our `run()` method. Note first that the `INITIAL_PROCESSING_TIME` delay incurred in the first time through the `run()` method causes a hiccup in the results, but in different ways for each timers. For the fixed-delay timer, the subsequent events occur at the regular `DELAY` intervals, as if nothing had happened. The fixed-rate timer, however, compensates for that one huge delay by speeding up the next couple of events until the average time equals the specified `DELAY`.

Note, also, that the normal `PROCESSING_TIME` delay spent sleeping in `run()` causes no problems for either timer. The delay between events is based on when the `run()` method is called, not how long the method took to process work. As long as the time spent in `run()` does not exceed the interevent delay, as it does in the case of the first time through our `run()` method, subsequent events occur regularly.

---

javax.swing.Timer

`Timer` was such a great name for a class implementing timing functionality that it was also used for the Swing class `javax.swing.Timer`.[7] This `Timer`'s functionality is similar to that of `java.util.Timer`, with a few important distinctions:

Callbacks on Swing Event Thread

This difference is probably the most important distinction between these two `Timer` classes, especially for Swing programmers.

---

7. And the class `javax.management.Timer`. Clearly, this is a class name whose time has come.

Tip: All callbacks for `javax.swing.Timer` occur on the Event Dispatch Thread (EDT).

This timer's integration with the EDT is particularly useful for Swing applications because GUI operations, such as blinking a cursor or pulsating a button, must happen on the EDT. Rather than receiving callbacks on an arbitrary thread and having to forward GUI-related operations to the EDT, applications using the Swing timer can simply perform the GUI operations directly in the callback method, knowing that they are on the proper thread already. For more information about thread management issues with these timers, see Chapter 2.

Fixed-Delay and Fixed-Rate Approaches

By default, the Swing timer uses the fixed-delay approach in which each callback occurs after a specified delay after the previous callback. Actually, it's a bit more involved than this. The thread that posts the events posts them at the specified delay regardless of what else is happening in the system or how long any particular event takes to process.

However, by default, the Swing timer *coalesces* timing events, much like it does with repaint requests as discussed in earlier chapters, so that some timing events may get thrown away if they are not serviced fast enough. This ends up having slightly different characteristics than the fixed-delay behavior of `java.util.Timer`. You can change this behavior by calling `setCoalesce(false)`, which would result in behavior similar to `java.util.Timer` running with fixed-rate delays: The system would catch up after hiccups because there would be additional pending requests on the queue that would get serviced sooner than the requested delay. We see both approaches illustrated in the next example.

Single Timer Thread

There is no danger of spawning arbitrary numbers of timing threads, since there is exactly one thread that creates all timer events.

Actions, Not Tasks

Instead of creating a `TimerTask` to receive the callbacks, Swing timer clients provide an `ActionListener` to the timer. This listener's `actionPerformed()` method is called for each timing event.

Example: SwingTimerDemo

The SwingTimerDemo application on the book's Web site shows how to use the Swing timer. This demo looks and performs much like UtilTimerDemo. In fact, most of the code is exactly the same. The only real differences are the following:

- SwingTimerDemo uses actionPerformed() instead of run() to receive the timing callbacks.

- SwingTimerDemo creates a javax.swing.Timer() with an ActionListener object, which is an instance of SwingTimerDemo() itself, instead of the TimerTask that java.util.Timer requires.

- The timer is started with timer.start() instead of the schedule() method of java.util.Timer.

The variables used are exactly the same as in UtilTimerDemo:

```
private static final int DELAY = 100;
private static final int DURATION = 5 * DELAY;
private static final int PROCESSING_TIME = 30;
```

Once again, we create and run two separate timers to show the difference in behavior due to coalescing. Here is the first timer:

```
// Run a default fixed-delay timer
timer = new Timer(DELAY, new SwingTimerDemo());
startTime = prevTime = System.currentTimeMillis();
timer.start();
```

This setup is similar to that of UtilTimerDemo, although there are a couple of important differences. First of all, the call to create the timer is different from that for java.util.Timer. This timer constructor takes the inter-callback delay and the ActionListener as arguments. In java.util.Timer, these parameters are passed into the schedule() method instead. Also, the timer is started differently here than in UtilTimerDemo. A Swing timer must be started manually by calling start(), whereas a java.util.Timer is started implicitly through scheduling the TimerTask object.

After sleeping for some time to let the first timer finish, the same as we did in UtilTimerDemo, we create and run a fixed-rate timer:

```
// Run a timer with no coalescing to get fixed-rate behavior
timer = new Timer(DELAY, new SwingTimerDemo());
startTime = prevTime = System.currentTimeMillis();
```

```
timer.setCoalesce(false);
timer.start();
```

This code is the same as the previous code except for the added call to setCoalesce(false), which tells the timer to post and handle all timing events and not to combine any duplicate requests that might occur.

The actionPerformed() method is nearly the same as UtilTimerDemo's run() method, although this time we stop our timer with a call to stop() instead of the cancel() method of java.util.Timer.

```
public void actionPerformed(ActionEvent ae) {
   long nowTime = System.currentTimeMillis();
   long elapsedTime = nowTime - prevTime;
   long totalTime = nowTime - startTime;
   System.out.println("Elapsed time - " + elapsedTime);
   if (totalTime > DURATION) {
     timer.stop();
   }
   prevTime = nowTime;
   try {
     if (firstTime) {
       Thread.sleep(INITIAL_PROCESSING_TIME);
       firstTime = false;
     } else {
       Thread.sleep(PROCESSING_TIME);
     }
   } catch (Exception e) {}
}
```

For comparison to the earlier UtilTimerDemo, here is the output from SwingTimerDemo:

```
Fixed Delay Times
Elapsed time = 105
Elapsed time = 299
Elapsed time = 101

Fixed Rate Times
Elapsed time = 102
Elapsed time = 201
Elapsed time = 31
Elapsed time = 70
Elapsed time = 101
```

Note that the results from the fixed-delay approach are slightly different from results for UtilTimerDemo. Coalescing events is not the same as simply issuing the next event at a set time after the previous event. But the results for fixed-rate are very similar to what we saw before. Removing the coalescing behavior causes the same catch-up behavior as the fixed-rate approach for `java.util.Timer`.

As you can see, using the Swing timer is quite similar to using the `java.util.Timer` object. The Swing timer tends to be easier to deal with in general for Swing applications. The lack of an extra `TimerTask` object simplifies programming the timer, and receiving the timing events on the EDT simplifies GUI-related operations.

Tip: `javax.swing.Timer` is a better mechanism in general for Swing applications than `java.util.Timer`, particularly because of its EDT-friendly timing event processing.

Resolution

The amount of time between events of a timer is called the *resolution*. The resolution determines the frame rate of an animation. For example, if an animation has a resolution of 30 ms, then the animation will achieve performance of about 33 fps (1,000 milliseconds/30 ms/frame = 33.3 fps).

Note: A thorough discussion of frame rates, animation, and the human visual system is slightly beyond the scope of this book. But in general, animations that want to appear smooth to the user should aim for a ballpark frame rate of 20 to 30 fps or more. At around this speed or greater, the human eye stops seeing separate events and sees smooth motion instead. For example, movies in the theater typically play at 24 fps. Of course, some animations may use much higher frame rates to get even smoother motion. Video games, for example, run at the refresh rate of computer monitors, which ranges from 60 times per second to 70, 75, 85, or even higher. And some animations appear perfectly smooth at much lower frame rates, as we see later in some fading animation examples. But 20 to 30 fps tends to be a nice number to shoot for in general.

There are a couple of important application elements that can prevent us from achieving our desired frame rate:

- *Performance:* If the system is not capable of doing everything we are asking of it for each animation frame, then we will necessarily spend longer doing the work of each frame. We will end up getting a lower frame rate, since we necessarily render fewer frames per second.

- *Timer resolution:* In some situations, we may need a very high frame rate, which requires a very low resolution. Depending on the timing mechanism we use, the timer may be unable to deliver that resolution.

For the first situation, performance, the solution depends on your situation, but you have the following choices:

- Optimizing the performance of what you are attempting to do, using appropriate techniques including the numerous tips and approaches covered in this book.

- Trying to do less in each frame, such as offloading non-GUI processing onto different threads or lowering the frequency of some operations.

- Setting your expectations lower and being satisfied with a lower frame rate. Remember, the goal is to make the animation smooth to the user; there is no hard rule as to how fast it has to run, as long as it looks good.

Tip: This is one of my favorite maxims of computer graphics in general: It just has to look good. There has been much work done over the decades to get computer graphics techniques ever closer to reality, which has enabled the onslaught of all of the computer-animated films in recent years. We can model light reflection, object surfaces, object movement, and anthropomorphized cars much more realistically, but at the end of the day, it usually matters only whether it looks good enough, not how "correct" it is.[8]

Tip: If you are shooting for a frame rate of 90 fps because that's what your favorite gore-game achieves, ask yourself whether your application actually requires that animation rate. Perhaps your favorite game benefits from the faster rate because of all the quick and extreme changes happening in every frame. Does your GUI application have that same dynamic? Or will your users detect smooth movement at a much lower rate? Remember: The main requirement is that your application has to look good, not achieve some theoretical perfection.

Tip: It is also worth noting that computer displays have a maximum refresh rate typically between 60 and 85 times per second. For example, many LCD displays generally have a refresh rate of only 60 Hz. Any animation running faster than that rate is therefore wasting cycles by updating a screen that is being viewed by the user at a slower rate.

---

8. My kids and mother couldn't give a hoot about physically correct lighting calculations, but they appreciate when something looks good.

For the second situation, timer resolution, we must understand how the timer you use affects the callback frequency. On one hand, most of the timing mechanisms that we use in this book's examples are low-resolution timers, so there is a definite limit for resolution beyond which we cannot effectively go. This limit means that we also have a limit for achievable frame rate, which generally does not match the high frame rates used by 3D video games.

On the other hand, the animations we deal with generally do not need super-high frame rates. Frame rates of 30 fps, or even 60 fps, are quite achievable with the current, easy-to-use mechanisms, and we have found these frame rates to be quite effective for dynamic content in Filthy Rich Clients. There are ways to achieve higher resolution in timers, but we leave that discussion for another time, since we have what we need for now with the built-in mechanisms of Java.

Even though the timing mechanisms built into Java are sufficient for our purposes, it is important to understand the resolution of the timers that we use so that we can understand the implications they have on frame rates and on possible animation artifacts that we may otherwise see.

In general, the built-in timing mechanisms of Java use the low-resolution timer of each native platform, which means that the resolution of the Java timers is limited by the resolution of these native timers. It also means that the resolution is platform-dependent, since all platforms use different mechanisms that may not have the same resolution. Fortunately, all of the different platforms have timers that perform well enough for our situation. For our investigations here, we use Windows XP running on a laptop.[9]

Note: As proof of the unpredictability of timing resolution, I offer my laptop.[9] I originally wrote and ran all of these tests on this system and got very consistent results, represented by the tables of timings that follow. I ran these tests originally when I was running Windows XP. Now I have Windows Vista installed and get *completely* different results. For example, my `sleep()` resolution is slightly worse than what we see in this chapter, while my `wait()` resolution is far better than what I experienced before. The resolution for `currentTimeMillis()` has improved and seems quite close to that of `nanoTime()`. Also, the resolution of `wait()` as well as the Swing timer that depends on `wait()` have improved and are close to the resolution of `sleep()`. All of this goes to show that if you really want to understand the resolution on your system, you'll need to do some testing yourself. Or, perhaps this is a better approach: Satisfy yourself that the results are good enough for your needs and go think about something else instead.

---

9. For comparison purposes, or just for anyone who really likes to know these things, my laptop has a 2-GHz Intel Pentium M processor with 2 GB of RAM and an ATI Mobility Radeon X300 graphics processor.

We examine the resolution of the different timing mechanisms explored previously with sample code that demonstrates the results (and which you could use to do similar investigations).[10]

Resolution of System.currentTimeMillis() and System.nanoTime()

System.currentTimeMillis() is, on Windows, built upon a low-resolution timing mechanism and returns times according to this native timer. We have found that this particular timing mechanism contributes more to artifacts than do the timers discussed later, so it is useful to understand the implications of this resolution.

On the Windows XP system tested, we found that currentTimeMillis() has a resolution of about 16 ms. This means that currentTimeMillis() will return values that are correct only to 16 ms boundaries.

For example, suppose we are measuring an activity that takes exactly 5 ms. We may get measurement results similar to the following:

Real time elapsed	currentTimeMillis elapsed time
0	0
5	0
10	0
15	0
20	16
25	16
30	16
35	32

Note that the timing mechanism does not round to the nearest 16 ms value but rather acts like a floor function, since the underlying timer increments only to the next 16 ms level when it has passed it. System.nanoTime(), on the other hand, appears from experience to be correct to within about 2 to 3 ms on this same system.

Now, let's look at a sample application that we use for the measurements discussed here. The TimeResolution application on the book's Web site has several functions in it that correspond to the different topics we explore in this chapter.

---

10. If you are sitting around late at night with nothing to do and decide that you need to figure out the resolution on that old Linux system you have, feel free to perform your own thorough investigation.

In the `measureTimeFunctions()` method of our application, we sleep for "increment" milliseconds each iteration and measure the elapsed time by both `currentTimeMillis()` and `nanoTime()`. Each time, we print out the elapsed time according to our internal counter, the amount we have supposedly slept so far, and our two measurements.

```
void measureTimeFunctions(int increment, int max) {
  long startTime = System.currentTimeMillis();
  long startNanos = System.nanoTime();
  long elapsedTimeActual = 0;
  long elapsedTimeMeasured = 0;
  long elapsedNanosMeasured = 0;
  System.out.printf("sleep   currentTimeMillis   nanoTime\n");
  while (elapsedTimeActual < max) {
    try {
      Thread.sleep(increment);
    } catch (Exception e) {}
    long currentTime = System.currentTimeMillis();
    long currentNanos = System.nanoTime();
    elapsedTimeActual += increment;
    elapsedTimeMeasured = currentTime - startTime;
    elapsedNanosMeasured =
        (currentNanos - startNanos) / 1000000;
    System.out.printf(" %3d          %4d          %4d\n",
                    elapsedTimeActual, elapsedTimeMeasured,
                    elapsedNanosMeasured);
  }
}
```

Here are the results for a run with `increment` set to 5 and `max` set to 50:

sleep	currentTimeMillis	nanoTime
5	16	8
10	16	15
15	31	21
20	31	27
25	31	33
30	47	38
35	47	44
40	63	50
45	63	56
50	63	62

You can see here that `currentTimeMillis()` is incrementing its values by 15 to 16 ms. You can also see that `nanoTime()` is much closer to the theoretical sleep() time, but that it's also not dead-on. In fact, you can see that the difference between nanoTime() and sleep() grows as the total sleep time increases. Given this result, it appears that our sleeps of 5 ms may in fact be taking longer. It's time to measure sleep().

Sleeping Resolution

To get an accurate measurement for Thread.sleep(), we must discount any inaccuracies in the times we get. We can do this by simply sleeping for a longer time to reduce the significance of any inaccuracies. For example, sleeping for a second would make even the 16 ms resolution of currentTimeMillis() good enough, since the inaccuracy of any particular measurement would be at most 16/1000, or 1.6%. But it's more likely that sleep() inaccuracies, which we are trying to determine here, would occur at smaller sleep intervals, so sleeping for a longer time would be somewhat beside the point. The workaround is to sleep for small increments but to do it many times successively. Then we can compare the theoretical sleep time, the amount we slept each time multiplied by the number of times we slept, to the measured sleep time, using currentTimeMillis() or nanoTime().

Here is our simple sleep measurement function:

```
private void measureSleep() {
  System.out.printf("                                    " +
                    "measured\n");
  System.out.printf("sleep time   iterations   total time" +
                    "   per-sleep\n");
  for (int sleepTime = 0; sleepTime <= 20; ++sleepTime) {
    int iterations = (sleepTime == 0) ? 10000 :
        (1000 / sleepTime);
    long startTime = System.nanoTime();
    for (int i = 0; i < iterations; ++i) {
      try {
        Thread.sleep(sleepTime);
      } catch (Exception e) {
      }
    }
    long endTime = System.nanoTime();
    long totalTime = (endTime - startTime) / 1000000;
    float calculatedSleepTime = totalTime / (float)iterations;
    System.out.printf("   %2d          %5d          %4d" +
                      "          %5.2f\n", sleepTime, iterations,
                      totalTime, calculatedSleepTime);
  }
}
```

In this function, we use `nanoTime()` to get as close as possible to the real time, but tests using `currentTimeMillis()` showed similar results because the larger inaccuracies of `currentTimeMillis()` were marginalized, as explained earlier. We sleep for as many times as necessary to get an accurate measurement. In general, the test sleeps for about a second or so. The exception is with a `sleepTime` of 0, which is going to be so quick that we threw in an extra order of magnitude to get a better measurement.

We can see from the following table how the experiment worked out. The main columns to pay attention to are the leftmost, the amount of time we tried to sleep, and the rightmost, the actual amount of time we slept. In general, the results show that `sleep()` is mostly accurate, at least much more so than `currentTimeMillis()` in our previous tests, although reality diverges from theory by 1 to 2 ms in general. As with our `currentTimeMillis()` findings, this inaccuracy becomes less important the longer we sleep: An inaccuracy of .74 ms for a sleep time of 20 (3.7%) is less important that the inaccuracy of 1.01 ms for a sleep time of 1 (101%). We can also see that sleeping for 0 is almost like not sleeping at all; doing it 10,000 times took only 10 ms. This is great if you don't want to sleep much, but it could get you into the same CPU-pegging situation that we were trying to avoid by calling `sleep()` in the first place. On the other hand, `sleep()` is a handy way to hand over control to other threads if they need it, so if you're okay with handing control over briefly but you want it back very soon, `sleep(0)` can be a reasonable alternative.

| | | measured | |
sleep time	iterations	total time	per-sleep
0	10000	10	0.00
1	1000	2007	2.01
2	500	1533	3.07
3	333	1343	4.03
4	250	1247	4.99
5	200	1192	5.96
6	166	1309	7.89
7	142	1192	8.39
8	125	1116	8.93
9	111	1100	9.91
10	100	1160	11.60
11	90	1086	12.07
12	83	1075	12.95
13	76	1048	13.79
14	71	1051	14.80

sleep time	iterations	measured total time	per-sleep
15	66	1079	16.35
16	62	1118	18.03
17	58	1024	17.66
18	55	1030	18.73
19	52	1035	19.90
20	50	1037	20.74

We can run this same test with `Object.wait(timeout)`. We do not discuss this mechanism of sleeping because it is not one we would typically use in our cases of interest. `Thread.sleep()` is convenient and direct. `Object.wait()` is more useful for cases in which another thread may want to wake this one up. Typically, a thread will put itself to sleep with `Object.wait()`, and another will wake it up with `Object.notify()`.

Even though we have not discussed `wait()`, it is useful to examine its resolution issues here because some of the mechanisms on which we depend use `wait()` under the hood,[11] so those other mechanisms are limited by the underlying resolution of `wait()`.

We can use the same code as `measureSleep()` except for a few minor differences:

```java
private synchronized void measureWait() {
  System.out.printf("                                    " +
              "measured\n");
  System.out.printf("wait time    iterations    total time" +
              "    per-wait\n");
  for (int sleepTime = 1; sleepTime <= 20; ++sleepTime) {
    int iterations = (sleepTime == 0) ? 10000 :
        (1000 / sleepTime);
    long startTime = System.nanoTime();
    for (int i = 0; i < iterations; ++i) {
      try {
        wait(sleepTime);
      } catch (Exception e) {}
    }
    long endTime = System.nanoTime();
    long totalTime = (endTime - startTime) / 1000000;
    float calculatedSleepTime = totalTime / (float)iterations;
```

continued

---

11. In particular, `javax.swing.Timer` uses `wait()` internally.

```
System.out.printf("  %2d          %5d          %4d" +
              "           %5.2f\n", sleepTime, iterations,
                 totalTime, calculatedSleepTime);
    }
  }
```

The differences between this method and the previous `measureSleep()` method include the following:

synchronized method

The use of `synchronized` ensures that this object, on which we call `wait()`, holds the monitor when `wait()` is called.

for (int sleepTime = 1;...)

`wait(0)` is equivalent to waiting until some other thread wakes us up, which is different from `sleep(0)`, which is equivalent to waking up almost immediately if no other thread needs to run in the meantime. We opted to skip the measurement at 0 because of this difference, so we start from `sleepTime=1` instead of `sleepTime=0` in this version. All we are after is a rough idea of resolution at low wait times, so having results from 1 to 20 is sufficient.

wait(sleepTime)

Instead of calling `Thread.sleep(sleepTime)`, we call `Object.wait(sleepTime)`. The semantics of `wait()` are a bit different. For one thing, our thread can be woken up by means other than the timeout. But in this case, it should be functionally equivalent to using `Thread.sleep()`, since there is no external mechanism to wake up our thread, so we will wake up after the `sleepTime` amount has expired.

Here are the results from running the `measureWait()` test:

wait time	iterations	measured total time	per-wait
1	1000	15753	15.75
2	500	7806	15.61
3	333	5233	15.71
4	250	3905	15.62
5	200	3124	15.62
6	166	2592	15.61
7	142	2217	15.61
8	125	1952	15.62
9	111	1733	15.61

wait time	iterations	measured total time	per-wait
10	100	1561	15.61
11	90	1405	15.61
12	83	1297	15.63
13	76	1185	15.59
14	71	1108	15.61
15	66	1046	15.85
16	62	1934	31.19
17	58	1811	31.22
18	55	1717	31.22
19	52	1614	31.04
20	50	1561	31.22

As you can see, these results are significantly different from those of `sleep()`. In our `sleep()` test, we saw that it was possible to `sleep()` for roughly within a millisecond or so of the requested duration . But here, we seem to be waiting for increments of nearly 16 ms. Does this ring a bell? It should. It is the same resolution we saw earlier in our `currentTimeMillis()` testing. It looks like `wait()` on our test system is falling prey to the same low-resolution clock that is used for `currentTimeMillis()`, which should help explain the results of our next and final resolution test: `measureTimer()`.

Timer Resolution

To measure the Swing timer, we use code similar to that which we used for the other timing mechanisms, although the logic is split into two functions because of the callback nature of timers. In one function, `measureTimer()`, we set up the timer and start it, then wait around until the measurements on that timer are done. Note that we once again use the technique of measuring the timer over a longer period of time to eliminate inaccuracies in our measurement mechanisms. We do this for every value that we want to test the timer against. In this case, we iterate through timer delay values of 0 to 20 ms, similar to the `sleep()` and `wait()` tests. Here is our `measureTimer()` function:

```
public void measureTimer() {
  System.out.printf("                                    " +
                  "measured\n");
  System.out.printf("timer delay    iterations    total time" +
                "    per-delay\n");
```

continued

```
for (int sleepTime = 0; sleepTime <= 20; ++sleepTime) {
  iterations = (sleepTime == 0) ? 1000 :
      (1000 / sleepTime);
  timerIteration = 1;
  timer = new Timer(sleepTime, this);
  startTime = System.nanoTime();
  timer.start();
  while (timerIteration > 0) {
    try {
      Thread.sleep(1000);
    } catch (Exception e) {}
  }
}
}
```

The `actionPerformed()` method receives regular callbacks until we stop the timer, which is done after the number of times called exceeds the number of iterations we wanted to run. We then measure the total time between when we started the timer and when it finished, and then calculate the actual delay time per callback.

```
public void actionPerformed(ActionEvent ae) {
  if (++timerIteration > iterations) {
    timer.stop();
    timerIteration = 0;
    endTime = System.nanoTime();
    long totalTime = (endTime - startTime) / 1000000;
    float calculatedDelayTime = totalTime / (float)iterations;
    System.out.printf("  %2d        %5d        %4d" +
                "        %5.2f\n", sleepTime, iterations,
                totalTime, calculatedDelayTime);
  }
}
```

Here are the results for the `measureTimer()` test:

wait time	iterations	measured total time	per-wait
0	1000	15884	15.88
1	1000	15640	15.64
2	500	7826	15.65
3	333	5217	15.67
4	250	3906	15.62
5	200	3124	15.62

wait time	iterations	measured total time	per-wait
6	166	2608	15.71
7	142	2218	15.62
8	125	1951	15.61
9	111	1734	15.62
10	100	1562	15.62
11	90	1406	15.62
12	83	1296	15.61
13	76	1249	15.43
14	71	1109	15.62
15	66	1045	15.83
16	62	1546	24.94
17	58	1827	31.50
18	55	1717	31.22
19	52	1624	31.23
20	50	1562	31.24

These results should look familiar; they look just like our wait() test results above. No matter how long a delay we specify, we usually get an actual delay equal to the next greater increment of ~16 ms.

As eerily foreshadowed[12] in the section on wait(), the low resolution of wait() is affecting the resulting low resolution of our Swing timer. The way that timer events are scheduled uses wait(), so it's not surprising, then, that we would see the same resolution results from this related timer.

Resolution about Resolution

So where does this leave us? What impact does the inaccuracy of any given timing facility have on our code or our programming practices? Not much.

Note: In general, our animations will be running at rates that make inaccuracies in the timing mechanisms insignificant.

---

12. I'm trying hard to build a sense of suspense and tension into a section on timing resolution analysis. Is it working?

For example, if we want to run an animation at a reasonable rate of 30 fps, `nanoTime()`'s and `sleep()`'s abilities of coming within a couple of milliseconds of the true time should be more than sufficient, and even the lower-resolution Swing timer and `currentTimeMillis()` time measurement have a far lower error boundary than this rate.

However, it is important to understand the issue of resolution so that if you are in a situation in which you need to run faster, to get accurate timing for your current frame rate, or to simply understand some of the timing results you are seeing, you can understand the limitations and workings of the timing mechanisms available to you. For example:

- Do not call `currentTimeMillis()` around a fast operation and automatically trust the result when it tells you that it took either 0 or 16 ms. Find a better way to measure the operation to make sure you are getting a reliable answer.

- Do not try to use the Swing timer for an animation that must run at greater than 60 fps[13] because, depending on your runtime platform, the timer may simply not call back into your code often enough to match that frame rate.

- If high, consistent frame rates are critical to your application, make sure you test the resolution of the timing facilities on which you rely for your target platforms. The examples we presented are specific to our Windows XP test system and do not reflect the behavior of these Java facilities on other platforms.[14]

The demo code shown previously is available on the book's Web site in the application `TimeResolution`. If you want to run tests on your target platform, this might be a good tool with which to start.

Animating Your Swing Application

Now that we have seen how to use the timing facilities in Java, we can discuss how to animate your Swing application. Beyond the timing facilities, there are two things to understand in animating Swing applications: animating graphics in general and animating GUIs in particular.

---

13. But, again, you do not need to use frame rates greater than this for Filthy Rich Clients. Games? Sure. GUI animations? More than 60 fps is overkill.

14. Such as the same test system running Windows Vista. It pays to test your code to see what's really going on.

Animated Graphics

We saw in Chapter 2 how to draw graphics into a Swing component. Animating graphics in a component uses the same techniques except that the graphics you draw vary over time, using timing facilities like the ones discussed in this chapter.

Recall our discussion of the exciting `OvalComponent` demo in Chapter 2. In this demo, we created a custom Swing component in which the following `paintComponent()` method rendered a gray oval:

```
public void paintComponent(Graphics g) {
  g.setColor(getBackground());
  g.fillRect(0, 0, getWidth(), getHeight());
  g.setColor(Color.GRAY);
  g.fillOval(0, 0, getWidth(), getHeight());
}
```

Example: AnimatedGraphics

What if we wanted to have the color of the oval change over time, between gray and black? We did this in the `AnimatedGraphics` demo on the book's Web site. The resulting code for `paintComponent()` looks much like the code above except that the color is variable, determined by a calculation performed at intervals of the animation. Here, the only change is the second call to `setColor()`, which uses the variable `currentColor` instead of the earlier hard-coded `GRAY` color:

```
public void paintComponent(Graphics g) {
  g.setColor(getBackground());
  g.fillRect(0, 0, getWidth(), getHeight());
  g.setColor(currentColor);
  g.fillOval(0, 0, getWidth(), getHeight());
}
```

First, we declare some variables that will be useful during the animation:

```
Color startColor = Color.GRAY;  // where we start
Color endColor = Color.BLACK;   // where we end
Color currentColor = startColor;
int animationDuration = 2000;   // animation will take 2 seconds
long animStartTime;             // start time for each animation
```

In order to vary the `currentColor` value, we create and start an animation in the constructor, using the Swing timer discussed earlier in this chapter. We store the time that we are starting in animStartTime so that we can determine how long we've run at any future point in time. We also set an initial delay just to give Swing a chance to get everything set up before we start running the animation.[15]

```
public AnimatedGraphics() {
  Timer timer = new Timer(30, this);
  // initial delay while window gets set up
  timer.setInitialDelay(1000);
  animStartTime = 1000 + System.nanoTime() / 1000000;
  timer.start();
}
```

Finally, we vary the value of currentColor in our timer callback method according to how much time has elapsed in our 2-second animation. Our color calculation is a simple linear interpolation between the start and end colors, according to the fraction of the animationDuration that has elapsed.

```
public void actionPerformed(ActionEvent ae) {
  // vary color between start and end values using
  // interpolation fraction below
  long currentTime = System.nanoTime() / 1000000;
  long totalTime = currentTime - animStartTime;
  if (totalTime > animationDuration) {
    animStartTime = currentTime;
  }
  float fraction = (float)totalTime / animationDuration;
  fraction = Math.min(1.0f, fraction);
  int red = (int)(fraction * endColor.getRed() +
      (1 - fraction) * startColor.getRed());
  int green = (int)(fraction * endColor.getGreen() +
      (1 - fraction) * startColor.getGreen());
  int blue = (int)(fraction * endColor.getBlue() +
      (1 - fraction) * startColor.getBlue());
  currentColor = new Color(red, green, blue);
  repaint();
}
```

Note that the repaint() call at the end of this method simply tells Swing to re-render the component. When Swing does so, our paintComponent() method is called and the currentColor that we calculated here is used when the oval is redrawn.

---

15. Waiting for Swing to get set up is just a workaround for this micro-demo. A typical Swing application would not need to wait because the Swing window would already be up and ready to go by the time any particular animation was started.

Admittedly, this is a simple example, but in its essence, animating graphics *is* a simple operation. We combine our knowledge of how to draw graphics into a Swing component and our knowledge of how to schedule timers and calculate in-between values to vary the rendering over time to create whatever graphics animation we desire. This example happens to use simple Java 2D graphics primitives, but it could just as easily have used more involved graphics like images, translucency, gradients, and complex shapes. The example could also have used more complex timing models. But more complex animations would all be based on the same simple principle of varying properties over time and rendering the scene with those varying properties.

Animated GUIs

Now that we know how to animate graphics rendering, let's learn how to animate GUI elements, bringing us closer to the effects that we use in Filthy Rich Clients. Recall in our discussion of the `TranslucentButton` demo in Chapter 2 that we created a custom button as follows:

```
public class TranslucentButton extends JButton {
  public TranslucentButton(String label) {
    super(label);
    setOpaque(false);
  }

  public void paint(Graphics g) {
    // Create an image for the button graphics if necessary
    if (buttonImage == null ||
        buttonImage.getWidth() != getWidth() ||
        buttonImage.getHeight() != getHeight()) {
      buttonImage = (BufferedImage)createImage(
          getWidth(), getHeight());
    }
    Graphics gButton = buttonImage.getGraphics();
    gButton.setClip(g.getClip());

    // Have the superclass render the button for us
    super.paint(gButton);

    // Make the graphics object sent to this
    // paint() method translucent
    Graphics2D g2d  = (Graphics2D)g;
    AlphaComposite newComposite = AlphaComposite.getInstance(
        AlphaComposite.SRC_OVER, .5f);
    g2d.setComposite(newComposite);
```

continued

```
    // Copy the button's image to the destination
    // graphics, translucently
    g2d.drawImage(buttonImage, 0, 0, null);
  }
}
```

In this case, we override `paint()` to render the button with a translucent effect, which we get by calling the superclass to paint the standard button to an image, altering the composite on the `Graphics` object and drawing the image to the now-translucent `Graphics` object.

What if we wanted to alter the translucency of the button over time? You will see later how we use very similar approaches to create dynamic effects, such as glowing, pulsing, or cross-fading between different states. These effects all build on approaches similar to the simple one we are about to demonstrate.

Example: FadingButton

The following example is available on the book's Web site in the `FadingButton` project. Just like our previous example with animated graphics, animating the button's translucency is as easy as altering the alpha value programmatically on the basis of a value we calculate during the animation. First of all, we make one small change to the `paint()` method:

```
AlphaComposite newComposite = AlphaComposite.getInstance(
    AlphaComposite.SRC_OVER, alpha);
```

As you can see, the only change here is that we use the calculated value alpha value instead of the previous hard-coded value `.5f`.

As in the previous animated graphics example, we set up some instance variables to help track our animation values:

```
float alpha = 1.0f;              // current opacity of button
Timer timer;                     // for later start/stop actions
int animationDuration = 2000;    // animation will take 2 seconds
long animStartTime;              // start time for each animation
```

We create the timer that runs the animation in our constructor, as in the previous demo. This time, however, we do not start the animation in the constructor. Since we're animating a button, let's use the button as a trigger to start and stop the animation. We do this by adding the button as an `ActionListener` and starting the timer in the `actionPerformed()` method.

```
public FadingButton(String label) {
   super(label);
   setOpaque(false);
   timer = new Timer(30, this);
   addActionListener(this);
}
```

Because we are listening to the button for actions, or mouse clicks, and listening to the timer for actions, or timing events, as well, there are two distinct parts of our actionPerformed() method. The first part is executed when there is a button click:

```
public void actionPerformed(ActionEvent ae) {
   if (ae.getSource().equals(this)) {
     // button click
     if (!timer.isRunning()) {
       animStartTime = System.nanoTime() / 1000000;
       this.setText("Stop Animation");
       timer.start();
     } else {
       timer.stop();
       this.setText("Start Animation");
       // reset alpha to opaque
       alpha = 1.0f;
     }
   } else {
     // second part, shown later...
   }
}
```

This code checks whether the animation is currently running. If not, it sets the current animStartTime, changes the button label, and starts the animation. If the animation is already running, it stops the animation, changes the button label, and resets our alpha variable to the default opaque value. Note that resetting the value to opaque is not actually necessary but is just a behavior we chose for this demo.

The second part of our actionPerformed() method is intended for handling the animation. This code is called when the timer events occur:

```
public void actionPerformed(ActionEvent ae) {
   if (ae.getSource().equals(this)) {
     // first part, shown earlier...
   } else {
     // timer event
     long currentTime = System.nanoTime() / 1000000;
```

continued

```
    long totalTime = currentTime - animStartTime;
    if (totalTime > animationDuration) {
      animStartTime = currentTime;
    }
    float fraction = (float)totalTime / animationDuration;
    fraction = Math.min(1.0f, fraction);
    // This calculation will cause alpha to go from
    // 1 to 0 and back to 1 as the fraction goes from 0 to 1
    alpha = Math.abs(1 - (2 * fraction));
    repaint();
  }
}
```

This code calculates the current fraction elapsed in our animation and sets the alpha value on the basis of this fraction. In this case, we want alpha to vary from 1 to 0 and back to 1 as the fraction goes from 0 to 1. After we have our new alpha value, we force a repaint(), which causes Swing to paint our button. Then, in our custom paint() method, we set the Composite according to the new alpha value and render the button appropriately. The resulting fading button is shown in Figure 12-4.

Figure 12-4   FadingButton demo: Checkerboard pattern can be seen through our translucent component.

Example: MovingButton

Now let's examine a slightly different GUI animation in which the button moves instead of fading. This new application is much like the previous FadingButton application except that clicking on the button causes it to animate down and back up by some amount over the same animation time of 2 seconds. This demo is also available on the book's Web site, under the project name MovingButton.

We start with the same code used earlier and make small changes to alter the translation of the Graphics object. First, here is the paint() method that enables us to move the button:

```
public void paint(Graphics g) {
  g.translate(0, translateY);
  super.paint(g);
}
```

This animation technique is simpler than the previous translucency. There is no need for an image to hold the intermediate results, no need to create a Composite object for achieving the translucency effect, and no need to copy the image to the screen—all we need to do is reposition the location where the Graphics object renders.

The actionPerformed() callback that calculates the translation is also relatively simple. The first part is mostly the same as in the previous FadingButton example except we reset the translation factor instead of the alpha factor when the animation is stopped:

```
public void actionPerformed(ActionEvent ae) {
  if (ae.getSource().equals(this)) {
    if (!timer.isRunning()) {
      animStartTime = System.nanoTime() / 1000000;
      this.setText("Stop Animation");
      timer.start();
    } else {
      timer.stop();
      this.setText("Start Animation");
      // reset translation to 0
      translateY = 0;
    }
```

The second part is similar to our translucency example except that we vary the translateY value over time instead of the alpha value:

```
    } else {
      long currentTime = System.nanoTime() / 1000000;
      long totalTime = currentTime - animStartTime;
      if (totalTime > animationDuration) {
        animStartTime = currentTime;
      }
```

continued

```
    float fraction = (float)totalTime / animationDuration;
    fraction = Math.min(1.0f, fraction);
    // translateY will go from 0 to MAX_Y and back to 0
    // as the fraction goes from 0 to 1
    if (fraction < .5f) {
      translateY = (int)(MAX_Y * (2 * fraction));
    } else {
      translateY = (int)(MAX_Y * (2 * (1 - fraction)));
    }
    repaint();
  }
}
```

But there is a disturbing rendering artifact that we see in the demo. The button is clipped to the original button area in the window, no matter where we reposition the button with our translation operation. For example, Figure 12-5 shows a screenshot of the demo in its starting position, with the button drawn in its original location.

Figure 12-6 shows a screenshot of the demo during the animation: The button has moved slightly down from the original location and has its bottom cut off by the clip area of the original button.

What's going on here? Why isn't our drawing area matching the area of the object we are drawing?

Tip: The problem shown in Figure 12-5 and Figure 12-6 for the MovingButton application is that there is a difference between an object being *drawn* in a different location and actually being *located* in a different location. In this application, we are not actually changing the location of the Swing button but merely the location of where that button is rendered.

Figure 12-5 MovingButton demo, before the animation starts.

Figure 12-6 `MovingButton` artifact: The translated button is clipped to the original button display area.

Swing tells us to draw a component whose bounds are known to Swing, and it sets up the clip area appropriately. In this case, it sets up the clip to correspond to the known location of the button. This clip area is different from the location in which we want to draw the animating button. How we decide to render our button inside that area is completely up to us—as long as we don't expect any rendering to happen outside of that area.

This problem did not come up in the previous `FadingButton` animation example because the effect of translucency did not change the location of the button but merely the appearance of the button in its normal location.

We clearly need a different approach for effects that alter the location of an object. There are several ways of attacking the problem, including the following:

Work at the `Container` Level

So far, we have been trying to alter rendering at the component level, where the component is restricted to the area set aside by the container. Instead, we could alter the rendering of the `Container`, the parent in which a component resides.

Change the Actual Position of a Component

Instead of modifying the rendering of a component, it is possible to move the component itself, and Swing will draw it in the correct place. This approach is complicated by `LayoutManagers`, since a non-null `LayoutManager` will want to position the component and may ignore attempts to move the component within the layout. There are ways to work around this constraint, such as using a null LayoutManager to begin with[16] or using a null LayoutManager temporarily during an animation. In any case, this solution tends to be more complex than we want to deal with for simple animations like the one here.

Use the GlassPane

One way to get the effect of moving a component absolutely without having to live within the constraints of the current LayoutManager is to use the GlassPane layer to render the component during the animation. This is the approach taken by some of the effects covered later in the book, such as those discussed in Chapter 18, "Animated Transitions."

For the purposes of keeping this example simple and showing how to solve the problem in a straightforward way, we use the first approach and work at the Container level.

Example: MovingButtonContainer

Our previous examples have subclassed the actual component of interest, in this case a JButton. In our subclass, we overrode paint() to alter the Graphics used to render the component.

Our new approach in the demo MovingButtonContainer, which resides on the book's Web site does something very similar, but instead of subclassing the component we want to move, we subclass the Container that our button lives within and do a similar override of paint() in the Container's class.

In this case, most of the code that we showed earlier is exactly the same. The only difference is the class in which that code is implemented. For example, our actionPerformed() method is exactly the same. It still listens for clicks on the button and calculates the translationY factor according to how long the animation has been running.

The button here is no longer a custom class but merely a standard JButton that we add to our new custom JComponent subclass. The paint() method is also quite similar; we need only alter the translation of the Graphics object and then

---

16. Using a null LayoutManager is not a great recommendation in general. LayoutManagers are quite useful, and it would be a shame to throw away their power just for this component-movement ability.

defer to the superclass to render our component. But in this case, that `paint()` method is in the `Container` subclass instead of in the `JButton` subclass.

```
public void paint(Graphics g) {
    g.translate(0, translateY);
    super.paint(g);
}
```

The call to the superclass to paint this component is now rendering the entire container. In this case, it will render the children of the container as well, including the button, and in the process of doing so it will draw the button in the translated position.

There are a few interesting items to note here in order to understand how things work:

Events

Clicks on the button are still received in the original location of the button, no matter where the button is actually being drawn. This is another example of the difference between where the button is *drawn* and where the button is physically *located*. As far as Swing is concerned, that button still resides where it always has, in its original, untranslated location. Any transformations performed on the `Graphics` object of the button or the container are irrelevant to where the button is located. Therefore, any button events will still occur through that original location. There are a couple of workarounds for this situation that are worth noting:

- *Disable:* We could disable clicks during an animation. Indeed, this seems like a reasonable idea in many situations.[17] And it's at least better than allowing clicks in the wrong area.
- *Transform:* We could transform input events just as we transform rendering so that clicks will be interpreted correctly based on the current rendering.

---

17. Romain and I went back and forth on this for entirely too many e-mails. As an engineer, it seems odd that you would not want to receive clicks on a GUI object at its visible location, no matter what was happening on the screen. But Romain pointed out that this brings up complicated user-experience issues. For example, if a button turns transparent, do you actually want the user to be able to click on this invisible object? Or if objects are moving around during an animation, do you want your user to be able to easily click on the wrong object? There is a strong usability argument for simply ignoring clicks entirely during animations, especially the kinds of animated transitions that we see later in chapters 17 and 18.

We do not go into detail here, but anyone interested in this approach should check out Alexander Potochkin's experimental JXTransformer project[18] in which he shows how to arbitrarily transform Swing transform components and their events.

Children

The translation that we apply in our container's paint() method will be applied to *all* children of this container. In this simple application, that's fine; the button is the only child we are drawing. But in a more complicated container, we would need to take a different approach unless we wanted to translate the rendering of all components in the container.

setOpaque(false)

We still need to set the opaque property to false for the button, just as we did in the FadingButton example. This is perhaps not obvious,[19] but it makes sense when you think about it. Comment out the call to button.setOpaque(false) in the demo code. Go ahead, I'll wait. . . . Now, run the application and move the mouse over the original area of the button—can you see a flicker of the original button while the animating button is being rendered elsewhere?

Tip: This artifact results from Swing performing an optimized rendering of the button when it thinks that it is completely opaque. When Swing updates the button for the mouseover state, it doesn't bother redrawing anything behind the button, including our container, because it knows that the button is opaque.

Why render everything behind the button when all it needs to do is update the rendering for the button itself to reflect that the button is in mouseover state? But in this case, we need to have the parent container perform a repaint in order to get the translation set correctly for our button rendering, so we must

---

18. http://weblogs.java.net/blog/alexfromsun/archive/2006/07/jxtransformer_t.html.

19. In fact, it was not obvious to me when I wrote the demo to go along with this section. I usually use setOpaque(false) in cases of translucent components or components with transparent regions (such as rounded corners). The idea of a nonopaque component that's completely opaque didn't occur to me until I saw the rendering artifacts and divined the optimization that Swing was using on its assumption of an opaque component.

somehow force Swing to re-render the container itself. This parent rendering is requested by telling Swing that the button is not opaque. If the button is set to be nonopaque, then any time Swing wants to draw the button, it will force a repaint of the contents behind the button. This repaint on the container will call our `paint()` routine, which will make things look correct.

Force `repaint()` When Done

Our previous example did not have to force a `repaint()` when the animation finished; we had just changed the text of the button, which forced the label region to repaint itself automatically. But in this case, changing the text of the button will force an update only of the button's physical area, *not the area where we may be drawing the button.* The effect that you get without the repaint is that the last animated position of the button may be left unerased in the window while the new, reset position of the button is drawn in the original location, as seen in Figure 12-7.

Figure 12-7   Artifact: The final animation rendering is not erased without a final call to `repaint()`.

The fix is to simply call `repaint()` after we call `timer.stop()` to ensure that we update our container appropriately.

With all of these fixes in the code for the various artifacts, we get what we originally wanted, a moving button, as shown in Figure 12-8.

Figure 12-8 Moving button, working as desired.

Summary

Animation is not hard to understand, and with the right approaches, timing utilities, and use of Swing and Java 2D, it is possible to perform very easy animations of graphical and GUI applications. In later chapters, we see how to expand on these simple animation ideas to create more complex animations and truly Filthy Rich Clients.

13

Smooth Moves

THIS chapter covers techniques that can help you create smooth, realistic, and effective animations. We discuss some of the artifacts that contribute to animations being choppy and some of the underlying causes of those artifacts. We talk about solutions to the issues as we go, and you can see some of the problems and solutions in the demo application called SmoothMoves, available on the book's Web site.

Background: Why Does My Animation Look Bad?

I was working on some animation code recently and ran into some artifacts that made the animation look choppy. In this particular example, there was an animation that faded a large scene in and out, and there was another animation that moved a small image in the view. The fade looked great, but the motion animation stuttered. The difference in visual quality between these animations seemed particularly odd to me, since the fade happened over the entire screen, whereas the moving animation occupied only a small portion of the screen.

It seemed obvious to me that the fading animation must have a higher frame rate than the motion animation, which must have been hitting some performance bottleneck. Some simple timing code in both animation loops contradicted this assumption. Strangely, I found that the fade was happening at a rate of about 10 frames per second (fps). As we discussed in Chapter 12, "Animation Fundamentals," smooth animations are typically 20 to 30 fps or more, so this rate seemed a bit on the slow side. Stranger still, I found that the motion animation was getting about 15 to 20 fps, a rate faster than the visually smoother fading animation.

So here was the quandary: Why did the large fading animation with a lower frame rate look better than the moving animation with the higher frame rate?

Then it dawned on me that I had discovered another example of *perceived performance*.

Tip: Perceived performance comes up often in the GUI application world, where the true performance of an application is often not as important as how fast the user thinks it is. This is why, for example, you should run your long, nongraphical operations on a separate thread from the GUI thread, so that if your application has to go out and query the database for several seconds, at least the GUI is not frozen while it waits for that action to finish. Make the application GUI snappy, and the user will be happier with the performance of the application.

In this case, I perceived the fading animation to be faster than the moving animation simply because it looked smoother. After this realization, I figured that it was time to investigate the factors that could affect the smoothness of an animation. What makes an animation appear choppy? And what can we do to reduce or eliminate choppiness?

What Makes Animations Choppy, and How to Smooth Them Out

Various elements contribute to choppy animations, some of which were factors in my application but all of which are worth considering whenever you develop animation code.

The demo application SmoothMoves, found on the book's Web site, demonstrates some of the problems and solutions that we discuss in this chapter. The application shows two animations: The animation on the left fades an object in and out, and the animation on the right moves a similar object back and forth. We can see the demo in action in Figure 13-1. The animations are run at the same frame rate, but the difference in choppiness between these animations is obvious when you run the application.

Many of the problems and solutions we discuss are implemented as options in the demo, which you can toggle with various keys while the demo is running. For each problem that can be manipulated with the demo, there is a "Demo"

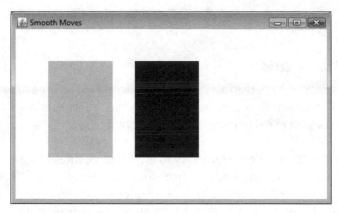

Figure 13-1 SmoothMoves demo: The rectangle on the left fades in and out while the rectangle on the right move back and forth.

section in this chapter that describes how to enable a potential solution in the application.

We can break down the choppiness factors into three main categories: timing, color, and vertical retrace.

Timing Is (Nearly) Everything

In general, you want your animations to be speedy. I don't mean that they should zip across the screen as fast as possible (you have to give the player the chance to actually hit the alien spaceship, don't you?), but rather that the animations should move quickly in small increments. There are various elements related to the speed at which an animation can run: raw performance, frame rate, consistency, realistic timing, and realistic movement.

Problem: Performance

Raw performance is one of the most important factors affecting animation smoothness and is probably the most obvious. The faster you run your animation, the smoother it tends to look because the amount of change between each frame of your object is smaller, and thus the eye tends to perceive the motion as more continuous.

Solution: Optimization One way to improve the performance of your application is by making your Swing and 2D code render faster. We discuss general solutions to performance issues in Chapter 5, "Performance," and throughout the book in general. Look first to those solutions if your problems are performance related.

Problem: Slow Frame Rate

Frame rate is closely related to performance. You want to make the time between sequential frames of your animation as short as possible, because slow frame rates contribute to slow perceived performance of the application.

Solution: Optimize the Resolution   One way to affect frame rate is to improve the performance of your rendering code, as we discussed previously. Another approach is to run your animation at a different resolution. At the core of your animation is a timer (discussed in Chapter 12), which causes timing events at specified intervals. You can set up this timer to call you every half-second, which would result in a very unanimated animation running at a whopping 2 fps. Or you can set it up to call you every 30 ms, which would give you a more reasonable 33 fps, assuming your application could complete its rendering in less than 30 ms in order to maintain this frame rate.

Run your application and determine, visually, an appropriate frame rate for smoothness. Remember that you want the interval to be as small as it needs to be to make your animations smooth without being too small and causing the application to demand too much of the CPU. See the section "Resolution" in Chapter 12 for more information on resolution constraints.

Demo: Increase or Decrease the Resolution   If you use the up and down arrow keys in the SmoothMoves application, you will change the resolution from its default down to 0 ms, or as quickly as Swing can animate it, and up to 500 ms, which is only 2 fps. It should be visually obvious that the moving animation gets *much* smoother as the resolution decreases and fps increases.

Problem: Consistency

Ideally, you will have as small a timer resolution as possible so that your animation can begin to render the next frame very quickly. However, if some frames require significantly more time to render, or if other things are happening in your program or on the system that make this frame rate unachievable, then you will end up with intermittent pauses in your animation. These pauses do not have to be very long to be noticeable to the user. Suppose that your animation runs swimmingly at 30 fps most of the time but takes a time hit of 100 ms, or three times your normal interframe delay, every fourth frame. The net result is that the user would see your animation pause and jump several times per second.

Solution: Set a Reasonable Resolution   An animation running at a consistent 20 fps is better than one running at 30 fps with occasional but noticeable lags and jumps. Just because some frames *can* run at a rate of 1,000 per second doesn't mean they should. Or, rather, don't try to run your animation at that rate just because you can achieve it sometimes. Instead, you should set a reasonable rate that you can achieve consistently.

> **Tip:** It is far better to set a frame rate that you know is achievable in most situations than to have a jumpy animation.

Problem: Realistic Timing

Related to consistency is use of time-based animation rather than speed-based animation. We discussed this topic in Chapter 12. A very simple animation engine updates the animation state to some next sequential step each time it is called. This behavior works on systems in which timing is very predictable, but it breaks down when run on differently configured systems or when events happen to perturb the timing between steps. It is far better to base an animation state on the real time that has elapsed. That way, the animation will always proceed in a logical fashion regardless of how much time passes between individual steps.

Solution: Use a Timer   Our discussion in Chapter 12 of the various timing facilities, ending with the `Timer` utilities, was no mistake. These timers are convenient utilities for ensuring that your animations can use a realistic timing scenario. Gone are the days of step-based animations that ran more quickly when you pushed the Turbo button on your PC. Welcome to the world of time-based animation.

Problem: Realistic Motion

The simplest motion to calculate is linear interpolation. That is, for any fraction of the elapsed animation, you move the object by that fraction between the starting and ending points of the animation. The code for this calculation is straightforward. For any starting value $x0$ and ending value $x1$, we can calculate the linearly-interpolated value x for any elapsed fraction between 0 and 1 as:

$$x = x0 + (x1 - x0) * fraction$$

Unfortunately, this calculation results in movement that looks unnatural to humans. We simply don't live in a linearly interpolated world. With effects like gravity, anticipation, acceleration, and deceleration,[1] we are used to objects

---

1. Not to mention, in my case, tripping, stumbling, falling, and crashing.

moving with a much different feel than a linearly interpolated animation would display. The other problem with linear interpolation is that it is very easy for our eyes to detect inconsistencies in movement in strictly linear motion. If an object is moving at a constant rate and pauses briefly, the pause will be quite obvious to the user. If, on the other hand, the object is moving in a nonlinear fashion, slight pauses are much harder to discern.

Solution: Nonlinear Interpolation   There are many ways to calculate nonlinear movement, depending on the kind of effect you want to achieve. Do you want the motion to speed up at the beginning and slow down at the end? Or have constant acceleration? Or have a gravity-like motion?

In simple terms, you want to take the fraction of time elapsed in your animation and perform a function on it to return a nonlinear value from that fraction. You can then perturb your motion on the basis of that nonlinear fraction instead. We talk more about nonlinear interpolation in our discussion of the Timing Framework in Chapters 14 and 15.

Demo: Bouncing Animation   You can toggle the linearity of object motion in the demo by hitting the L (for linear) key on your keyboard, which toggles the movement between the default linear motion and a motion that is more like a bounce: the animation decelerates up to the halfway point and accelerates back to the start. It is particularly interesting that changing this behavior makes the moving animation on the right appear smoother but has little effect on the smoothness of the fading animation.

Color: What's the Difference?

The effect of color on the animation is perhaps less obvious than performance issues, but it turned out to be the largest contributor to the choppiness I witnessed in my original investigation. For example, in the demo application, the display pixels affected by each of the two animations are changing at some rate, and that rate is perceived to be smoother in the case of the fading animation.

Tip: The apparent smoothness of an animation is closely related to the rate of change of the pixel colors affected.

Let's take a step back and think about what makes an animation smooth in general. It is fairly obvious that having a higher frame rate results in a smoother animation. Let's see why.

Imagine trying to animate an image from the left side of this page to the right over the course of one second. You could simply move it from left to right in one step. The image sits over on the left until the animation begins, at which time you erase it from the left side and draw it on the right side. You've just animated that movement at a whopping 1 fps. Of course, it's only "animated" in the technical sense. It didn't really animate at all, it simply performed a single movement. I think you'll agree that that animation would be just a bit choppy.

Let's try for something a little better. Let's divide the total distance into 10 steps and perform the animation by moving the image to each of those steps in turn, ending up at the same place as before at the end of a second. This looks a little better. At least it looks like the image is moving this time instead of just appearing in the end location. Now we're getting a more reasonable 10 frames per second, which is a rate that at least allows us to consider it an animation—but it's still pretty choppy.

Now let's take it up another order of magnitude. Imagine dividing the space into 100 equal parts and doing the same as before: We copy the image to each place along the way, reaching the end position at the end of a second. Now we're getting somewhere; the image is moving *much* more smoothly than before, at a rate of 100 fps. You may still notice some choppiness, but you can at least consider this an "animation."

The key that made this image movement an animation was increasing the frame rate and decreasing the amount of movement per interval so that each step was small enough that the overall movement began to appear smooth to our eyes. This interval-decreasing was done in the time and space dimensions, decreasing the time between steps and the space between each movement. Now imagine doing the same for color.

In particular, think about the color of each pixel being affected by an animation. How much do they change between each step? For each step, do we have large numbers of pixels changing drastically or small numbers of pixels undergoing minor changes?

In the first case, in which we moved the object from the left to the right in one single frame, we changed all of the pixels at the origin, erasing them to the background color, and all of the pixels at the final destination, changing them from the background color to the image color. Many pixels underwent significant change in one step, twice the number of pixels in the image, in fact. In the final animation, however, in which we moved the object gradually from the left to the right, the only pixels affected in each step were those on the leading and trailing edges of the object. The changes to those pixels may have been just as drastic, since the pixels were changing between the background and foreground colors in one step, but because far fewer pixels were affected in each step, the animation appeared much smoother than the first attempt.

Tip: In order to smooth out an animation, we want to *minimize the amount of color change per pixel* in each step of the animation.

Let's think about the animations in the original application in which I noticed these artifacts. In that animation, the fade occupied the entire window of 800 × 800 pixels, and the motion animation occupied a much smaller area of only about 200 × 50 pixels. In the fading animation, each pixel was modulating between the original color and the new color at a rate of 10 fps. In the extreme case of a pixel moving between black, (0,0,0) in RGB space, and white, (255, 255, 255) in RGB space, the change for every step would be 10 percent of that color difference, or (25.5, 25.5, 25.5). We can calculate this Euclidean distance in RGB space as:

$$distance = sqrt(25.5^2 + 25.5^2 + 25.5^2) = 44.17$$

Alternatively, we could use the HSB (hue, saturation, brightness) representation of these colors and calculate our color difference in that space instead.[2] Black has an HSB value of (0, 0, 0) and white has an HSB value of (0, 0, 1). Every step in gray between these values is proportional in brightness to the percentage change, so a 10 percent increment in RGB color difference would be a change of (0, 0, .1) in HSB space. This gives us the following distance calculation in the HSB color space:

$$distanceHSB = sqrt(0 + 0 + .1^2) = .1$$

---

2. A complete description and treatment of color spaces and the human visual system is way beyond the scope of this chapter, this book, and anything else that I will probably ever write. There are various things about RGB space that make it less ideal than other color spaces when speaking of colors with relation to how our eyes perceive them. The HSB color space is good to use here instead because the change in color that we see here is purely in the brightness factor of HSB, since we are only varying between black and white. So it is interesting to see how the calculations work out in this alternative color space that is more closely aligned with how we perceive things. A full treatment of the subject would go much further, but the intent here is to give a sense of what's going on and to leave a deep-dive into the subject to other references.

By the way, HSB is a handy alternative in Java, since there are easy methods in `Color` to convert from and to RGB and HSB, such as `Color.RGBtoHSB()` and `Color.HSBtoRGB()`.

Meanwhile, the moving animation was changing pixels between the background color and the object color in one step for all of the pixels affected by each movement step of that animation. In the extreme case of a black object and white background, pixels would change as much as (255, 255, 255) in each step, for a Euclidean distance of ten times the fading amount, or 441.7 in RGB space:

$$distance = sqrt(255^2 + 255^2 + 255^2) = 441.7$$

Performing this distance calculation in HSB space, given the values of (0, 0, 0) and (0, 0, 1) for black and white, gives us the following:

$$distanceHSB = sqrt(0 + 0 + 1^2) = 1$$

By either the RGB or HSB calculation, each pixel in the moving animation, in the extreme case of black–white color difference, is changing 10 times the amount of any pixel in the fading animation.

One of the interesting things in this investigation is that the amount of color change of individual pixels appears to be *much* more significant than the amount of color change in the application window overall. That is, a large color change happening over a small number of pixels is *far* more detectable than a small change happening across a large number of pixels. The fading animation occupied the entire 800 × 800 window. At 10 fps fading from black to white, this means there were 640,000 pixels changing by 44.17 in RGB space or .1 in HSB space for each frame of the animation. It seems reasonable to think that all of that color change would be easily detectable by our eyes.

Meanwhile, the moving animation affected only an area of about 200 × 50, or 10,000 pixels. Also, the moving animation did not actually affect every pixel in that area, since it involved only some objects shifting slightly every time. Assuming that the scrolling animation affected only a quarter of the pixels in that region, there were only about 2,500 pixels affected each frame. In the extreme black–white case again, we have a color change of 441.7 in RGB space for each of these pixels. That's 44.17/pixel change for 640,000 pixels versus 441.7/pixel change for only 2,500 pixels. Using a comparison in HSB space, this is .1/pixel change for 640,000 pixels versus 1/pixel change for the smaller 2,500-pixel area. By numbers alone, it seems the fade effect is much more significant. Nevertheless, the fade looked far smoother.

I'm going to go out on a limb here and make this wild claim:

Tip: The amount of change of any single pixel is more significant than the total change over a group of pixels.

Imagine it this way: If you have an entire screen of a million pixels changing by just one incremental color value, it will be far less noticeable than a single pixel in the middle of the screen flickering between color extremes.

Playing around with the SmoothMoves demo can help you verify the color difference issue for yourself, but let's look at some pictures from a different application to make the situation clearer. The screenshots presented here come from the ColorDifference application on the book's Web site. This application draws two different black rectangles with some white space separating them, as seen in Figure 13-2.

The application runs a timer in the background that animates changes for both black rectangles. For the rectangle on the left, the color is toggled between black, with RGB values (0, 0, 0), and a color that is 1 percent brighter, with RGB values (3, 3, 3). The rectangle on the right continues to draw with a black background, but every other frame it also draws a 4 × 4 white square in the middle. We can see this alternating frame of the animation in Figure 13-3.

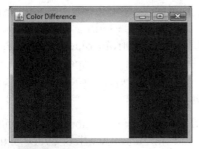

Figure 13-2 ColorDifference application: The same black rectangle is drawn on both the left and right of the application window.

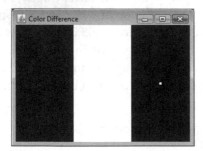

Figure 13-3 ColorDifference: In this alternate frame of the animation, the rectangle on the left is drawn with a slightly lighter color than before, and the rectangle on the right has a white square drawn in the middle. Which one looks more noticeably different from its previous version in Figure 13-2?

The question for you is: Which of these rectangles looks more obviously different from its previous version?

The answer should be obvious: The rectangle on the right is clearly different from its previous version. You simply can't miss that white square in the middle of all of that black. Meanwhile, you can study the versions of the rectangle on the left for some time and still not see the difference.

In terms of the numbers of pixels affected, or the raw amount of change in RGB space, the rectangle on the left is clearly affecting more pixels. The entire rectangle of 20,000 (100 × 200) pixels on the left is having its color shifted by 1 percent. Meanwhile, the only change to the pixels on the right are from that single square in the middle of 16 pixels, or less than .1 percent of the total pixels in that black rectangle area. But the impact of the changes on the right to far fewer pixels is significantly greater than that of the changes on the left. Once again, we see that the amount of change to individual pixels has greater effect than the total change over a large group of pixels.

Maybe it comes from our ability to edge-detect very well. Or maybe it's from ancient instinct, evolved through millennia of being hunted by flickery pixels in the wastelands of Cro-Magnon times. I have no idea, but I do know that's what it looks like, and in computer graphics, it's all about how it looks.

Various factors contribute to color difference problems. They are presented next along with solutions and "Demo" sections.

Problem: Object Color versus Background Color

One of the largest contributing factors to color difference during an animation is the colors that the pixels are changing between. If a black object is moving on a white background, the user sees the maximum color shift possible for each pixel that changes during every animation frame. On the other hand, if that object were very light gray on a white background, then the user would see far less color change, and the animation would appear far smoother.

Solution: Minimize Contrast   One approach is to change the color of the object or of the background color. This is not really a general solution for most cases, but it is interesting to note the effect that this change has on perceived smoothness. An object that is closer to the background color causes the pixels to shift less as it moves around on that background; the background pixels do not need to shift as much in RGB space to represent the object color, and this difference in color shift results in smoother perceived movement for the object.

Demo: Lighter Object Color Hitting the C key in the SmoothMoves application toggles the object color between its default black, seen in Figure 13-4, and a
light gray, seen in Figure 13-5. Note how the lighter color causes less pixel color
shift during the animation and results in a smoother resulting animation.

Problem: Hard Edges

Again, imagine a black object moving on a white field. If the edge of the object
is straight, then the pixels on the edge would change be between black and
white, causing the maximum RGB shift possible. But what if this black object
had edges that blended between the internal color, black, and the background
color, white? In this case, the pixels affected during movement would shift
through gray shades between black and white, and each individual pixel color

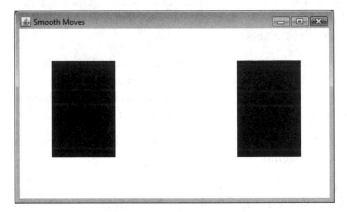

Figure 13-4 Default black color contrasts sharply with white background pixels.

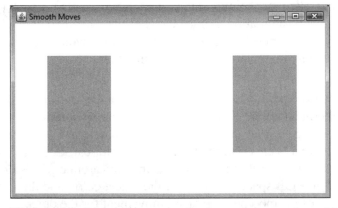

Figure 13-5 Lighter gray color has less contrast against white background pixels.

change would be far less than the black–white shift on the edge of the original object.

Solution: Antialiasing   One approach is to use antialiasing. Instead of using an object with hard edges that sharply contrast with the pixels the object moves over, you could soften those edges by fading out the object color translucently on the edges. Doing so has the net effect of a smoother blend to the object color and back to the background color as the object moves around over the background.

Demo: Antialiasing   Hitting the A key in the SmoothMoves application toggles the antialiasing setting from no antialiasing, the default, to antialiased, where the outside edges of the object are drawn with increasing translucency from opaque to transparent through an external edge 5 pixels wide, as seen in Figure 13-6. The choppy effects along the edge are much harder to detect when this option is enabled.

Problem: Straight Edges

This problem is related to the hard edges issue. Picture the black rectangle against the white background in the SmoothMoves demo. The rectangle will create a perceptibly more choppy animation than one with a less linear shape. One thing you will notice is that hard-edge movement trips up your eyes more than irregular-edge movement. The eye is very good at detecting artifacts in a column of pixels that marches along, but tracking artifacts in an irregular shape is more difficult, making artifacts easier to disguise with nonlinear shapes.

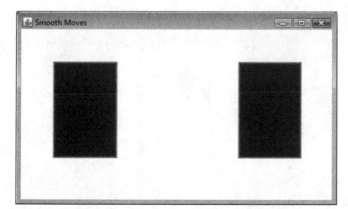

Figure 13-6   Antialiased edges provide smooth transition from the black interior color to the white background color.

Solution: Curves and Irregular Edges   This solution works well with modern user interfaces, which tend to have fewer rectangles and more curves than previous generations of GUIs. It doesn't take much to reduce the number of hard and straight edges in your applications: rounded corners, oval buttons, images for icons. All of these are viable elements in a modern user interface and are apt to enable smoother animations than do rectangular UI elements.

Demo: Use an Image   Hitting the I key in the `SmoothMoves` application swaps out the default rectangle for a far more interesting image of Duke, seen in Figure 13-7. Even with all other factors in the demo set to the default, Duke appears to have a much smoother animation simply because there are no hard edges for our eyes to detect while the image is moving.

Problem: Jumpy Motion

This effect is related to the hard edges issue. As the object moves around, all of the pixels change between the background color and the full object color in one step.

Solution: Motion Blur   As with the antialiasing solution proposed, the more we can do to smoothly transition pixels up to and down from the object color as the object moves through the pixels, the more we can minimize the color differences of each individual pixel. One approach to this problem is to simulate "motion blur," smearing the object as it moves. Blurring causes an automatic transition from the object color to the background color on the trailing edge of the object movement.

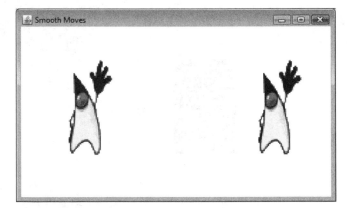

Figure 13-7   Duke substitutes for the black rectangle to show that motion of irregular edges appears smoother.

Note: Motion blur is not just a computer graphics hack; we have been seeing motion blur in movies for decades. Take a look at any individual movie frame during a scene with movement. Chances are very good that the objects that are moving in that scene will be blurry in the frame. The camera that took that frame recorded a range of positions occupied by the moving object during that frame. When these frames are run in sequence, our eye does not see blurriness, but instead sees smooth movement of the objects. Without the effect of blurring on the individual frames, we would see much choppier movement, more like what we see in the old movies from the 1920s. In those older movies, each frame was a distinct, crisp picture, which does not create a smooth animation nearly as well as the blurred photos of modern movies. This film technique made its way into computer graphics, so scenes in an animated film are now rendered with motion blur to create the same smooth motion effect that we see in live-action films. Art imitates life.

Motion blur in graphics is implemented by drawing ghost images of the object as it moves around. There are various ways to do motion blur, some more correct than others and some faster than others. The demo offers a very simple approach, drawing trailing versions of the object translucently in locations recently occupied by the object. The effect is similar to the cursor trails available as an option on some desktop systems. This effect does not impact the rate of color change for the pixels on the leading edge of the object movement. Because we are still drawing the object in its current location with its true colors, the background pixels still shift immediately to that color as the leading edge of the object moves over those pixels. But blurring the past locations of the objects allows a smoother transition back to the background color from the object color.

Demo: Motion Blur Hitting the B key in the SmoothMoves application toggles motion blur between off, the default, and on. Hitting the numbers 1 through 9 changes the number of ghost images painted, for shorter or longer ghost trails in the motion blur. An example of this effect can be seen in Figure 13-8. Note that this effect is more pronounced with smaller timing resolutions; if successive positions of the object are sufficiently far away from each other, as they are with a large resolution, then the effect is less smooth and more confusing. But with a small resolution and an accordingly tight motion blur trail, the effect is a smooth ramp-down from the object color to the background color in a way that fools our eyes, since motion blur is such a natural way of seeing smooth animation.

Vertical Retrace: That Syncing Feeling

Another major factor that was noticeable in my original investigations was the impact of the *vertical retrace* of the display. This has little to do with the problems

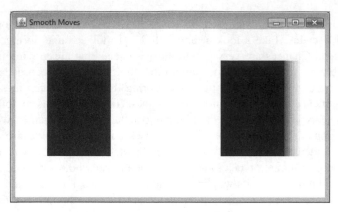

Figure 13-8 Motion blur using trailing ghost images provides a smooth transition from the object color to the background color. Here, the object is moving from right to left.

and solutions discussed previously, so I'm putting this issue in its very own section.

Here is the problem: A typical computer display updates the screen from video memory at some frequency, typically 60 times per second for LCD displays and anywhere from 60 to 90 times per second for older-style monitors. You can think of this as a linear process whereby every pixel on the screen is updated one by one, left to right, and top to bottom. It's done so fast and seamlessly that you would not usually notice it happening. But fast animations on the screen can cause an artifact called *tearing* that makes vertical retrace an issue.

Imagine that the vertical retrace is in the middle of refreshing the screen, and it happens to be refreshing the pixels in the area where your application is copying pixels to the screen. The effect will be that the pixels below and to the right of the refresh location will show up in their new location, but the pixels to the left and above that location will still be shown in their old location. This artifact happens because the refresh has already updated the pixels above and to the left, and is only updating the pixels to the right and below on this refresh cycle. This effect does not last long. It is fixed by the next refresh, which will be in only one-sixtieth of a second for a typical LCD display. Since the artifact is not permanent, you might not even notice or be disturbed by it. And the effect is visible only on animations of moving objects; anything that stays in the same place, such as the fading animation in SmoothMoves, is unaffected by this artifact. But if your user interface is moving things constantly, and if those animations are happening in large increments, then the tearing will be so obvious that it will add to any perception of a choppy animation.

This is a graphics book; we should show this effect with a picture. Suppose we are trying to move our image between a position in frame 1 and a different position in frame 2, as seen in Figure 13-9.

Now suppose that the vertical retrace, represented by the horizontal line, is happening right in the middle of this area as the object is being drawn in the position it occupies in frame 2, as seen in Figure 13-10.

The net result is that the user sees frame 2 very briefly as having a torn object in it until it is fixed by the next refresh.

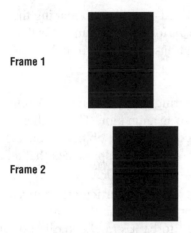

Frame 1

Frame 2

Figure 13-9   Position of the object in two successive frames of an animation.

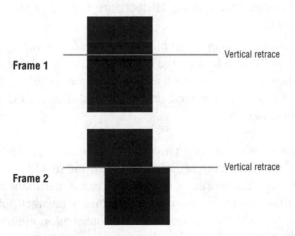

Frame 1   ──────── Vertical retrace

Frame 2   ──────── Vertical retrace

Figure 13-10   The object is drawn to the position in frame 2 of the animation as the vertical retrace line is just passing through that same area.

The problem is that copies to the screen do not, by default, pay any attention to the state of the vertical retrace process. So it is entirely possible, even likely, that animations will run into this rather jarring, if transient, artifact.

Solution: Don't Worry About It

What kind of solution is that? *Don't worry about it?* I just got done explaining that this is a noticeable factor, and if you have run the SmoothMoves demo, you may have noticed it already. And now you're just supposed to forget about it?

Yes. And no.

For one thing, all of the tips we discussed should contribute to making the vertical retrace effects less noticeable. There are various workarounds for this issue, mostly related to the same problems and solutions described for color, including the following:

- *Minimizing color differences:* The tearing artifact of vertical retrace is made worse by high-contrast changes in an animation. The smaller the difference is between the background color and the object color, the less noticeable will be the tearing artifact. All of the approaches that address high-contrast changes are applicable here.

- *Minimizing linear shapes:* The tearing artifact is particularly noticeable in objects like the rectangle in our example and in the SmoothMoves demo. Our eyes notice that what is supposed to be a straight line is no longer straight. Vertical straight lines are particularly susceptible to this artifact, since the tearing occurs along vertical, not horizontal, lines. If the object has irregular edges instead, then tearing artifacts are harder to spot and therefore less disturbing.

- *Minimizing distance between frames (or increasing the frame rate):* The further an object moves between frames, the more obvious any tearing artifacts. Figure 13-10 shows a pretty horrid tear that consumes nearly a third of the object width. If that object moved only one pixel instead, the tear would be far less noticeable.

For the most part, this artifact should simply go away, or at least be negligible, in your animations. But what if you wanted to actually do something to address this artifact? There is a Windows-specific workaround that you can experiment with in the original article that this chapter is based on: http://today.java.net/pub/a/today/2006/02/23/smooth-moves-solutions.html. This article has pointers to source code and a variation on the SmoothMoves demo that shows how you can potentially work around the vertical retrace artifact. (Hint: We use a small bit of native code to wait until the vertical retrace is between refreshes to update the Swing window.)

We do not include that approach here because it is, frankly, a hack;[3] the solution is for Windows only, and even so, it is neither a general nor a complete fix. It is actually still possible to see the artifact, depending on where the window is on the screen (this factor is discussed further in the original article).

There is no good general approach for a Swing application because Swing is at the mercy of the window system and cannot control when the vertical refresh happens. There is a solution for some situations, using a `FlipBufferStrategy`. `BufferStrategy` is a mechanism by which you can double-buffer your application, much like Swing does. In fact, Swing uses a `BufferStrategy` internally as its double-buffering solution.[4] You can create a `BufferStrategy` for your top-level window, calling the following method in `Window` and its subclasses:

```
public void createBufferStrategy(int numBuffers)
```

By default, `createBufferStrategy` attempts to create a `FlipBufferStrategy`. `FlipBufferStrategy` uses graphics hardware facilities to ensure that the screen is only updated between vertical refreshes. In this approach, an application's back buffer is actually swapped with the front buffer (a process that is usually called a *flip*). This switch happens so quickly that it can be scheduled to occur between the vertical retrace events.

`FlipBufferStrategy` is not, however, always available by default. It is available if the `OpenGL` rendering pipeline, described in Chapter 5, is enabled. It is

---

3. Here is a philosophical tangent: What is a hack? There is a fine line between a hack and a cool bit of code. And that line can vary widely between contexts. In this case, the fix to the vertical retrace artifact was perfectly valid for the article I wrote. Articles tend to be short-lived descriptions that point out items of interest to the current audience. I figured it was fair game to show something that Windows developers might want to play around with. At the very least, it's an interesting exploration into how this bit of arcane graphics technology works. But books tend to sit on the shelves a bit longer than articles ride on Web site front pages, so the solution should be a bit more robust and generally applicable. Since the "fix" here is so platform-specific (Windows, pre-Vista), in contrast with the cross-platform nature of Java, and since it is actually not a complete fix (we cannot prevent Swing from copying to the screen during a vertical retrace but merely try to time it a bit better), it just didn't make the "no hacks, please" bar for inclusion in the book. But feel free to check out the article and demo at the URL provided if you want to learn more about it. My little hack is lonely and would appreciate the company.

4. Note that Swing uses a `BltBufferStrategy` by default, not a `FlipBufferStrategy`. So just because Swing is using a `BufferStrategy` to double-buffer the application doesn't mean that Swing will fix the tearing artifacts automatically.

also available on UNIX/X11 platforms in general. On Windows, with the default rendering pipeline enabled, FlipBufferStrategy is available only for applications running in full-screen mode, and UI applications are typically windowed applications. I would not advocate using full-screen mode for your GUI applications just to access this one piece of technology.

> **Tip:** Since Swing already manages double-buffering for your application, you generally should not do your own double-buffering in addition to Swing's. BufferStrategy is mentioned only by way of completeness for anyone who really needs vertical retrace sync behavior and is on a platform or rendering pipeline that can provide it. FlipBufferStrategy is not a general solution for Swing v-sync behavior.

The other solution is a long-term solution, but it's a good one: *the operating system will fix it.* This sounds trite and optimistic, but in fact the solution is already partially here today. On the Macintosh, the solution is built into recent versions of OS X. On Windows, the solution is in Windows Vista, which has been available since early 2007.

On these operating systems, and probably others from other vendors eventually, the desktop that the user sees is actually double-buffered, just like Swing itself. Application windows are actually drawn to offscreen video memory and composited together onto the back buffer of the screen. This back buffer is then swapped with the screen buffer, in exactly the same process as the FlipBufferStrategy, thus completely avoiding the vertical retrace issue.[5]

So in the medium and long terms, the vertical retrace issue simply goes away. In the short-term, on the platforms that do not fix the problem for you, minimize choppy animation artifacts as you would for the other problems we've discussed, and these fixes will all contribute to fewer vertical retrace artifacts as well.

---

5. I find it amusing to think about all of the buffers involved in a Swing application on Vista. First, there's the screen (that's 1). Then there's the back buffer for the screen (2). Then there's the offscreen representation of the Swing window (3). Then there's Swing's back buffer (4). In some cases, we may have an extra buffer to account for different kinds of rendering to the window (5). That's a quintuple-buffered application—some serious buffering! Note that this is all just an internal implementation detail of Swing and the operating system; these extra buffers are not adding performance overhead from extra copies, since the speed of copies and flips between these buffers are at hardware-accelerated GPU speeds.

SmoothMoves: The Demo

The SmoothMoves demo is mentioned in several places in this chapter, and you are encouraged to go to the book's Web site to run the demo and look at the code directly. But it is worth discussing the basic implementation and operation of the demo, since it shows some functionality of Swing and Java 2D graphics and animation in action.

Creating the Graphics Objects

Before rendering, the application creates the graphics objects that it will render to the screen. In all cases, the application creates an image that will be copied later using drawImage() during the animation. In the default case, the contents of this image are created by rendering a solid black rectangle. Here is the image-creation routine:

```
void createAnimationImage() {
  GraphicsConfiguration gc = getGraphicsConfiguration();
  image = gc.createCompatibleImage(imageW, imageH,
      Transparency.TRANSLUCENT);
  Graphics gImg = image.getGraphics();
  gImg.setColor(Color.BLACK);
  gImg.fillRect(0, 0, imageW, imageH);
  gImg.dispose();
}
```

First, we get the GraphicsConfiguration object from the component, which we will need to create a compatible image, as discussed Chapter 5. Note that we create the image to be translucent. That capability is not actually needed in the default case, since the default image is an opaque black rectangle. But we use the translucency of the image with some of the application options discussed later. We then get the Graphics for the object, set the color, and fill the rectangle with solid black.

Running the Timer

The next step is to start a timer, which runs the animation loop:

```
private void startTimer(int resolution) {
  if (timer != null) {
    timer.stop();
```

continued

```
      timer.setDelay(resolution);
    } else {
      timer = new Timer(resolution, this);
    }
    timer.start();
}
```

This method creates a `Timer` object, if none exists, with the given resolution and `ActionListener`, the `SmoothMoves` instance itself. If a timer already exists, this code stops that timer and sets a new resolution value on it. It then starts the timer. The resolution used is set at runtime to either the default for the demo, 50 ms, or a new value set by the user during program execution with the arrow keys.

The timer calls into the `actionPerformed()` method at intervals determined by the resolution we set on the timer.

```
public void actionPerformed(ActionEvent ae) {
    long currentTime = System.nanoTime() / 1000000;
    long totalTime = currentTime - cycleStart;
    if (totalTime > CYCLE_TIME) {
        cycleStart = currentTime;
    }
    float fraction = (float)totalTime / CYCLE_TIME;
    fraction = Math.min(1.0f, fraction);
    fraction = 1 - Math.abs(1 - (2 * fraction));
    animate(fraction);
}
```

In this method, we calculate a fraction of the animation that has elapsed, according to the `CYCLE_TIME` variable. Note that a single animation cycle will move or fade the object to one extreme and back, so we calculate the fraction accordingly. The fraction will go from 0 to 1 as we approach the halfway mark of our cycle and 1 to 0 as we approach the full cycle time. We reset `cycleStart` to our current time whenever we exceed the maximum `CYCLE_TIME` so that `totalTime` always reflects the time elapsed in the current cycle.

After we have the timing fraction, we call `animate()` to alter the values that we care about during the animation:

```
public void animate(float fraction) {
    opacity = fraction;
    int prevMoveX = moveX;
    moveX = moveMinX + (int)(.5f + fraction *
        (float)(moveMaxX - moveMinX));
    repaint();
}
```

Here, we set the opacity to the fraction value so that our object will vary between completely transparent, 0, and completely opaque, 1. We calculate the moveX value, which is the location at which the moving image will be drawn, as the linear interpolation between the minimum and maximum X values with the given timing fraction (the added .5f is for rounding). After we set these values, we call repaint() to force the application to render itself.

Rendering

Finally, let's look at the meat of the application: rendering the graphics during the animation. There are three main tasks in the paintComponent() method: erasing to the background color, drawing the fading animation, and drawing the moving animation.

Erasing the Background

This step is simple; we just erase to white, like so:

```
g.setColor(Color.WHITE);
g.fillRect(0, 0, getWidth(), getHeight());
```

Drawing the Fading Animation

In this step, we use the current value of opacity, calculated by our animate() function, to create a new AlphaComposite object and set it on the Graphics2D object. Then we render our existing image using this Graphics2D object.

```
Graphics2D gFade = (Graphics2D)g.create();
gFade.setComposite(AlphaComposite.SrcOver.derive(opacity));
gFade.drawImage(image, fadeX, fadeY, null);
gFade.dispose();
```

Note that we create and dispose a new Graphics2D object here, cloned from the Graphics object passed into paintComponent(). Doing so allows us to set the composite on the Graphics object without having to worry about resetting it when we are done, so the rendering of other objects using the original Graphics object does not suffer side effects of this change. The opacity variable is set during the calls to animate(), described earlier. fadeX and fadeY are constant instance variables that declare where the fading image will be drawn.

Render the Moving Animation

This step is straightforward:

```
g.drawImage(image, moveX, moveY, null);
```

We simply copy the image into the appropriate location, determined by the moveX and moveY parameters. moveY is constant: We are moving the object only in the X direction. moveX is set during each call to animate(), as seen previously.

Rendering Options

The tasks just discussed are all that we need for the default behavior of the application. They create the image, set up the timer, and paint the two animations forever. But there is more to this demo. There are keyboard commands that you can use while the application is running to try out different approaches to rendering to mitigate the choppiness and see the results. We covered these inline in the earlier discussion of problems and solutions, but here is the comprehensive list of options for the demo:

I (Image)

This option toggles the rendered object between a solid rectangle and an image. Using this option gives your object an irregular shape, which makes it harder to see some of the rendering artifacts seen when using the solid black rectangle. The code to create this image is in createAnimationImage():

```
image = gc.createCompatibleImage(imageW, imageH,
    Transparency.TRANSLUCENT);
Graphics2D gImg = (Graphics2D)image.getGraphics();
if (useImage) {
  try {
    URL url = getClass().getResource("duke.gif");
    Image originalImage = ImageIO.read(url);
    gImg.drawImage(originalImage, 0, 0,
                   imageW, imageH, null);
  } catch (Exception e) {
      System.out.println("Problems loading image file: " + e);
  }
}
gImg.dispose();
```

Note that we simply substitute these contents for the black rectangle contents we created earlier. At rendering time, we just draw the same image to the window that we drew before, but this time that image contains Duke instead of the black rectangle.

C (Color)

This option toggles the color between the default, black, and light gray. You should notice that the moving animation appears much smoother simply by decreasing the contrast, or color distance, between the object color and the background color. The code to change the object color is in `createAnimationImage()`:

```
Color graphicsColor;
if (alterColor) {
    graphicsColor = Color.LIGHT_GRAY;
} else {
    graphicsColor = Color.BLACK;
}
gImg.setColor(graphicsColor);
gImg.fillRect(0, 0, imageW, imageH);
```

B (Blur)

This option toggles our simple motion blur effect, which causes the painting code to render a trail of translucent ghost images in recent object locations. Notice how the choppy artifacts on the trailing edge of the object are greatly decreased. The code to create this effect is in `paintComponent()`. First, here is the setup code to create the arrays of blur values:

```
if (motionBlur) {
    if (prevMoveX == null) {
        // blur location array not yet created; create it now
        prevMoveX = new int[blurSize];
        prevMoveY = new int[blurSize];
        trailOpacity = new float[blurSize];
        float incrementalFactor = .2f / (blurSize + 1);
        for (int i = 0; i < blurSize; ++i) {
            // default values, act as flag to not render these
            // until they have real values
            prevMoveX[i] = -1;
            prevMoveY[i] = -1;
            // vary the translucency by the number of the ghost
            // image; the further away it is from the current one,
            // the more faded it will be
            trailOpacity[i] = (.2f - incrementalFactor) -
                i * incrementalFactor;
        }
    }
}
```

Next, we render each ghost image:

```
Graphics2D gTrail = (Graphics2D)g.create();
for (int i = 0; i < blurSize; ++i) {
    if (prevMoveX[i] >= 0) {
        // Render each blur image with the appropriate
```

continued

```
        // amount of translucency
        gTrail.setComposite(AlphaComposite.SrcOver.
                            derive(trailOpacity[i])));
        gTrail.drawImage(image, prevMoveX[i],
                        prevMoveY[i], null);
    }
  }
  gTrail.dispose();
```

Finally, the ghost locations are updated at the end of the `paintComponent` method:

```
if (motionBlur) {
  // shift the ghost positions to add the current position
  // and drop the oldest one
  for (int i = blurSize - 1; i > 0; --i) {
    prevMoveX[i] = prevMoveX[i - 1];
    prevMoveY[i] = prevMoveY[i - 1];
  }
  prevMoveX[0] = moveX;
  prevMoveY[0] = moveY;
}
```

It is worth noting again that there are various ways of implementing motion blur, some of which are much more complex, time-intensive, and physically correct than this simple approach. I was after a simple blur to show the visual effect of motion blur on smoothing out the animation, and thus chose to implement a simple solution. You may want to experiment with more involved approaches in your code.

1 to 9

These numbers toggle the length of the motion blur, from 1 ghost image to 9. The more images, the more gradual the transition from the object color to the background color and the less obvious the artifacts of the trailing edge. But with more ghost images comes a potentially longer and less realistic trail behind the object. The code for this effect is shown earlier in the section "B (Blur)." This toggle affects the `blurSize` variable in that code.

A (Antialiasing)

This option toggles the use of antialiasing on the solid rectangle image. The edges of the rectangle are now drawn with translucency that gradually fades out to completely transparent. Like the motion blur effect discussed previously, anti-aliasing results in a smoother transition from the object color to the background color. But in this effect, the blur is on all sides of the object and not just the trailing edge, as in the motion blur effect. The approach used is quite simple. We draw increasingly faded outlines at the edges of the rectangle, as shown in this code from `createAnimationImage()`:

```
if (useAA) {
  gImg.setComposite(AlphaComposite.Src);
  int red = graphicsColor.getRed();
  int green = graphicsColor.getGreen();
  int blue = graphicsColor.getBlue();
  gImg.setColor(new Color(red, green, blue, 50));
  gImg.drawRect(0, 0, imageW - 1, imageH - 1);
  gImg.setColor(new Color(red, green, blue, 100));
  gImg.drawRect(1, 1, imageW - 3, imageH - 3);
  gImg.setColor(new Color(red, green, blue, 150));
  gImg.drawRect(2, 2, imageW - 5, imageH - 5);
  gImg.setColor(new Color(red, green, blue, 200));
  gImg.drawRect(3, 3, imageW - 7, imageH - 7);
  gImg.setColor(new Color(red, green, blue, 225));
  gImg.drawRect(4, 4, imageW - 9, imageH - 9);
}
```

Up and Down Arrows

The animation starts off at a somewhat slow frame rate, but the rate can be increased or decreased by pressing the up and down arrows on your keyboard. Each click increments or decrements the resolution by some number of milliseconds, to a minimum of 0 and maximum of 500.

L (Linearity)

This option toggles the interpolation mode of the animation. By default, the animation moves in a linear fashion. The L key toggles the animation to use a simple nonlinear sine function instead. The sine function gives the motion a "bouncing" effect. Notice how this nonlinear movement makes it more difficult to track individual frame discrepancies. It is more difficult for the eye to predict exactly where the object is supposed to be when the motion is nonlinear than it is when the motion is linear.

Summary

As you start to work with animations, you may notice some artifacts and want your animations to run faster, better, smoother, cooler. The tips in this chapter may help you to identify and fix some of the problems you see in these animations. One of the keys to Filthy Rich Clients is not just making your GUIs move but making them more dynamic and making users believe in the realistic and smooth motion they see in the application. Ensuring that your animations are smooth and realistic is an important part of developing these applications.

14

Timing Framework: Fundamentals

Introduction

When you first start working with animations in Swing, you quickly realize two things about the built-in timers:

- Their simplicity makes building any kind of animation possible.
- Their simplicity makes building any kind of animation incredibly difficult.[1]

That is, with a time-based callback mechanism like javax.swing.Timer, you can perform any time-based task, such as varying Swing component characteristics over time, and thus animate your GUI. But the details of implementing such animations are prohibitively tedious, so most developers skip this step and opt for the static component behavior that most GUI toolkits provide by default.

---

1. The timers illustrate the classical trade-off between simplicity and power. Sure, the ancient Egyptians could build the pyramids and Sphinx with just a bunch of rocks, but it took monumental efforts and lots of cheap labor to get it done. The English seem to have taken a more practical stance on the problem in constructing Stonehenge and similar monuments, where the finished product is just a small pile of large stones. The end result is not quite as impressive, but it must have been a far sight easier to build than the pyramids. The same trade-off is made in most "rich client" applications today: Applications either skip animations entirely or implement only rudimentary animations because the process of building more powerful ones is so tedious and time-consuming and the software industry lacks the cheap labor that abounded in ancient Egypt.

This problem became evident when I first started experimenting with animations in Swing and Java 2D. I just kept writing the same boilerplate code over and over again to get the basic functionality that all of my animations required. This experience was the inspiration for the Timing Framework.

Note: The Timing Framework is a library that is being developed in a project at http://timingframework.dev.java.net. We have taken a specific version of the library and put it on the book's Web site so that all text in the book and all code in the book's demos match the version of the framework available there. So if you want to use the version of the framework that we discuss in the book, use the one on the book's Web site. If you want to use the latest/greatest version of the library, or you just want to see what's happening with ongoing development of the framework, check out the project site on java.net.

The Timing Framework is a set of utility classes that provides a much more capable animation system that handles many of the details that you would otherwise need to implement in your application. The purpose of the library is to enable you to create powerful animations in Swing without worrying about the low-level implementation details.

The motivations for all of the features in the Timing Framework were twofold:

- *Handle common tasks:* Much of the code that we write in animating graphics and GUIs is necessary for nearly all animations. For example, most time-based animations need to figure out what fraction of the animation has completed at any given time during the animation, so why not simplify things by calculating that fraction automatically?

- *Simple API:* In providing more capabilities for animations, we do not want to create an API that is prohibitively complex. It should be as easy to use as possible.

The framework has a few distinct levels of functionality. At the core of the framework is the `timing` package, with the fundamental building blocks that all of the other pieces use. This group of classes provides the equivalent of the built-in `Timer`s but with significantly increased functionality. We cover this functionality in this chapter.

An additional level of functionality is provided in the `triggers` and `interpolation` packages. Triggers associate animations with specific events and automate starting animations on the basis of those events. Property setters in the `interpolation` package provide the ability to animate properties of Java objects and to define complex models of how those properties are interpolated between different values. We cover triggers and property setters in Chapter 15, "Timing Framework: Advanced Features."

Core Concepts

Several key concepts and properties are embedded in the central classes used by the Timing Framework:

- *Animator:* This class encapsulates most of the functionality discussed in this chapter, but it is worth discussing it separately so that we can see how an `Animator`, and the animation it defines, is created and run.

- *Callbacks:* An application must have a means to be notified of events during the animation. In this way, an application can be involved in the animation to perform appropriate actions based on the state of the animation. Event notification is handled through callbacks to an interface that application code may implement. This mechanism is similar to what we saw earlier in our discussion of the built-in Java timers, except that the Timing Framework has more callbacks with more information to enable more flexibility in your animations.

- *Duration:* The duration value defines the length of time that the animation will last. An animation stops automatically when this duration has elapsed. You may also specify that an animation should run indefinitely.

- *Repetition:* Some animations are intended to run once and then finish. Others may run indefinitely. Still others may run with a finite duration and then repeat when they are done.

- *Resolution:* The resolution of an animation controls the frame rate of the animation. This concept was discussed at length in Chapter 12, "Animation Fundamentals."

- *Starting behavior:* An animation may not want to start with the default behavior of moving forward from the beginning. It may instead want to run backwards or start from some other point than the beginning. It may also want to delay for some time before starting.

- *Ending behavior:* By default, an animation holds its final value when it is stopped. You might choose, instead, to have an animation reset to the start state when finished.

- *Interpolation:* The easiest kind of interpolation is linear interpolation, which we discussed in earlier chapters. But there are other kinds of interpolation that we can apply to give the animation nonlinear behavior.

Animator

Animator is the core class of the entire framework. Users of the Timing Framework create Animators with information that details the animations they want to run. The properties that define an animation are set through a combination of the constructors, which enable setting the most common properties, and other methods in the class. Animations are started and stopped by calling methods in this class. Finally, this class is responsible for issuing ongoing animation events while the animation is running, which is discussed in the next section, "Callbacks."

Creation

Animators are created through one of the three constructor methods:

Animator(int duration)

This method takes only a duration parameter, discussed later, which controls how long the animation will run. Note that this constructor takes no TimingTarget parameter. Callers would typically add one or more TimingTarget objects later via the addTarget() method; otherwise the Animator will run but will issue no events.[2]

Animator(int duration, TimingTarget target)

This variant, the most common, takes a duration and a TimingTarget. The TimingTarget, discussed in the section "Callbacks," contains the methods that will be called with animation events as the animation runs.

Animator(int duration, double repeatCount, Animator.RepeatBehavior repeatBehavior, TimingTarget target)

This final variant takes the same duration and target parameters as before, but also takes two other parameters that control how the animation is repeated over time, as discussed in the section "Repetition."

---

2. This is the animation equivalent of the great woodsy philosophical question: "If a tree falls in the forest and no one is around to hear it, does it make a sound?" The parallel question for Animator might be, "If an Animator runs and there is no TimingTarget around to receive the events, does it do anything?" We may never really know.

Control Flow

There are several methods that control the running and stopping of the animation. Note that, as discussed in the section "Duration," animations may stop automatically. But animations may also be programmatically halted by some of the methods of `Animator` described here.

void start()

This method starts the animation, which results in callbacks to the `TimingTarget` `begin()` and `timingEvent()` methods, as described in the section "Callbacks."

void stop()

This method stops the animation, which results in a call to the `end()` method of `TimingTarget`, notifying any targets that the animation has completed.

void cancel()

This method is like `stop()` except that `TimingTarget.end()` will not be called for any targets. It's like pulling the plug on the animation instead of letting it stop normally.

void pause()

This method pauses a running animation, which stops the animation in its current state until and unless a later call to `resume()` is issued.

void resume()

This method resumes an animation that has been paused. The animation will continue from its previously paused state, as if no time had passed between `pause()` and `resume()`. This method has no effect on an animation that has not been paused.

boolean isRunning()

This method queries whether the animation is currently running.

Controlling a Running Animation

It is worth noting that most of the parameters that control an animation, such as the duration and repetition parameters, make sense only on a non-running animation. Once an animation is running, it is not clear how changes to these parameters should be interpreted. Therefore, most of the methods of Animator that set these parameters, except where noted, will throw an exception if called while an animation is running.

Callbacks

TimingTarget

Animations in the Timing Framework run by having the animation code in Animator call back into one or more TimingTarget implementations. A TimingTarget object exists to receive timing events from an Animator. The TimingTarget object is the connection between the animation running through Animator and the animation actually doing something. The callback methods in TimingTarget are given information about the current animation state and can set up object state, calculate new property values, or do anything else appropriate for the situation.

When you set up an Animator, you give it one or more TimingTarget objects through one of the constructors for Animator and through the addTarget() method of Animator. As the animation runs, the Animator object calls the methods in each of its TimingTarget objects.

The TimingTarget interface has four different event methods to implement:

```
public interface TimingTarget  {
    public void begin();
    public void end();
    public void repeat();
    public void timingEvent(float fraction);
}
```

void begin()

This method is called by Animator when the animation is first started. It allows the timing target to perform any necessary setup prior to running the animation.

void end()

This method is called when the animation is finished, either because the animation completed naturally by running for the specified duration and number of repetitions or because the stop() method was called on this target's Animator. This method allows the target to perform any necessary cleanup operations. The end() method can be used as a mechanism to help sequence animations together. For example, a target can use the `end()` call to signal that some other dependent animation should start. Note, however, that triggers provide an even easier mechanism for this functionality, as we see in Chapter 15.

void repeat()

This method is called during a repeating animation, every time the animation begins another repetition. Repeating animations are discussed later.

void timingEvent(float fraction)

This method is the most important method in this interface and, in fact, in the entire framework.[3] `timingEvent()` provides the target with the fraction, from 0 to 1, of the animation that has elapsed. The target can then use this information to change whatever properties need to be changed during the animation and to schedule a repaint if necessary.

The fraction value is directly related to the `duration` property. If `Animator` is given a duration of 2 seconds, then an animation that issues a `timingEvent()` one second after starting would call `timingEvent()` with a fraction value of .5.[4]

The fraction is a useful value to have. If you want to animate some variable linearly between start and end values, it is important to know what fraction of the animation has elapsed. If the animation is halfway through, then you know to set your variable to halfway between its start and end values.

Some of the parameters of `Animator`, such as the start direction and the reversing behavior, may make an animation run backwards. When this happens, the fraction values received in `timingEvent()` run in reverse, too. That is, the fraction always represents the elapsed fraction of the animation from the start to the end. An animation running in reverse starts at the end point and runs in reverse. So, for example, an animation that starts at the end and runs in reverse will issue values from 1 down to 0.

---

3. In fact, this method was the original inspiration for the entire framework. I just got so tired of recoding the same "how much of my animation has elapsed?" logic in every animation, it seemed like a much easier mechanism was called for—one that would have the timer give me the fraction instead of my having to compute it by querying the system time and calculating it from starting times, durations, and so on. So it doesn't look like much, but the whole library grew from this one small method.

4. Note that some nondefault properties of `Animator`, such as a nonlinear `Interpolator` or a non-zero starting fraction, would change this simple example. We discuss these properties later.

TimingTargetAdapter

The `TimingTargetAdapter` class is a simple implementation of `TimingTarget`, providing empty methods for that interface. This class is provided as a utility for subclasses that want to receive only specific `Animator` events and do not want to implement all of the `TimingTarget` methods just to get the one or two that they really care about.

Duration

The discussion of `timingEvent()` relates directly to the `duration` property, because the fraction elapsed of an animation is calculated from the time elapsed so far and the total duration of that animation. The duration is specified in either one of `Animator`'s constructors, as seen previously, or in the following method:

```
setDuration(int duration)
```

Both the `setDuration()` method and `Animator`'s constructors set the duration for the animation in milliseconds. For example, an animation is assigned a duration of 2 seconds through a constructor, like this:

```
Animator myAnimation = new Animator(2000);
```

or through a later assignment to an existing animation:

```
myAnimation.setDuration(2000);
```

There is one additional, important value that a duration may have: `Animator.INFINITE`, which tells `Animator` that this animation should run indefinitely. Note that such animations will still call `timingEvent()` on a regular basis, but the fraction value in that call will be meaningless because there can be no elapsed percentage of an infinite amount of time.[5]

An important concept to note in relation to `duration` is that all animations are tracked in `Animator` in fractional time. That is, an animation, regardless of actual duration, may be thought of in terms of the percentage that the animation has elapsed at any time. So any animation, other than one of `INFINITE` duration, has a fractional duration of exactly 1. Calls to `timingEvent()` during the animation will use a fractional value instead of an actual duration. This mechanism tends to be easier to deal with for callers, which get more useful information

---

5. This is why, when you are in a meeting or lecture that seems to drag on forever, you keep looking at the clock and the minute hand has not moved at all. In fact, the meeting is of infinite duration and elapsed time has no meaning.

from knowing that an animation is one-quarter elapsed than that it is 500 ms into whatever its total duration may be. The concept of the elapsed fraction comes up often. We typically discuss animations in terms of this fraction instead of the total duration simply because that is what Animator keeps track of and reports to its targets, and because it is much more powerful and useful to Animator's users.

Repetition

A repeated animation is a common pattern. Repetition can take the form of running the same animation over and over, like an indefinite progress bar whose status always crawls from the left to the right. A repeating animation can also be constantly reversing, like a pulsating button that has a glow effect in which the glow is constantly glowing toward full intensity and then dimming back down to some default state. Instead of constructing separate animations for each repetition or creating one large animation that handles all of the repetitions as an implementation detail, the framework provides the ability to define the core animation and then parameters for how that animation should be repeated.

There are two properties of Animator that control repetition: the number of times the animation should be repeated and the behavior upon each repetition. These properties are controlled through the following constructor and methods:

```
Animator(int duration, double repeatCount,
         Animator.RepeatBehavior repeatBehavior,
         TimingTarget target)

void setRepeatCount(double repeatCount)

void setRepeatBehavior(Animator.RepeatBehavior repeatBehavior)
```

In this constructor and these methods, the repetition behavior is controlled through the repeatCount and repeatBehavior variables. repeatCount is simply the number of times that the animation should be repeated. This value can be fractional, such as 2.5, to indicate that the animation may stop partway through. repeatCount can also, like the duration value, take the value Animator.INFINITE, which indicates that the animation should repeat indefinitely.

repeatBehavior can have a value of either RepeatBehavior.LOOP or RepeatBehavior.REVERSE. LOOP repeats the animation in the same direction every time. When the animation reaches the end, it starts over from the beginning. So, for example, the animation fraction being passed into timingEvent() calls will go from 0 to 1, then 0 to 1, and so on, until repeatCount is reached or the animation is otherwise stopped. REVERSE creates an animation that reverses direction whenever it reaches the end of an animation. For example, the animation fraction passed into timingEvent() calls will go from 0 to 1, 1 to 0, 0 to 1, and so on.

Resolution

The resolution of `Animator` controls the amount of time between each call to `timingEvent()`. The default used by `Animator` is reasonable for most situations, so developers should not need to change the value in general, but changing it is a simple matter of calling `setResolution()`:

```
void setResolution(int resolution)
```

This method sets the number of milliseconds between each call to `timingEvent()`. Recall from our discussion of resolution in Chapter 12, "Animation Fundamentals," that the actual resolution may be dependent on such factors as the internal timing mechanism being used and the runtime platform. The Timing Framework currently uses the Swing timer internally, and its resolution is thus constrained to the resolution of that timer for now.[6]

Start Behavior

There are three factors about the starting state of the animation that you can control: the start delay, the direction, and the initial fraction.

Start Delay

Some animations may wish to have an initial delay before commencing. The amount of this delay is controlled through the `setStartDelay()` method:

```
void setStartDelay(int startDelay)
```

where the `startDelay` value is in terms of milliseconds.

Start Direction

By default, an animation runs forward when it starts. The initial direction can be changed to run the animation in reverse instead. This setting is controlled through the `setStartDirection()` method:

```
void setStartDirection(Animator.Direction startDirection)
```

where `startDirection` can have the value of either `Direction.FORWARD`, which is the default behavior, or `Direction.BACKWARD`.

---

6. A late addition to the Timing Framework added the ability to use an external timer. So while the framework still uses the Swing timer by default, it is now possible to supply a timer with a different resolution. See the JavaDocs for `TimingSource` in the framework for more information, but note that most users should not need anything but the default timer.

Start Fraction

By default, an animation begins at fraction 0. This setting can be changed to start from any point during the animation by calling `setStartFraction()`:

```
void setStartFraction(float startFraction)
```

where `startFraction` is a value from 0 to 1, representing the fraction elapsed of the animation. Note that to run an animation from the end to the beginning, the caller should set the initial fraction to 1 and the direction to `BACKWARD`. An example of this behavior is shown in the `FadingButtonTF` demo later.

End Behavior

By default, an animation will hold its final value when it finishes. For example, an animation that finishes a normal forward cycle from 0 to 1 will hold the value 1 at the end. This can be changed to reset to 0 at the end instead by calling `setEndBehavior()`:

```
void setEndBehavior(Animator.EndBehavior endBehavior)
```

where `endBehavior` can have the value of either `EndBehavior.HOLD`, which is the default behavior, or `EndBehavior.RESET`, which sends out a final `timingEvent()` with a fraction of 0 at the end of the animation.

Demo: FadingButton Reprise

We're not quite done with the core `Animator` features. We still need to cover the important area of `Interpolator`. But it's time for a break to see some of the concepts in action.

Let's look at what we can do with just the classes that we have covered so far. We have many classes in the framework yet to cover, but the power and flexibility of just the basic `Animator` and `TimingTarget` classes provides enough to enable simple code that drives powerful animations. In particular, think of the things that we had to do with the built-in timers to animate our GUIs in previous chapters or the things that seemed unapproachably tedious, like cyclic, repeating animations.

For a simple example, let's revisit the `FadingButton` demo that we discussed Chapter 12. While the application is not terribly complex, it is a useful example for showing how using `Animator` helps make animations easier to program.

Recall in that example that we defined a custom JButton subclass with various methods for rendering the button translucently and animating the value of alpha. First, there were some instance variables to help track state:

```
float alpha = 1.0f;              // current opacity of button
Timer timer;                     // for later start/stop actions
int animationDuration = 2000;    // animation will take 2 seconds
long animationStartTime;         // start time for each animation
```

In the constructor, we created the Timer object that ran the animation:

```
timer = new Timer(30, this);
```

Finally, we had an actionPerformed() method that served two purposes: It caught clicks on the button and used them to start and stop the animation, and it also received Timer events and animated the value of alpha with the following code:

```
public void actionPerformed(ActionEvent ae) {

    // ... code to handle button clicks not shown here ...

    long currentTime = System.nanoTime() / 1000000;
    long totalTime = currentTime - animationStartTime;
    if (totalTime > animationDuration) {
        animationStartTime = currentTime;
    }
    float fraction = (float)totalTime / animationDuration;
    fraction = Math.min(1.0f, fraction);
    // This calculation will cause alpha to go from 1 to 0
    // and back to 1 as the fraction goes from 0 to 1
    alpha = Math.abs(1 - (2 * fraction));
    repaint();
}
```

Now that we have the power of Animator, let's see how the code changes. You can see and run the code for this version, called FadingButtonTF, on the book's Web site. First of all, we need fewer instance variables:

```
float alpha = 1.0f;              // current opacity of button
Animator animator;               // for later start/stop actions
int animationDuration = 2000;    // each cycle takes 2 seconds
```

We do not need to track the animationStartTime because we no longer need to calculate the fraction of the cycle elapsed. Animator does this for us.

The constructor is similar to what it was before, although the declaration for Animator is a bit different from that of Timer:

```
animator = new Animator(animationDuration/2, Animator.INFINITE,
                        RepeatBehavior.REVERSE, this);
```

There are a few interesting bits about this call. First of all, we are using a duration of only half of animationDuration. This difference is because of how this new animation will be handled. Previously, each individual animation would consist of both the fade-out and fade-in portions, which we wanted to last for 2 seconds. With Animator, we can declare a more interesting reversing animation that reverses every second, which gives us the same result. Also, we see that we are going to be repeating infinitely, which is the same behavior as in the earlier Timer example. We declare a REVERSE behavior so that the animation reverses direction every time it repeats. And finally, we pass in this as the TimingTarget that will be called with timing events. Our object implements the TimingTarget interface in order to catch timingEvent() calls, just as the previous version of the demo received events from Timer in its actionPerformed() method.

Additionally, since we want to start at an opaque value and animate toward transparency, we need to make sure that we link up the animation fraction and our alpha value correctly. Both values vary between 0 and 1 over the course of the animation, so we're almost there. But since our animation starts at 0 by default and we want our alpha value to start at 1, or fully opaque, these values are going to run opposite of each other. We can either have alpha represent the inverse of the fraction, so that alpha would be 1 when fraction was at 0, or we can use additional facilities in Animator to start the animation at the end, playing backwards. This will ensure that the animation fraction starts at the same value as we want for our alpha. We add the following code to set the Animator properties accordingly:

```
animator.setStartFraction(1.0f);
animator.setStartDirection(Direction.BACKWARD);
```

Finally, let's see the actual animation code for this new version of the demo. This time, the code is in the timingEvent() method, which is the target for Animator's timing events, instead of the old actionPerformed() method. Compare the code in actionPerformed() to this approach for timingEvent():

```
public void timingEvent(float fraction) {
  alpha = fraction;
  repaint();
}
```

Note that we do not need to calculate the fraction elapsed of the animation, because it is given to us. Also, the flexibility in how we defined the animation, starting at the end and running backwards in the first animation, simplified our alpha calculation to simply equal the fraction itself. A screenshot of the application is seen in Figure 14-1.

Figure 14-1   FadingButtonTF: same as the FadingButton demo, but with less code.

This new version of the demo behaves exactly like the old one, but with less code. The demo is, by design, very simple, so it does not really show off the power of the Timing Framework as much as the simpler code that is possible, even for very easy animations. But it would help for us to develop a more interesting demo that shows off more about the framework. We develop this demo, The Racetrack Demo, throughout this chapter and the next one so that you can see how the different elements of the framework work together to create more interesting and complex animations.

The Racetrack Demo

This demo can be found on the book's Web site in the various projects ending with Race. There are several versions of the application that correspond to the different features of the framework that we discuss in this chapter and the next.

Background

First, we should explain how the application works in general. There are four main classes in the demo package in use in all of the versions of this application:

ControlPanel: This is the panel with the Go and Stop buttons that you can see at the bottom of the window in Figure 14-2. These buttons are added as listeners elsewhere in the application to start and stop the race appropriately.

TrackView: This is the part of the application that handles drawing the car in the current position and orientation on the track. Other code may call this class to set the position and rotation of the car, and the paintComponent() method of this class handles drawing the car appropriately.

RaceGUI: This class simply creates and manages the TrackView and ControlPanel objects inside a JFrame.

*Race: Each variation of this demo that we will see is called *Race, according to what it demonstrates. For example, the first version we will see is called BasicRace. These classes handle the setup of the animation and the changing of the car properties during the animation.

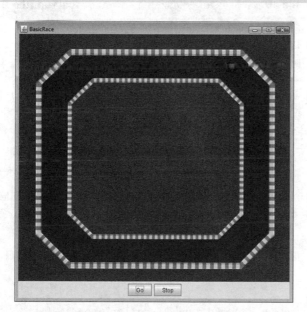

Figure 14-2 The Racetrack Demo.

Now that we understand the overall architecture, let's see how the program actually works. We do not go into the details of the ControlPanel and TrackView classes because they are quite simple and somewhat irrelevant for our discussions. Instead, we cover the code in the *Race classes; that is where the animations occur.

BasicRace

BasicRace is the simplest version of the demo: It runs the car down the first stretch of the track over some amount of time, showing how to use the basics of Animator to perform this task.

There are some constants and instance variables that BasicRace uses:

```
public static final int RACE_TIME = 2000;
Point start = TrackView.START_POS;
Point end = TrackView.FIRST_TURN_START;
Point current = new Point();
Animator animator;
```

The start and end constants come from TrackView, which keeps track of the eight corners of the race track. The variable current is used for storing the position of the car. And the animator is, of course, the Animator that runs the show.

First of all, BasicRace is constructed. It creates a RaceGUI object that holds the track and the control panel. It adds itself as a listener to the buttons in the control panel so that it knows when to start and stop the race. And it creates the Animator object, which will call our BasicRace object with timing events during the animation:

```
public BasicRace(String appName) {
  RaceGUI basicGUI = new RaceGUI(appName);
  basicGUI.getControlPanel().addListener(this);
  track = basicGUI.getTrack();
  animator = new Animator(RACE_TIME, this);
}
```

When one of the buttons is clicked, the actionPerformed() method is called, which stops the current animation if Stop was clicked and starts a new one if Go was clicked:

```
public void actionPerformed(ActionEvent ae) {
  if (ae.getActionCommand().equals("Go")) {
    animator.stop();
    animator.start();
  } else if (ae.getActionCommand().equals("Stop")) {
    animator.stop();
  }
}
```

The heart of the animation is in the implementation of the `TimingTarget` methods. `BasicRace` extends `TimingTargetAdapter`, which implements all `TimingTarget` methods, and `BasicRace` chooses to override only this one method:

```
public void timingEvent(float fraction) {
    // Simple linear interpolation to find current position
    current.x = (int)(start.x + (end.x - start.x) * fraction);
    current.y = (int)(start.y + (end.y - start.y) * fraction);

    // set the new position; this will force a repaint in TrackView
    // and will display the car in the new position
    track.setCarPosition(current);
}
```

The `timingEvent()` method is where the meat of the demo is. This method simply calculates the current position of the car as a linear interpolation from the starting point to the end point, based on the fraction elapsed in the animation. Then it sends this car position to the `TrackView` object, which redraws the race track with the car in the new location.

That's it for the simplest version of the race. It doesn't do much, but you can watch the car run down the first stretch of the track, all powered by just a few lines of code. We will see additional functionality added to the demo as we go through the other sections in this chapter.

Interpolation

Haven't you sometimes wished you could change time, slow it down, reverse it, accelerate it, or just stop it altogether? That wasn't exactly the motivation for the interpolation features of the framework, but these are some of the things you can do with interpolation, at least in the context of your animations.

We saw in Chapter 13, "Smooth Moves," that nonlinear behavior of animations is a good thing; acceleration, deceleration, and other techniques create a more natural and smoother animation for the viewer.

By default, `Animator` reports linear fraction values in its calls to `timingEvent()`. That is, for any time elapsed t in an animation of length *duration*, the default value for the elapsed fraction will be *t/duration*. `TimingTarget` objects are, of course, free to use the fraction value to do whatever they want; thus they can calculate nonlinear movement values given a linear time value. But wouldn't it be nice if the Timing Framework handled the pesky details?

There are actually two mechanisms for controlling the linearity of the timing fraction. The first mechanism, acceleration/deceleration, is quite easy to understand and may be the best to use in many situations. The second mechanism, Interpolator, is more involved, but also much more powerful.

Acceleration and Deceleration

The acceleration and deceleration parameters control whether there are periods of acceleration or deceleration in the animation. They control the value of the fraction passed into `timingEvent`. In a period of acceleration, which is always at the beginning of an animation, the fraction is increasing faster than the fraction based on the real elapsed time during the animation. In a period of deceleration, which is always at the end of an animation, the opposite is true; the fraction is increasing slower than the fraction based on real time elapsed.

Setting these values on an `Animator` is easy. Simply call the appropriate set methods before the animation begins:

```
setAcceleration(float acceleration)
setDeceleration(float deceleration)
```

Both methods take a value from 0 to 1 that represents the fraction of the animation that should be spent accelerating or decelerating. Note that the two periods are exclusive from each other. An animation cannot be accelerating and decelerating in the same time period of an animation, so (*acceleration* + *deceleration*) ≤ 1 by necessity. These constraints are illustrated in Figure 14-3. Calling either method with values that disobey these constraints results in an `IllegalArgumentException`.

During the period of acceleration, the speed increases at a constant rate of acceleration. The opposite is true for the deceleration period. As the figure shows, all

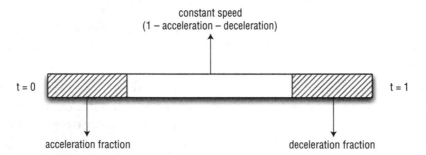

Figure 14-3 Acceleration, deceleration, and default (constant) fractions add up to 1, the total duration of an animation.

animations have an initial fractional period of acceleration, whose default length is 0, followed by some fractional period of constant speed, whose default length is 1, or the entire animation, and they end with a fractional period of deceleration, whose default length is also 0.

Think of the default situation, with no acceleration or deceleration, being an animation that goes from 0 to the full speed of the animation at the start and then from full speed back to 0 at the end. The graph of speed over time is shown in Figure 14-4.

For comparison, imagine an animator `anim` with an acceleration period of .4 and a deceleration period of .2. We would set these parameters with the following statements:

```
anim.setAcceleration(.4f);
anim.setDeceleration(.2f);
```

This animation would ramp up smoothly from 0 to full speed over the first 40 percent of the animation, cruise at constant speed for another 40 percent of the animation, and then ramp down from full speed to 0 over the final 20 percent. The graph of speed over time for this animation would resemble Figure 14-5.

This acceleration/deceleration approach provides an experience of a smoother animation compared to the sudden on/off speed behavior of the default behavior.

If we map the interpolated value over time, we get the graph in Figure 14-6. The straight line is linear interpolation, for comparison.

If you recall from the beginning of this discussion, the value of the `timingEvent()` fraction is being altered by the acceleration and deceleration values. So the

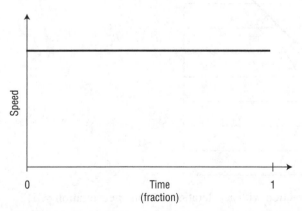

Figure 14-4 Default animation behavior, with no acceleration or deceleration: The speed of animation is constant.

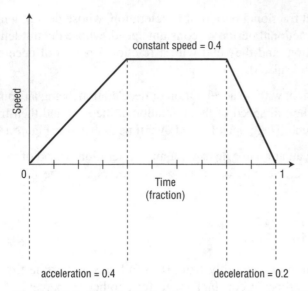

Figure 14-5 Speed of animation with acceleration (.4) and deceleration (.2) factors.

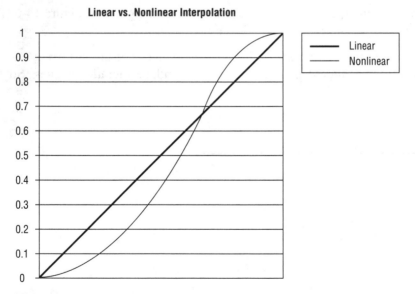

Figure 14-6 Interpolated fraction with acceleration = .4 and deceleration = .2, compared to linear time (straight line).

elapsed fraction values that you receive in your `timingEvent()` method will be nonlinear and will enable you to easily calculate nonlinear values accordingly. For example, if you look at the graph in Figure 14-6, you can imagine what impact this might have on object movement calculations. If the interpolated fraction, represented by the curved line, is being interpolated in this way while linear time, represented by the straight line, marches on, then your calculations on object movement will be affected the same way. If you do a parametric, linear calculation on your object based on the incoming pre-interpolated fraction, then your object will have slowly accelerating movement to begin with, will eventually be going faster than linear movement, and will then slow toward the end as it reaches the final destination. This holds not just for acceleration and deceleration but for the more general methods of interpolation as well.

Tip: Nonlinear motion can be created by performing simple linear interpolation calculations using nonlinear timing values.

Tip: Acceleration/deceleration is an easy way to tap into nonlinear movement for your animations; just tell `Animator` to accelerate and decelerate the timing fraction, and your simple linear calculations take on this advanced, realistic nonlinear motion.

Interpolator Race

ONLINE DEMO

Now let's see how to apply our new knowledge of acceleration and deceleration to our `Racetrack` demo to get a little more realistic motion out of that car.

In the previous version of the demo, `BasicRace`, the car looked pretty good rolling down the track, but it seemed fairly unrealistic.[7] In particular, it was strange how the car went from 0 to full speed immediately and then simply halted suddenly at the end of the first stretch. Wouldn't it be more realistic to accelerate up to full speed and then have some period of slowing down at the end?

For this demo, we want to reuse as much of `BasicRace` as possible. Therefore, we simply create `NonLinearRace` as a subclass of `BasicRace`. This new class has no functionality in it at all apart from a `main()` method to launch the application

---

7. Except for the rendering style of the track and car, which I think you'll agree are very realistic.

and a constructor. The constructor defers to the superclass, BasicRace, to do its work and then makes two minor adjustments:

```
public NonLinearRace(String appName) {
   super(appName);
   animator.setAcceleration(.5f);
   animator.setDeceleration(.1f);
}
```

These calls into the animator object set the acceleration period to half of the animation duration and the deceleration to the last 10 percent. The result is that the car speeds up to full speed over the first half and then slows down to 0 right at the end.

The reason we can make this change to have nonlinear movement so easily is, as we explained earlier, setting the acceleration and deceleration values changes how the fraction is interpolated against real time. During the first half of the animation, the animation fraction is accelerating, or increasing faster than the real elapsed fraction of time in our animation. When we take this fraction and compute the new location of the car, in our existing BasicRace.timingEvent() method, our calculation results in the new location also being interpolated at that accelerating rate. Similarly, use of the decelerating fraction toward the end results in decelerating movement in our standard position calculations. So even though we use simple, linear, parametric calculations for the car position in BasicRace.timingEvent(), our use of acceleration and deceleration changed the results of those calculations into more realistic nonlinear results by using a nonlinear timing fraction.

Run the demo. I think you will agree that the car's movement looks a lot better than it did in BasicRace.[8] And with only these two lines of code to make it work, it was well worth the effort.

Interpolator

Interpolator is a general and powerful mechanism for interpolating timing values. Interpolator is, as we mentioned earlier, somewhat more involved than acceleration and deceleration. Or at least it can be. It is actually quite easy to get complex behavior from Interpolators without doing much work. And there is

---

8. I would put a picture here to show you, but it would look exactly the same as the earlier picture of BasicRace. It is so difficult to get across time-based animation nuances when we have only individual pictures to work with. We could spend the rest of the book on a flip-book animation of the result. Maybe if we hadn't gotten around to writing anything more, that's what we would have done here. But now you'll have to satisfy your curiosity by going to the book's Web site and running the demo directly.

plenty of built-in behavior handled for you in the existing `Interpolator` implementations. It all depends on what you want to do.

First, the API details: `Interpolator` is a deceptively simple interface consisting
of just one method:

```
float interpolate(float fraction)
```

This method takes a fractional value from 0 to 1 and returns a fractional value
from 0 to 1.

Tip: The complexity in `Interpolator` comes from its open-endedness; you can do
anything you want in this method and return values that have a huge impact on the
resulting animation.

However, there is built-in structure to `Interpolator` and its subclasses so that
you can get powerful effects without going completely into unknown territory.

The idea behind `Interpolator` is that it interpolates the timing fraction itself;
the value passed into `interpolate()` is the elapsed fraction of time in the current animation. The fractional value returned from `interpolate()` will be used
by clients of the animation to calculate values based on the fraction.

Usage

An `Interpolator` object is set, implicitly or explicitly, on an `Animator` object.
By default, `Animator` uses a `LinearInterpolator`, supplied by the system, and linear interpolation is therefore the default for `Animator`. But the user of an `Animator`
can change the interpolation through the following method:

```
public void setInterpolator(Interpolator interpolator)
```

Types of Interpolators

While the power of implementing your own `interpolate()` method might be
appealing and even exciting, like standing at the edge of the Grand Canyon, it
may be a bit too much, like slipping while standing at the edge of the Grand
Canyon. Typical uses of interpolation can be much more constrained and therefore more approachable.

There are four different ways of using `Interpolator`:

- Linear interpolation, using the built-in `LinearInterpolator` class
- Discrete interpolation, using the built-in `DiscreteInterpolator` class

- Spline-based interpolation, using the built-in SplineInterpolator class
- Custom interpolation, using a class that you define

Linear Interpolation

Linear interpolation, as discussed in various places previously, is a means of calculating a value between two boundary values by using the fraction elapsed between the values as the multiplier of their difference, as seen in this standard parametric equation:

```
v = v0 + t * (v1 - v0)
```

All that is needed to perform a linear interpolation on the values, then, is to have the fraction *t* be the fraction of time elapsed in the interval. This is exactly what the built-in LinearInterpolator class does. As mentioned, Animator uses linear interpolation by default; it does so by using LinearInterpolator.

LinearInterpolator exposes the interpolate() method of the Interpolator interface, which performs the following simple functionality:

```
public float interpolate(float fraction) {
    return fraction;
}
```

It may seem a bit redundant to even have this class and method; if we are only returning the value we are given, then are we supplying anything but overhead here?[9] The answer, obviously, is yes; we are supplying a general framework such that any other interpolation mechanism may easily be substituted for the default interpolator and the system will carry on perfectly with the new interpolator. Bit-twiddlers, in whose company I occasionally count myself, may want to optimize this special case out of general principle, but the overhead of a single function call is insignificant compared to the flexibility it affords.

---

9. One might compare this to the way that kids clean their rooms, by simply shuffling objects from one location to another. They are not actually cleaning anything but merely moving things around so that it looks different. And, amazingly, it takes them *so long* to do it. The metaphor for LinearInterpolator goes even a step further, however, since returning the same fractional value is like kids picking up the objects and then putting them back exactly where they were before. So not only did they spend all day at the task, but it looks exactly the same at the end as it did at the beginning. However, as with LinearInterpolator, this rabid inactivity has a purposefulness that is difficult to fathom from the outside; eventually the parents will step in and assist to get the job done. Kids aren't dumb.

The LinearInterpolator class has one more method that allows users to get at the single instance of this class:

```
static LinearInterpolator getInstance()
```

Because LinearInterpolator provides such a simple and standard implementation of the interpolate() method, there is no reason for more than one of these objects in the runtime. There is also no reason for users to subclass LinearInterpolator; thus it was made final. Instead, users of linear interpolation should just get the singleton and use it as appropriate.

Discrete Interpolation

Discrete interpolation is a means of stepping, as opposed to sliding, from one value to the next, as illustrated in Figure 14-7.

On the left of the figure, we see linear interpolation as the value slides smoothly between 2 and 6 as the time varies from 0 to 1. On the right, we see discrete interpolation as the value holds the value 2 until the time reaches 1, when the value switches to the end value of 6.

The framework provides discrete interpolation through the cleverly named DiscreteInterpolator class. Like LinearInterpolator, DiscreteInterpolator is a singleton and provides a similar method to get at the DiscreteInterpolator instance:

```
static DiscreteInterpolator getInstance()
```

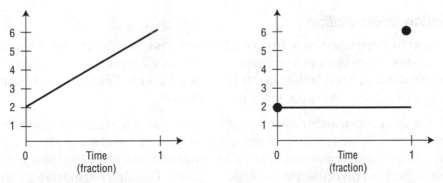

Figure 14-7 Linear versus discrete interpolation. Linear interpolation takes on values between 2 and 6, while the discrete interpolation maintains the original value until the end.

The implementation of `DiscreteInterpolator` is, like `LinearInterpolator`, quite simple:

```
public float interpolate(float fraction) {
  if (fraction < 1.0f) {
    return 0;
  }
  return 1.0f;
}
```

Basically, this method returns a fractional value that represents the start of the animation, which is always zero until the very end of the animation. This result ensures that calculations based on this interpolation will end up with the value at the beginning of the interval except when the interval is completed, exactly as illustrated in Figure 14-7.

The utility of `DiscreteInterpolator` may seem somewhat limited. In fact, it does not appear as though animations using discrete interpolation are really animating at all. They just switch to a different value at the end of the animation. The utility of `DiscreteInterpolator` will make a little more sense when we revisit it later in the section on `KeyFrames` in Chapter 15. Here, we are discussing interpolation over an entire animation. As we will see later, it is possible to create an animation that consists of several smaller intervals. `DiscreteInterpolator`, like any other `Interpolator`, can be used for each of these smaller intervals. When this happens, it is easier to see some more interesting use cases for discrete interpolation, as the intervals may be used, for example, to animate between index values for an array. But for now, we are just working on the basics: `DiscreteInterpolator` causes an animation to hold the beginning value until the animation reaches the end.

Spline Interpolation

`LinearInterpolator` and `DiscreteInterpolator` are simple to explain and understand. They perform a very basic operation on the input value and return a very simple value. The next built-in interpolator that we discuss, `SplineInterpolator`, is not as trivial. It is, however, much more interesting.

Defining a custom interpolator is, essentially, defining a function $f(t)$, which will return some sensible value for any given value t. `SplineInterpolator` allows an application to define such a function through the use of Bézier splines, which are smooth curves defined by four control points. Defining $f(t)$ in this way allows the user can get quite complex and arbitrary control functions through manipulating just a handful of parameters. And by enforcing some simple constraints about how we use splines, we can further reduce the amount of information that we need from the caller so that only a couple of parameters need to be supplied in order to define a spline curve.

A Bézier spline is defined by two *anchor points*, where the beginning and end of the curve are located, and two *control points*, which control the path that the curve takes between the two anchor points. You can think of the control points as "pulling" the curve toward them, although the math is a bit more involved than that. One of the constraints that we will impose is that the anchor points for our splines will always be at (0, 0) and (1, 1). Because these points are predefined by the system, the user needs to supply only the two control points for each spline to define the curve.

It is probably easier to see some examples of what we mean than to get buried in words and equations. Here are some diagrams that show different spline curves, all with anchor points at (0, 0) and (1, 1), but with different control points, as noted in the diagrams (Figures 14-8 through 14-11).

As you can see, the diagrams are attractive, and it is apparently very easy to create interesting functions and curves with just these two values for control points—but what do the diagrams mean?

As you have probably guessed, the curves define the interpolation for the timing fraction used by `Animator`. The spline defines the curve along which the input parameter, the real elapsed fraction of the animation, travels. The interpolated

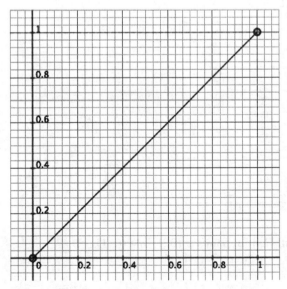

Figure 14-8 Linear interpolation: Control points at (0, 0) and (1, 1).

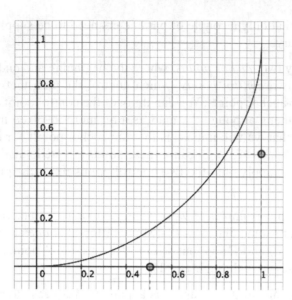

Figure 14-9   Constant acceleration: Control points at (.5, 0) and (1, .5).

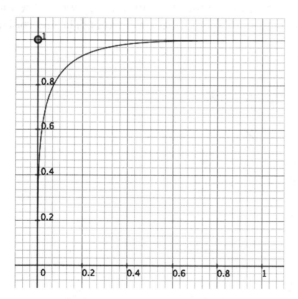

Figure 14-10   Fast in, slow out: Control points at (0, 1) and (0, 1).

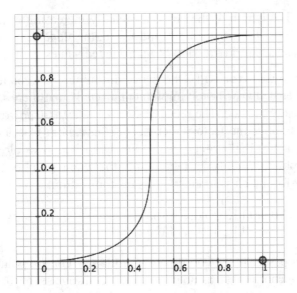

Figure 14-11 Ease in, ease out: Control points at (1, 0) and (0, 1).

value is calculated as the y-value, the vertical axis in the diagrams, at the given point on the curve. That is, the input value of the elapsed fraction of the animation is interpreted as the length traveled along our spline curve. From that length, we can calculate where we are on the curve and return the resulting y-value.

One way to think about splines is to visualize a diagram of the curve and see how fast the curve is moving in the y-direction at any given point; that will give you some feeling for how quickly the animation fraction is being interpolated at that value.

Let's look at how this works in the "ease-in, ease-out" curve, shown in Figure 14-11. The curve starts out with a very shallow slope, proceeding much faster in x than in y; this results in interpolated values that are far less than the original values for this beginning part. Around $x = .4$, the slope picks up, going vertical at the halfway point. After this point, the y-values are greater than the x-values, and each small increment in the original value will result in a larger increment in the interpolated value. Note, however, that the interpolated value will come from an interpolation on the *length* of the curve, not the x-values. So while the spline curve might look like we're going to increase hugely in interpolated values in this near-vertical area, the truth is that we are increasing in the interpolated values greater than original values but not as much as the y-versus-x

comparison might indicate. The length of the curve is steadily increasing in this area as well, just not as rapidly as the *y*-values. Around $x = .6$, the slope decreases dramatically and we get much slower progression of interpolated values.

Let us look at the `SplineInterpolator` API. One major difference between this class and the other predefined `Interpolator` implementations is that there is a public constructor and no factory method. The other classes, `LinearInterpolator` and `DiscreteInterpolator`, offer the factory method `getInstance()` because they are both singletons. For `SplineInterpolator`, however, it is possible to vary the effects of the interpolator widely; in fact, that is the whole point of the class, so it has a constructor for the class to enable this customization:

```
public SplineInterpolator(float x1, float y1,
                          float x2, float y2)
```

In this constructor, the caller passes in the coordinates for the two control points, `(x1, y1)` and `(x2, y2)`. The anchor points, as noted earlier, are always set at (0, 0) and (1, 1). The coordinates must always be in the range [0, 1], because splines are always contained in the (0, 0) to (1, 1) square area. This is another simplifying constraint that suits the use case of interpolating the elapsed fraction which is also always defined to be in the range [0, 1].

Besides the constructor, `SplineInterpolator` defines the `interpolate()` method from the `Interpolator` interface. This method uses the spline created by the constructor to calculate the appropriate interpolation for the caller at runtime.

Demo: SplineInterpolatorTest

Now let's see some code. There is a simple demo on the book's Web site called `SplineInterpolatorTest`, which looks like this:

```
public class SplineInterpolatorTest extends TimingTargetAdapter {

    private long startTime;
    private final static int DURATION = 5000;

    public void begin() {
        startTime = System.nanoTime() / 1000000;
        System.out.println("Real\tInterpolated");
        System.out.println("----\t------------");
    }
```

```
  public void timingEvent(float fraction) {
    long currentTime = System.nanoTime() / 1000000;
    long elapsedTime = currentTime - startTime;
    float realFraction = (float)elapsedTime / DURATION;
    System.out.println(realFraction + "\t" + fraction);
  }

  public static void main(String args[]) {
    Animator animator = new Animator(
        DURATION, new SplineInterpolatorTest());
    SplineInterpolator interpolator = new SplineInterpolator(
        1f, 0f, 0f, 1f);
    animator.setInterpolator(interpolator);
    animator.setResolution(DURATION / 10);
    animator.setStartDelay(1000);
    animator.start();
  }
}
```

The point of SplineInterplatorTest is to compare the elapsed fraction, in real time, to the elapsed fraction when using a sample SplineInterpolator. SplineInterpolatorTest extends TimingTargetAdapter, since we really want to implement only two of the TimingTarget methods: begin() and timingEvent().

In main(), we set up the Animator to run for a specific DURATION:

```
Animator animator = new Animator(
    DURATION, new SplineInterpolatorTest());
```

We then set the interpolator for the animation using a SplineInterpolator with the same control points (1, 0), and (0, 1) as the ease-in, ease-out spline represented in Figure 14-11.

```
SplineInterpolator interpolator = new SplineInterpolator(
    1f, 0f, 0f, 1f);
animator.setInterpolator(interpolator);
```

We set the resolution at one tenth the total duration to avoid being buried in values; we want just enough to plot a basic curve:

```
animator.setResolution(DURATION / 10);
```

We set a startDelay of 1 second to make sure that our application is set up and ready to go before the animation kicks in:

```
animator.setStartDelay(1000);
```

Finally, we start the animation:

```
animator.start();
```

In the `begin()` method, called by `Animator` when the animation starts, we record the current time in milliseconds for later use in tracking the elapsed fraction in real time:

```
startTime = System.nanoTime() / 1000000;
```

In the `timingEvent()` method, we calculate the real elapsed fraction, using the original `startTime` and the current time:

```
long currentTime = System.nanoTime() / 1000000;
long elapsedTime = currentTime - startTime;
float realFraction = (float)elapsedTime / DURATION;
```

We then output this `realFraction` value compared to the fraction value we received in the `timingEvent()` callback. This is the comparison between the elapsed fraction of real time and the post-interpolated fraction according to `Animator`. The comparison allows us to see how the interpolation changes over time given this `SplineInterpolator`.

A sample run of this program resulted in the following output:

Real	Interpolated
0.00	0.00
0.10	0.01
0.20	0.06
0.30	0.17
0.40	0.33
0.50	0.50
0.60	0.67
0.70	0.83
0.80	0.94
0.90	0.99
1.00	1.00

We can see in the table that the interpolated values change more slowly at the start of the animation and more quickly after the midway point. A plot of the points helps visualize this curve more clearly (Figure 14-12).

Now we can begin to have a clearer image of how this interpolation works over time. As we start into the animation, our elapsed fraction increments very slowly,

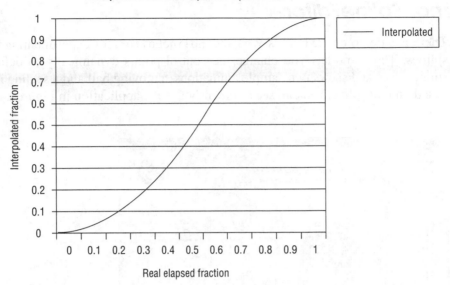

Figure 14-12 Real versus interpolated fraction for control points (1, 0) and (0, 1), as represented by the ease-in, ease-out spline in Figure 14-11.

which is the "ease-in" part. Around a quarter of the way through the animation, the rate picks up and we start interpolating faster than the original values. Then at the end of the animation, we slow down in our interpolation, incrementing the interpolated values at a slower rate than our input values. This is the "ease-out" portion of the animation.[10]

Note that the part in the middle where the curve is essentially straight looks quite different from the middle section of our spline curve in Figure 14-11. The spline curve shows a nearly vertical climb in *y*, whereas this curve is closer to, albeit steeper than, 45 degrees. This is the crucial part to understand with the spline curve representation. We should not compare the *x*-versus-*y* plot in the spline curve graphs but rather the curve-length-versus-*y* plot. That can be harder to see intuitively, but it gets easier over time with practice, with sample plots like we just did, and with simply playing around with splines.

---

10. This curve is similar to the curve you would get with a default linear interpolator and acceleration/deceleration factors of .5. You can see that splines are a more powerful and more general mechanism, but that acceleration and deceleration are a simpler way to express an important subset of this functionality.

Demo: SplineEditor

There is a demo on the book's Web site, SplineEditor, for experimenting with splines. The demo lets you change the control points dynamically to define a spline curve and shows two sample animations, a moving ball and a scaling icon, based on that spline. You can see a screenshot of the application in Figure 14-13.

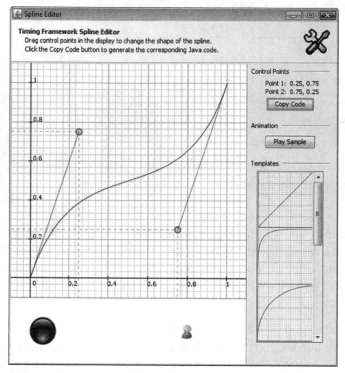

Figure 14-13 SplineEditor demo: You create the spline by changing the control points and watch the effect on the interpolated animations at the bottom.

There is a lot of detail about splines in general, Bézier splines in particular, and how interpolation calculations are actually performed internally in the framework, but I defer to other sources for that information. This book is mostly about using all of these pieces to get Filthy Rich effects. As long as you understand the basic functionality of splines, at least enough to be able to define the interpolations you want, then you understand enough to use them for Filthy Rich Clients.

Feel free to chase down more details about them in many references, both online and in books. There are numerous resources for understanding the math behind Bézier splines, including computer graphics books such as the canonical graphics reference *Computer Graphics: Principles and Practice* by James D. Foley, Andries van Dam, Steven Feiner, and John F. Hughes. A graphics book that I found more helpful in this situation was *The Geometry Toolbox for Graphics and Modeling* by Gerald E. Farin and Dianne Hansford. There are also numerous online resources that explain the concepts and math fundamentals and allow interactive spline manipulation in applets. Just do a search with your favorite search engine on "spline applet." Most of all, I defer to the Synchronized Multimedia Integration Language (SMIL) specification, which can be found online at www.w3.org/TR/SMIL/. `SplineInterpolator` and other elements in the Timing Framework were implemented specifically to be compatible with SMIL. The method of defining and calculating splines is the same for SMIL as for the Timing Framework.

Custom Interpolation

All of the `Interpolator` classes we discussed are predefined in the Timing Framework. But there is one more mechanism for `Interpolator` that is worth mentioning: You can define your own.[11] All you need to do is implement the single `interpolate()` method and return any value you want between 0 and 1, according to whatever interpolation you think would be interesting.

For example, you could provide a simple inverse interpolator with the following class:

```
public class Inverter implements Interpolator {

  // return the inverse of the input fraction
  public float interpolate(float fraction) {
    return 1.0f - fraction;
  }

}
```

---

11. It is perhaps the bane of our entire industry that it is always more fun for engineers to write their own stuff than to use what someone else has already written. But heck, why buck the trend? In this case, I hope that the built-in classes provide most or all of what you would ever need, but if you want to do anything not handled by one of them, it's easy enough to do. And with only one `Interpolator` method to implement, it's not as though you're going to spend the next several years implementing your own custom `Interpolator`. At least I hope not.

Of course, there are other ways to achieve this simple inverse effect, such as setting the direction of REVERSE for an Animator, but this will do for a simple example of custom interpolation.

For a slightly more interesting example, you could provide simple sine-curve behavior with the following class:

```
public class SineInterpolator implements Interpolator {

  public float interpolate(float fraction) {
    return (float)Math.sin(fraction * Math.PI);
  }
}
```

You can see that it's really up to you and your mathematical imagination here; what kind of effect do you want? Something cyclic? discrete? gravity-based? erratic? random? You can implement your own Interpolator implementation to suit your needs.

Summary

The core functionality covered in this chapter is powerful enough to create great animations. Just the ability to create animations of finite durations with repeating behavior and have your code called with the elapsed animation fraction is a big step up from the built-in timers. With Interpolators thrown in, there are plenty of great animated effects that you can create. But read on; the next chapter details more functionality that makes animations even easier and more powerful.

15

Timing Framework: Advanced Features

IN Chapter 14, "Timing Framework: Fundamentals," we covered the core features of the Timing Framework. These fundamentals can be thought of as the framework's equivalent of the built-in timer facilities, only much more powerful and flexible.

But now that we have these kinds of capabilities, why stop?[1] In particular, given our goal of providing an easy-to-use animations framework, we would like to have very simple APIs that enable more capabilities for the user of the framework. While some of the features described in this chapter, particularly the KeyFrames discussion, can get somewhat involved, most of the functionality that users need are embedded in very easy-to-use APIs that make animation creation and running trivial.

There are two major additional areas of advanced functionality in the framework: *triggers* and *property setters*.

Triggers

Triggers are a simple combination of the Timing Framework and Java's EventListener paradigm, enabling automatic starting of animations based on

---

1. As a great man (Spiderman's uncle) once said, "With great power comes great responsibility." But I'm sure that he actually meant, "With great power comes great insatiability for more power."

specified events in the system. It is not necessary to use triggers to get this functionality. You are free to set up your own event system for starting animations. But triggers save effort and code and make it much easier to automate animations, leaving you free to concentrate on core application logic instead of animation scheduling logic.

The main idea behind triggers is that they catch and handle environmental events, GUI events, timing events, or custom events that you define. Triggers start animations when those events occur. You can, for example, schedule an animation to start when a mouse is hovering over a button in your GUI or when the mouse clicks on a button. Triggers also allow you to sequence separate animations. For example, one animation can be set up to start as some other animation ends.

The triggers API has two audiences. One audience is the users of the API, allowing declaration of triggers to start animations based on certain events. The other audience is the extenders of the API, allowing creation of new triggers that handle events not yet built into the framework. We look primarily at the usage aspects of the API. Developers wishing to create their own custom triggers need only look at the source code for the simple triggers that exist already and model their own after those examples.

First we look at the general concepts and superclasses in triggers. Then we examine how these concepts apply in the various built-in triggers provided by the framework.

Concepts and Usage

Using any type of trigger is straightforward:

Creation

Triggers are created by calling either the constructor or the `addTrigger()` factory method of the appropriate `Trigger` subclass. For the constructor, you provide information about the `Animator` you want the trigger to run, the event that should cause the trigger to fire, and whether you want the trigger to "auto-reverse," which is discussed later. For the factory method `addTrigger()`, you also provide an object that you want the trigger to add itself to as a listener.

Adding Listeners

Each built-in trigger implements a specific event listener. For example, the `ActionTrigger` implements `ActionListener`, and the `FocusTrigger` implements `FocusListener`. Each trigger can be added to one or more objects as a listener on those objects. For example, an `ActionTrigger` can be added to an object that produces `ActionEvents`, such as a button. To enable the trigger to fire when a specific button is clicked, you would call `addActionListener(actionTrigger)` on that button.

The `addTrigger()` factory methods add listeners automatically. You pass in the object that you want the trigger to listen to, and it will add the listener appropriately.

Firing

Firing, or starting the animation, is something that happens automatically on the basis of information you provided to the factory method or constructor. The listener receives events from the object you specified, and when the right event comes its way, it starts the `Animator` you specified.

Disarming

You may cancel a trigger at any time by calling the `disarm()` method of a trigger.

Auto-Reversing

Some triggers have the ability to auto-reverse the animation. Auto-reversing means that when an opposite event is received from the event you specified in the constructor or in `addTrigger()`, the animation will be stopped and started in reverse at the same point. This functionality can be useful for tasks such as automatically causing a roll-off animation by specifying an auto-reversing rollover animation.

Note: The key concept behind triggers is that all of the work is in the setup: You create a trigger, and it handles any later actions appropriately without further assistance from you.

Now let's look at the two superclasses in the triggers package.

Triggers Superclasses

Trigger

This class is the superclass of all the built-in triggers and any custom triggers that you might want to implement. It holds common constructors, variables, and information that subclasses will need. `Trigger`'s methods are not used directly by application developers except for the single `disarm()` method:

```
public void disarm()
```

This method disables a trigger; any future events that would have triggered the animation of this trigger will no longer have any effect.

TriggerEvent

This superclass is set up to provide a way for `Trigger` subclasses to specify events specific to those triggers. This mechanism enables `TriggerEvents` to be accessed by the `Trigger` superclass in a generic way, which offloads some of the logic from `Trigger` subclasses. Application developers will not typically call `TriggerEvent` directly, but will instead deal with one of the simple subclasses that define events specific to a particular `Trigger` subclass.

There is one public method in `TriggerEvent`, called `getOppositeEvent()`. Even though this method is public, it is not intended to be called directly by applications. Instead, it is a utility method that subclasses will override and that will be called by `Trigger` in the process of running an auto-reversing animation.

The Built-In Triggers

So much for the superclasses. We now discuss the specific triggers that come with the library and that you may want to use in your applications. All of the triggers have the same pattern between their constructors and factories. The factories are called `addTrigger()` and take one extra argument that is used to specify an object to which the trigger adds itself as a listener.

To help you understand how to use triggers in an application, we show screenshots and code from the ingeniously named `Triggers` demo on the book's Web site. This application shows five colored spheres plus a couple of buttons for controlling the demo, as shown in Figure 15-1.

Each sphere in the demo has an associated animation that causes it to bounce down to the bottom of the window and back. The sphere painting and animating functionality is embedded in the separate `SpherePanel` class, which creates the animation and handles painting for a single sphere. The creation of these panels with specific sphere images is seen here:

```
action = new SpherePanel("yellow-sphere.png");
focus  = new SpherePanel("blue-sphere.png");
armed  = new SpherePanel("red-sphere.png");
over   = new SpherePanel("green-sphere.png");
timing = new SpherePanel("gray-sphere.png");
```

The `Animator` is defined through a `PropertySetter`, using multiple values to move it from the top of the screen to the bottom and back. We have not yet seen

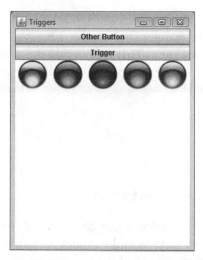

Figure 15-1 Triggers demo. Various triggers have been set on the Trigger button. Each trigger causes a different sphere to bounce down to the bottom of the window and back.

property setters, but they're coming soon, so here is a tantalizing preview of how they work:

```
bouncer = PropertySetter.createAnimator(1000, this, "sphereY",
    0, (PANEL_HEIGHT - sphereImage.getHeight()), 0);
bouncer.setAcceleration(.5f);
bouncer.setDeceleration(.5f);
```

Here, the Animator is given a duration of one second, during which it changes the value of the property sphereY in the SpherePanel object from 0 to the bottom of the panel and back. We set acceleration and deceleration properties on the Animator to give it a bouncing motion.

Painting the sphere in the proper location is handled in this simple paintComponent() method in SpherePanel:

```
@Override
protected void paintComponent(Graphics g) {
    g.setColor(Color.white);
    g.fillRect(0, 0, getWidth(), getHeight());
    g.drawImage(sphereImage, sphereX, sphereY, null);
}
```

For each of the following built-in triggers, we will see how each trigger kicks off this same animation for the different spheres in the Triggers demo window.

ActionTrigger

`ActionTrigger` is the simplest trigger in the framework because it handles only one type of event: `java.awt.event.ActionEvent`. This means that this trigger does not need a `TriggerEvent` because the only event that causes the trigger to fire is implicit.

Constructor

```
ActionTrigger(Animator animator)
```

Factory

```
addTrigger(Object source, Animator animator)
```

The `animator` is the animation that will be started when an `ActionEvent` is received. The object argument in the factory method is the object to which this trigger will add itself as a listener. Note that `Object` is a more generic source than the other `Trigger` subclasses use because there are various unrelated classes that can send events to an `ActionListener`. It is the responsibility of the caller of `addTrigger()` to provide an `Object` that has an `addActionListener()` method so that `ActionTrigger` can call that method successfully.

Example

Suppose you have a `JButton` and `Animator` as follows:

```
JButton button;
Animator anim;
```

You could have `anim` start automatically when `button` is clicked as follows:

```
ActionTrigger.addTrigger(button, anim);
```

Demo: Triggers

In the `Triggers` demo, clicking on the Trigger button animates the bouncing motion of the first sphere, as shown in Figure 15-2. The code to create this trigger is as follows:

```
ActionTrigger.addTrigger(triggerButton, action.getAnimator());
```

where `action` is the `SpherePanel` that contains the leftmost sphere and the associated `Animator`.

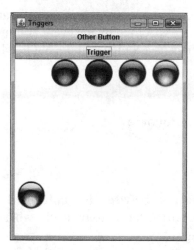

Figure 15-2 ActionTrigger: First sphere animates when the Trigger button is clicked.

FocusTrigger

FocusTrigger starts animations according to whether a component gains or loses focus. This trigger implements the FocusListener interface and is added, either by the caller or implicitly in the factory methods, as a listener to a component. Future focus events on that component will cause the animation to begin.

Constructors

```
FocusTrigger(Animator animator, FocusTriggerEvent event)
FocusTrigger(Animator animator, FocusTriggerEvent event,
            boolean autoReverse)
```

Factories

```
addTrigger(JComponent component, Animator animator,
            FocusTriggerEvent event)
addTrigger(JComponent component, Animator animator,
            FocusTriggerEvent event, boolean autoReverse)
```

The animator is the animation that will be started when the event is received. The event is one of the following:

- FocusTriggerEvent.IN, when the component receives focus
- FocusTriggerEvent.OUT, when the component loses focus

See the JavaDocs for FocusListener for more information on these events; they map exactly to those in the FocusListener interface. The autoReverse flag is used to specify that the trigger should stop, reverse, and restart the animation when it receives the opposite event from the one specified by the event argument. The component argument in the factory methods is a Swing component to which this trigger will add itself as a listener.

Example

Suppose you have a JButton and Animator as follows:

```
JButton button;
Animator anim;
```

Suppose further that anim animates a transition between the unfocused and focused states of the button. You could have anim start automatically when the button receives focus by calling the following:

```
FocusTrigger.addTrigger(button, anim, FocusTriggerEvent.IN, true);
```

The final argument tells addTrigger() to make this an auto-reversing trigger. This means that an IN event will cause anim to start as usual, and a subsequent OUT event will cause anim to stop, reverse, and restart at the same point.

Demo: Triggers

The second sphere is animated whenever the Trigger button receives focus, as seen in Figure 15-3. This trigger is the reason for Other Button in the demo, as it creates another GUI object to receive focus. Hitting the Tab button or clicking the mouse on either button changes focus appropriately. The code to create this trigger is as follows:

```
FocusTrigger.addTrigger(triggerButton, focus.getAnimator(),
                        FocusTriggerEvent.IN);
```

where focus is the SpherePanel that contains the second sphere and the associated Animator.

MouseTrigger

MouseTrigger starts animations on the basis of mouse events in a component. This trigger implements the MouseListener interface and is added, either by the caller or implicitly in the factory methods, to a component. Future mouse events

Figure 15-3 `FocusTrigger`: Second sphere animates when Trigger button receives focus.

on that component will cause the animation to begin. These events can be useful for running animations according to a component's rollover state, when the mouse is hovering over the component, or armed state, when the mouse has been pressed but not released in the component.

Constructors

```
MouseTrigger(Animator animator, MouseTriggerEvent event)
MouseTrigger(Animator animator, MouseTriggerEvent event,
            boolean autoReverse)
```

Factories

```
addTrigger(JComponent component, Animator animator,
           MouseTriggerEvent event)
addTrigger(JComponent component, Animator animator,
           MouseTriggerEvent event, boolean autoReverse)
```

The `animator` is the animation that will be started when the event is received. The event is one of the following:

- `MouseTriggerEvent.ENTER`, when the mouse enters a component's area
- `MouseTriggerEvent.EXIT`, when the mouse leaves a component's area
- `MouseTriggerEvent.PRESS`, when the mouse button is pressed in a component's area

- MouseTriggerEvent.RELEASE, when the mouse button is pressed in a component's area is released

- MouseTriggerEvent.CLICK, when the mouse button is clicked, pressed, and released in a component's area

See the JavaDocs for MouseListener for more information on these events; they map exactly to those in the MouseListener interface. The autoReverse flag is used to specify that the trigger should stop, reverse, and restart the animation upon receiving the opposite event from the one specified by the event argument. The component argument in the factory methods is a Swing component to which this trigger will add itself as a listener.

Example

Suppose you have a JButton and Animator as follows:

```
JButton button;
Animator anim;
```

Suppose further that anim animates a transition between the default and rollover states of the button. You could have anim start automatically when the button receives a mouse-entered event by calling the following:

```
MouseTrigger.addTrigger(button, anim,
    MouseTriggerEvent.ENTER, true);
```

The final argument tells addTrigger to make this an auto-reversing trigger. This means that an ENTER event will cause anim to start as usual, but an EXIT event will cause anim to stop, reverse, and restart at the same point.

Demo: Triggers

There are two animations in the Triggers demo tied to MouseTrigger. The first animation is started when the Trigger button is "armed," which happens when the button is pressed, as seen in Figure 15-4. The other animation begins when the mouse is "over" the Trigger button, as seen in Figure 15-5. The code to create these triggers is as follows:

```
MouseTrigger.addTrigger(triggerButton,
    armed.getAnimator(), MouseTriggerEvent.PRESS);
MouseTrigger.addTrigger(triggerButton,
    over.getAnimator(), MouseTriggerEvent.ENTER);
```

where `armed` and `over` are the `SpherePanels` that contain the third and fourth spheres and the associated `Animators`.

Figure 15-4 `MouseTrigger`: Third sphere is animated when Trigger button is pressed.

Figure 15-5 `MouseTrigger`: Fourth sphere is animated when mouse is over Trigger button.

TimingTrigger

`TimingTrigger` is useful in sequencing separate animations. It allows you to specify that one `Animator` object should start when another stops, repeats, or starts. This trigger implements the `TimingTarget` interface and is added, either by the caller or implicitly in the factory methods, to an `Animator` object.

Constructors

```
TimingTrigger(Animator animator, TimingTriggerEvent event)
TimingTrigger(Animator animator, TimingTriggerEvent event,
             boolean autoReverse)
```

Factories

```
addTrigger(Animator source, Animator animator,
          TimingTriggerEvent event)
addTrigger(Animator source, Animator animator,
          TimingTriggerEvent event, boolean autoReverse)
```

The argument `animator` is the animation that will be started when the event is received. The event is one of the following:

- `TimingTriggerEvent.START`, when a source animation begins
- `TimingTriggerEvent.STOP`, when a source animation ends
- `TimingTriggerEvent.REPEAT`, when a source animation repeats

See the JavaDocs for `TimingTarget` for more information on these events; they map exactly to the `begin()`, `end()`, and `repeat()` methods in the `TimingTarget` interface. The `autoReverse` flag is used to specify that the trigger should stop, reverse, and restart the animation upon receiving the opposite event from the one specified by the event argument. The `source` argument in the factory methods is an `Animator` to which this trigger will add itself as a target.

Example

Suppose you have two animations as follows:

```
Animator anim1, anim2;
```

Suppose further that you want `anim2` to start when `anim1` stops. You could set up this sequence as follows:

```
TimingTrigger.addTrigger(anim1, anim2, TimingTriggerEvent.STOP);
```

Demo: Triggers

The last sphere is animated whenever the animation on the first sphere, which is triggered by clicking on the Trigger button, stops. This `TimingTrigger` animation is seen in Figure 15-6. The code to create this trigger is as follows:

```
TimingTrigger.addTrigger(action.getAnimator(),
    timing.getAnimator(), TimingTriggerEvent.STOP);
```

where `action` is the `SpherePanel` that contains the leftmost sphere and the associated `Animator` and `timing` is the `SpherePanel` that contains the rightmost
sphere.

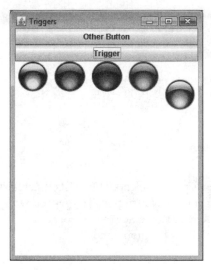

Figure 15-6 `TimingTrigger`: The rightmost sphere is animated when the animation on
the leftmost sphere, started by clicking on Trigger, completes.

Demo: TriggerRace

It is time to revisit our racetrack demo from Chapter 14. Now that we understand
triggers, we can simplify the code that we saw previously in `NonlinearRace` and
create another version, `TriggerRace`, also found on the book's Web site. In particular, we can automate the race to start when the Go button is clicked. We still need
our `actionListener` to stop the race, but starting the race based on the Go button
is much easier. Instead of setting up an `ActionListener` on `goButton` and implementing the logic in our `actionPerformed()` method to start the race, we simply
do the following:

```
ActionTrigger.addTrigger(goButton, animator);
```

This trigger handles clicks on the `goButton` inside the `ActionTrigger` and starts
our race automatically.

The complete functionality of `TriggerRace` is as follows:

```java
public class TriggerRace extends NonLinearRace {
  public TriggerRace(String appName) {
    super(appName);
    JButton goButton = controlPanel.getGoButton();
    ActionTrigger trigger = ActionTrigger.addTrigger(
        goButton, animator);
  }

  public void actionPerformed(ActionEvent ae) {
    if (ae.getActionCommand().equals("Stop")) {
      animator.stop();
    }
  }
  // main() method deleted for brevity
}
```

This class, like `NonLinearRace` itself, depends on the functionality of its superclass for setting up the race, and then adds a trigger on the Go button. Triggers currently only start animations, so we still need a mechanism, the `actionPerformed()` method, to stop the animator when the user clicks the Stop button.

Property Setters

Property setters are a great mechanism for specifying animations that automatically alter object properties over time without having to involve you and your application code in the process. Just like triggers, property setters are all about providing mechanisms for callers to set up an animation and then performing the tasks of the animation automatically. But where triggers handle the functionality of starting animations, property setters handle the core functionality of actually modifying objects during the animation, which is a powerful thing to have automated.

 Note: Property setters take animations from the world of manually handling animation events and changing properties on the fly in your application code to the more automated, declarative world of specifying animations in terms of what you want to animate and letting the property setter do the work for you.[2]

---

2. The difference between using property setters and not is a bit like the difference between taking a cab and driving a car. They may both get you to your destination, but one method requires you to do a lot more of the work. Hopefully property setters are a little safer and less adrenaline-producing than a typical cab ride, however.

Generally, you will be creating or using animations for your applications in which you will vary object properties over time: the translucency of a component, the placement of a button, the text in a label, and so on. Using the core `Animator` and `TimingTarget` classes, you now know how to perform these animations, and you can do so in a much easier way than by using Java's built-in timers. But most of these types of operations can be automated by property setters, using simple definitions of how objects should be modified over time.

That is, instead of your application code manually doing the work of altering values over time according to some formula, you can let the Timing Framework do it for you. For example, suppose you want to change some integer property `myInt` from a value of 0 to a value of 10 in a linear fashion over a period of a second. You might do so with the core Timing Framework facilities as follows:

```java
public class MyIntAnim {
  private int myInt;
  public void setMyInt(int newValue) {
    myInt = newValue;
  }

  public MyIntAnim() {
    // Set up the animation
    TimingTarget myTarget = new TimingTargetAdapter() {
      public void timingEvent(float fraction) {
        setMyInt((int)(fraction * 10));
      }
    };
    Animator anim = new Animator(1000, myTarget);
    anim.start();
  }
}
```

In this demo, found on the book's Web site under `MyIntAnim`, the implementation of `timingEvent()` calls the `setMyInt()` method to vary the value of `myInt` as the animation runs.

Property setters allow you to simply specify the object and property you want to modify, and let the framework change the property's value for you. For this example, the code in the constructor could be simplified to just the following, which you can see in the `MyIntAnimPS` demo on the book's Web site:

```java
public MyIntAnimPS() {
  // Set up the animation
  Animator anim = PropertySetter.createAnimator(
      1000, this, "myInt", 0, 10);
  anim.start();
}
```

Note that this version has no implementation of `timingEvent()`, because that functionality is embedded within the `PropertySetter` itself. This means that all your code needs to do is tell `PropertySetter` what you want to vary and how you want to vary it, and the setter takes care of the rest.

In order to handle this functionality for you, property setters have some important constraints. Most of them are related to the mechanism used to do this work: reflection. Property setters take the information you provide and construct a callback mechanism into the object you specify using reflection. This mechanism requires certain important assumptions about the property and object specified.

First of all, the system must have access to the object and property you specified, which implies several things:

Public

The object must have public access. Since the `PropertySetter` will be calling into this object from a different package, the object must have access that allows this call to happen. If you hand in a private object to `PropertySetter`, then the system will attempt to get the information it needs from that object and will fail due to access privileges.

Setter

The property must be the name of a property that is accessible through a public JavaBean-like `set*()` method. In the example with the property `"myInt"`, the `PropertySetter` expects to find the method `setMyInt(int)` in the object `this`. If such a method is not found in the object, `PropertySetter` will fail as it tries to set up the reflection mechanism for future calls to that method.

Getter

A `get*()` method may also be needed. One usage of `PropertySetter` requires just one value for your variable, as opposed to the two values used in the above example. Specifying just one value tells the system to use the current value, whatever it is when the animation starts, as the starting value for the property. In order to do this, the system must be able to call an appropriate `get*()` method for the property to query its current value. For example, if we had specified only the end-value of 10 for `myInt` like this:

```
Animator anim = PropertySetter.createAnimator(
    1000, this, "myInt", 10);
```

then the `PropertySetter` would have expected to find, in `this`, the method

```
public int getMyInt()
```

Known Types

The types of values provided to PropertySetter must be in a type that the system understands. The system currently knows of various common built-in types, such as all of the primitive types plus the Object equivalents: int and Integer, float and Float, and so on. The system also knows of a few more common GUI types, such as Point, Dimension, and Rectangle. If you are providing values for a type of which the system is not aware, PropertySetter will throw an exception at creation time. In this case, you must provide the system with a way of understanding and interpreting that type: You must provide an appropriate Evaluator object, which we discuss later.

Now let's see the classes used in property setters. In particular, let's go over PropertySetter itself, Evaluator, and KeyFrames and its related classes.

PropertySetter

PropertySetter is, not surprisingly, the main class that you interact with when dealing with property setters in the Timing Framework. You use this class to declare the object and property that you want to modify and the manner in which you want the property to be modified over time. You can declare a separate Animator that defines the animation parameters, but PropertySetter also has utility createAnimator() factory methods, as we saw earlier, for creating both the PropertySetter and Animator that are needed to drive the animation.

PropertySetter implements the TimingTarget interface, which is how it handles the timing events from the associated Animator in order to modify properties.

Constructors

There are three constructors for PropertySetter and three parallel factory methods.

```
PropertySetter(Object object, String propertyName,
                 T... params)
```

This constructor takes an object, which holds the property to be modified, the name of the property to be modified, and a list of values. The funky T notation is an indicator that *generics*, a feature of the Java language since JDK 5.0, are at play. Another giveaway of J2SE 5.0+ features is the "..." notation of the varargs feature. Varargs may be familiar to old C/C++ hackers, but the feature is new in the Java language since J2SE 5.0. These two features together mean that there can be an arbitrary number of parameters (because of varargs) of any type (because of generics). Part of the magic here is that the system knows how to interpret arbitrary types, which is accomplished through the Evaluator class that we discuss later.

An example of how this constructor is used is as follows. Suppose, to use our earlier MyIntAnimPS example again, that you want the property setter to vary the integer property myInt of the object this between 0 and 10. You might call the constructor like this:

```
new PropertySetter(this, "myInt", 0, 10);
```

The number of values provided here is worth discussing. The typical case for most animations is two values: the value at which the property starts and the value to which it will animate. A degenerate case uses a single value, which will be used as the final value, where the starting value will be determined dynamically when the animation begins. But it is also possible to provide three or more values. So what do these additional values mean?

Multiple values in the PropertySetter constructor mean that the property will take on each of these values in the course of the overall animation, moving from one value to the next over the full duration of the animation. The length of time spent in the intervals between the values will be equal by default. For example, if three values are provided, the property will start at the first value, at an elapsed animation fraction of 0; reach the second value halfway through the animation, at an elapsed animation fraction of .5; and reach the final value at the end, at an elapsed animation fraction of 1. We can see how this works in Figure 15-7.

In Figure 15-7 we can see how prop takes on the values 10, 20, and 100 at times that evenly divide the duration. That is, prop equals 10 at time $t = 0$, 20 at $t = .5$, and 100 and $t = 1$. We can also see how prop takes on values that are linearly interpolated between the values for times that lie between 0 and .5 and .5 and 1.0. This is the default interpolation behavior for the simple case in which PropertySetter

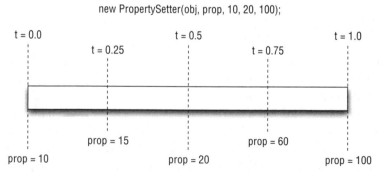

Figure 15-7 PropertySetter with three values supplied in the constructor.

is constructed with values only. We see later how we can vary this default interpolation behavior.[3]

PropertySetter(Object object, String propertyName, Evaluator evaluator, T... params)

This constructor is exactly like the one before except that this one takes an `Evaluator`. This class is provided when you want to provide your own mechanism for calculating values in between the ones you provide in `params`. One important reason to provide a custom `Evaluator` is for interpolating between types that are unknown to the framework. Another possible use case for a custom `Evaluator` is for providing a different calculation of in-between values than the framework provides by default.

We describe `Evaluator` in more detail later. For now, suffice it to say that `Evaluator` provides a means of calculating values that lie in between the values provided in the constructor.

PropertySetter(java.lang.Object object, String propertyName, KeyFrames keyFrames)

This final constructor is the most powerful and flexible because it takes a `KeyFrames` structure instead of simple values. `KeyFrames` are described completely later in the chapter. Briefly, `KeyFrames` provide a mechanism to describe not only the values that the property should take on during the animation but also the times at which those values are assigned and the manner of interpolating between those values. `PropertySetter` ends up using a `KeyFrames` structure internally. The other constructors that do not take a `KeyFrames` object make more assumptions about the elements in `KeyFrames`, and the resulting animations are therefore simpler. A more complex animation may be constructed by creating a custom `KeyFrames` object. For example, `KeyFrames` is important in creating a multistep animation, with more than just simple from and to values.

Factory Methods

There are three parallel factory methods in `PropertySetter` that are exactly like the constructors just described but with one important difference: They also take a `duration` parameter, and they return an `Animator` object. Calling one of these factory methods is equivalent to calling one of the `PropertySetter` constructors and then creating an `Animator` using the simple constructor that takes a `duration` and

---

3. Extra credit for anyone who guessed that the `Interpolator` class has something to do with this.

a TimingTarget. Here, the PropertySetter created in the factory method is set as a target for the Animator. For example, to animate the myInt property of **this** from 0 to 10 over a period of one second, we could either do this:

```
PropertySetter ps = new PropertySetter(this, "myInt", 0, 10);
Animator anim = new Animator(1000, ps);
anim.start();
```

or this:

```
Animator anim = PropertySetter.createAnimator(
    1000, this, "myInt", 0, 10);
anim.start();
```

There is no functional difference between these approaches; the factory methods are provided merely as a convenience for common cases.

TimingTarget Methods

The only other methods in PropertySetter are from the TimingTarget interface. To be completely accurate, they are overrides of TimingTargetAdapter methods, which PropertySetter subclasses:

```
void begin()
void timingEvent(float fraction)
```

These methods are not intended for public use by your code but rather are there for use by Animators that use this PropertySetter as a TimingTarget. These methods are the means by which PropertySetter turns all of the setup information passed into its constructor or factory method into the action of modifying the property during an animation.

Demo: SetterRace

Now, let's see how using property setters affects the racetrack demo that we saw in Chapter 14. This version is found on the book's Web site in the application SetterRace.

Recall from the original BasicRace that setting up and running the animation consisted of creating the animator in the constructor:

```
animator = new Animator(RACE_TIME, this);
```

and changing the position of the car in the `timingEvent()` method:

```
Point start = TrackView.START_POS;
Point end = TrackView.FIRST_TURN_START;
Point current = new Point();

public void timingEvent(float fraction) {
  current.x = (int)(start.x + (end.x - start.x) * fraction);
  current.y = (int)(start.y + (end.y - start.y) * fraction);
  track.setCarPosition(current);
}
```

Now let's see how we handle that same functionality in `SetterRace`. Here is the call to create the `Animator` in the constructor:

```
animator = PropertySetter.createAnimator(RACE_TIME,
    basicGUI.getTrack(), "carPosition",
    TrackView.START_POS, TrackView.FIRST_TURN_START);
```

And that's it. Here, we are creating a `PropertySetter` with:

- `RACE_TIME`: the duration for the animation
- `basicGUI.getTrack()`: the object that will have its property modified
- `"carPosition"`: the name of the property we wish to animate
- `START_POS` and `FIRST_TURN_START`: the values we wish to animate from and to

The `PropertySetter` handles the rest, automatically calculating and setting the value of `carPosition` as the animation runs.

Evaluator

Evaluator is a simple class for calculating intermediate values for specific types:

```
public abstract class Evaluator<T> {
  Evaluator();
  abstract T evaluate(T v0, T v1, float fraction);
}
```

This class is used by `PropertySetter`, discussed earlier, and `KeyValues`, discussed later, for calculating values in between boundary values during the course of an animation. For example, in the `SetterRace` example, the `PropertySetter` takes two `Point` values for the starting and ending positions of the car. An `Evaluator` that knows how to interpolate between `Point`s is responsible for calculating the intermediate values of `carPosition` during the animation.

There are several Evaluators built into the system that understand many of the core types that GUI and graphics animation code might care about. The primitive types, int, long, short, float, double, and byte, are covered, as are many types of concern to graphics and GUI developers, such as Rectangle2D, Point2D, Dimension, and Color. Each Evaluator performs simple linear interpolation between values of the specified type:

v = v0 + ((v1 - v0) * fraction)

For example, here is the implementation of the evaluate() method of EvaluatorFloat, which gets called by the system whenever floating-point values need to be interpolated:

```
public Float evaluate(Float v0, Float v1,
                      float fraction) {
   return v0 + ((v1 - v0) * fraction);
}
```

For a slightly more interesting example that works on a more complex object, here is the built-in Evaluator for Dimension2D, which is used to interpolate between Dimension and Dimension2D values:

```
public Dimension2D evaluate(Dimension2D v0, Dimension2D v1,
                            float fraction) {
   double w = v0.getWidth() +
       ((v1.getWidth() - v0.getWidth()) * fraction);
   double h = v0.getHeight() +
       ((v1.getHeight() - v0.getHeight()) * fraction);
   Dimension2D value = (Dimension2D)v0.clone();
   value.setSize(w, h);
   return value;
}
```

More built-in Evaluators can be seen in the source code for Evaluator in the Timing Framework project on the book's Web site.[4]

There are two cases in which you may want to implement your own Evaluator:

- The system has no support for some type that you are using.
- You want to perform a custom evaluation on some type.

_____

4. To spare you the gripping suspense, all of the built-in Evaluators are exactly like the two examples we just saw. They simply take in boundary values of some type plus a fraction and then compute a simple linear interpolation appropriate for that type.

New Evaluator Type

Although the system supports many built-in types, it may not support some type that you need. For example, the system does not currently support the type AffineTransform, so if you want to support interpolating between transform objects, you could supply your own Evaluator to KeyValues that would be called by the system to interpolate intermediate AffineTransform values:

```
class EvaluatorTransform extends Evaluator<AffineTransform> {
  public AffineTransform evaluate(AffineTransform v0,
                                  AffineTransform v1,
                                  float fraction) {
    // Insert your interpolation here
  }
}
```

Then you can use your Evaluator when creating your PropertySetter for some object, "propName", and AffineTransform objects xform0 and xform1:

```
PropertySetter ps = PropertySetter(object, "propName",
          new EvaluatorTransform(), xform0, xform1)
```

Custom Evaluator

You might also be interested in supplying your own Evaluator for a custom interpolation between values. For example, the code inside the evaluate() method in EvaluatorTransform could really return anything of type AffineTransform, which makes Evaluator an interesting place to plug in custom behavior. We already discussed the more general mechanism for providing arbitrary interpolation, Interpolator, in Chapter 14, but Evaluator is an alternative means of providing custom interpolation. Given the two input values and fraction, your implementation is free to return whatever result makes it happy.

Usually, Evaluators are supplied automatically by the framework as needed. When a PropertySetter is created with values of a given type, the system searches for an Evaluator that knows how to interpolate between values of that type. If you use a type that is unknown to the system, or you wish to use your own Evaluator for some other reason, you can use the PropertySetter constructor or factory method that takes an Evaluator argument. Similarly, you can supply a custom Evaluator to the KeyValues.create() routine, discussed later, to have that KeyValues object use your Evaluator instead of any default supplied by the framework.

KeyFrames

Key frame is a term from traditional animation that defines an object's state at a particular point in time. At any time between two key frames, the object's state can be interpolated from its states at the surrounding key frames. For example, suppose we want to animate Duke between two key frames defined for times t = 0 and t = 1, where the position and rotation are defined for each key frame. Calculating the position and rotation for Duke for any time in between these key frames is straightforward. In Figure 15-8, we show a sample frame calculation at t = .5.

In the Timing Framework, each key frame defines a time from 0 to 1 in the elapsed animation and a value associated with that time. A KeyTimes structure holds the times, a KeyValues structure holds the values, and a KeyFrames object holds these KeyTimes and KeyValues objects. These structures work hand in hand with the property-setting capabilities. The values defined are for the property that we wish to alter over time, and the times correspond to the elapsed times during the animation when the property should take on the associated values. During the animation, if the current fraction equals one of the times in the KeyTimes structure, then the object's property will be set to the corresponding value in KeyValues. If the current fraction is between two times in the KeyTimes structure, the value will be interpolated between the values at the two surrounding times.

There is an additional element that makes KeyFrames even more powerful and flexible: Interpolator. For every interval of time defined by the KeyTimes structure, there is an associated Interpolator. Just as with Animator overall, the default Interpolator for each interval is LinearInterpolator. But KeyFrames

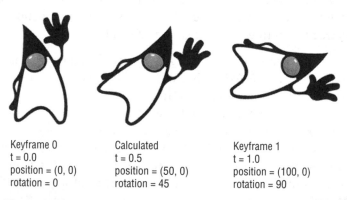

Keyframe 0
t = 0.0
position = (0, 0)
rotation = 0

Calculated
t = 0.5
position = (50, 0)
rotation = 45

Keyframe 1
t = 1.0
position = (100, 0)
rotation = 90

Figure 15-8 Interpolating position and rotation at t = .5 between key frames at t = 0 and t = 1.

can be created to use different Interpolators for its intervals instead, making for much more interesting animation behavior.

We can picture, with the help of Figure 15-9, a KeyFrames object as a series of time/value pairs, along with Interpolator objects that define how values get interpolated between the specified times.

As we mentioned earlier, KeyFrames uses linear interpolation by default. So for any fraction f between 0 and 1, where f lies between the times t_{n-1} and t_n in the KeyTimes object, and x_{n-1} and x_n are the values in the KeyValues object that correspond to t_{n-1} and t_n, we can calculate the appropriate value $x(f)$ for the property at f as follows:

```
t = (f - tn) / (tn - tn-1);
x(f) = xn-1 + t * (xn - xn-1);
```

This is exactly the calculation being performed in Figure 15-7. For (f = .75), we get a value t_{n-1} of .5 and t_n = 1, and values of x_{n-1} and x_n of 20 and 100 respectively. This gives us the following equations:

```
t = (f - tn-1) / (tn - tn-1)
  = (.75 - .5) / (1 - .5)
  = (.25 / .5)
  = .5
x(f) = xn-1 + t * (xn - xn-1)
     = 20 + .5 * (100 - 20)
     = 20 + 40
     = 60
```

One of the powerful things with KeyFrames is the ability to modify the interpolation for each interval. The above interpolation is the default behavior if none

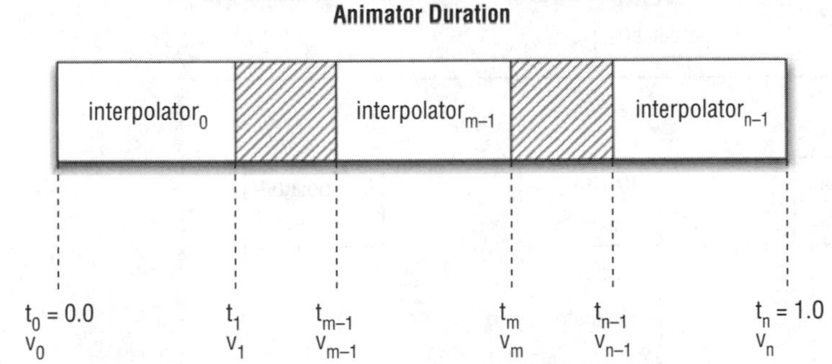

Animator Duration

Figure 15-9 KeyFrames are specified by times (t), values (v), and interpolators (interp). Note that the intervals need not be of equal length in time.

other is specified, but the creator of a KeyFrames object can use Interpolator and Evaluator to customize this behavior.

Helper Classes: KeyValues, KeyTimes, Evaluator, and Interpolator

In order to better understand the KeyFrames class, it is helpful to understand the classes that it depends on and how they all fit together, as the flow chart in Figure 15-10 illustrates.

Figure 15-10 shows how data moves through the system during an animation. An Animator object sends timing events to a PropertySetter, which is a TimingTarget. The PropertySetter holds a KeyFrames object internally, even if the PropertySetter was not created explicitly with a KeyFrames object. The KeyFrames object is queried for an appropriate value given the elapsed fraction of the animation, f. KeyFrames calculates and returns the proper value on the basis of information from KeyTimes, KeyValues, Evaluator, and Interpolator. This value is then sent to the appropriate setter method in the object with which PropertySetter was created.

We have already seen how Evaluator and Interpolator work. Let's see how the additional helper classes of KeyFrames are constructed and how they help store and retrieve the necessary information.

KeyValues   KeyValues is a class that exists to hold an arbitrary number of values of any type.

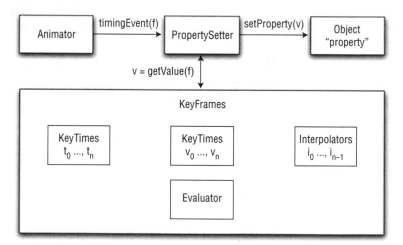

Figure 15-10 Flow of data during an animation.

Tip: All values in a KeyValues object must be of the same type. Creating KeyValues with objects of different types can lead to problems with the system not knowing how to interpolate between values of some generic superclass type.

You can create a KeyValues object with one of two factory methods:

```
static <T> KeyValues<T> create(T... params)
```

If the generics syntax (<T>) in this method confuses you, you're not alone.[5] Fortunately, you really don't need to understand generics in order to use this method. In fact, your calling code won't have any generics syntax in it at all. For example, you could create a KeyValues object to hold integers 1, 2, and 3 like this:

```
KeyValues values = KeyValues.create(1, 2, 3);
```

The reason that the <T> syntax is in the method declaration is that the method uses the generics language feature to create a KeyValues object of the appropriate type, depending on the type of the parameters used in the call. One non-generics alternative would be to create a single KeyValues class that just held Objects, which would then need to be cast and instanceof-ed at runtime in a continuing effort to figure out what the objects were. Another possibility would be to have numerous subclasses and constructors of KeyValues that were type-specific. Generics allows us to have the same functionality as type-specific versions without all of the API litter. We just have to deal with a little <> syntax to get there.

One thing to note is that KeyValues depends on another JDK 5.0 feature called *autoboxing*[6] to choose the type most appropriate for the values you pass in. Autoboxing provides us the ability, for example, to pass in parameters of type int and have them cast automatically into the Object type Integer.[7] This action should have no impact on your code. You can pass in values of type int or Integer, and

---

5. I'm right there with you. I don't believe generics help make this code very readable. However, it does help tremendously in being able to have a compact API without a lot of type-specific subclasses that would otherwise be necessary. For more information on Generics in general, check out the release notes for J2SE 5.0, when this feature was first introduced: http://java.sun.com/j2se/1.5.0/docs/guide/language/generics.html.

6. http://java.sun.com/j2se/1.5.0/docs/guide/language/autoboxing.html.

7. Life before autoboxing was sometimes truly and inexplicably painful. I know that an int is an Integer. You know that an int is an Integer. Surely, the compiler can figure it out, right? Well, now it can.

these values can be used to act on variables that are of type int or Integer. But this implicit use of autoboxing helps explain the background to some of the type-conversion details that follow.

The main thing to understand with this method is that it needs to be called with types that are all the same. Otherwise, the system may make some bad guesses as to what you mean. For example, suppose you try to create the same KeyValues object as before with values 1, 2, and 3, but you pass in a double for one of the values:

```
KeyValues values = KeyValues.create(1, 2, 3.0);
```

You won't get a KeyValues object that holds ints. You won't even get one that holds doubles. You'll get one that holds objects of type Number. KeyValues will automatically pick the most general Object type that fits all of the parameters. In this case, the ints will be autoboxed to Integer and the double to Double. The common superclass of these is Number, so that is what the compiler will choose for the type of this KeyValues instance that you create. This KeyValues<Number> object is probably not the result you were looking for. In particular, this object may be unable to do anything useful with the resulting types, because there may be no Evaluator available that can interpolate between values of this more general type.

Tip: There is no Evaluator for values of type Number. Be sure to supply values all of the same type unless you are supplying an Evaluator to your KeyValues object that knows how to interpolate between types that the system does not understand.

The solution here is to create KeyValues objects with parameters of the same type. In the previous situation, you should either call:

```
// returns KeyValues<Integer>
KeyValues values = KeyValues.create(1, 2, 3);
```

or

```
// returns KeyValues<Double>
KeyValues values = KeyValues.create(1.0, 2.0, 3.0);
```

but not

```
// returns KeyValues<Number>
KeyValues values = KeyValues.create(1, 2, 3.0);
```

Finally, it is worth noting that if KeyValues is used to operate on a property assigned in PropertySetter, then the types used in KeyValues should be the same as the type of that property. So if you have a property of type Dimension, you should create a KeyValues with parameters of type Dimension. Similarly, if you have a property of type int or Integer, you need to create a KeyValues object with ints or Integers. Mixed or double variants will not suffice for this situation. The result of a mismatch is that the system may fail to call your property-setting method, since it will not be able to find a method that takes the type that KeyValues has stored.

The other factory method for KeyValues is quite similar, but takes one extra parameter:

```
static <T> KeyValues<T> create(Evaluator evaluator, T... params)
```

Evaluator tells KeyValues how to interpolate between values of the type passed in to params. We saw the Evaluator class earlier, in our discussion of PropertySetter. That earlier usage of Evaluator actually boils down to exactly this usage: PropertySetter creates a KeyValues object internally, and if you give PropertySetter an Evaluator, it will create the KeyValues with that Evaluator. Most uses of KeyValues will probably not need this capability, because the system has several Evaluators stored already for common types.[8] But there may be cases in which your application either needs to use a type that the system does not know about or you want to provide an Evaluator that performs a custom interpolation between types. In either case, you would supply a custom Evaluator to KeyValues.

KeyTimes KeyTimes is a very simple class, especially compared to the type-specific details we just covered in KeyValues. KeyTimes just stores a collection of floating-point values that represent the times at which the values in KeyValues

---

8. In fact, this is where the whole discussion of types and getting KeyValues to store the correct type really kicks in. If KeyValues cannot effectively determine the type of your parameters, such as in the (1, 2, 3.0) case, then it may search for, and fail to find, an appropriate Evaluator for that type. KeyValues, at the API level, is all about storing values. It's just a place for you to store the values for your key frames. But internally, KeyValues is used to calculate intermediate values between these stored values during animations. If it cannot determine the type, it cannot pick an appropriate Evaluator and cannot calculate intermediate types. Don't worry about it too much. You probably won't actually run into the problem, or if you do it will be in the form of obvious compile-time errors, like the inability to find an Evaluator, or runtime errors, like the inability to find a property setter with the KeyValues type. I'm just covering the details here so that if and when you do see the errors, you'll know why.

should hold true for the `KeyFrames`. There are some important constraints to `KeyTimes` that are worth noting:

Times Are Fractional

All time values are in the range [0,1] and represent the elapsed fraction of an animation. For example, if you have an `Animator` with a 3-second duration, a `keyTime` value of .5 would represent 1.5 seconds in this particular animation. But if you use that same `KeyTimes` structure on an `Animator` with a duration of 10 seconds, a .5 time value would represent 5 seconds in that second animation.

Times Are Monotonically Increasing

`KeyFrames` advance forward in time, and `KeyTimes` reflect that constraint.

Times Begin at 0, End at 1

`KeyFrames` must know what to do for all time values between 0 and 1, inclusive, so there must be times, and associated values, for the start and end points of 0 and 1. For example, a `KeyTimes` structure with only 2 entries would have the times 0 and 1 only.

Number of Times Must Equal Number of Values

The number of times supplied in a `KeyTimes` structure must equal the number of values supplied in a `KeyValues` structure with which it will be used. `KeyFrames` matches up the values and times and expects to have the same number of each.

The constructor, and only method, for `KeyTimes` is simple:

```
public KeyTimes(float... times)
```

To use a `KeyTimes` class, simply call the constructor and pass in the times at which you will have `KeyFrame` information. Note the `varargs` notation in this constructor, which matches similar `varargs` parameters in other methods discussed previously and allows this constructor to take an arbitrary number of parameters.

Interpolator   We discussed `Interpolator` earlier, in the context of `Animator`. `Animator`'s `Interpolator` object is responsible for interpolating the elapsed fraction of the animation. By default, `Animator` uses `LinearInterpolator`.

Similarly, each interval during a KeyFrame animation uses a LinearInterpolator by default, but it is possible to provide an alternate Interpolator to use instead.

The default facilities provided by KeyFrames will interpolate between values that you supply, but they will do so in a linear fashion. If you want to change this behavior, you must supply a different Interpolator for KeyFrames to use.

Interpolators come into play in the intervals between the times specified in KeyTimes. Just as an Interpolator determines how an elapsed fraction is interpolated for Animator, an Interpolator determines how an elapsed fraction is interpolated for an interval in KeyFrames. KeyFrames can be created with a single Interpolator, which will be used for all intervals, or with a set of Interpolators whose size is equal to the number of intervals. Each Interpolator will interpolate across an interval as if that interval were a complete animation in the range [0, 1].

For an example of how Interpolators operate on intervals, let's look at DiscreteInterpolator. We saw in Chapter 14 that this interpolator returns an interpolated value of 0 during an animation and 1 when the animation finishes. When applied to the intervals of KeyFrames, the interpolator effectively creates an animation that moves discretely between the values in the KeyValues structure, without interpolating between them.

For example, suppose we want to create an animation in which a variable moves through, but not between, the values from 2 to 6, as shown in Figure 15-11.

We could create this animation using KeyFrames created as follows:

```
KeyValues keyValues = KeyValues.create(2, 3, 4, 5, 6);
KeyFrames keyFrames = new KeyFrames(keyValues,
    DiscreteInterpolator.getInstance());
```

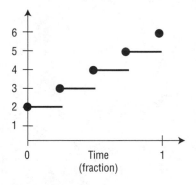

Figure 15-11   Discrete Animation from 2 to 6.

Note that discrete interpolation need not happen on sequential values, as in this example. To see how you can use `DiscreteInterpolator` to animate between nonsequential values, check out the `DiscreteInterpolation` demo on the book's Web site. This application sets up a `KeyFrames` object just as we did previously, except that the values are nonsequential:

```
KeyValues keyValues = KeyValues.create(2, 6, 3, 5, 4);
KeyFrames keyFrames = new KeyFrames(keyValues,
    DiscreteInterpolator.getInstance());
```

An `Animator` is created to animate between these values over a duration of a second, using a `PropertySetter` that calls into the `DiscreteInterpolation` demo class to set the value of `intValue` during the animation:

```
Animator anim = PropertySetter.createAnimator(1000,
    new DiscreteInterpolation(), "intValue", keyFrames);
anim.start();
```

The property-setting method for `intValue` records the new value and prints it out:

```
public void setIntValue(int intValue) {
   this.intValue = intValue;
   System.out.println("intValue = " + intValue);
}
```

The output from the program looks like this, with repeated entries replaced by [...] for brevity:

```
intValue = 2
intValue = 2
[...]
intValue = 2
intValue = 6
intValue = 6
[...]
intValue = 6
intValue = 3
intValue = 3
[...]
intValue = 3
intValue = 5
intValue = 5
[...]
intValue = 5
intValue = 4
```

Note that there are duplicate values for every interim value except the final value of 4. In graph form, the animation looks like the chart in Figure 15-12.

KeyFrames: The Class

Now that we have seen how the component pieces of KeyFrames work, we can see how they fit together in constructing and running the KeyFrames object itself.

Constructors   The constructors for KeyFrames range from simple to complete, reflecting the different ways in which developers might use KeyFrames. Internally, all constructors get turned into the same information we saw in Figure 15-9: a series of times, values, and interpolators. The difference between the constructors is merely what the KeyFrames assume as a default versus what the caller specifies explicitly.

At the simple end of the spectrum, the caller can use a constructor that requires only a series of values, in the form of a KeyValues object:

```
public KeyFrames(KeyValues values)
```

These values become the $(v_0, \ldots, v_n)$ values in Figure 15-13. The times $(t_0, \ldots, t_n)$ default to an even split of the interval [0, 1], so for $(n + 1)$ values, each time value t is $(1/n)$ more than the previous one. For example, if the caller provides three values (v0, v1, v2), we will have three corresponding times at 0, .5, and 1.0:

The interpolation mechanism for this constructor defaults to simple linear interpolation, as noted earlier. That is, interpolation in each of the two intervals defined by this case will use the default LinearInterpolator.

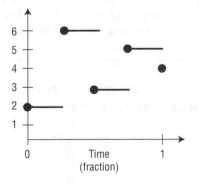

Figure 15-12 DiscreteInterpolation demo: Values in a discrete interpolation need not be sequential.

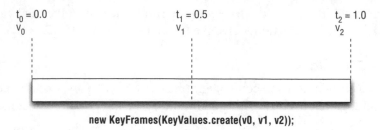

new KeyFrames(KeyValues.create(v0, v1, v2));

Figure 15-13 KeyFrames for simple case with three values.

There is one special case worth calling out. It is possible to define a KeyFrames object with only one value. Or, to be more accurate, it is possible to define a KeyFrames object that uses a KeyValues object with only one value, like so:

```
KeyFrames kf = new KeyFrames(KeyValues.create(v));
```

It does not make sense to have a KeyFrames object with only one value, because KeyFrames are all about intervals, not single values.[9] In this case, KeyFrames actually does create an interval internally, with the first value and time assumed. This is a "to" animation for which you provide only the final value to animate toward. The initial value is determined dynamically whenever the animation begins. We saw something similar in our discussion of single-value PropertySetters. Internally, these cases are the same, since PropertySetter creates a KeyFrames structure to hold the property value information used during the animation.

Tip: Don't go overboard. It is worth noting that although all KeyFrames constructors take one or an arbitrary number of values, a typical use case normally has just two values: the value animating from and the value animating to. The ability to pass in more than two values with the magic of the varargs language feature makes it easier to create multistep animations—but that does not mean you have to actually do so. Feel free to create simple animations with just two values.

The next constructor takes the same KeyValues structure but also lets you supply the times at which these values should be assigned to the property:

```
public KeyFrames(KeyValues keyValues, KeyTimes keyTimes)
```

---

9. A KeyFrame with only one time/value pair would be as useful as having a single glove (pop stars from other planets excepted), or a single nostril, or a single sip of coffee. It's just not enough.

In this constructor, the number of values in keyValues must match the number of times in keyTimes. This constraint should be somewhat obvious from the earlier discussions, because KeyFrames consists of a set of matched time/value pairs. Each value in keyTimes, starting at 0, incrementing monotonically, and ending at 1, is the time in the animation cycle at which the corresponding value in keyValues will be assigned.

Figure 15-14 shows a sample KeyFrames created with four value/time pairs.

In the interval between each of the times in keyTimes, the value is interpolated linearly, as in the previous constructor, using the default LinearInterpolator of KeyFrames.

The third constructor is like the first, supplying only values, but this variant also supplies a set of interpolators to be used in the intervals:

```
public KeyFrames(KeyValues values,
                 Interpolator... interpolators)
```

In the first and second constructors, the lack of Interpolator objects for the intervals meant that the default LinearInterpolator object would be assigned for every interval between the values in KeyValues. In this version, the caller supplies a set of Interpolator objects to be used for all intervals. These Interpolators can include built-in singleton interpolators, LinearInterpolator or DiscreteInterpolator, instances of the SplineInterpolator class, or completely custom Interpolators. There should be either one Interpolator, which will be used for all intervals, or exactly one less Interpolator than the number of values in KeyValues, since the number of intervals is one less than the number of values.

As in the first KeyValues-only constructor, this version computes an evenly spaced set of KeyTimes to be used.

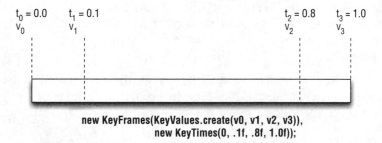

new KeyFrames(KeyValues.create(v0, v1, v2, v3)),
new KeyTimes(0, .1f, .8f, 1.0f));

Figure 15-14 Creating KeyFrames with multiple values and times. The number of times supplied must equal the number of values.

The final, most flexible constructor puts all of the elements together and accepts values, times, and interpolators:

```
public KeyFrames(KeyValues values, KeyTimes times,
                 Interpolator... interpolators)
```

This constructor is exactly like the previous one that took values and interpolators except that the times are supplied explicitly to KeyFrames instead of calculated to be evenly spaced. The resulting KeyFrames object will be essentially something like what is pictured in Figure 15-9, with the caller supplying values $(v_0, \ldots, v_n)$, times $(t_0, \ldots, t_n)$, and interpolators $(interp_0, \ldots, interp_{n-1})$.

KeyFrames Methods   There is one single method, other than the constructors, in KeyFrames:

```
int getInterval(float fraction)
```

This is a simple utility method that returns the interval for any given fraction from 0 to 1. It is sometimes useful to be able to query the KeyFrames object in a multistep animation to help figure out which interval an animation is in at any given time. This capability is used, for example, in the MultiStepRace demo we are about to see.

Demo: MultiStepRace

Let's take one last look at our racetrack demo and how it changes given what we now know about KeyFrames. This time, we take advantage of multistep animations to make the car race around the entire track. You can find this version on the book's Web site under MultiStepRace.

Just as in the previous version, SetterRace, we use PropertySetter to handle the animation. Also, just as in that previous version, all of the work is in the setup of the Animator. The runtime processing of the animation is handled for us by the Timing Framework.

In multistep animations, we need to define the KeyFrames that will handle all of the time/value pairs and interval interpolators. First, let's define the values that carPosition will assume in going around the track:

```
Point values[] = {
  TrackView.START_POS,
  TrackView.FIRST_TURN_START, TrackView.FIRST_TURN_END,
```

```
      TrackView.SECOND_TURN_START, TrackView.SECOND_TURN_END,
      TrackView.THIRD_TURN_START, TrackView.THIRD_TURN_END,
      TrackView.FOURTH_TURN_START,
      TrackView.START_POS};
   KeyValues keyValues = KeyValues.create(values);
```

The code for the key times, not shown here but available in the demo on the book's Web site, calculates the distance in every leg of the journey and bases the times on those distances. There are other ways to get the times, some of them probably more correct, but this will do for now. Once we have stored those times in an array, we can create our `KeyTimes` object:

```
   KeyTimes keyTimes = new KeyTimes(times);
```

If we created the `KeyFrames` object now, with just these values and times, the car would go around the track, but it would look terribly unrealistic. Not only would the car start off at full speed, but it would take the turns and other stretches of the track at that same speed. With the ability to set interpolators for every leg of the journey, we should be able to do better than this. There are basically four different kinds of nonlinear movement that we will account for in this demo:

Initial acceleration: At the start of the race, the car begins at a speed of zero and accelerates up to full speed.

Turns: All turns are taken with the same dynamic of starting off slower and accelerating through the turn.

Straightaways: Except for the initial stretch, where the car is starting from a dead stop, the car will start off a little slower coming out of the turn and then accelerate.

Final stretch: On the final turn, we want the car to slow down even more as it comes to rest.

We should note one important thing about the different sections of the race. In order to be more realistic, we should make sure that the speeds at the end of one segment and the beginning of another are close to each other. Otherwise, we may end up with disjoint behavior. For example, the car may slow down through a turn and then hit a straightaway where it is suddenly going much faster. This constraint gives us something to aim for when setting up our `SplineInterpolator` objects.

Tip: It is worth pointing out that we used the `SplineEditor` demo, discussed earlier and available on the book's Web site, to help visualize these interpolators and get appropriate acceleration behavior. You might want to do the same when playing with `SplineInterpolator`, especially if you're new to splines and they do not yet feel intuitive to you.

These interpolation behaviors are set up in the following `SplineInterpolators`:

```
Interpolator initialSpline = new SplineInterpolator(
    1.00f, 0.00f, 0.2f, .2f);
Interpolator curveSpline = new SplineInterpolator(
    0.50f, 0.20f, .50f, .80f);
Interpolator straightawaySpline = new SplineInterpolator(
    0.50f, 0.20f, .50f, .80f);
Interpolator finalSpline = new SplineInterpolator(
    0.50f, 0.00f, .50f, 1.00f);
```

Finally, we can set up our `KeyFrames` object with the values, times, and interpolators defined previously:

```
KeyFrames keyFrames = new KeyFrames(keyValues, keyTimes,
    initialSpline, curveSpline,
    straightawaySpline, curveSpline,
    straightawaySpline, curveSpline,
    straightawaySpline, finalSpline);
```

And now that we have our `KeyFrames`, we can create our `PropertySetter`:

```
PropertySetter modifier = new PropertySetter(basicGUI.getTrack(),
    "carPosition", keyFrames);
```

Note that we did not use the utility factory method of `PropertySetter` to create our `Animator`. Because we wish to add repeating behavior to the race, we construct our own `Animator` instead.

```
animator = new Animator(RACE_TIME, Animator.INFINITE,
                        RepeatBehavior.LOOP, modifier);
```

Now we can run our race and get the result shown in Figure 15-15.

Did you notice anything wrong in Figure 15-15? Perhaps you noticed that the car looks ready to crash through the track wall?

The problem is that we are not rotating the car through the turns. The current setup of `KeyFrames` handles the position of the car but not the rotation. We need to do a little more work. We need another set of `KeyFrames` to handle rotation.

First of all, we need some values for our rotation:

```
keyValues = KeyValues.create(360, 315, 270, 225, 180,
                             135, 90, 45, 0);
```

These rotation values align with the positions we set up earlier. So, for example, the car starts at a rotation angle of 360 degrees. This is equivalent to a rotation of 0 but means that the car will spin the correct way when rotating to the next angle.

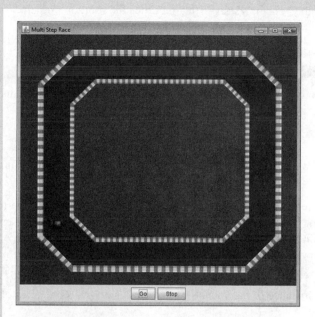

Figure 15-15 `MultiStepRace` with faulty steering wheel.

The other angles are all 45 degrees from each other as the car goes into the turn and then onto the next straightaway, ending up back at the starting rotation.

We would like to interpolate the rotations just as we did the motion, although here we need just two splines to control rotation. The straightaway interpolation will make the car go straight for most of the way and then start rotating toward the end of the stretch. The curve interpolation will turn quickly at first and then slow down the rotation toward the end, as if the car were skidding through each turn.

```
Interpolator straightawayTurnSpline = new SplineInterpolator(
    1.0f, 0.0f, 1.0f, 0.0f);
Interpolator curveTurnSpline = new SplineInterpolator(
    0.0f, 0.5f, 0.5f, 1.0f);
```

We use the same `keyTimes` as before, so we can now create our rotation `KeyFrames`:

```
keyFrames = new KeyFrames(keyValues, keyTimes,
    straightawayTurnSpline, curveTurnSpline,
    straightawayTurnSpline, curveTurnSpline,
    straightawayTurnSpline, curveTurnSpline,
    straightawayTurnSpline, curveTurnSpline);
```

And we can create the PropertySetter that modifies the rotation property on the car over time:

```
modifier = new PropertySetter(basicGUI.getTrack(),
    "carRotation", keyFrames);
```

Finally, we can use the multitarget capabilities of Animator to simply add this new PropertySetter as a target of the original Animator that we created:

```
animator.addTarget(modifier);
```

Now the scene, shown in Figure 15-16, looks correct, with the car actually turning through the curves.

There is one final element to add to make this demo complete: sound. Unfortunately, we could not figure out a way to embed an audio experience in the screenshots, so you will either have to download and run the demo from the book's Web site or make your own sound effects as you look at the screenshots on these pages. But we can at least show you how the sound effects were implemented.

First, we create an instance of the SoundEffects class with our KeyFrames object:

```
soundEffects = new SoundEffects(keyFrames);
```

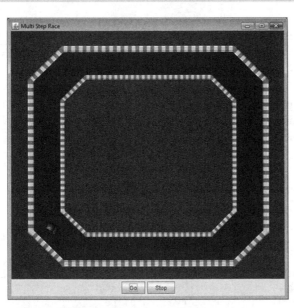

Figure 15-16 MultiStepRace with working steering wheel.

This class implements `TimingTarget` so that it can react to timing events during the animation. At construction time, `SoundEffects` caches the `keyFrames` variable and sets up some sound resources for the straightaways and turns:

```
this.keyFrames = keyFrames;

URL url = SoundEffects.class.getResource("sounds/vroom.wav");
drivingClip = java.applet.Applet.newAudioClip(url);

url = SoundEffects.class.getResource("sounds/drift.wav");
turningClip = java.applet.Applet.newAudioClip(url);
```

The key to making the sound effects work is in knowing which interval the car is in at any point in the animation. To track this information, we use the `KeyFrames.getInterval()` method discussed earlier. For any elapsed fraction in the animation, we can query what interval we are in and change sound effects as appropriate. We play the `drivingClip` all of the time, but when we enter a turn we also play the `turningClip` sound. For example, here is the code that plays the turning sound on the first turn:

```
if (keyFrames.getInterval(fraction) == 1) {
  turningClip.play();
}
```

Check out the `SoundEffects` code for more details, but the main logic is shown here.

Now that we have created our `SoundEffects` object, which implements `TimingTarget`, we can add it as another target to our original `Animator`:

```
animator.addTarget(soundEffects);
```

Finally, we can set up our `Animator` to start upon a click on the Go button with an `ActionTrigger`, as we saw earlier in the `TriggerRace` version:

```
ActionTrigger trigger = ActionTrigger.addTrigger(goButton, animator);
```

Now the application is ready to go, and the car is ready to roll. Note that all of the work described here was performed at construction time. The animation is completely set up and simply waiting for events. First, it waits for the Go button click to start the animation. Then the various `TimingTargets`, the `PropertySetters` for moving and rotating the car, and the `SoundEffects` object for playing the audio, wait for timing events and perform their tasks appropriately.

Now we can sit back and enjoy the race. Over and over. That red car wins every time.

Summary

We hope this brief introduction to the Timing Framework has enabled you to see what the framework has to offer in building complex and interesting animations in any easy fashion. Go to the book's Web site. Play with the demos. Check out the code. Once you start using the framework, you will agree that it makes it much easier to create GUI animations. And with animation creation this easy, there is no reason not to starting adding animated touches to your Filthy Rich Clients.

Part IV

Effects

16

Static Effects

STATIC effects are nonanimated graphical effects that you can apply to make your application look better. Static effects are very important to Filthy Rich Clients. They are used to improve the appearance of an application, and they serve as the basis for more complex, animated visual effects. This chapter does not present all of the static effects you may use in your user interface but focuses on a few of the most common effects.

Blur

A blur effect is an image filter that removes finer details from a picture, blending the graphics together to get a smoother, less crisp view.

Motivation

Blur may be used when your user interface contains design elements that might distract the user's attention. A blur effect reproduces a natural visual effect known as *depth of field*. When your eyes focus on a very specific point in space, everything else in the scene appears blurry. You can test this effect by moving very close to an object, the top edge of this book for instance, and focusing your vision on that object. You will notice that the background and surrounding objects lose their details.

Photographers were the first to use blur effects as an artificial element of design. *Bokeh* refers to out-of-focus areas in an image; it is produced with a camera lens with focal length and aperture set to obtain a shallow depth of field. This technique is very common in macro or portrait photography because it emphasizes the primary subject.

The pictures in Figure 16-1 and Figure 16-2 show how effective blur can be in focusing the viewer's attention on the primary subject.

While user interfaces are not photographs, the same ideas apply. Many video games use blur effects when a menu is shown. The menu shows on top of the game itself, but in order to avoid too much visual clutter and player distraction, the background is blurred.

The demo called `Blur`, available on this book's Web site, shows how to use a blurred background to focus the user's attention on a progress bar, as seen in Figure 16-3.

Figure 16-1   The blur, or bokeh, emphasizes the importance of the bishop and the pawn.

Figure 16-2   The blurred background helps the viewer concentrate on the subject.

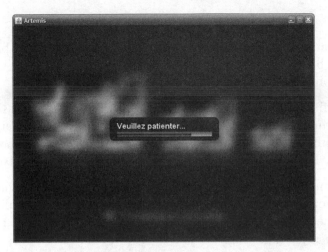

Figure 16-3 The blurred background draws the user's attention to the progress bar.

Blur effects may also be used to convey information without distracting the user. In such situations, the effect is subtler than in the progress bar example. Figure 16-4 shows the main screen of Aerith, available online in source and binary form at http://aerith.dev.java.net. On this screen, the two category labels, Tasks and Albums, are slightly blurred. When users see this screen, they can read the labels without being distracted by them, thus effectively focusing their attention more on the interactive elements.

Figure 16-4 A slight blur on the category labels helps convey the information without distracting the user.

Simple Blur

There are many variations of blur filters, including box blur, Gaussian blur, motion blur, and lens blur. The first two of these are particularly useful for user interfaces and can be implemented using a `ConvolveOp`.

The purpose of a blur filter is to remove details from the source image. The easiest way to do it is to compute the weighted average color value of a pixel and its neighbors. Herein lies the difference between most blur effects: Which pixel neighbors are used to produce the final result, and what weight is associated with each pixel?

The box blur is the simplest blur that you can implement. A box blur is defined by a radius, which specifies how many neighbors on each side of the source pixel must be included in the computations. The formula to find the size of a box blur kernel given a radius r is the following:

```
kernelWidth = radius * 2 + 1
kernelHeight = radius * 2 + 1
```

According to this formula, a 3×3 kernel represents a box blur of radius 1.

A box blur uses the same weight for each pixel, making sure that the luminosity, or brightness, is preserved. Therefore, all of the pixel weights must add up to 1. The formula to find the weight of all of the pixels is as follows:

```
weight = 1 / (kernelWidth * kernelHeight)
```

According to this formula, the weight of each pixel for a box blur of radius 1 is one ninth. The resulting kernel is the following:

$$
kernel = \begin{bmatrix} 1/9 & 1/9 & 1/9 \\ 1/9 & 1/9 & 1/9 \\ 1/9 & 1/9 & 1/9 \end{bmatrix}
$$

The name *box blur* comes from the shape of the kernel. Because all of the weights are the same, it has a boxlike pattern.

Constructing the appropriate kernel and `ConvolveOp` in Java is straightforward with the previous formulas:

```java
public static ConvolveOp getBlurFilter(int radius) {
  if (radius < 1) {
    throw new IllegalArgumentException("Radius must be >= 1");
  }
```

```
    int size = radius * 2 + 1;
    float weight = 1.0f / (size * size);
    float[] data = new float[size * size];

    for (int i = 0; i < data.length; i++) {
      data[i] = weight;
    }

    Kernel kernel = new Kernel(size, size, data);
    return new ConvolveOp(kernel);
  }
```

You many now apply a blur effect on any `BufferedImage`:

```
    BufferedImage image = // load image
    image = getBlurFilter(5).filter(image, null);
```

Unfortunately, this approach is quite slow. On my test system, an Intel CoreDuo 2.0 GHz with 2 GB of RAM running on Mac OS X, a box blur of radius 10 takes one second to complete when applied to a 640×480 picture.

Because of the mathematical properties of convolve operations and matrices, a box blur can be implemented in a much more efficient way. The above code uses a 3×3 kernel when the blur radius is 1. The resulting filter executes at least nine operations per pixel in the source image. A better approach splits the 3×3 kernel into two smaller kernels, one 3×1 kernel and one 1×3 kernel:

horizontal kernel $= [1/3 \quad 1/3 \quad 1/3]$

$$\textit{vertical kernel} = \begin{bmatrix} 1/3 \\ 1/3 \\ 1/3 \end{bmatrix}$$

Through the wonders of matrix multiplication, we can see that performing these two operations on any pixel is equivalent to the original 3×3 kernel. Multiplying the vertical kernel by the horizontal kernel gives us our original 3×3 matrix with all elements equal to one ninth.

Because we now use two kernels, we must also use two convolve operations:

```
    image = getBlurFilter(radius, 0).filter(image, null);
    image = getBlurFilter(0, radius).filter(image, null);
```

Each of these calls executes only three operations per pixel instead of nine, giving the same blur effect with a total of only six operations per pixel. On the same test system as before, a box blur of radius 10 with a split kernel blurs a 640×480 picture in only 150 ms.

The source code of both box blur implementations can be found in the project called BoxBlur on this book's Web site.

The two-kernels approach is much more efficient than the original 3×3 kernel approach, but it can be further improved. The implementation just shown filters the image twice, once for each separate kernel. A more efficient approach performs the horizontal and vertical convolve operations in a single filter.

The demo called FastBlur on this book's Web site offers a very efficient implementation of a box blur. The algorithm used is similar to using two kernels, but everything is done in a single filter. The execution speed is also independent of the blur radius. On the same test machine as before, a fast blur filters a 640×480 picture in about 50 ms, regardless of the radius size. Figure 16-5 shows an image blurred with a fast blur of radius 100.

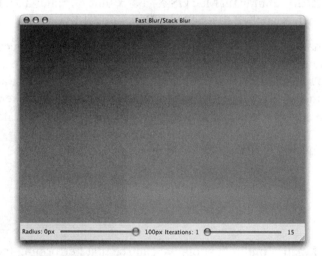

Figure 16-5 FastBlur with a radius of 100. The execution speed of this approach is independent of the radius size. But note that a blur with such a large radius makes the image impossible to recognize.

Gaussian Blur

Box blur effects are interesting because they are easy to understand and relatively fast. However, they tend to produce bad results with high-contrast images that contain sharp edges. Figure 16-6 shows a dark screen with a white arrow. The contrast between the arrow and the background is strong, and a box blur performs poorly, as shown in Figure 16-7.

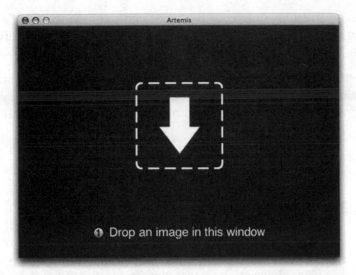

Figure 16-6 The white arrow contrasts sharply with the dark background.

If you look at Figure 16-7, at the place where the white arrow used to be, you will notice a rectangular pattern. On this picture, it is impossible to recognize the white arrow or even the dashed rectangle surrounding it.

A different type of blur effect can help in such situations. A Gaussian blur works similarly to a box blur: It is a weighted average of pixels implemented as

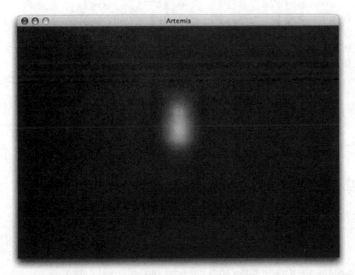

Figure 16-7 A box blur produces an unpleasant result from scenes with high contrast.

a convolve operation. The only difference lies in the choice of the weight of each pixel. A Gaussian blur computes the weights using a normal, or Gaussian, distribution. Figure 16-8 shows what a Gaussian distribution looks like.

The curve shows the weight of each pixel in a kernel, where the pixel at the center is represented by the center of the curve. The source pixel, the one at the center of the kernel, has the highest weight. The further a pixel is from the center, the lower is its weight.

The equation of a Gaussian distribution is the following:

$$G(u, v) = \frac{1}{\sqrt{2\pi\sigma^2}} e^{-(u^2 + v^2)/2\sigma^2}$$

In this formula, u is the horizontal distance from a pixel to the center, v is the vertical distance from a pixel to the center, and σ (sigma) is the standard deviation. You can set the standard deviation to any number, but the following value, where r is the radius of the kernel, generates good results:

$$\sigma = \frac{r}{3}$$

Here is a kernel constructed with the value we calculated for sigma and a radius of 3:

```
0.000    0.001    0.003    0.004    0.003    0.001    0.000
0.001    0.007    0.033    0.054    0.033    0.007    0.001
0.003    0.033    0.147    0.242    0.147    0.033    0.003
0.004    0.054    0.242    0.399    0.242    0.054    0.004
0.003    0.033    0.147    0.242    0.147    0.033    0.003
0.001    0.007    0.033    0.054    0.033    0.007    0.001
0.000    0.001    0.003    0.004    0.003    0.001    0.000
```

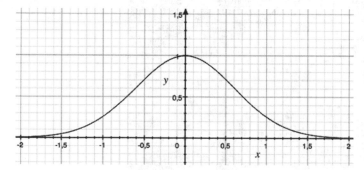

Figure 16-8   A Gaussian distribution is often called a bell-shaped curve.

The Gaussian distribution gives the kernel a circular shape. The center value, denoted in bold, is the highest. The weights furthest from the center are the lowest. You may also notice that this kernel is perfectly symmetrical.

For the same reason as before with the box blur, we are able to split this kernel into two smaller kernels. Instead of using a 5×5 kernel, we use one 5×1 kernel and one 1×5 kernel.

Here is the code to create such kernels:

```
public static ConvolveOp getGaussianBlurFilter(int radius,
        boolean horizontal) {
  if (radius < 1) {
    throw new IllegalArgumentException(
          "Radius must be >= 1");
  }

  int size = radius * 2 + 1;
  float[] data = new float[size];

  float sigma = radius / 3.0f;
  float twoSigmaSquare = 2.0f * sigma * sigma;
  float sigmaRoot = (float)
      Math.sqrt(twoSigmaSquare * Math.PI);
  float total = 0.0f;

  for (int i = -radius; i <= radius; i++) {
    float distance = i * i;
    int index = i + radius;
    data[index] = (float) Math.exp(-distance / twoSigmaSquare)
              / sigmaRoot;
    total += data[index];
  }

  for (int i = 0; i < data.length; i++) {
    data[i] /= total;
  }

  Kernel kernel = null;
  if (horizontal) {
    kernel = new Kernel(size, 1, data);
  } else {
    kernel = new Kernel(1, size, data);
  }
  return new ConvolveOp(kernel, ConvolveOp.EDGE_NO_OP, null);
}
```

As with a box blur, you must apply the horizontal kernel and then the vertical kernel to produce the desired result:

```
BufferedImage image = // load image
image = getGaussianBlurFilter(radius, true)
    .filter(image, null);
image = getGaussianBlurFilter(radius, false)
    .filter(image, null);
```

 You can find a complete implementation in the project called `GaussianBlur` on the book's Web site.

Figure 16-9 shows the result of a Gaussian blur of radius 12 applied to the picture in Figure 16-6. The effect looks much better than the previous attempt with a box blur. The user can actually see the dashed rectangle and the arrow in this version.

Tip: Faster Gaussian Blurs by Approximation. In contrast to box blurs, Gaussian blurs cannot be implemented in a very efficient manner. However, it is possible to simulate a Gaussian blur by applying a box blur several times. If you use this technique, remember to use a smaller radius for the box blur.

The `FastBlur` demo, from this book's Web site, contains a box blur implementation called `StackBlurFilter` that lets you choose the number of times the blur is applied. A box blur with three iterations produces a nice approximation of a Gaussian blur.

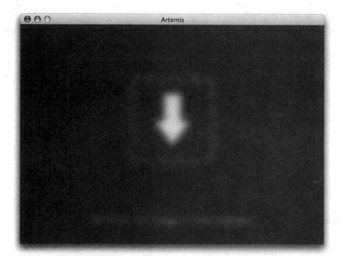

Figure 16-9 Gaussian blur effects generate visually pleasing results and retain more information from the original high-contrast elements in the scene.

Performance Trick

As you may have guessed, blurring is an expensive operation, which can make it difficult to use in animations. You won't have any problem with small pictures, like icons or banners, but you might want better performance in some specific cases.

Java 2D offers a simple and easy way to improve the performance of any blur filter. Remember that blurring an image is really about losing details. Java 2D already contains a similar operation: image resizing. When you scale an image down to a smaller size and then back to its original size, you are effectively losing details because of the color information necessarily lost during the scaling operations. If you use a bilinear or bicubic rendering hint, then Java 2D will interpolate the missing pixel data by averaging the values in the neighborhood of each pixel. Hey, that sounds almost like a blur operation!

The idea is to let Java 2D and its highly optimized rendering paths do part of the work for us. For example, if you want to blur an image with a blur of radius 15, you can instead scale the image to half its size, apply a smaller blur of radius 7, and finally scale the picture back to its original size. There are two ways that we gain performance with this approach. First of all, we are operating on an image with one quarter of the original pixels, so we are doing only a quarter of the operations that we would have done on the original image. Second, each pixel operation is faster because the radius is smaller.

Here is what the code looks like with this trick:

```
public static BufferedImage blurImage(BufferedImage image) {
   image = changeImageWidth(image, image.getWidth() / 2);
   image = getGaussianBlurFilter(radius / 2, true).
        filter(image, null);
   image = getGaussianBlurFilter(radius / 2, false).
        filter(image, null);
   image = changeImageWidth(image, image.getWidth() * 2);
}

public static BufferedImage changeImageWidth(
    BufferedImage image, int width) {
   float ratio = (float) image.getWidth() /
      (float) image.getHeight();
   int height = (int) (width / ratio);

   BufferedImage temp = new BufferedImage(width, height,
      image.getType());
   Graphics2D g2 = temp.createGraphics();
```

continued

```
g2.setRenderingHint(RenderingHints.KEY_INTERPOLATION,
    RenderingHints.VALUE_INTERPOLATION_BILINEAR);
g2.drawImage(image, 0, 0,
    temp.getWidth(), temp.getHeight(),
    null);
g2.dispose();

    return temp;
}
```

This code is available in the GaussianBlur project from the book's Web site. On my machine, a Gaussian blur of radius 20 without this performance tweak takes 280 ms to filter a 640 × 480 picture. Dividing the width of the picture by two before applying a Gaussian blur of radius 10 on the same picture takes only 90 ms. The images produced by these two techniques are so close that the user cannot tell the difference.

Blurring is an effective tool that you can use in many situations. You can generate high-quality results quickly without hindering your application's performance.

Reflection

Reflections are used to simulate a reflective surface, like a shiny metal plane or a wet floor.

Motivation

At the time that this book is being written, reflections are very popular among graphic designers. They can be seen everywhere, from software GUIs to advertisements in the street. There are two main reasons to use reflections.

First, reflections are an easy way to simulate a surface supporting an object. Doing so with other graphics techniques is harder because it requires advanced drawing skills. Most of the time, reflections are also less graphically intrusive than, for instance, drawing a realistic floor with the appropriate backdrop. Figure 16-10 shows how this effect is used in iTunes 7 to make it look like the album covers lie on the same "wet floor."

The second and most important reason reflections are used in GUIs is because they look cool.

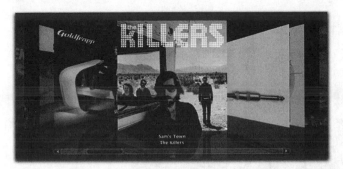

Figure 16-10 iTunes 7 album covers browser.

Drawing Reflections

The code required to draw reflections in Java is explained in Chapter 7, "Gradients." Reflections are also used in the demo called `RepaintManager`, presented in Chapter 11, "Repaint Manager."

The `SwingX` project, available at http://swingx.dev.java.net, offers a class called `ReflectionRenderer` that you can use to easily generate reflections. The following code snippet shows how to use this class:

```
ReflectionRenderer renderer = new ReflectionRenderer();
BufferedImage image = loadImage();
image = renderer.appendReflection(image);
```

The `appendReflection()` method returns the original image and its reflection in a single image. Another method, `createReflection()`, returns only the reflection.

Blurred Reflections

Reflections can be made a little more realistic by adding a blur effect. If you look at the reflections of the cars on a wet road on a rainy day, you will notice they are distorted and blurry. Figure 16-11 and Figure 16-12 show the difference between a regular, clean reflection and a blurry one.

Blurring the reflection requires only applying a blur filter on the generated reflection. The `ReflectionRenderer` class can take care of that for you, as in the following example:

```
ReflectionRenderer renderer = new ReflectionRenderer();
renderer.setBlurEnabled(true);
BufferedImage image = loadImage();
image = renderer.appendReflection(image);
```

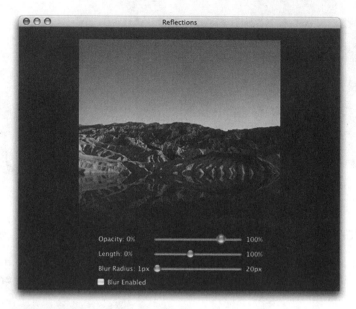

Figure 16-11   A regular reflection.

Figure 16-12   A blurry reflection.

A complete example of how to use the `ReflectionRenderer` class and how to generate blurry reflections can be found on this book's Web site in the project called `BlurryReflection`.

Drop Shadows

Drop shadows are one of the oldest and most widespread computer graphics effects. They simulate lighting in a user interface.

Motivation

In the real world, every object casts a shadow when illuminated by a light source. In the 2D world[1] of user interfaces, there is no light source, so shadows do not naturally occur. But drop shadow effects are very commonly used in user interfaces.

Probably the most important reason for using drop shadows in a user interface is to simulate depth. Windowing systems usually add drop shadows to pop-up menus or mouse cursors to give the impression that these objects are floating above the applications. Mac OS X casts drop shadows from every window onto the items below the windows. The focused window casts a longer drop shadow to give the impression of being closer to the user than the other windows. Figure 16-13 shows this difference.

Drop shadows are also sometimes used to better distinguish elements that sit on a cluttered background. Windows and Mac OS X render the text of the desktop's icons with a drop shadow to make it easy to read, no matter what background picture you choose, as seen in Figure 16-14.

And do not forget that drop shadows simply look cool.[2]

---

1. At the time this book is being written, GUIs are still very much 2D, and it is very likely that they will remain 2D for quite a while. Some desktop windowing systems, like Mac OS X and Windows Vista, are able to apply some 3D effects, but the desktops are still essentially 2D interfaces. Three-dimensional GUIs have the powerful advantage of being able to easily autogenerate drop shadows for any object. But despite years of ongoing research into 3D interfaces, desktop interaction remains an essentially 2D-oriented task.
2. Coolness is an important factor of Filthy Rich Clients. Never underestimate the power of cool for an application that you want your users to enjoy using.

Figure 16-13   The focused window has a stronger drop shadow to make it stand out.

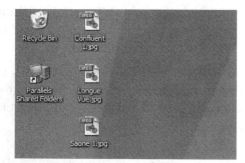

Figure 16-14   Windows XP casts drop shadows under the desktop icons' text to make reading easier.

Simple Drop Shadow

Drop shadows can be implemented in different ways. The easiest way consists of drawing the same thing twice. First, paint the primitive with a translucent black color, which becomes the drop shadow behind the object. Then draw the primitive naturally, which is the actual object itself. Do not forget to offset the position of the drop shadow by a few pixels if you want the user to see it. See Figure 16-13 and Figure 16-14 for examples of this offset effect.

The following code snippet demonstrates how to paint a drop shadow for a rectangle:

```
Graphics2D g2 = // obtain a Graphics2D
Composite oldComposite = g2.getComposite();

// the drop shadow is 50% transparent
g2.setComposite(AlphaComposite.SrcOver.derive(0.5f));
g2.setColor(Color.BLACK);

// offset the drop shadow by (5, 5) pixels
g2.translate(5, 5);
g2.fillRect(0, 0, 100, 100);

// restore the graphics state
g2.translate(-5, -5);
g2.setComposite(oldComposite);

// paint the original subject
g2.setColor(Color.GREEN);
g2.fillRect(0, 0, 100, 00);
```

This technique works fine for simple shapes. However, casting shadows in this manner for complex drawings requires many Graphics state changes that will clutter your code. Also, this approach makes it impossible to cast a shadow for images with transparent areas. The shadow would be improperly drawn for the transparent areas. Indeed, the only shape you can use to draw a shadow under an image, which is an inherently rectangular primitive, is a rectangle. Finding the shape of the nontransparent pixels in an image requires more work.

Chapter 6, "Composites," offers a solution to the problem of creating shadows for more complex shapes and images. Creating a drop shadow for an arbitrary shape or picture can be done with the AlphaComposite.SrcIn, as shown in the following code snippet:

```
public static BufferedImage createDropShadow(
    BufferedImage image) {
  BufferedImage shadow = new BufferedImage(
      image.getWidth(), image.getHeight(),
      BufferedImage.TYPE_INT_ARGB);

  Graphics2D g2 = shadow.createGraphics();
  g2.drawImage(image, 0, 0, null);
```

continued

```
        g2.setComposite(AlphaComposite.SrcIn);
        g2.setColor(Color.BLACK);
        g2.fillRect(0, 0, shadow.getWidth(),
                    shadow.getHeight());

        g2.dispose();

        return shadow;
    }
```

The original subject is first painted onto a new translucent image. After setting the SrcIn composite, this code fills a black rectangle over the entire picture. This operation paints black only in the nontransparent destination pixels.

Such drop shadows are not realistic enough, though. The two previous code snippets produce very sharp shadows, as in the example shown in Figure 16-15. But real-world shadows always have soft edges, because shadows are cast by the many large and diffuse light sources in nature. Sharp shadows are produced only by point light sources, like spotlights, which do not occur naturally in the world. If we want user interfaces to look more realistic, we should improve the rendering of our drop shadows.

Figure 16-15   Duplicating the drawing results in sharp shadows.

Realistic Drop Shadow

Our drop shadow is not perfect yet. We still need to smooth edges to make it look more realistic. A blur filter is the easiest way to achieve this:

```
    public static BufferedImage createDropShadow(
        BufferedImage image, int size) {
      BufferedImage shadow = new BufferedImage(
          image.getWidth() + 4 * size,
          image.getHeight() + 4 * size,
          BufferedImage.TYPE_INT_ARGB);

      Graphics2D g2 = shadow.createGraphics();
      g2.drawImage(image, size * 2, size * 2, null);
```

```
g2.setComposite(AlphaComposite.SrcIn);
g2.setColor(Color.BLACK);
g2.fillRect(0, 0, shadow.getWidth(), shadow.getHeight());

g2.dispose();

shadow = getGaussianBlurFilter(size, true).
    filter(shadow, null);
shadow = getGaussianBlurFilter(size, false).
    filter(shadow, null);

return shadow;
}
```

Figure 16-16 and Figure 16-17 show the difference between hard- and smooth-edged drop shadows.

The code shown for drop shadows is fast enough for most situations. However, it requires between 20 and 100 ms on my test system, depending on the radius used to smooth the shadow. The project called DropShadow, available on this book's Web site, offers both this implementation and a faster one.

The second implementation, written by Sébastien Petrucci for the SwingX project, does everything in one step. Instead of first painting a black shadow and then blurring it, the ShadowRenderer class blurs the original image and replaces all color information by a black color at the same time.

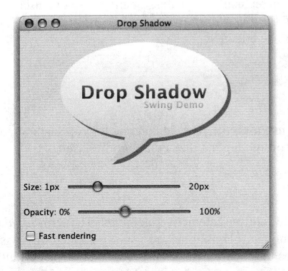

Figure 16-16 The sharp drop shadow behind the caption bubble lacks realism.

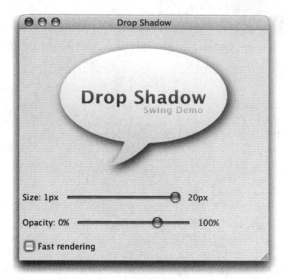

Figure 16-17   A smooth drop shadow behind the caption bubble looks more realistic.

 Note: Fast drop shadow. The ShadowRenderer's algorithm is, in fact, a modified implementation of the fast box blur algorithm that we saw earlier in this chapter. As a result of this speedup, ShadowRenderer can generate a drop shadow in 2 ms on my test computer, compared to 100 ms for the slower approach.

Drop shadows add a touch of realism and professionalism to your user interfaces. Drop shadows are subtler than most effects and do not require a lot of work from the programmer to be effective.

Highlights

Highlights simulate lighting in a user interface. In contrast to drop shadows, they do not simulate a side-effect of lighting but the actual lighting itself.

Motivation

Highlights are used mainly to indicate interactive elements. The term *highlight* covers a wide variety of techniques. Highlights are usually applied on a visual element when the user moves the focus or the mouse over that element. Putting the emphasis on interactive elements is vital in graphics-rich applications like

Web pages and Filthy Rich Clients. These applications may use nonstandard widgets, so they must help the user drive the interface.

Showing that an element, such as a button or a link, is interactive is often achieved with one of the following techniques:

- Changing a grayscale icon to a colored icon (example: toolbar buttons)
- Adding a border to an icon (example: toolbar buttons)
- Changing an element's color (example: links in a Web page)
- Changing the decoration of an element (example: links in a Web page)
- Increasing an element's brightness (example: toolbar buttons)
- Lighting the element

In this section, you will learn how to implement the last two techniques. Figure 16-18, Figure 16-19, and Figure 16-20 show some examples of highlights in common applications.

Figure 16-18 This Web page changes the background and the border of the highlighted item.

Figure 16-19 Safari, the Mac OS X default Web browser, changes the background and the color of the highlighted bookmark in the toolbar.

Figure 16-20 Word 2004 for Mac OS X adds a border to the highlighted button in its toolbars.

Figure 16-21   Windows Vista uses text highlighting in every window title bar.

Highlights may also be used to improve text readability. Windows Vista offers translucent windows, which can make text on those windows difficult to read. To counter that effect, the window system highlights window titles and the contents of some text fields, as shown in Figure 16-21.

Brightening

You should increase the brightness of interactive pictures and text to emphasize to the user that the current element is particularly important or active.

Brightening Text

To increase the brightness of text in Swing, you need to modify its color. The java.awt.Color class offers an interesting method called brighter() that seems to match our need. This method can be used to increase the brightness of any color:

```
JButton button = new JButton("Brighter");
label.addActionListener(new ActionListener() {
  public void actionPerformed(ActionEvent e) {
    JButton button = (JButton) e.getSource();

    Color c = button.getForeground();
    c = c.brighter();

    button.setForeground(c);
  }
});
```

This solution works, but it gives you very little control over the effect. The Color class uses an undocumented, predefined brightening factor. In Sun's current Java SE implementation, this factor is 30 percent. Since this factor is not part of the API, it might differ from one Java implementation to another.

You may, instead, get better control over brightness with other methods from the Color class: RGBtoHSB() and getHSBColor(). RGBtoHSB() converts a color encoded with RGB (red, green, and blue) components to the same color encoded with HSB (hue, saturation, and brightness) components. To increase the brightness of a color, you can simply change the value of the brightness component in the HSB format. The second method, getHSBColor(), turns a set of HSB components into a new instance of Color.

The following code increases the brightness of a button's text by 100 percent. Note that HSB components are values between 0.0 and 1.0.

```
Color color = button.getForeground();
int r = color.getRed();
int g = color.getGreen();
int b = color.getBlue();

float[] hsb = Color.RGBtoHSB(r, g, b, null);

hsb[2] = Math.min(1.0f, hsb[2] * 2.0f);
Color brighter = Color.getHSBColor(hsb[0], hsb[1], hsb[2]);

button.setForeground(brighter);
```

The complete source code for text brightening is available in the project called Brightness on this book's Web site.

Aerith (http://aerith.dev.java.net) also contains an example of how to use brightening on text. Figure 16-22 shows a section of the main screen of Aerith. When the mouse cursor is over an interactive element, the text becomes white, as opposed to the light gray color of the other text elements. The effect is subtle, but powerful enough to be noticed by the user.

Brightening Images

To increase the brightness of a picture, you must use the RescaleOp image filter. This filter was explained in detail in Chapter 8, "Image Processing." As a reminder,

Figure 16-22 The View Photos label is brighter than the others because the mouse cursor is hovering above it.

here is a method that shows how to increase the brightness of a JLabel's picture:

```
public static void increaseImageBrightness(JLabel c,
            BufferedImage image) {
  // we use an image with an alpha channel
  // therefore, we need 4 components (RGBA)
  float[] factors = new float[] {
      1.4f, 1.4f, 1.4f, 1.4f
  };
  float[] offsets = new float[] {
      0.0f, 0.0f, 0.0f, 0.0f
  };
  RescaleOp op = new RescaleOp(factors, offsets, null);
  BufferedImage brighter = op.filter(image, null);
  c.setIcon(new ImageIcon(brighter));
}
```

The source code for this effect is also available in the Brightness project from this book's Web site.

Spotlighting

Increasing the brightness of an element is effective, but it does not always look nice. This technique can turn a suitable darker color into an unattractive brighter one. Another solution for highlighting an active element is to add a real lighting effect to the element that you want to emphasize. Aerith[3] uses this technique on buttons, as shown in Figure 16-23 and Figure 16-24.

There are two different ways to implement these lighting effects. The first technique relies on radial gradients. You can refer to the Chapter 7 to learn more about using radial gradients.

The second technique for this highlighting effect is a little more interesting. Instead of drawing a radial gradient on the element, you must draw a picture. In the examples shown in Figure 16-23 and Figure 16-24, the code simply paints the image of a white, blurry ellipse in the background.

Compared to brightening, this technique has one drawback: You cannot achieve this effect without subclassing the component and adding some code to the paintComponent() method.

---

3. I hope you are used to reading references to Aerith by now.

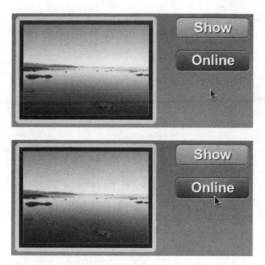

Figure 16-23 When the mouse moves over a button, a spotlight is added in the background of the button.

Figure 16-24 The navigation path at the top of the window adds spotlights in the background to show that the user can interact with these elements.

The project called SheddingLight on this book's Web site contains an example of a button that becomes highlighted on mouseover events. The highlighting code is short and simple:

```java
@Override
protected void paintComponent(Graphics g) {}
  Graphics2D g2 = (Graphics2D) g;

  // paint background

  if (getModel().isRollover()) {
    g2.setRenderingHint(RenderingHints.KEY_INTERPOLATION,
        RenderingHints.VALUE_INTERPOLATION_BILINEAR);
    g2.drawImage(buttonHighlight, 2, 2,
              width - 4, height - 4, null);
  }

  // paint text
}
```

In this snippet, the variable buttonHighlight holds the picture of a white, blurry ellipse. When this image gets drawn on the button, it is resized to cover the entire background, which ensures that the effect is independent from the size of the button.

Text Highlighting for Better Readability

Text highlighting, as seen in Windows Vista for example, can be implemented in three different manners. The obvious solution is to paint a picture behind the text, akin to the previous highlight code. This approach does not work very well, however, because the generic highlight does not match the shape of the text.

The second solution consists of painting the text in an offscreen image, blurring it, and painting the result prior to painting the real text. For this approach, please refer to the "Blur" section earlier in this chapter.

The third solution is the most interesting. It requires only a few lines of code, it looks good, and it's much faster than blurring an offscreen picture. This technique is used in the project called TextHighlighting on this book's Web site to produce the effect shown in Figure 16-25.

When the user presses the Show Dialog button, located at the bottom of the frame, a new internal window appears. This window title mimics an effect seen in Windows Vista with the Aero theme. The content of the internal window shows a blurred version of the parent frame, as if seen through a frosty glass

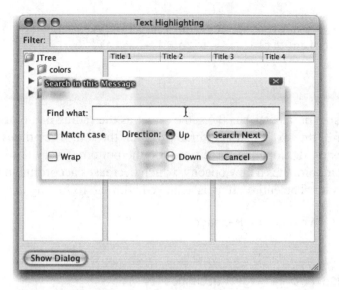

Figure 16-25 The highlight makes the internal window's title easier to read.

pane.[4] Because of this translucency effect, the title of the window might become hard to read in some situations.

To improve the text's readability, a highlight is drawn around it. As this example shows, highlights do not need to be white; you can use any color you wish. If you look closely at this highlight, you will notice that it looks like a blurred version of the text. The code actually simulates a blur effect by painting the text several times:

```
private void drawTextHighlight(Graphics2D g2, String title,
                               int size, float opacity) {
  g2.setColor(Color.BLACK);

  for (int i = -size; i <= size; i++) {
    for (int j = -size; j <= size; j++) {
      double distance = i * i + j * j;
      float alpha = opacity;
      if (distance > 0.0d) {
        alpha = (float) (1.0f /
            ((distance * size) * opacity));
      }
```

continued

4. Note that all of the techniques used to create frost effect for this internal window have been presented in the book already. The blur and drop shadow effects were discussed earlier in this chapter. The color tint filter was discussed in Chapter 8.

```
            g2.setComposite(
                AlphaComposite.SrcOver.derive(alpha));
            g2.drawString(title, i + size, j + size);
        }
    }
}
```

In this method, the size parameter has the same effect as the radius in a blur filter. With a radius of 3, the text is painted three times on the left, three times on the right, three times on the top, and three times on the bottom. Every time the code paints the text, it computes a new opacity, which decreases according to the distance from the center. The entire effect is achieved with the following code:

```
String title = "Search in Message";
int size = 3;

g2.translate(x, y);
Composite oldComposite = g2.getComposite();

drawTextHighlight(g2, title, size, 0.8f);

g2.setComposite(oldComposite);
g2.setColor(Color.WHITE);
g2.drawString(title, size, size);

g2.translate(-x, -y);
```

This painting technique is not limited to text. It may be similarly applied to arbitrary drawing primitives. To use this technique with pictures containing transparent or translucent areas, you must first tint it with an opaque color. This can be done easily with the ColorTintFilter shown in Chapter 8.

Highlights are a cheap and efficient way to point out interactive elements or to improve the readability of specific elements in a user interface. Highlights are even more important when your GUI contains customized visual components that do not look like traditional widgets; they can significantly assist the user in navigating a new UI experience.

Sharpening

A sharpen effect is an image filter that recovers finer details from a picture, enhancing the edges in the scene to make a crisper, sharper view.

Motivation

Professional digital photographers know how important it is to master digital sharpening tools. No matter how good your digital camera and lenses are, your photos will always look soft in some places. This softening is due to the loss of information that happens when the photons captured by the camera are turned into pixels. Sharpening filters help compensate for this softness by emphasizing the edges in the picture. Figure 16-26 shows a comparison between the photograph as taken by a digital camera and a digitally sharpened copy. The brick patterns are much softer on the original picture.

Sharpening's utility is not constrained to digital photography, however. It can be used any time you want to increase the sharpness of an image that looks too soft.

In Chapter 4, "Images," you learned how to scale down an image to give a visually pleasing result. Unfortunately, the result is always softer than the original image because the filtering used in scaling the image blends neighboring pixels. You can therefore use a sharpening filter to further improve the downscaled image by enhancing some details.

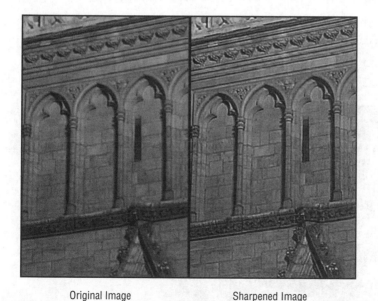

Original Image   Sharpened Image

Figure 16-26 The picture on the left shows what the camera produced. The picture on the right was digitally sharpened.

Simple Sharpen

A sharpening filter works by increasing the contrast around edges. Edges, in digital images, can be defined as darker pixels next to lighter pixels. To increase the contrast, we simply need to make dark values darker and light values lighter.

We discussed sharpening in Chapter 8. The technique proposed for sharpening relies on a ConvolveOp and a simple kernel:

```
BufferedImage dstImage = null;
float[] sharpen = new float[] {
     0.0f, -1.0f,  0.0f,
    -1.0f,  5.0f, -1.0f,
     0.0f, -1.0f,  0.0f
};
Kernel kernel = new Kernel(3, 3, sharpen);
ConvolveOp op = new ConvolveOp(kernel);
dstImage = op.filter(sourceImage, null);
```

This kernel works by subtracting the value of pixels that are adjacent to each pixel in the image. When a pixel is dark and surrounded by bright pixels, it becomes darker. On the contrary, when the pixel is bright and surrounded by dark pixels, it becomes brighter. To better understand this result, look at Figure 16-27.

This diagram represents an area of pixels in an image. Columns 2 and 3 represent an edge because the lighter tonal values in column 3 are next to darker tonal

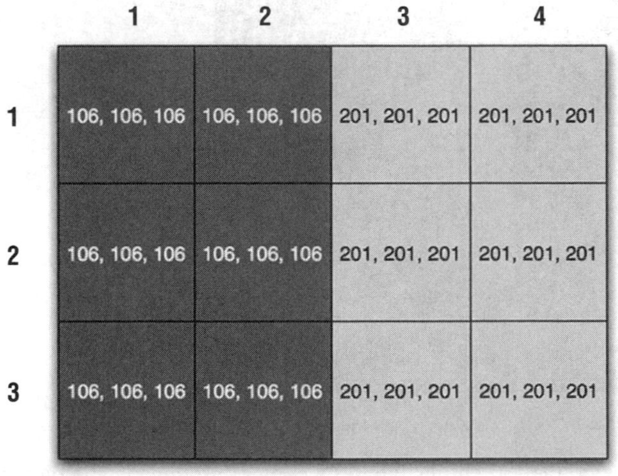

Figure 16-27 Pixel columns 2 and 3 represent an edge in a picture. The values indicate the RGB color of each pixel.

values from column 2. Now let's see the effect of the sharpening filter by applying the kernel on a dark pixel, located at (2, 2):

```
result = (1, 1) *  0 + (1, 2) * -1 + (1, 3) *  0 +
         (2, 1) * -1 + (2, 2) *  5 + (2, 3) * -1 +
         (3, 1) *  0 + (3, 2) * -1 + (3, 3) *  0
```

If we replace each pair of coordinates by the corresponding pixel's color value, the result becomes, for each RGB color component:

```
result = 106 *  0 + 106 * -1 + 201 *  0 +
         106 * -1 + 106 *  5 + 201 * -1 +
         106 *  0 + 106 * -1 + 201 *  0

result = 11
```

The new pixel's color is therefore (11, 11, 11), a very dark gray, almost black. If we apply the same kernel on a bright pixel, for instance the pixel located at (2, 3), we get the following result:

```
result = 106 *  0 + 201 * -1 + 201 *  0 +
         106 * -1 + 201 *  5 + 201 * -1 +
         106 *  0 + 201 * -1 + 201 *  0

result = 296
```

Because 296 does not fit on 8 bits, the value is clamped to 255, and the new pixel's color is (255, 255, 255), a pure white. Figure 16-28 shows the result of

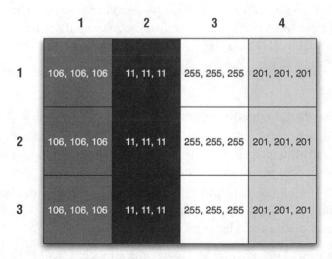

Figure 16-28 Sharpening this image increases the contrast around the edge.

the sharpening operation on the image presented in Figure 16-27. The contrast has been increased around the edge between columns 2 and 3.

> **Note: Sharpening Kernels.** The sharpening kernel used in this example is not the only kernel you can use to sharpen a picture. Just make sure to use lower values for the surrounding pixels, and remember to preserve the image brightness by choosing values that add up to 1.0.

This sharpening technique is simple to use but very limited. First, you cannot easily choose the amount of sharpening that you want to apply on an image. All pixels in the image will be equally affected by the sharpening. As a result, pixels that are not part of an edge will be modified, which can produce disturbing artifacts in noisy images. We need a better solution.

Unsharp Masking

Unsharp mask is the name of the image filter that most digital photographers use to sharpen their photographs. This name sounds a bit confusing at first: Why use an *un*sharp mask to sharpen an image?

The idea behind the unsharp masking technique (also called USM) is to subtract a blurred copy of the image, the unsharp mask, from the original image. USM filters start by applying a Gaussian blur to a copy of the original image. This copy is compared to the original, and if the difference is greater than a predefined threshold, the images are subtracted.

Because the user can set the threshold, it becomes possible to apply the sharpening filter only on image elements that differ more from each other than the rest of the image. This leaves out small details like noise.

USM filters found in graphics editing tools like Adobe Photoshop usually include three settings:

- *Amount:* This percentage controls how much contrast is added to the edges.
- *Radius:* This setting controls the radius of the Gaussian blur used for creating the mask and affects the size of the edges you want to enhance. Thus, a small radius enhances small-scale details.
- *Threshold:* This setting controls how far apart adjacent tonal values have to be for the filter to be applied. The threshold can therefore be used to sharpen pronounced edges and leave subtle ones untouched.

Reading the "Blur" section of this chapter and reviewing Chapter 8 will help you understand how to implement a USM filter.

Sharpening a Downscaled Image

An example of a USM filter implemented in Java can be found in the project called `UnsharpMask` on this book's Web site. This demo loads a 1024 × 673 image, scales it down to 300 × 197 using a progressive bilinear algorithm, and applies a USM filter, as shown in Figure 16-29.

Figure 16-29 The `UnsharpMask` demo reproduces Photoshop's settings for unsharp masking.

The `UnsharpMaskFilter` class extends `AbstractFilter`, detailed in Chapter 8. After applying a Gaussian blur of the specified radius on the original image, `UnsharpMaskFilter` calls the following method to subtract the images wherever the tonal value is greater than the threshold:

```
static void sharpen(int[] original, int[] blurred,
   int width, int height, float amount, int threshold) {

   int index = 0;

   int srcR, srcB, srcG;
   int dstR, dstB, dstG;

   amount *= 1.6f;
```

continued

```
for (int y = 0; y < height; y++) {
  for (int x = 0; x < width; x++) {
    int srcColor = original[index];
    srcR = (srcColor >> 16) & 0xFF;
    srcG = (srcColor >>  8) & 0xFF;
    srcB = (srcColor      ) & 0xFF;

    int dstColor = blurred[index];
    dstR = (dstColor >> 16) & 0xFF;
    dstG = (dstColor >>  8) & 0xFF;
    dstB = (dstColor      ) & 0xFF;

    if (Math.abs(srcR - dstR) >= threshold) {
      srcR = (int) (amount * (srcR - dstR) + srcR);
      srcR = srcR > 255 ? 255 : srcR < 0 ? 0 : srcR;
    }

    if (Math.abs(srcG - dstG) >= threshold) {
      srcG = (int) (amount * (srcG - dstG) + srcG);
      srcG = srcG > 255 ? 255 : srcG < 0 ? 0 : srcG;
    }

    if (Math.abs(srcB - dstB) >= threshold) {
      srcB = (int) (amount * (srcB - dstB) + srcB);
      srcB = srcB > 255 ? 255 : srcB < 0 ? 0 : srcB;
    }

    int alpha = srcColor & 0xFF000000;
    blurred[index] = alpha | (srcR << 16) |
        (srcG << 8) | srcB;

    index++;
  }
 }
}
```

This algorithm is a lot simpler than it looks. Parameters include pixels from the original image, pixels from the blurred copy, the amount, and the threshold. Pixels of the original image are called srcColor and are decomposed as srcR, srcG, and srcB in the code. Similarly, blurred pixels are called dstColor and are decomposed as dstR, dstG, and dstB.

Each color component from the original image is compared to the corresponding color component from the blurred copy. When the difference is greater than or equal to the threshold, then the pixel will be sharpened. Sharpening happens by adding to the original image the difference between the two images multiplied by the amount. With a positive difference, the pixel becomes brighter, and with a negative difference, the pixel becomes darker. Pixels with a difference below the threshold are left untouched, thus preserving subtle edges.

Tip: Clamp the Results. Because the sharpening operations can cause large values to be added to or subtracted from the color components, the result might be negative or greater than 255. To prevent rendering artifacts in the resulting image, remember to clamp the values in the [0…255] range, as in this example.

Tip: Sharpening and Performance. Unsharp masking is not an expensive operation when you keep the radius small. With a radius of 1 pixel, an unsharp mask filter is almost as fast as a simple sharpen filter implemented with a `ConvolveOp`.

Figure 16-30 shows a comparison between the original image and the sharpened image, using the default settings: 70 percent of amount, two pixels of radius, and two levels of threshold.

Sharpening your downscaled images can greatly improve their appearance. However, such an operation can produce many odd-looking artifacts when used with high values for the amount and radius settings.

Sharpening, more than any other visual effect, must be subtle. The `UnsharpMask` demo will help you choose the appropriate settings easily. Change the values and click the image to show the original image instead of the sharpened result. A

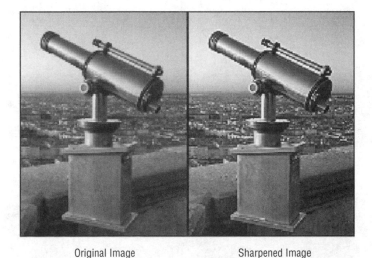

Original Image   Sharpened Image

Figure 16-30 Comparison between the original image and the sharpened image.

setting that seems to have no effect whatsoever is easier to see when the results are compared to the original image.

Summary

Creating impressive user interfaces becomes easier with visual effects such as those presented in this chapter. You should, however, use them carefully. It is very tempting to use them in too many places and clutter the user interface. Whenever you want to use one of these effects, think about what it means to the users and whether or not it will help them appreciate your application.

17

Dynamic Effects

LIFE does not stand still; neither should your applications. User experience can usually be improved by adding simple animations to your user interfaces. Animations are powerful, maybe too powerful. You must use them wisely so as not to distract or annoy the users.[1]

This chapter offers a variety of dynamic, or animated, effects that you can use in your applications. I should, however, emphasize that animations must be short and simple. That is the most important thing to understand about animated effects.[2]

All of the effects presented in this chapter are built upon the animation capabilities that were introduced earlier in Chapter 14, "Timing Framework: Fundamentals," and Chapter 15, "Timing Framework: Advanced Features." The graphics behind the effects are built upon the Swing and 2D elements developed in the Part I of this book. If you read these earlier chapters,[3] you should have no problem whatsoever understanding the source code for all of these effects.

---

1. Whenever I see an application with annoying animations, I can't help thinking that the developers are just using them as a vengeance against annoying users. This, of course, makes the users angrier and eventually even more annoying—which results in the next version of the application having even more annoying animations. And on it goes.
2. Before you read further in this chapter, go outside and repeat the following until you are drooling or getting really cold: "Animations must be short and simple."
3. If you didn't read those chapters yet, what are you doing here? That's like reading the last page of a mystery first. Or eating dessert before dinner. Or taking the final after skipping class all term. If you want to go back and catch up on that material now, go ahead. We'll wait.

Motion

Whenever you change an element's location in a user interface, that element should move smoothly, not teleport.

Motivation

Eons ago, hairy human beings used to hunt for food with powerful weapons like nails and teeth. This task was not easy. Silly creatures with longer nails and teeth thought that the hairy human beings were the food and made hunting even more difficult. Because our ancestors did not enjoy dying, they became very good at detecting movement in order to better detect and avoid these other creatures.

Unfortunately, our brain is not as good at quickly detecting the differences between two similarly detailed scenes. Usually, when a user interface needs to change the location of an element, it happens instantly. The user can easily notice that something has changed yet cannot to say what exactly has changed.[4] By changing things abruptly, the application disrupts our excellent spatial sense.

I call this the "undo/redo syndrome." Whenever I find myself using an application that teleports elements around, I use the undo and redo actions until I can finally tell what elements have moved and where exactly they went. Teleportation would be a great means of transportation, but it is a truly awful usability scenario.

The solution to this problem is obvious. You just have to go down to the street and see how people and vehicles move from one point to another. They move smoothly across all the points in space that separate them from their destination. Our brain is so used to this kind of movement that your applications should take a hint from what happens in reality.

Mac OS X successfully uses motion in a variety of situations. For instance, when you minimize a window to the Dock, which is the equivalent of Windows' taskbar, an animation plays to show you where the window is going. Figure 17-1 shows this animation.

Exposé, an application that displays all of the currently open windows, behaves similarly. When the user activates Exposé, all of the windows on the screen move and shrink smoothly to form a tiled pattern, as shown in Figure 17-2. If

---

4. You have probably observed this same problem in real life. Whenever a new restaurant opens up in a place where there used to be some other store or restaurant, it's almost impossible to remember what used to be there. If only the switch had occurred in an animated way, we may have found it easier to track the change.

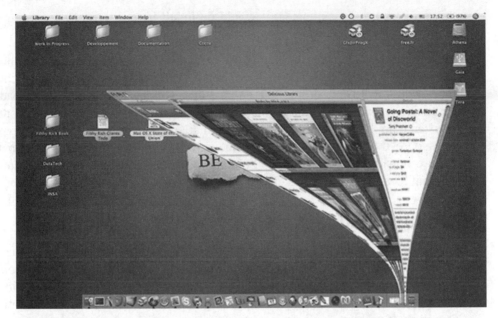

Figure 17-1 A minimized window smoothly moves to the bottom of the screen on Mac OS X.

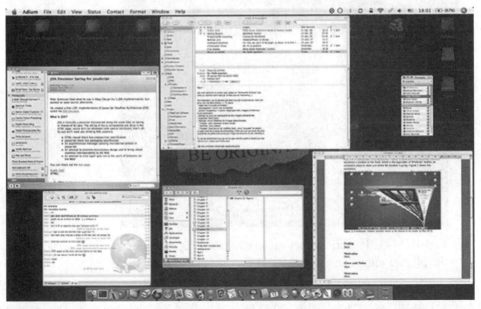

Figure 17-2 Mac OS X's Exposé mode shows all of the windows at once to let you pick one easily.

this effect were not animated, it would be much harder to quickly choose the window you want.

Drag and drop is another interesting use of motion. When a user interface allows the user to drag an element around and drop it on a specific location, the user interface often fails to correctly handle failed drops. This lack of feedback can lead to confusion or bad assumptions on the part of the user. Using animation in this situation can help. For example, Aerith lets you mark waypoints on a map and drop pictures onto these waypoints, as seen in Figure 17-3. However, if you drop the picture outside of a waypoint, an animation shows the picture going back to its original location to make you clearly understand that the drop operation failed.

Going, Going, Gone

Moving things around is simple with the Timing Framework. Every Swing component has a property called `location`, which lets you get and set the position of the widget in its parent container. Thanks to the Timing Framework's ability to interpolate `Point` instances, implementing an animated motion requires only a few lines of code.[5]

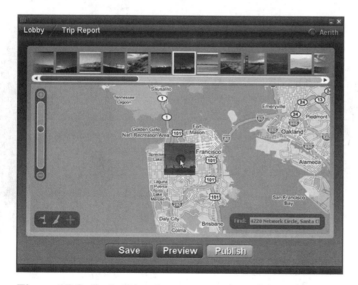

Figure 17-3 In Aerith, when an operation of dropping a picture onto a waypoint fails, the picture moves smoothly back to the picture bar at the top.

---

5. I actually complained to Chet about the simplicity of the implementation. The Timing Framework makes animations so easy that I don't have anything to explain when I show the code of the effect, thus making me feel a bit useless.

Figure 17-4 shows a simple user interface in which two buttons lie to the right of a text area. This application provides the user with the ability to change the layout by moving the buttons to the left side of the text area instead, as shown in Figure 17-5.

When the user clicks one of the buttons in the toolbar to change the layout, the components do not change location instantly. Instead, the buttons move smoothly from one side of the window to the other.

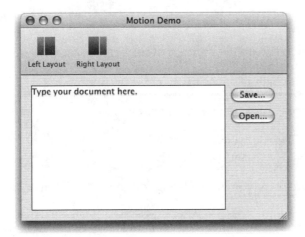

Figure 17-4 The toolbar buttons allow you change the layout of the text area and buttons.

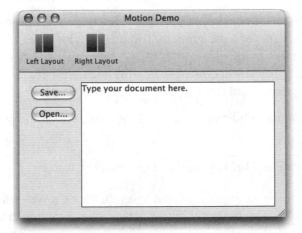

Figure 17-5 The transition between this layout and the previous one is animated.

To implement this animation, you need three classes from the Timing Framework: Animator, PropertySetter, and ActionTrigger. The following snippet shows how to set up a trigger on the Left Layout button to move the Save... and Open... buttons to the left of the window and the text area to the right.

```
Animator leftAnimator = new Animator(200);
leftAnimator.setAcceleration(0.3f);
leftAnimator.setDeceleration(0.2f);

leftAnimator.addTarget(new PropertySetter(
    saveButton, "location",
    new Point( 16, saveButton.getY())));

leftAnimator.addTarget(new Propert ySetter(
    openButton, "location",
    new Point( 16, openButton.getY())));

leftAnimator.addTarget(new PropertySetter(
    textArea, "location",
    new Point(16 + saveButton.getWidth() +
            6, textArea.getY())));
```

First, this snippet creates an Animator instance with duration of 200 ms.

Tip: Keep the Animation Short. Any animation of duration between about 16 ms and 200 to 300 ms follows the rule, "Animations should be short and simple."

To make the motion more natural, you need nonlinear interpolation, which is easily done via the acceleration and deceleration properties of the animator.

The rest of the code creates one PropertySetter per component that needs to be moved. Each of these setters uses the property location. The single value passed to the PropertySetter is the destination of the component. When the animation starts, the Timing Framework interpolates the location between the starting location of the component and the specified destination.

Finally, a trigger is added on the Left Layout button to start the animation upon a user's click:

```
ActionTrigger.addTrigger(leftLayoutButton, leftAnimator);
```

**ONLINE
DEMO**

The complete source code of this example is available on this book's Web site in the project called Motion. This example should prove how easy it is to implement motion in your user interface with the Timing Framework's PropertySetter.

Note: Automating Motions. The motion effect is most appropriate when you need to move one or only a few elements. It is better and easier to use the Animated Transitions library, presented in Chapter 18, "Animated Transitions," when you need to change the location of many elements at once or when you don't know exactly which elements will move between application states.

Fading

Whenever you need to make an element appear or disappear, you should do so gradually, not abruptly.

Motivation

Human beings have a good spatial sense, which can be easily thrown off when new elements are added to or removed from a user interface instantaneously. In the same way that motion can be used to avoid dumbfounding the user when an element changes its location, fading effects can be used to soothe the user's spatial sense.

Note: Fade-In and Fade-Out. There are actually two different fading effects, called fade-in and fade-out. The latter is the one we usually refer to when we use the verb *to fade*. A visual element fading out gradually grows fainter and finally disappears.

The fade-in effect has the exact opposite result: A visual element fading in appears and gradually grows clearer.

Fading effects are versatile and can be used in a wide variety of situations. Windows XP, for instance, fades pop-up menus in and out when you invoke them with the mouse's right button. Similarly, Apple's Aperture, shown in Figure 17-6, fades palettes and tooltips in and out. In these examples, the fading effects enhance the user experience by making the user interface smoother and gentler to the eyes.

Fading effects can also be used to change the contents of an element. The most common usage can be found in picture slideshows. When the next image needs to be displayed, the current image fades out and the new image fades in. However, fading effects are too often limited as a means to create a transition between two pictures. You can also use them to change the value of a text field or

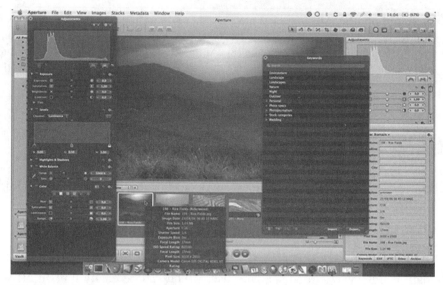

Figure 17-6 The black palettes and tooltips of Aperture fade in and out when invoked.

a label. For instance, when you are watching a picture album in Aerith and proceed to the next slide, as shown in Figure 17-7, the current label fades out and the new label fades in.

Fading between different values can be applied to an entire frame with all of its child widgets. As such, you can use fading effects to create transitions between

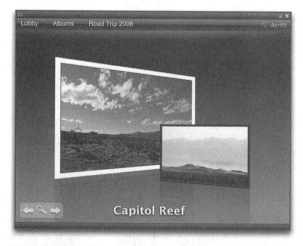

Figure 17-7 The picture's caption fades between old and new labels as the next image is displayed.

two screens. Figure 17-8, Figure 17-9, and Figure 17-10 show how Aerith fades its loading screen out to progressively show the main menu.

Fading Strategies

Fading effects can be implemented in two different ways. A regular fading effect relies on the opacity, or translucency, of the element. When you want to fade the entire element, you need to be in control of the painting code. Indeed, you must

Figure 17-8 Aerith loading screen.

Figure 17-9 When the user is authenticated, the loading screen progressively fades out.

Figure 17-10   The main menu appears progressively as the loading screen fades out.

use an `AlphaComposite.SrcOver` instance on the `Graphics` to change the opacity of the element.

When you cannot change the painting code, there is a simple workaround. The `Color` class provides an alpha channel, which is always understood by Swing. Therefore, if you can change the color of an element, you can change its opacity. Note that if you change the alpha channel of a component's background color, you must make sure that the component is nonopaque; see the discussion of `setOpaque()` in Chapter 2, "Swing Rendering Fundamentals," for more information on this topic.

AlphaComposite Fading

The `AlphaComposite` class makes the implementation of a fading effect simple. The example called `Fading`, which you can find on the book's Web site, displays a help balloon, as shown in Figure 17-11, to entice the user to click the Next button to display the next picture. When the user clicks the button, the help balloon fades out and disappears.

The painting code for the help balloon is the following:

```
@Override
protected void paintComponent(Graphics g) {
  Graphics2D g2 = (Graphics2D) g.create();
```

```
    Point p = nextButton.getLocationOnScreen();

    p.x += nextButton.getWidth() / 2 - 16;
    p.y += nextButton.getHeight() / 2 -
            helpImage.getHeight() + 10;

    SwingUtilities.convertPointFromScreen(p, this);

    g2.setComposite(AlphaComposite.SrcOver.derive(alpha));
    g2.drawImage(helpImage, p.x, p.y, null);
}
```

Figure 17-11 The help balloon fades out when a user clicks the Next button.

The last two lines are the most interesting part of this snippet. The component, a glass pane, sets an `AlphaComposite.SrcOver` instance with an opacity value of `alpha`. This value is an instance variable that can be queried and modified with the appropriate getter and setter:

```
public void setAlpha(float alpha) {
  this.alpha = alpha;
  repaint();
}

public float getAlpha() {
  return this.alpha;
}
```

These two methods are used to animate the fading effect with the help of the Timing Framework. When the user clicks the Next button, a new `Animator` is created and started:

```
Animator animator = new Animator(100);
animator.addTarget(new PropertySetter(glass, "alpha", 0.0f));
animator.setAcceleration(0.2f);
animator.setDeceleration(0.4f);
animator.start();
```

The `PropertySetter` changes the value of the alpha property of the glass object, an instance of the class that paints the help balloon, from its current value to 0.0f. When alpha reaches the value 0.0f, the help balloon disappears. Finally, the animation is made nonlinear by using acceleration and deceleration.

Color Fading

Run the `Fading` project and press the Next and Previous buttons. You should notice that the value of the text field, located at the top of the window, smoothly changes as the pictures change. Because we cannot modify the painting code of the text field, at least not without extending the `JTextField` class, we must use the foreground color property to perform the fading effect.

To fade out the current text and fade in the new text, you must use a series of `KeyFrames`. The `KeyFrames` are used to make the color change from fully opaque to transparent and finally back to fully opaque. The following code snippet shows how to create a property setter that changes the foreground color of a `JTextField` to make the text fade out then fade in:

```
KeyFrames keyFrames = new KeyFrames(
  KeyValues.create(
    new Color(0.0f, 0.0f, 0.0f, 1.0f),
    new Color(0.0f, 0.0f, 0.0f, 0.0f),
    new Color(0.0f, 0.0f, 0.0f, 1.0f)
  ));
PropertySetter setter = new PropertySetter(
  titleField, "foreground", keyFrames);
```

Because we did not specify the time fraction of each `KeyFrame`, the Timing Framework will divide the time equally between each `KeyFrame`. The first `KeyFrame` will happen when the elapsed fraction of the animation equals 0.0, the second when the elapsed fraction equals 0.5, and the last when the elapsed fraction equals 1.0. As a result, the text will become totally transparent halfway through the animation.

Finally, you need to create an `Animator` and a `TimingTarget` that will change the text when the color has become transparent so that the user cannot see the change happen:

```
Animator animator = new Animator(200, setter);
animator.addTarget(new TimingTargetAdapter() {
  private boolean textSet = false;

  public void timingEvent(float fraction) {
    if (fraction >= 0.5f && !textSet) {
        titleField.setText(text);
        textSet = true;
    }
  }
});
animator.start();
```

As soon as the animation is more than halfway through, and if the text has not been changed already, the `TimingTarget` sets a new value on the text field.

This technique works with numerous Swing components, like `JTextArea`, `JLabel`, and `JComboBox`. To animate a value change in any Swing text component, you can use the following method:

```
setTextAndAnimate(myTextField, "New Text");
// ...

public static void setTextAndAnimate(
    final JTextComponent textComponent,
    final String text) {
  Color c = textComponent.getForeground();

  KeyFrames keyFrames = new KeyFrames(KeyValues.create(
    new Color(c.getRed(), c.getGreen(), c.getBlue(), 255),
    new Color(c.getRed(), c.getGreen(), c.getBlue(), 0),
    new Color(c.getRed(), c.getGreen(), c.getBlue(), 255)
  ));
  PropertySetter setter = new PropertySetter(textComponent,
    "foreground", keyFrames);

  Animator animator = new Animator(200, setter);
  animator.addTarget(new TimingTargetAdapter() {
    private boolean textSet = false;
```

continued

```
    public void timingEvent(float fraction) {
      if (fraction >= 0.5f && !textSet) {
        textComponent.setText(text);
        textSet = true;
      }
    }
  });
  animator.start();
}
```

Cross-Fading

Cross-fading is a common variation of the fading effect. A cross-fade is actually a fade-in of one element and a fade-out of a different element happening at the same time. In the Fading demo we saw earlier in Figure 17-11, the pictures are cross-faded when you press the Next and Previous buttons:

```
@Override
protected void paintComponent(Graphics g) {
  Graphics2D g2 = (Graphics2D) g.create();

  g2.setComposite(AlphaComposite.SrcOver.derive(1.0f - alpha));
  g2.drawImage(firstImage, 0, 0, null);
  g2.setComposite(AlphaComposite.SrcOver.derive(alpha));
  g2.drawImage(secondImage, 0, 0, null);
}
```

As you can see, a cross-fade is implemented by using an alpha value for one element and an inverse value (1.0 – alpha) for the other element. Cross-fade can be implemented only when you control the painting code because both elements, the old one and the new one, must be painted at the same time. As such, you cannot rely on the color-fade technique.

Fading Made Easy

SwingX (www.swinglabs.org) is a library of advanced Swing components that can be used to make fading effects easier to implement. The JXPanel class, which works as a substitute for Swing's JPanel, supports translucency thanks to its getAlpha() and setAlpha() methods. Even better, all of the components inside a JXPanel inherit the translucency. Combined with the Timing Framework, this class lets you fade entire forms in and out with just a few lines of code.

Pulse

A pulse is an animation that is played repeatedly forward and backward.

Motivation

Pulsating effects have two primary purposes. Their repeated animation helps attract the user's attention. They can also be used to denote indeterminate progress.

The Alloy look and feel for Swing, available from www.incors.com, offers an example of a pulsating effect used to attract the user's attention. A dialog's default button contains an animated inner glow, shown in Figure 17-12, which distinguishes that button from other buttons. Mac OS X also uses a pulsating effect for the same reason.

Word 2004 for Mac uses a pulsating effect to notify users when they are using a feature that might not be compatible with previous Word versions; the background of a toolbar button pulsates from transparent to red and back.

Aerith relies on a pulsating effect to create an indeterminate progress indicator. When the application starts, the user can enter a Flickr (www.flickr.com) account name, and Aerith attempts to authenticate the user. Because this process involves a network operation, there is no reliable way to predict how long it will take to complete. An indeterminate progress indicator shows the user that the application is still running and will continue the current task for an unknown period of time. Figure 17-13 shows this indeterminate progress indicator, which is a glow that gradually appears and disappears behind the logo.

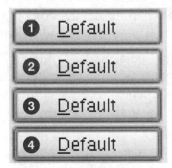

Figure 17-12   The Alloy look and feel uses a pulse effect by drawing an inner glow on the border.

Figure 17-13   Aerith's indeterminate progress indicator uses a pulsating effect.

Note that pulsating effects can break the rule[6] that animations should be short and simple. A fast animation conveys an impression of urgency to the user. That urgency might be what you intend when, for example, you want to attract the user's attention to an error in the application. When you want to use a pulsating effect as an indeterminate progress indicator, however, the animation is paced more slowly to show users that everything is fine and that they should not feel pressured. In this case, the duration between repetitions of the animation can be between 500 milliseconds and 1 second.

It is equally important to use subtle transitions between the extreme states of the pulse. For instance, don't make a pulse effect go from full red to full green. The animation should be enough for the user to notice the effect but not enough to be jarring or nauseating.

Feel My Pulse

One of the easiest pulse implementations works by animating a glow behind the element you want to emphasize. Thanks to your studious reading of every page of this book so far, you already know how to generate a glow for any visual element.

A glow is simply a blurred copy of the original item, tinted to increase the brightness. The project called `Pulse` from the book's Web site reuses techniques covered in Chapter 8 and in the "Blur" section of Chapter 16, "Static Effects."

Figure 17-14 shows the original picture that we want to animate with a pulsating glow. The glow itself is shown in Figure 17-15. The final application paints the original picture on top of the glow to produce the result seen in Figure 17-16.

---

6. I would never have imposed this rule on you at the beginning of this chapter if I didn't have the intention of breaking it at some point.

Figure 17-14   The element that we want to animate with a pulsating glow.

Figure 17-15   The glow generated from the original picture.

Figure 17-16   The picture and its glow.

The following code snippet shows how to generate the glow from the original picture:

```
// "image" is the original picture
// "glow" is the glow of "image"

// Create an image with the same dimensions
// as the original picture
glow = GraphicsUtilities.createCompatibleImage(image);

// Duplicate the original picture
g2 = glow.createGraphics();
g2.drawImage(image, 0, 0, null);
g2.dispose();

// Apply a two-pass Gaussian blur filter
BufferedImageOp filter = getGaussianBlurFilter(24, true);
glow = filter.filter(glow, null);
filter = getGaussianBlurFilter(12, false);
glow = filter.filter(glow, null);

// Turn the image white
filter = new ColorTintFilter(Color.WHITE, 1.0f);
glow = filter.filter(glow, null);
```

The original picture is first duplicated and then blurred with a Gaussian blur filter. To increase the brightness of the picture and make it white, this piece of code applies a ColorTintFilter, described in Chapter 8. As constructed here, the ColorTintFilter replaces the color of every pixel in the image with the color white, preserving the transparency.

When the glow is ready, you paint it behind the original picture:

```
@Override
protected void paintComponent(Graphics g) {
  int x = (getWidth() - image.getWidth()) / 2;
  int y = (getHeight() - image.getHeight()) / 2;

  Graphics2D g2 = (Graphics2D) g.create();

  g2.drawImage(glow, x, y, null);
  g2.drawImage(image, x, y, null)
}
```

To make the glow pulsate, we just need to vary its opacity. The glow is the result of a blur operation, which means that the pixels located the furthest from the original edges are also the pixels with the lowest alpha values. Thus, if we paint the glow with an `AlphaComposite.SrcOver` instance and progressively decrease its alpha value, the farthest pixels will disappear first, as shown in Figure 17-17. The painting code must be changed as follows:

```
g2.setComposite(AlphaComposite.SrcOver.derive(getAlpha()));
g2.drawImage(glow, x, y, null);
g2.setComposite(AlphaComposite.SrcOver);
g2.drawImage(image, x, y, null);
```

To animate the glow, the alpha value must gradually change from 0.0 to 1.0, then from 1.0 to 0.0, and so on. The Timing Framework allows creating animations that repeat infinitely and that reverse when they reach the end of each repetition:

```
PropertySetter setter =
  new PropertySetter(this, "alpha", 0.0f, 1.0f);
Animator animator = new Animator(600, Animator.INFINITE,
  Animator.RepeatBehavior.REVERSE, setter);
animator.start();
```

Figure 17-17 The white border shows the boundaries of the glow when alpha = 1.0. When alpha is lower, pixels disappear on the edges.

Contrary to the other animations presented in this chapter, this one will not stop unless you call `animator.stop()`.

Automatic Glow

A popular variation of the glow effect is called *bloom*. This effect can be seen in many modern video games. The bloom is a diffuse halo around bright areas in the scene. Figure 17-18 shows the same game, Quake 3, without and with the bloom effect. The bloom was exaggerated to emphasize the difference.

Bloom can be applied effectively on all kinds of graphics, like logos and splash screens, as shown in Figure 17-19.

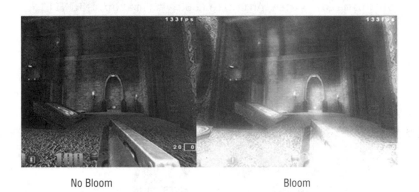

No Bloom   Bloom

Figure 17-18   Quake 3 without and with the bloom effect.

Figure 17-19   A bloom effect applied on Aerith's splash screen.

A bloom effect is created by a progression of blur effects. In our sample, we use a series of six steps to create the effect. These steps are illustrated in Figure 17-20 to Figure 17-26. The original picture that we start from is shown in Figure 17-20.

1. A bright-pass filter is applied to the original image to keep only the brightest pixels. The result is shown in Figure 17-21.
2. The filtered image is blurred with a Gaussian blur of radius 2. The result is shown in Figure 17-22.

Figure 17-20   The original image on which we apply the bloom.

Figure 17-21   The bright-pass filter keeps only the brightest pixels.

Figure 17-22   A Gaussian blur of radius 2 is applied to the filtered image.

3. Step 2 is repeated with a Gaussian blur of radius 5. The result is shown in Figure 17-23.

4. Step 2 is repeated with a Gaussian blur of radius 10. The result is shown in Figure 17-24.

5. Step 2 is repeated with a Gaussian blur of radius 20. The result is shown in Figure 17-25.

Figure 17-23   A Gaussian blur of radius 5 is applied to the filtered image.

Figure 17-24   A Gaussian blur of radius 10 is applied to the filtered image.

Figure 17-25   A Gaussian blur of radius 20 is applied to the filtered image.

6. The original images and the four blurred copies are composed in a single image by adding their values. The result is shown in Figure 17-26.

Figure 17-26 The final bloom effect.

The Gaussian blur implementation used in this effect is presented in Chapter 16. The AddComposite used to generate the final image of the bloom is explained in the Chapter 6, "Composites."

The bright-pass filter relies on a single algorithm. For each pixel in the image, it compares the luminance to a threshold. When the luminance is lower than the threshold, the pixel is not bright enough and is made completely black. The formula to compute the luminance of an RGB pixel in the YCC[7] color space is the following:

```
luminance = 0.2125 * red + 0.7154 * green + 0.0721 * blue
```

The complete source code of the bright-pass filter and of the bloom effect can be found in the project called Bloom on this book's Web site.

> **Note: High-Performance Bloom.** Because the bloom effect involves several Gaussian blurs, the performance can be disappointing on large images. Even though the Bloom demo from this book's Web site uses several performance tricks explained in this chapter, the algorithm is almost unusable on animated graphics.

Video games provide high-performance bloom effects by implementing them using pixel shaders. All of the work is deferred to the GPU, which can run shaders quite fast and get good performance for these types of operations. The project called

---

7. YCC is a convenient color space to use when dealing with the luminance values of colors, as we are doing here.

BloomOpenGL available on this book's Web site contains an OpenGL implementation of the bloom effect that runs much faster than the pure Java 2D version. This demo requires the Java bindings for OpenGL (JOGL) library to compile and execute. JOGL is available for Mac OS X, Windows, Solaris, and Linux and can be found at http://jogl.dev.java.net.

Palpitating Pulse

Pulsating effects also work on regular Swing components. For instance, the project called PulseField on the book's Web site shows how to create a pulsating border for a text field, as shown in Figure 17-27.

The pulsating effect is painted by an implementation of the Border interface. The pulsating border draws a blue rectangle with a thickness varying between 0.0 and 2.0 and an opacity ranging from 0.0 to 1.0:

```java
public static class PulsatingBorder implements Border {
  private float thickness = 0.0f;
  private JComponent c;

  public PulsatingBorder(JComponent c) {
    this.c = c;
  }

  public void paintBorder(Component c, Graphics g,
        int x, int y, int width, int height) {
    Graphics2D g2 = (Graphics2D) g.create();
    g2.setRenderingHint(RenderingHints.KEY_ANTIALIASING,
                        RenderingHints.VALUE_ANTIALIAS_ON);

    Rectangle2D r = new Rectangle2D.Double(x, y,
        width - 1, height - 1);
    g2.setStroke(new BasicStroke(2.0f * getThickness()));

    g2.setComposite(AlphaComposite.SrcOver.
        derive(getThickness()));
    g2.setColor(new Color(0x54A4DE));
    g2.draw(r);
  }

  public Insets getBorderInsets(Component c) {
    return new Insets(2, 2, 2, 2);
  }

  public boolean isBorderOpaque() {
    return false;
    }
```

```
  public float getThickness() {
    return thickness;
  }

  public void setThickness(float thickness) {
    this.thickness = thickness;
    c.repaint();
  }
}
```

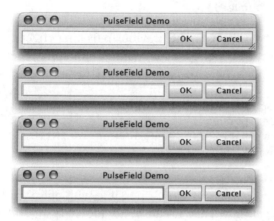

Figure 17-27 The text field contains a pulsating inner border.

Because the thickness is defined as a float value, it is important to enable anti-aliasing on the Graphics2D surface. It allows Java 2D to draw lines that are less than one pixel wide by using clever antialiasing tricks. You should also note that the border's constructor takes a component as a parameter. This component is used in the setThickness() method to force a repaint during the animation.

Note: Custom Components. Forcing a repaint during an animation is an important point in some of our Filthy Rich Clients that use custom components. In this case, changing the value of the internal thickness variable does not otherwise cause any repaint to occur.

This is one of the situations in which our code knows that a repaint needs to happen even though Swing does not. If we change state that Swing knows about, such as the text of a label or the size of a button, then a repaint will happen automatically. But if we change state local to our subclass of a Swing component and that state affects the rendering of the component, then we must alert Swing to that fact and cause a repaint.

The border can be installed on any rectangular Swing component. In the `PulseField` example, the border is installed on a `JTextField`. Creating a compound border containing both the existing border and a pulsating border preserves the existing border. The pulsating border is designated as the inner border:

```
JTextField field = new JTextField(20);

PulsatingBorder border = new PulsatingBorder(field);
field.setBorder(new CompoundBorder(
    field.getBorder(), border));
```

The animation code is exactly the same as in the previous pulsating effect example. All you need to do is create a `PropertySetter` and an infinitely repeating `Animator`:

```
PropertySetter setter =
      new PropertySetter(border, "thickness", 0.0f, 1.0f);
Animator animator = new Animator(900, Animator.INFINITE,
      Animator.RepeatBehavior.REVERSE, setter);
animator.start();
```

This example barely scratches the surface of what's possible with pulsating borders in Swing. It shows, however, how easy it can be to add such an effect to existing components. Pulsating effects can also be very interesting to use with the Timing Framework's triggers. You could, for example, start a pulsating effect when the mouse enters the boundaries of a component or when a component gains focus.

Spring

Animate launch actions with a spring effect to show the user that the application is working.

Motivation

Users are accustomed to launching applications and documents in a desktop environment, usually by double-clicking an icon. Most of the time, there is no visual feedback to confirm that the launch is actually taking place. When you double-click an icon on your Windows XP desktop, the only thing that indicates that you performed the action correctly is that the mouse cursor switches to an hourglass briefly. The problem is that the hourglass is associated with many meanings other than launching an application.

Mac OS X uses another technique, called the spring effect. When you double-click a document or an application on the desktop or in a folder, you can see the icon grow and fade out, as shown in Figure 17-28. This animation gives the impression of "launching" the icon upward, toward the user.

This effect is very good at providing visual feedback for a launch action. It can also be successfully used to indicate that an element can be clicked to launch an action. On Aerith's main screen, for instance, a spring effect plays when the user moves the mouse over the clickable elements, as show in Figure 17-29.

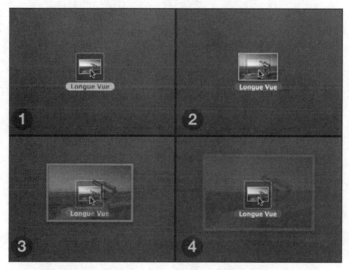

Figure 17-28   The spring animation on Mac OS X when the user double-clicks a document.

Figure 17-29   A spring effect plays when the mouse is over the element.

If you have read the rest of this book, you should be able to understand how to implement a spring effect. Let's see how it might look in code.

Spring Fever

You will find an implementation of a spring effect in the project called Spring on the book's Web site. The example displays a launch window in which the user can choose among various applications to launch, as shown in Figure 17-30.

Because a spring effect requires increasing the size of the clicked element, this implementation paints the animation on a glass pane. The glass pane needs an image, the boundaries of the original image, a magnifying factor, and the current zoom level:

```
public static class SpringGlassPane extends JComponent {
  private static final float MAGNIFY_FACTOR = 1.5f;

  private Rectangle bounds;
  private Image image;

  private float zoom = 0.0f;
}
```

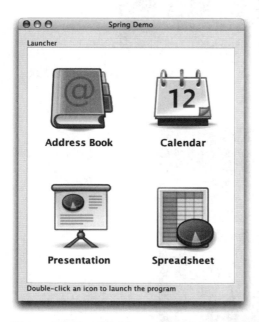

Figure 17-30   Clicking any of the icons triggers the spring effect.

During the animation, the glass pane increases the size of the image by MAGNIFY_FACTOR * zoom. Thus with a MAGNIFY_FACTOR of 1.5, when zoom equals 0.0, the image is painted with the original size, and when zoom equals 1.0, the image is 150 percent larger.

Because we would also like the image to fade out during the animation, we can reuse the zoom value. The opacity of the image is alpha equals 1.0 minus zoom. Thus, when zoom equals 0.0, the image is totally opaque (alpha = 1.0) and when zoom equals 1.0, the image is totally transparent (alpha = 0.0).

The painting code for the effect is as follows:

```
@Override
protected void paintComponent(Graphics g) {
  if (image != null && bounds != null) {
    // Increase the image size
    int width = image.getWidth(this);
    width += (int) (image.getWidth(this) *
        MAGNIFY_FACTOR * getZoom());

    int height = image.getHeight(this);
    height += (int) (image.getHeight(this) *
        MAGNIFY_FACTOR * getZoom());

    // Center the image on the original element
    int x = (bounds.width - width) / 2;
    int y = (bounds.height - height) / 2;

    // Draw the translucent, blown-up image
    Graphics2D g2 = (Graphics2D) g.create();
    g2.setRenderingHint(RenderingHints.KEY_INTERPOLATION,
        RenderingHints.VALUE_INTERPOLATION_BILINEAR);

    g2.setComposite(AlphaComposite.SrcOver.derive(
        1.0f - getZoom()));
    g2.drawImage(image, x + bounds.x, y + bounds.y,
                 width, height, null);
  }
}
```

This method first computes the new size of the image and the new location so that the spring effect is always centered over the original image. The method then sets up a bilinear interpolation on the Graphics2D surface to ensure that the image will look good once magnified on screen. Finally, the code uses an

AlphaComposite.SrcOver instance, whose alpha value is 1.0 minus zoom, as suggested earlier, to draw the translucent image.

The animation starts when the application passes an image and the boundaries of the clicked element to the glass pane:

```
public void showSpring(Rectangle bounds, Image image) {
    this.bounds = bounds;
    this.image = image;

    Animator animator = PropertySetter.createAnimator(
        250, this, "zoom", 0.0f, 1.0f);
    animator.setAcceleration(0.2f);
    animator.setDeceleration(0.4f);
    animator.start();

    repaint();
}

public float getZoom() {
    return zoom;
}

public void setZoom(float zoom) {
    this.zoom = zoom;
    repaint();
}
```

Once again, the animation code is very simple, thanks to the Timing Framework. The animator changes the value of the zoom property between 0.0 and 1.0 over a period of 250 ms. To improve the quality of the effect, the animator uses a nonlinear interpolation, as described by the acceleration and the deceleration factors.

The result of the spring effect in the Spring project is shown in Figure 17-31.

In this example, the spring effect is painted over the clickable item to enforce the impression of launching an application. When you use the spring effect to highlight an element on mouseover, it is preferable to paint the effect behind the element, as in Figure 17-29. The difference is subtle, but users should not get the impression that they have actually launched something—only that it is possible to launch something with that element.

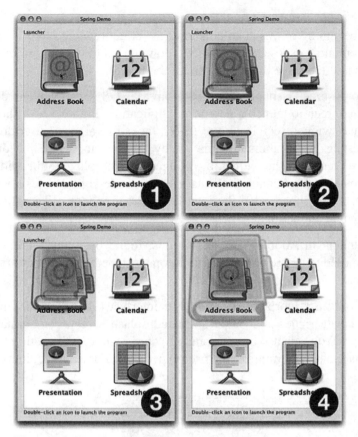

Figure 17-31 The spring effect in action.

Morphing

Morphing is a visual effect that changes one shape into another through a seamless transition.

Motivation

In contrast to all of our previous dynamic effects, morphing is not widely used in traditional user interfaces, mainly because of the obvious difficulty of morphing one arbitrary shape into another.

Mac OS X offers two examples of how to use morphing in a user interface. Figure 17-1, at the beginning of this chapter, shows the effect rendered by Mac OS X when the user minimizes a window. The window moves to the bottom of the screen and morphs at the same time into a small thumbnail.

Figure 17-32 shows some Dashboard widgets from Mac OS X that you can drag and drop onto the screen to launch a new mini-application. Figure 17-33 shows what the Dictionary widget, seen in Figure 17-32, looks like after the user drops it. What's interesting is the animation played by the system before the drop occurs. While the user drags the widget, the widget icon morphs into the widget itself. In the case of the Dictionary, the square icon seamlessly becomes a wide rectangle. Figure 17-34 shows what the icon being dragged looks like halfway through the morphing animation.

Morphing is common in Adobe Flash animations, found on many Web sites, because it can be used to create complex animations. Adobe Flash refers to morphing as *shape tweening*.

You can successfully use morphing in your user interfaces. For instance, morphing can help create richer and better-animated splash screens or animated About dialog boxes. You can also use morphing to convey more information than with a regular shape and thus improve the user experience. For example, imagine

Figure 17-32   Dashboard widgets in Mac OS X.

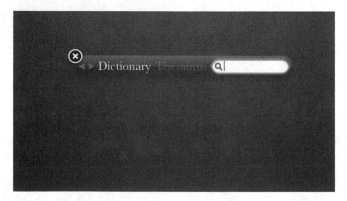

Figure 17-33   The Dictionary widget as it appears after being dropped on the screen.

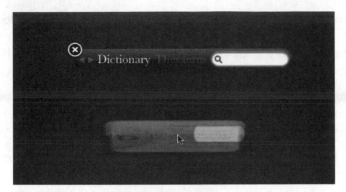

Figure 17-34 The widget icons morphs into the widget.

a delete button that morphs into a trashcan when the mouse is over it, enforcing the idea that the button disposes of something.

Morphing Buttons

The project called `Morphing` on the book's Web site contains a simple application that lets the user navigate back and forth between two pictures. Figure 17-35 shows what the user interface looks like. The user can press the two Backward and Forward buttons to flip through the pictures. Because those buttons have a standard shape, the user is most likely to understand that they should be pressed.

Figure 17-35 The two buttons can be pressed to navigate through the pictures.

Wouldn't it be more interesting to graphically show the user what each button is supposed to do? Most user interfaces would simply add an icon in each button, in this case perhaps arrows pointing to the left and right. Icons can be distracting, however, and it is hard to find a set of icons that works well across operating systems.

It is also possible to change the shape of the buttons themselves and paint them as arrows. Unfortunately, arrow shapes are not very common for buttons, and the user might be confused as to their purpose.

Another solution is to use morphing. When the mouse pointer enters the button, the button morphs into an arrow pointing in the appropriate direction, as shown in Figure 17-36. This effect is animated to make the transition look smooth. Figure 17-37 shows what the button looks like in the middle of the morphing sequence.

The `Morphing` example is based on the `Morphing2D` class, written by Jim Graham,[8] member of the Java 2D team at Sun Microsystems, and the class is available under the LGPL license in the `SwingX` project (http://www.swinglabs.org).

Figure 17-36   The button turns into an arrow when the mouse is over it.

---

8. The `Morphing2D` class is complicated, and it would not be possible to explain its 600 lines of code in detail here. Every `Shape` is made of segments, which can be straight lines, quadratic curves, or Bézier curves. The idea behind `Morphing2D`'s algorithms is to match all of the segments of the start shape to all of the segments of the end shape. If there are not enough segments in either shape, new segments must be interpolated from the existing ones. Those of you who love mathematics or feel courageous enough should read `Morphing2D.java`. I did when I committed the class to `SwingX` and did very simple code refactoring. I stopped when I started drooling, and it took me a few days to recover from the damage that my brain suffered. Superman's weakness is kryptonite. Mine is mathematics.

Figure 17-37 Mid-morph: The rounded rectangle morphs seamlessly into an arrow.

Morphing2D implements the java.awt.Shape interface and can therefore be used like any other Java 2D shape, such as Rectangle and Ellipse2D. A Morphing2D instance is created with two other Shape instances, which represent the start and end shapes. The setMorphing() method controls the amount of interpolation, or morphing, between the two shapes. When the morphing amount is 0.0, only the start shape shows. When the morphing amount is 1.0, only the end shape shows. Any other value between 0.0 and 1.0 will show a shape that is a mix between the start shape and the end shape.

The following code comes from the DirectionButton class and shows how to create a Morphing2D shape that starts with a rounded rectangle and ends with an arrow pointing to the left:

```
private Morphing2D createMorph() {
  // Start shape is a rounded rectangle
  Shape sourceShape = new RoundRectangle2D.Double(2.0, 2.0,
      getWidth() - 4.0, getHeight() - 4.0, 12.0, 12.0);

  // End shape is a left pointing arrow
  GeneralPath.Double destinationShape =
      new GeneralPath.Double();
  destinationShape.moveTo(2.0, getHeight() / 2.0);
  destinationShape.lineTo(22.0, 0.0);
  destinationShape.lineTo(22.0, 5.0);
  destinationShape.lineTo(getWidth() - 2.0, 5.0);
  destinationShape.lineTo(getWidth() - 2.0, getHeight() - 5.0);
```

continued

```
        destinationShape.lineTo(22.0, getHeight() - 5.0);
        destinationShape.lineTo(22.0, getHeight());
        destinationShape.closePath();

        return new Morphing2D(sourceShape, destinationShape);
    }
```

Note that the two shapes can be of arbitrary size and location. To paint the morphing shape, proceed as you would with any other Java 2D shape:

```
    @Override
    protected void paintComponent(Graphics g) {
        Graphics2D g2 = (Graphics2D) g.create();

        LinearGradientPaint p;
        p = new LinearGradientPaint(0.0f, 0.0f, 0.0f, getHeight(),
                    new float[] { 0.0f, 0.5f, 0.501f, 1.0f },
                    colors);
        g2.setPaint(p);

        Morphing2D morph = createMorph();
        morph.setMorphing(getMorphing());

        g2.fill(morph);
    }
```

The morphing animation relies entirely on the TimingFramework. An animator is created to change the value of the button's morphing property between 0.0 and 1.0. This animator is attached to a MouseTrigger that takes care of playing the animation when the mouse enters the button's boundaries:

```
    private void setupTriggers() {
        Animator animator = PropertySetter.createAnimator(
            150, this, "morphing", 0.0f, 1.0f);
        animator.setAcceleration(0.2f);
        animator.setDeceleration(0.3f);

        MouseTrigger.addTrigger(this, animator,
            MouseTriggerEvent.ENTER, true);
    }

    public float getMorphing() {
        return morphing;
    }

    public void setMorphing(float morphing) {
        this.morphing = morphing;
        repaint();
    }
```

The last parameter of the addTrigger() method tells the Timing Framework to reverse the animation when an opposite event is received by the trigger. In this case, the event opposite to MouseTriggerEvent.ENTER is MouseTriggerEvent.EXIT. Automatically, the arrow morphs back to a rounded rectangle when the mouse exits the button's boundaries.

> **Note: Leaving the Animation Partway Through.** The Timing Framework also handles events that occur during the animation. For instance, if the mouse exits the button when the animation has played for only 40 percent of the total duration, the reverse animation starts at 40 percent of the total duration.

Morphing is an impressive visual effect underused in today's user interfaces. There are many situations in which it can be useful. For instance, imagine a combo-box morphing into its drop-down menu when clicked. Morphing2D and the Timing Framework let you add this kind of effect very easily into your applications.

Summary

Dynamic visual effects are very efficient mechanisms to spice up your user interfaces. They improve the user experience by providing a better visual feedback on what the application is doing, and they also make your product look great. You should not, however, abuse them. Animated effects must be used for specific purposes and be as seamless and natural as possible. Always think about the added value for the end user when you implement a new animation in your user interface.

18

Animated
Transitions

THIS chapter[1] introduces a library called Animated Transitions. This library works in conjunction with the Timing Framework library, described earlier. Like the Timing Framework library, the Animated Transitions library is available on the book's Web site. This chapter details the motivations for the Animated Transitions library as well as how to use the API. We discuss example applications that show what the library can do.

Animating Application State Segues

Picture a typical forms-based application. The user is presented with a GUI consisting of various widgets such as text fields, buttons, list boxes, and checkboxes, which they fill out, select, and click appropriately. The user then clicks on the ever-present Submit button, which usually results in this GUI disappearing and,

---

1. We weren't actually sure where to place this chapter. Animated Transition is kind of an Effect that you can use in your applications, so it belongs in the Effects section. But it's also an animation-enabling library, so it belongs in the Animations section. In the end, we decided to place it here in the Effects section because it's more of a nifty effect than a base library like the Timing Framework. But if we could put links in a book, we would put a link here from Part III. I tried to link the chapter using UNIX symlinks, like this: `ln -s PartIII/Chapter18 PartIV/Chapter18`. But the book had a page fault.

after some delay, being replaced by a completely different GUI. More text fields, more information, more buttons, and often more confusion for the user.

They puzzle over the new GUI for a bit. Then they proceed to fill out the information, click another Submit button, and thus continue on their journey in this fascinating application until either the server crashes or they retire.

This application is typical of HTML-based Web applications in which the GUIs tend to be very static and the capabilities of the browser container tend to be more limited than, say, a rich-client toolkit. But this experience is really the same in most client-server applications, regardless of language and toolkit. It is simply the easiest and most obvious way for such applications to work. Users complete information required by the application, they submit this information, the server thinks about it and sends a response, and then the application displays the results and asks for more information.

This may be the most straightforward way for the developer to write the application. But is it the easiest way for the user to use the application? And is the ease of development for the programmer worth the trade-off in the poor user experience?

The difficulty for users comes in the form of being constantly confronted with new GUIs that they must decipher before proceeding. And hopefully, the users don't take a break away from the display. Or click a button they didn't mean to. Or blink. They may be faced with some screen they have not seen before, and they may not know how they got there—or how to get back to where they were before.

The Big Idea

What if you could maintain some logical connection between these different application states? What if moving from one screen of the application to another happened in a way that flowed smoothly and logically, so that users could see how they got *here* from *there* and how they might even get back to where they were before? More importantly, what if keeping these logical connections between the application states made it easier for users to figure out what they were supposed to do on each screen, and they were therefore more productive in their use of your application?

Tip: Maintaining a logical and visual connection between application states is the idea behind Animated Transitions. An application GUI animates between its different states to create a smoother and more logical flow for the user.

The old model of application transitions consists of abrupt erasures of the current screen followed by painting of entirely new screens with potentially radically different appearance. The new model of animated transitions makes state transitions smoother by moving things around on the screen in a seamless fashion to make it more obvious how the different screens and application states relate to each other.

For example, imagine a search engine with an initial screen consisting of some explanatory text, a Search label, and a text entry field, as seen in Figure 18-1. Typing text into the search field and hitting Enter causes the GUI to change to a screen that shows the results of the search. A traditional version of this application might simply erase the first screen and replace it with a screen that holds the results of the search. It would be easy, and typical, to at least include another text entry field and Search label on this second screen, as shown in Figure 18-2.

Figure 18-1   Simple search engine GUI.

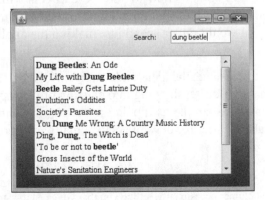

Figure 18-2   Results of search.

What if the first screen did not just disappear but instead transitioned smoothly into the second screen? For example, the text entry field and Search field could move themselves to the top of the screen while the search results faded or moved into view. If this happened, chances are better that users would automatically know where to go to enter a new search. They would see the search field component move up to the top, so they would know where that entry field was on the new GUI. Also, if the connection between the old GUI and the new GUI with the results listing was made in a very obvious way, it would be much clearer to users that *this* page full of information came from *that* initial search page.

Of course, this example is very simple, and the need for connecting the screens is probably less critical. But typical forms-based applications, such as enterprise database applications or online shopping sites, are much more complicated, and it is easy to get lost in all the new and old GUI objects popping in and out between all the application screens. Even in these more complex applications, we could apply the smooth transition approach to make these screen changes much more user friendly:

- Move and scale components that are shared between screens.
- Fade or slide in GUI objects that are appearing.
- Fade or slide out GUI objects that are disappearing.

The holdup, of course, is complexity of implementation. A little more pain for the developer will usually pay off well if it makes things better for the user. But a lot more pain for the developer usually means it simply won't happen, regardless of any potential user benefits. Many GUI programmers may view the kinds of things discussed here as too complicated to implement. Animation, fading, sliding, scaling—for someone used to using a GUI builder to place components, or coding components with a layout manager, it is probably not obvious how to accomplish these effects. It is also not obvious how to add these effects without throwing your application into contortions and spending a lot more development time on whizzy animations that you would rather spend just making the application logic work correctly.[2]

What developers need is a way to encapsulate the ideas and actions involved in animated transitions into a system that they can easily plug into existing or new applications. If we can make this behavior as simple as flipping a switch, or calling a method or two, maybe we can make it easier for developers to actually incorporate

---

2. I, for one, really like the idea of spending most of my development time on whizzy effects. But then there's that pesky reality bell that chimes occasionally, telling you that you need to actually finish the application in order to get paid.

it into their applications. And if we can make it radically easier, maybe applications will actually start using this capability on a regular, instead of exceptional, basis.

Help is on the way.

Animated Transitions: The Library

Please welcome the Animated Transitions library, a framework for making transitions between different application states smooth and easy. All that it requires from you and your application is a little bit of setup to tell it what you want to transition, and the library takes care of the rest.

Animated Application State

Typical effects in Swing applications are limited to individual components, such as buttons that pulsate, scrolling lists that expand smoothly, and images that fade in or out. While these effects are interesting and useful, imagine the potential when you can do these kinds of things at the application level instead of the component level.

> **Tip:** Animated transitions encompass more than simply animating the translucency of a button or the location of some other component. They comprise all of this and more for potentially every component in the application.

Imagine an application that has several simple components in its GUI: text entry fields, labels, icons, buttons, and so on. Clicking on a Submit button causes the application to switch to a different screen where many of these elements are the same, but they are in different locations, or they are of different sizes, or they are in different orientations. Meanwhile, many of the components on the first screen went away and some new components joined the GUI. What if we could animate all of these transitions or whatever subset was deemed interesting and productive for this application?

GUI States

A key concept in animated transitions is that an application changes state several times in its lifetime. Entering data on one screen causes a query to some database, which results in data and entry fields displayed on a different screen of the application. Entering data or otherwise interacting with that new screen causes the application to show a different screen, again with a different set of GUI components.

Whether these screens are static, with content that is predetermined at code-writing time, or dynamic, with content that is determined at runtime by processing user data, the application will understand these conditions as different states. And if it can understand and separate these separate states of the application, it can work with the Swing effects that we discuss here. It can make the screen transitions smoother and more effective than the typical transitions that re-create the GUI completely in traditional GUI applications.

The animated transitions framework centers on the ability of an application to define these different *screens* or *states* of an application. In particular, it cares only about two states of an application at any given time: the current state of the application that the user is about to leave and the next state that the user is about to enter into. Given this before and after information, the framework can calculate and render an animation that transitions smoothly between these two states.

The API

The basic usage of the Animated Transitions framework is simple. You create a ScreenTransition object, which manages the transition for you, and then tell it to start(). Here are the ScreenTransition constructors:

```
public ScreenTransition(JComponent transitionComponent,
                        TransitionTarget transitionTarget,
                        Animator animator)

public ScreenTransition(JComponent transitionComponent,
                        TransitionTarget transitionTarget,
                        int duration)
```

The transitionComponent parameter is the container in your GUI in which the transition takes place. The transitionTarget parameter is an object that receives callbacks during the transition. The animator parameter in the first constructor describes the actual animation. You can optionally provide a duration, as in the second constructor, and the ScreenTransition will construct its own Animator object internally. Note that the container you provide does not need to encompass the entire client area of your application window. You can have the transitions occur in subcomponents of your window.

The container that you provide to ScreenTransition can be set up normally, including the use of LayoutManagers as necessary. There is no special layout constraint when using transitions, which the later examples will demonstrate.

You call ScreenTransition.start() when you want the transition to begin:

```
public void start();
```

Once start() is called, ScreenTransition is in control and your application will only need to respond to a single callback. The rest of the details are handled by the framework. The callback you must implement is the method setupNextScreen(), defined in the TransitionTarget interface:

```
public interface TransitionTarget {
   public void setupNextScreen();
}
```

This method is called after your call to start(), when the framework needs you to arrange your container's GUI according to what you want it to look like when the transition ends. In this method, you add, remove, resize, and arrange the components in the application container to suit the application's needs. From this revised GUI in the container, ScreenTransition infers the state of the components that it needs to animate to during the transition. After you return from setupNextScreen(), the transition begins. The framework has everything that it needs to calculate and run the animation and then put the application in the final screen state when it is finished.

Example: SearchTransition

Let's use our earlier search engine GUI as an example. We'll see if we can improve the experience with animated transitions. The code for this application is found in the SearchTransition project on the book's Web site.

On the first screen of the application, there is a simple label and text entry field, along with some textual instructions, as seen in Figure 18-3. Once the user enters text into the field and hits Enter, a second screen appears that displays the search results along with the repositioned label and text entry field.

Without animated transitions, the application would behave as follows:

- The user enters text in the text field and hits Enter.
- The text-entry screen is erased, and the results screen appears.

With animated transitions, the application could connect the experience of the two screens more smoothly:

- The user enters text in the text field and hits Enter.
- The label and text field smoothly move into place at the top right of the results screen.
- The instructions fade or move out of the view.
- The results fade or move into view.

What we have in this transition are components that are undergoing one of three state changes:

- Some elements change their position between screens (the label and text field).
- Some elements go away between the first and second screens (the instructions).
- Some elements come into view between the first and second screens (the results).

The process of the transition is shown in Figure 18-3 through Figure 18-7.

It is certainly possible to animate each of these elements individually. Using what we know about animations, the Timing Framework, Swing components, Java2D, and animated effects rendering, we could create for each element separate custom animations that do the right thing: move, scale, fade, or whatever. But given the myriad of effects that we might need and the large numbers of elements and screens that a typical application has to manage, this seems like a lot

Figure 18-3   Start screen of application: awaiting user input.

Figure 18-4 User enters search phrase.

Figure 18-5 Mid-transition: the search label and entry field are moving, the results are fading and moving in, and the instructions arc fading out.

Figure 18-6 Still transitioning.

Figure 18-7 Transition complete: the second screen is now displayed.

of work for a developer. The result would probably be that the work would not get done, or not even get started, which helps explain why there are not more applications using animated transitions out there today.

Let's see how we can use the Animated Transitions library to get the job done. SearchTransition simulates an application with two screens. The user navigates from one screen to the other by hitting the Enter key in the text field. First, let's look at the GUI in each of these two screens.

For the first screen, shown in Figure 18-3, we have a label, a text entry field, and some instructions. The application defines these as simple components:

```
JLabel instructions = new JLabel("Search and ye shall find...");
JLabel searchLabel = new JLabel("Search:");
JTextField searchField = new JTextField("");
```

We set up the positions of these components in the method setupSearchScreen():

```
private void setupSearchScreen() {
  // assignment of searchX/searchY/etc. variables omitted
  add(instructions);
  add(searchLabel);
  add(searchField);
  instructions.setBounds(instructionsX, instructionsY,
                         INSTRUCTIONS_W, INSTRUCTIONS_H);
  searchLabel.setBounds(searchX, searchY, LABEL_W, LABEL_H);
  searchField.setBounds(fieldX, fieldY, FIELD_W, FIELD_H);
}
```

Tip: We happen to use a null LayoutManager in this application, which is merely a simplification for this trivial example. Real applications with complex, attractive, and robust GUIs should use real LayoutManagers instead.

We similarly define the additional scroll pane component used in the second screen, shown in Figure 18-7:

```
JEditorPane results = new JEditorPane("text/html",
   "My Life with <b>Dung Beetles</b><br/>" +
   "<b>Beetle</b> Bailey Gets Latrine Duty<br/>" +
   "Evolution's Oddities<br/>" +
   "Society's Parasites<br/>" +
   "You <b>Dung</b> Me Wrong: A Country Music History<br/>" +
   "Ding, <b>Dung</b>, The Witch is Dead<br/>" +
   "'To be or not to <b>beetle</b>'<br/>" +
   "Gross Insects of the World<br/>" +
   "Nature's Sanitation Engineers<br/> +" +
   "Why are they here?<br/> +" +
   "</body></html>");;
JScrollPane scroller = new JScrollPane(results);
```

Yes, we hard-code the results for this demo.[3]

We define the placement of all of the GUI elements in the second screen in the method setResultsScreen():

```
public void setupResultsScreen() {
   // assignment of searchX/searchY/etc. variables omitted
   add(searchLabel);
   add(searchField);
   add(scroller);
   searchLabel.setBounds(searchX, 10, LABEL_W, LABEL_H);
   searchField.setBounds(fieldX, fieldY, FIELD_W, FIELD_H);
   scroller.setBounds(RESULTS_X, resultsY,
                   getWidth() - (2 * RESULTS_X),
                   getHeight() - resultsY - 20);
}
```

---

3. I tried to implement a complete, searchable knowledge base on insects just for this demo, but alas, there were too many bugs. But it makes me wonder: Do they hard-code the results in real search engines too? It would explain why they're so fast. With all of the junk on the Web, how would we ever know?

We create our ScreenTransition object as follows:

```
Animator animator = new Animator(500);
animator.setAcceleration(.2f);
animator.setDeceleration(.4f);
ScreenTransition transition = new ScreenTransition(this,
    this, animator);
```

This transition lasts for a half-second, it accelerates for the first 20 percent, and it slows down for the final 40 percent. We use this, the JComponent that holds the GUI components, as the container for the transition. We also use this, which implements the TransitionTarget interface, as the target of the transition's callback to set up the next screen.

We use the Enter key as the event to display the results screen, so we add a KeyListener and implement an actionPerformed() method as follows:

```
public void actionPerformed(ActionEvent ae) {
    // Change currentScreen, used in setupNextScreen() callback
    currentScreen = (currentScreen == 0) ? 1 : 0;
    transition.start();
}
```

Starting the transition results in a callback to our setupNextScreen() method, which is implemented as follows:

```
public void setupNextScreen() {
    removeAll();
    switch (currentScreen) {
      case 0:
        setupSearchScreen();
        break;
      case 1:
        setupResultsScreen();
        break;
      default:
        break;
    }
}
```

The removeAll() function simply removes all components from the container, which is an easy way to clear out the state between screens and set things up cleanly. An alternative approach would be to figure out the difference in GUI state between the current screen and the next screen and to remove, add, and rearrange components individually, as appropriate. But removing everything and setting up all components for the next screen seems a bit easier, at least in this situation.

The `switch` statement calls the appropriate `setupSearchScreen()` or `setupResultsScreen()` method, as described previously, depending on which screen we are transitioning from. This is a simple mechanism that assumes we are toggling between these two screens. A real application would have more involved logic here to determine what the next screen should look like.

Our code review of `SearchTransition` is nearly complete. As we saw earlier, the API of `AnimatedTransitions` is very simple. Most of the functionality is hidden from view. The framework figures out internally how components change between screens and runs the animated transition between those changes. In particular, if your application can use the standard transition effects of the library and does not need custom effects, all you need is explained earlier: create a `ScreenTransition`, `start()` it, and handle `setupNextScreen()` appropriately.

There is, however, one more piece to our `SearchTransition` demo that is key to part of its functionality. It uses a custom effect for the sliding/fading results screen. To show you how your application can do something similar, we need to discuss effects.

Effects

By default, the Animated Transitions library uses standard effects for components during the animation.

- Components that go away use a fading-out effect.
- Components that appear use a fading-in effect.
- Components that move and/or resize use a moving/scaling effect.

While these effects work well as defaults, it seems reasonable to expect that developers may want to supply custom effects for their applications.

In order to simplify customizing the behavior of transitions, the effects used by the library were implemented as pluggable objects. So while the framework currently uses certain standard effects by default, it can easily be configured to use custom effects that you supply instead.

Let's look at the Effects API and how you can use it to create and use custom effects in your applications.

Effects: The API

There are two different uses of the Effects API: instantiating and using existing effects and creating custom effects. We cover both of these topics.

Instantiating Effects   First, let's look at the various effects that the current framework offers:

Move

This effect renders the component at a position that moves from the component's starting point in the first screen to its end point in the second screen.

Scale

This effect renders the component by resizing it between the starting and ending sizes of the component in the two screens. Because scaling can cause some components, especially those with text or whose internal layout changes with their size, to alter their appearance as their size changes, use of this effect triggers an internal flag that tells the system to render the component during the animation instead of using a snapshot image of the component. Scaling an image of the component produces results that don't look right in general, causing distortion during the transition and a disturbing "snap" to the real look when the transition completes and the real component is rendered. Rendering the actual component during the animation solves this problem and eliminates the artifacts.

FadeIn

This effect renders the component in varying degrees of translucency, from invisible to completely opaque, as the component fades into place between the first and second screens.

FadeOut

This is the opposite of the FadeIn effect, rendering the component from completely opaque to invisible as the transition runs between the first and second screens.

Rotate

This effect can be used to spin a component by some specified degrees around a given center of rotation.

Unchanging

This effect does nothing and is simply a utility for having an effect that causes the component to be rendered in its original state during the transition.

Instantiating one of these effects is easy, requiring a simple call to its constructor. Most of these effects have a default constructor that takes no arguments. For example, to create a Move effect, you would simply call this:

```
Move moveEffect = new Move();
```

The data for the appropriate start and end states is set in the effect by the framework when the transition begins, so no additional information is needed at construction time. Some of the effects take additional information if they require more than the component's position and size. For example, the Rotate effect needs to know the angle and center of rotation. You can create this effect with a given rotation center, like this:

```
Rotate rotateAroundXY = new Rotate(degrees, x, y);
```

where (x, y) is a position relative to the origin of the component that it is applied to.

You can also create a Rotate effect with a center that is calculated for you on the basis of the center of a given component:

```
Rotate rotateAroundCenter = new Rotate(degrees, component);
```

Using Effects   Once you have an Effect object, you must tell the framework how and when to use it. This is done through the EffectsManager's setEffect() method:

```
static void setEffect(JComponent component, Effect effect,
                      TransitionType transitionType)
```

setEffect() takes the component to be rendered with this effect, the effect to be used, and the TransitionType under which the effect should be used. The transition type is one of the following:

- **TransitionType.APPEARING:** This transition occurs when the component is in the second screen, but not the first.

- **TransitionType.DISAPPEARING:** This transition occurs when the component is in the first screen, but not the second.

- **TransitionType.CHANGING:** This transition occurs when the component is in both screens.

The effects set on the components in this way are set globally for the application. They are not specific to any current or future transition. To remove an effect for a component and transition type, call the setEffect() method with null for the effect.

For example, to install the rotation effect that we created previously, we would do the following:

```
EffectsManager.setEffect(component, rotateAroundCenter,
                         TransitionType.CHANGING);
```

This code tells the framework to use the rotateAroundCenter effect on this particular component when that component is on both screens of a transition.

When the transition starts, the system figures out whether and how each component in the container is changing between the two current screens. From that information, the framework determines the TransitionType to use. The EffectsManager is then queried to see if a custom effect is installed for this component/TransitionType pair. If no such custom effect is set in the system, the library falls back to the default for each TransitionType:

- FadeIn for APPEARING
- FadeOut for DISAPPEARING
- Move, Scale, or Move/Scale for CHANGING

Speaking of the Move/Scale effect, one more built-in Effect that is useful to know about is CompositeEffect. This effect does nothing on its own but instead uses multiple child effects to create a new effect that is a combination of all of its child effects. So, for example, the Move/Scale effect is actually a CompositeEffect that performs both a Move and a Scale operation on the component during the transition.

There are two constructors for CompositeEffect:

```
CompositeEffect composite = new CompositeEffect();
CompositeEffect composite = new CompositeEffect(someEffect);
```

The only difference is whether it starts out with an initial child effect. Additional effects are added by calling the addEffect() method:

```
composite.addEffect(someOtherEffect);
```

For example, the framework internally creates a `Move/Scale` effect as follows:

```
Effect move= new Move();
Effect scale = new Scale();
CompositeEffect composite = new CompositeEffect(move);
composite.addEffect(scale);
```

Creating Custom Effects   As we mentioned earlier, it is possible to create your own custom effects and to tell the `EffectsManager` to use those effects during transitions. The effects provided in the framework so far should cover the basics, but there are many more effects possible.

The API for creating custom effects is fairly simple. There are four main things that your effect might consider doing, most of which are optional:

- **Constructor:** If your effect takes any custom parameters, such as a position to start from or a color, then you need a specialized constructor to set these values. You can see custom parameters used earlier in the `Rotate` example, where the effect required the degrees and center of rotation.
- **init():** The framework calls your effect's `init()` method at the start of any transition using the effect. You may need to override it to create any special animation properties. For example, you can create `PropertySetters` in `init()` to animate any custom parameters during the transition. The `Animator` object that `ScreenTransition` uses is passed into `init()`, so you can add new targets to the animator, such as new `PropertySetter` objects, at this time.
- **setup():** This method is called during each animation frame of the transition to set up the `Graphics` object appropriately for rendering this effect.
- **paint():** This method is called after the call to `setup()`. It is the method in which the rendering of the object actually occurs.

> **Tip:** Most of these methods are optional for `Effect` subclasses. The `init()` method is really the only one that you need to override in general, depending on your situation. For example, the `Effect` superclass handles the `setup()` and `paint()` for components that simply need to draw themselves using the known position and size of the component.

For an idea of how you might go about building a custom effect, let's look at the code for some of the built-in effects in the system.

Move Effect Implementation   The Move effect simply moves a component from its start position to its end position over the course of the transition.

Move defines two constructors: one takes no arguments, expecting that its states will be set up later when the transition is initialized, and the other takes start and end states:

```
public Move() {}

public Move(ComponentState start, ComponentState end) {
  setComponentStates(start, end);
}
```

The animation to change the component's location over time is set up in Move's init() method with a PropertySetter targeting the location property in the Effect superclass:

```
public void init(Animator animator, Effect parentEffect) {
  Effect targetEffect = (parentEffect == null) ?
      this : parentEffect;
  PropertySetter ps;
  ps = new PropertySetter(targetEffect, "location",
      new Point(getStart().getX(), getStart().getY()),
      new Point(getEnd().getX(), getEnd().getY()));
  animator.addTarget(ps);
  super.init(animator, null);
}
```

The logic with parentEffect handles the situation in which the Move effect is part of an overall CompositeEffect. In that case, Move varies the location of the CompositeEffect instead of its own location, since it is actually the CompositeEffect that will later be rendered.

The PropertySetter is a simple object that varies the location from its starting point to its ending point. The setter is then assigned as a target on the animator object, which is the animator used by ScreenTransition to run the overall transition.

For rendering, Move requires no functionality beyond that in the Effect super-class. Effect automatically translates the Graphics2D object in Effect.setup() to the proper location, which is being animated by the PropertySetter created in Move.init(). Effect then renders a snapshot of the component in Effect.paint().

And that's all. Move was implemented with just these methods.

For a slightly more involved example, let's look at Rotate.

Rotate Effect Implementation   The Rotate effect rotates a component around a rotation center by a specified number of degrees. It has three constructors to handle different situations:

```
public Rotate(int degrees, int xCenter, int yCenter)
public Rotate(int degrees, Component component)
public Rotate(ComponentState start, ComponentState end,
              int degrees, int xCenter, int yCenter)
```

The first constructor provides the angle and center for the rotation, but no start and end states. Rotate, like all effects, expects these to be provided later at transition initialization time.

The second constructor is provided as a utility variant on the first, which fixes the center of rotation at the center of the given component. Calling this constructor is equivalent to the following:

```
Rotate(degrees,
        component.getWidth()/2, component.getHeight()/2);
```

The third constructor is the same as the first except that it provides the start and end states for the component. Normally, this version is not needed because the start and end states are determined and set dynamically by the framework.

Rotate differs from Move because it must store and track variables beyond those provided in the Effect superclass. Rotate also needs to expose a public setter method to be called by PropertySetter during the transition to vary the current rotation variable:

```
private double radians;
public void setRadians(double radians) {
  this.radians = radians;
}
```

Rotate's init() method is similar to Move.init() except that Rotate does not care about any CompositeEffect, which knows nothing about the radians variable. It must set the value in this local class instead:

```
public void init(Animator animator, Effect parentEffect) {
  PropertySetter ps;
  ps = new PropertySetter(this, "radians", 0.0, endRadians);
  animator.addTarget(ps);
  super.init(animator, null);
}
```

A simple PropertySetter is created in this method and added as a target to the transition's Animator object. This PropertySetter varies the value of the rotation radians from 0 to endRadians, which equals the "degrees" passed into the constructor, converted to radians.

Unlike Move, which lets the Effect superclass handle the translation to the appropriate location in its setup() method, Rotate must override setup() in order to modify the Graphics state to account for the rotation:

```
@Override
public void setup(Graphics2D g2d) {
  g2d.translate(xCenter, yCenter);
  g2d.rotate(radians);
  g2d.translate(-xCenter, -yCenter);
  super.setup(g2d);
}
```

Here, the Graphics2D object is translated by the center of rotation and back, as we saw earlier in Chapter 3, "Graphics Fundamentals." The Graphics2D object is rotated by the radians that are being animated by the PropertySetter. Finally, it calls super.setup() to perform any other setup steps necessary in the Effect superclass.

Like Move, Rotate chooses to not override Effect.paint() because it requires no special rendering beyond that which Effect.paint() already provides. The component itself, or a snapshot image of the component, will be rendered appropriately using the Graphics2D object that has had its state altered by the rotation operation.

Example: SearchTransition Revisited: Customization

Now that we understand how effects work and how to create custom effects, it is time to revisit our SearchTransition example to see how we implemented the custom effect for the results screen.

By default, a component with a TransitionType of APPEARING uses the standard FadeIn effect. For this application, we want the results to move up into place as well as fade in, so we need a custom effect to make this work.

We can already rely on the built-in FadeIn effect to do the fading. What we need, then, is a CompositeEffect that uses FadeIn as one of its child effects.

But we also need a new effect to move the component into place. The framework has a Move effect already, but that effect works only on components that exist in both screens and thus have a location on both screens to move between. In our case, we want to move a component that does not exist on the first screen of the transition. We want an effect that moves a component from a given location to its dynamically determined end state. We define a new MoveIn subclass of Effect that handles this functionality.

First, we use a variable to store the initial location that we want to move from:

```
private Point startLocation = new Point();
```

Next, we have the constructor that sets the value of our start location:

```
public MoveIn(int x, int y) {
    startLocation.x = x;
    startLocation.y = y;
}
```

And finally, we have the overridden init() method that sets up the animation:

```
public void init(Animator animator, Effect parentEffect) {
    Effect targetEffect = (parentEffect == null) ?
        this : parentEffect;
    PropertySetter ps;
    ps = new PropertySetter(targetEffect, "location",
        startLocation,
        new Point(getEnd().getX(), getEnd().getY()));
    animator.addTarget(ps);
    super.init(animator, parentEffect);
}
```

This init() method is very similar to the one that we saw for the built-in Move effect. The logic with parentEffect is the same as we described before, which handles the case in which there is a CompositeEffect, as in this situation. The animation is run by creating a simple PropertySetter from the startLocation, set at construction time, to the end location, set dynamically by the system, and adding this property setter to the animator. Finally, we call the superclass's init() method to make sure that everything is initialized appropriately for this effect.

Now that we have our MoveIn effect, we create the overall effect that we want by creating a CompositeEffect based on this MoveIn effect and the built-in FadeIn effect. We create this effect in our setupBackgroundAndEffect() method, which is called by the paintComponent() method whenever the height of our component has changed. This dependency on the height of the component comes from the nature of our MoveIn effect, which needs to move the component in from the bottom of the window. So if the height of the window changes, we must re-create the effect to make sure we change things accordingly.

```java
private void setupBackgroundAndEffect() {
    // init the background gradient according to current height
    bgGradient = new GradientPaint(0, 0,
                                   Color.LIGHT_GRAY.brighter(),
                                   0, getHeight(),
                                   Color.DARK_GRAY.brighter());
    // init resultsEffect with current component size info
    MoveIn mover = new MoveIn(RESULTS_X, getHeight());
    FadeIn fader = new FadeIn();
    moverFader = new CompositeEffect(mover);
    moverFader.addEffect(fader);
    EffectsManager.setEffect(scroller, moverFader,
        EffectsManager.TransitionType.APPEARING);
    prevHeight = getHeight();
}
```

The GradientPaint created here is not related to our transition but is a nice demonstration of using a rich background for this simple application.[4]

We instantiate the MoveIn effect with the starting location that we want: the *x*-value is the same as that used for the final location of the results component and the *y*-value is equal to the bottom of the container. These values ensure that MoveIn slides the component in vertically from the bottom of the window.

We create the desired fading-in effect simply by using the built-in FadeIn effect. And we create our CompositeEffect by constructing it with the mover effect and then adding the fader effect.

Finally, we register our custom moverFader effect with the system by setting it on the results component, scroller, with the APPEARING transition type. This tells the EffectsManager to use this particular effect whenever this component is undergoing a transition that makes it appear on the next screen.

That's all there is to this demo. There is some other simple Swing code in SearchTransition to create and display the application window, but all of the interesting transition logic is covered here. Obviously, this application is quite limited in scope, and a real application would be much more involved. On the other hand, you can see how easy it is to add transition capabilities, including custom effects, to an otherwise standard Swing application.

---

4. Never miss an opportunity to enrich your application's interface.

Example: ImageBrowser

The SearchTransition demo was graphically limited so that we could focus on the basic functionality of the Animated Transitions library. But it is worth seeing another application that drives home the point about the ease and utility of the library in a more graphically rich way. The following example can be found in the ImageBrowser project on the book's Web site.

Most of us have probably used some kind of photo-browsing software, whether it is a desktop application or an online utility. A standard control in the interface of these applications is the zoom factor, where you can change the size of the picture thumbnails that you are looking at. Adjusting the zoom is typically done through a slider, which is dragged back and forth to make the thumbnails of the pictures larger or smaller.

When thumbnails are resized, it affects how everything in the GUI is laid out. All of the thumbnails change size, so they all must reposition themselves accordingly. Wouldn't it be nice if these layout changes were animated to smoothly transition between the before and after states of the resize operation?

ImageBrowser is a simple application that reads in all of the images from a directory and displays their thumbnails, as seen in Figure 18-8. There is a slider on the bottom to control the current thumbnail size. As the slider is moved, the thumbnail sizes change. This resize event forces the LayoutManager, a FlowLayout, to reposition all of the images accordingly.

The Animated Transitions library is used to animate the transition between any two before and after screens. For example, we can see the transition as the thumbnails from Figure 18-8 are resized larger in the successive screenshots in Figure 18-9, Figure 18-10, and Figure 18-11. Notice how, for example, the picture on the right-hand side of the top row in Figure 18-8 moves down gradually to its final position as the second picture in the second row of Figure 18-11. Meanwhile, all of the other images are moving toward their final positions, and all pictures are scaling up gradually to their new thumbnail sizes.

Most of the animated transition functionality taking place in ImageBrowser was discussed earlier, with both the SearchTransition demo and the descriptions of the Animated Transitions API. However, there are a couple of important pieces in this application that are worth pointing out.

First of all, note that this demo, unlike SearchTransition, uses a LayoutManager. SearchTransition opted for a null LayoutManager just to simplify placement of the components in specific areas of its window. But in ImageBrowser, the LayoutManager is a key piece of functionality in the application. I certainly

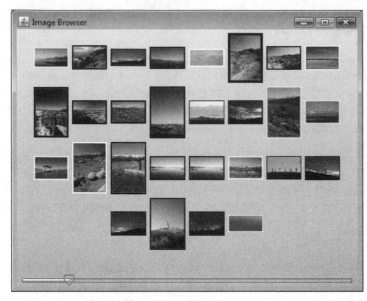

Figure 18-8 ImageBrowser demo: Animated transitions occur when the user changes the size of the picture thumbnails.

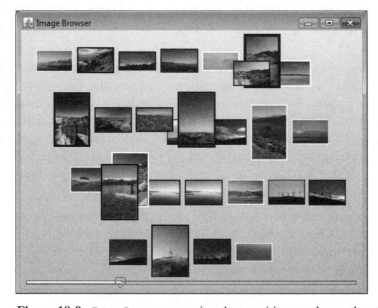

Figure 18-9 ImageBrowser: starting the transition to a larger thumbnail size.

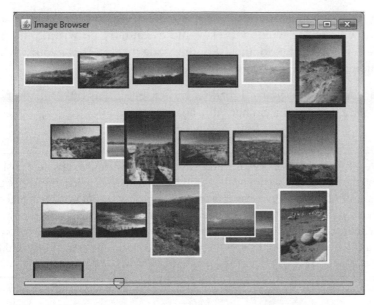

Figure 18-10 `ImageBrowser`: nearly done with the transition.

Figure 18-11 `ImageBrowser`: done with the transition.

don't want to have to reposition all of the thumbnails according to how large they are and how large the window is. I would essentially be writing my own `LayoutManager` in order to do that. So the code uses `FlowLayout`, which arranges the pictures nicely in left-right/top-bottom order.

This is an important point to make. I made it earlier, but it was rather theoretical, since we didn't see it in action. So here it is again:

Tip: Animated Transitions works well with a `LayoutManager`. It uses absolute positioning during the transition to animate the components to their new locations, sizes, and orientations. But it is perfectly capable of respecting any layout system in place in either or both of the before and after screens. In fact, layout managers in the two screens need not even be the same. One layout manager could be used in the before screen, and a different one could be in the after screen, and the transition would work just fine.

Another important point that this application demonstrates is about where the transition happens in the window. In `SearchTransition`, the transition occupied the entire window, but this need not be the case:

Tip: Transitions can happen in any container within the application window. The transition need not occupy the entire Swing window but can instead be constrained to any container within that window.

In this case, we wish to run the transition only on the picture viewing area. The area containing the slider is separate from the picture viewer and is not included in the transition animation.

Another point to make is that we're using a slightly modified version of progressive bilinear scaling, introduced in Chapter 4, "Images." This technique allows us to get very good image scaling quality while also getting good performance. The scaling approach is critical to getting decent performance and quality in this kind of application, since all of these thumbnails obviously require a lot of scaling from the original images.

Now, having discussed why this application is interesting, let's see a bit of the code that makes it work. We won't go over all of the code here, so please check out the book's Web site for all of the details. But we'll see how the most interesting parts work, especially with respect to animated transitions.

GUI Structure

The window consists of a JFrame, which contains a JSlider on the bottom for controlling the thumbnail size, and our custom JComponent ImageBrowser, where the images are shown:

```
JFrame f = new JFrame("Image Browser");
f.setLayout(new BorderLayout());
ImageBrowser component = new ImageBrowser();
f.add(component, BorderLayout.CENTER);
JSlider slider = new JSlider(1, 400 / SLIDER_INCREMENT,
    currentSize / SLIDER_INCREMENT);
f.add(slider, BorderLayout.SOUTH);
```

Pictures and ImageHolder

The pictures in the view are actually JLabel objects with ImageIcons set on them. These ImageIcon objects are created with images that we load in from a directory on disk. For each image, we create an ImageHolder object, which stores multiple versions of the image from the original size down to a very small size. We scale the original down by half, scale that new version down by half, and so on, until we reach MIN_SIZE, storing each resulting scaled image along the way. Here is the constructor for ImageHolder, which takes an Image, stores it, and then creates and stores all downscaled versions in an ArrayList.

```
private List<BufferedImage> scaledImages =
    new ArrayList<BufferedImage>();

ImageHolder(BufferedImage originalImage) {
  int imageW = originalImage.getWidth();
  int imageH = originalImage.getHeight();
  scaledImages.add(originalImage);
  BufferedImage prevImage = originalImage;
  while (imageW > MIN_SIZE && imageH > MIN_SIZE) {
    imageW = imageW >> 1;
    imageH = imageH >> 1;
    BufferedImage scaledImage = new BufferedImage(imageW,
        imageH, prevImage.getType());
    Graphics2D g2d = scaledImage.createGraphics();
    g2d.setRenderingHint(RenderingHints.KEY_INTERPOLATION,
        RenderingHints.VALUE_INTERPOLATION_BILINEAR);
    g2d.drawImage(prevImage, 0, 0, imageW, imageH, null);
    g2d.dispose();
    scaledImages.add(scaledImage);
  }
}
```

In graphics, storing prescaled versions of an original image is known as a *mip-mapping*. The technique is commonly used in games, where textures that are applied to 3D objects in the game may be stored at several different sizes. In our case, as in 3D games, there are two reasons for taking this approach: quality and speed.

The quality issue was raised in Chapter 4. By successive downscaling by 50 percent using bilinear filtering each time, we can achieve high quality for very small thumbnails without the performance hit that some other scaling approaches require.[5]

The speed issue is not just for this initial downscale but also for scaling operations for future thumbnail sizes. Whenever the user chooses a new thumbnail size, the application must provide an image of that size to the JLabel in the form of a new ImageIcon. It could always downscale from the original image, but it is much faster to simply downscale from some image that is already close to the size we need. ImageHolder retains these different scaling sizes of the original image for just this purpose. Whenever we need to supply a new thumbnail size, we simply ask ImageHolder for that size and ImageHolder scales from the most appropriate prescaled version. For example, here is the code that sets an ImageIcon on a JLabel from a new image of size currentSize requested from an ImageHolder object:

```
label[i].setIcon(
    new ImageIcon(images.get(i).getImage(currentSize)));
```

We can see this getImage() operation here, where ImageHolder takes the width desired and returns a version of the image that has been proportionally scaled to fit that width:

```
BufferedImage getImage(int width) {
  for (BufferedImage scaledImage : scaledImages) {
    int scaledW = scaledImage.getWidth();
    // This is the one to scale from if:
    // - the requested size is larger than this size
    // - the requested size is between this size and
    //    the next size down
    // - this is the smallest (last) size
    if (scaledW < width || ((scaledW >> 1) < width) ||
        ((scaledW >> 1) < MIN_SIZE)) {
```

---

5. If you skipped or forgot that section, go back and read it. Or at least remember this message: Don't use getScaledInstance(). The progressive bilinear approach used here, and discussed in depth in the earlier chapter, gives similar quality in a fraction of the time.

```
        if (scaledW != width) {
            // Create new version scaled to this width and
            // scale the height proportionally
            float scaleFactor = (float)width / scaledW;
            int scaledH = (int)(scaledImage.getHeight() *
                scaleFactor + .5f);
            BufferedImage image = new BufferedImage(width,
                scaledH, scaledImage.getType());
            Graphics2D g2d = image.createGraphics();
            g2d.setRenderingHint(
                RenderingHints.KEY_INTERPOLATION,
                RenderingHints.VALUE_INTERPOLATION_BILINEAR);
            g2d.drawImage(scaledImage, 0, 0, width, scaledH, null);
            g2d.dispose();
            scaledImage = image;
        }
        return scaledImage;
    }
}
// shouldn't get here
return null;
}
```

ScreenTransition

The setup of the ScreenTransition object is quite similar to what we saw before for the SearchTransition application. We create an Animator, set some nonlinear behavior on it to make the animation look good, and then create the ScreenTransition object. We use our custom ImageBrowser component as both the TransitionTarget for the setupNextScreen() callback and the container for the transition animation:

```
Animator animator = new Animator(500);
animator.setAcceleration(.1f);
animator.setDeceleration(.4f);
ScreenTransition transition = new ScreenTransition(
    this, this, animator);
```

When a slider event occurs, our class gets a callback to the stateChanged() method. This method sets the value of our currentSize variable, which controls the width of our thumbnails. Then it calls transition.start():

```
public void stateChanged(ChangeEvent ce) {
    currentSize = slider.getValue() * 25;
    transition.start();
}
```

At the start of the transition, we get a callback to our `setupNextScreen()` method, which resizes all of our thumbnails by setting new `ImageIcons` based on images that `ImageHolder` creates for us according to the new `currentSize`. This sets up the next screen that the transition will animate to, and the animation then runs to completion:

```
public void setupNextScreen() {
    for (int i = 0; i < images.size(); ++i) {
        label[i].setIcon(
            new ImageIcon(images.get(i).getImage(currentSize)));
    }
    revalidate();
}
```

One final piece is worth calling out here: We use a custom effect to perform our `Move/Scale` effect on the thumbnails. The library, by default, actually uses an effect that is very similar except for one important aspect: It forces the component to redraw itself every frame. This approach to rendering avoids the image tricks that most other effects use, where we simply manipulate a predrawn image of the component during the transition. The forced-redraw approach happens by default for any `Scale` effect because scaling many components looks awful by default, causing artifacts during the transition. But in this case, our `JLabel` *is* an image, so scaling the component using image tricks works perfectly. So we create a custom `Move/Scale` effect that tells the system that it's okay to use images during the transition via the `setRenderComponent()` method:

```
Effect effect = new Move();
Effect scaleEffect = new Scale();
effect = new CompositeEffect(effect);
((CompositeEffect)effect).addEffect(scaleEffect);
effect.setRenderComponent(false);
EffectsManager.setEffect(label[i], effect,
    TransitionType.CHANGING);
```

The main code for this application is covered previously. But be sure to check out the application on the book's Web site for all of the details. It's a pretty good application to start from for playing around with some of the effects and functionality of the Animated Transitions library. So go play, already!

Animated Transitions: Under the Hood, or How Do You Get Swing to Do That?

Ignore the man behind the curtain.
—*The Wizard of Oz* by Frank L. Baum

Everything you need to use the library is presented in the previous sections of this chapter. But if you're like us, and if you managed to get this far in a book on Swing and graphics, you are probably curious how some of this stuff actually works. There are a lot details about how Animated Transitions does its job. For the really nitty-gritty stuff, we encourage you to check out the source code to the library on the book's Web site. But here are some details that Swing programmers might find interesting about how we got Animated Transitions to do the right thing.

Setting Up the Next Screen—*Quietly*

The first question that might occur to a Swing programmer is, How can we define the next screen with all of the proper layout details, but without the user seeing what we're doing? That is, when `setupNextScreen()` is called, your code will have to set up the components in the container properly, including Swing validation. But doing so normally means that the user would see the components being rearranged on the screen before the animated transition runs.[6]

Fortunately, there are ways to perform a Swing layout validation without causing onscreen updates that are visible to the user. We tried a couple of approaches while implementing the framework, and both seemed to work well.

Hide in Plain Sight

This approach uses the glass pane of the window to hide the details of layout. When the transition process starts, the framework automatically determines the current screen information and creates an image that is a snapshot of this screen, like a Hollywood backdrop with a painting of a castle that takes the place of a real castle in the distance. It paints this image into the frame's glass pane and

---

6. I'd probably call an effect like this a "bug" instead of an "animated transition."

then makes the glass pane visible. The image is opaque so that nothing below shows through. Then the framework tells the application to rearrange the application window according to the layout in the next screen. This layout happens dynamically but is hidden from the user by the opaque glass pane. As far as the user can tell, the application is still in the first screen state.[7]

Hide Out of Sight

The second approach, which is used in the current implementation, makes the application's container invisible prior to layout. This approach works the same as the first one except that the user sees a different container set up to look just like the previous screen instead of the true container for the components. Meanwhile, the framework asks the application to perform the layout changes necessary for the second screen, which all occurs dynamically offscreen.

Tip: The real trick here is that layout of a container can be performed even on a non-visible container.

Once the layout changes are completed for the second screen, the framework can determine the component information that it needs from the container and can then run the animation. Note that the transition is necessarily quick in nature so that there are no unexpected results, such as the user clicking on an image of the application state and not getting a response from the components in that image.

Getting Layout to Lay Off: Animating Layout Changes

A second question that might occur to a Swing programmer at this point is, How do you animate a layout that changes between the screens? This problem seems particularly tricky when there are layout managers involved, since they control component position and size. Just as we cannot absolutely position a component in a particular (non-null) layout manager and expect that position to override the constraints imposed by the layout manager, we would have difficulty animating

---

7. The metaphor of the Hollywood backdrop breaks down here. A backdrop fakes the stuff *behind* the action, but this glass pane trick is faking the stuff in *front*. What we're talking about here is more like the curtain on a stage, which hides what the stagehands are doing to change scenes. But whereas a curtain is obviously a cover over the scene, the image we're talking about here actually looks like the scene itself. So it's a backdrop *and* a curtain.

the positions of components between screens if the animation had to adhere to layout constraints.

The mechanism for this problem is actually fairly straightforward and involves disconnecting the actual layout in the two screens from the animation of the GUI components during the transition. The solution is to run the transition animation in a separate container that exists solely for running the animation. This container is set up with a null, or absolute, layout manager so that all components inside of it *can* be moved and resized absolutely. During the animation, this animation container is the one that the user will see instead of the original application container. When the transition is complete, the animation container is replaced by the true application container, which now contains the layout of the second screen. These container switches are transparent to the user[8] because, by definition, the animation container looks exactly like the application container's first screen at the start of the animation and exactly like the application container's second screen at the end of the animation.

Making Swing Sing: Performance

Besides all of the performance tips covered throughout this book, one of the keys to making Animated Transitions perform well is the use of intermediate images, discussed in Chapter 5, "Performance."

> **Tip:** You don't need to re-render the actual component during the animation if it looks the same in every frame. Instead, you can render an image of the component. After all, Swing's lightweight components are basically images anyway. And if we can use an image instead, copying that image around instead of re-rendering a complex component will gain real performance and will help make transitions smoother.

---

8. "transparent to the user" here means "unknown by the user," and not anything related to graphical transparency or Swing opacity.

    Clearly, we need more words in English to express things in a less ambiguous way. The whole approach to overloading in the English language is not applied in a very systematic way. Perhaps if words were declared `final` by default, it would have avoided much confusion over the years. Unfortunately, due to backwards compatibility constraints, we cannot now change or remove meanings without breaking existing applications, such as books and speech. It may be time to introduce a more completely and consistently designed version, which I will dub "English 2.0." This was attempted some centuries ago in America, but those changes, such as simplifying the spelling of some words like "colour" to the easier "color." are now seen as minor optimizations and Ease of Use changes, and resulted in merely an update release, "English 1.0.1." We need far more radical and useful changes next time around.

Some effects, like scaling, will disable this approach, since it does not work with what those effects need to do. We discussed earlier some of the issues regarding scaling images of components versus rendering components. But many effects, such as the Move effect, use the intermediate images approach with great success.

Summary

Animated Transitions can provide great, simple animation effects with very little effort on your part. Even custom effects require only a small amount of effort, depending on what you are trying to accomplish. Check out the AnimatedTransitions library on the book's Web site, play with the demo applications, and let those transitions roll. Let's get moving!

19

Birth of a Filthy Rich Client

CREATING a good-looking, easy-to-use application requires a lot of work. The previous chapters provided you with the technical knowledge you need to build such applications, but programming is not enough. Visual design plays a crucial role in the birth of a Filthy Rich Client.

This book cannot pretend to fulfill the role of a user interface design library. However, we can at least show you how we created the Aerith demo that you have already seen screenshots of in the previous chapters. Our hope is to deliver tips that will help you get from a design scribbled on a piece of paper to a functional Java program.

Aerith

Aerith was born at Sun Microsystems as a demo for JavaOne 2006, the largest Java conference in the world, held every year in San Francisco. The idea of this demo was to show a mashup[1] of Web Services in a rich client and to show the results in a keynote in order to reach as many developers as possible. The team also wanted to make it look very good to prove how cool Swing can be.

---

1. Chet decided to call Aerith a "smashup," for "Swing mashup."

Between two and three people worked on Aerith over the span of two weeks, with more than 80 percent of the work achieved during the first week.[2] The core team included Richard Bair, Joshua Marinacci, and myself, Romain Guy. We also received a lot of help[3] from various members of the Swing and Java 2D teams, including Chet Haase, Chris Campbell, and Scott Violet.

This short development cycle was made possible by all of the work previously done by the team and presented in this book. Most visual effects, such as reflections and drop shadows, and supporting libraries, such as the Timing Framework, were already available to us. After reading this book, you will find yourself in the exact position we were in when we started Aerith.[4,5]

After a successful presentation at JavaOne 2006, Sun Microsystems decided to release the source code under the BSD license at https://aerith.dev.java.net/.

Note that Aerith is not a finished application. It was developed in a very short time purely as a technology demo. So there are some rough edges to the application and the project. Nevertheless, it is a great demonstration of many of the Filthy Rich Clients effects we discuss in this book, as well as other great Java and Swing technologies, so it is well worth a closer examination.

Running Aerith

To get Aerith running, follow these steps:

- Download and install Java SE 6 or better (http://java.sun.com or http://java.com).
- Download and install JOGL (http://jogl.dev.java.net) in the Java SE 6 extension directory (C:\Program Files\Java\jre1.6.0\lib\ext on Windows, /Library/Java/Extensions on Mac OS X).
- Download and install NetBeans 5.5 or better (http://www.netbeans.org).
- Check out the code for Aerith using Subversion (http://subversion.tigris.org): `svn check out https://aerith.dev.java.net/svn/aerith/trunk aerith` (username: `guest`).
- Open the aerith/ directory in NetBeans as a project.

---

2. The first week included very short nights.
3. And pizza from our manager, Jeff Dinkins.
4. You actually benefit from better APIs, since many of the building blocks of Aerith were in a much earlier stage of development than they are now.
5. Hopefully, you will get more sleep while working on your applications than we did while working on Aerith.

- Resolve broken references (you will need to specify your Java SE 6 installation in the project properties).
- Hit the Run button.

Note: User Name? Upon startup, Aerith requires a Flickr (http://www.flickr.com) user name. Because of time constraints,[6] Aerith works only with Flickr accounts that include at least five photo sets, or albums. If you do not have a Flickr account, or if your Flickr account does not meet this requirement, use the name romainguy.

Finding Your Way Around

All of the classes containing animations and visual effects are located in these two packages:

- `com.sun.javaone.aerith.g2d`, which contains graphics-oriented support classes. For example, this package has utilities to generate drop shadows.
- `com.sun.javaone.aerith.ui`, which contains all of the GUI code.

Workflow Paper Design

Designing your application on paper is the first thing you must do before delving into the code. While this will sound natural to most of you, the process of designing on paper plays a different role in the creation of a Filthy Rich Client than in a more typical GUI application.

Starting with paper design does not mean that you draw UML diagrams on paper before writing the code. It means that you diagram the overall features and workflow of the application to get a better sense of what you intend the user to do. Designing on paper helps you identify where and how to include visual effects in your application.

Figure 19-1 and Figure 19-2 show how Aerith's workflow was designed on paper.

The actual workflow, defined in Figure 19-2, is interesting because it makes clear that no two "screens" can be shown at the same time. It also indicates that the

---

6. And lack of sleep, caffeine, and pizza.

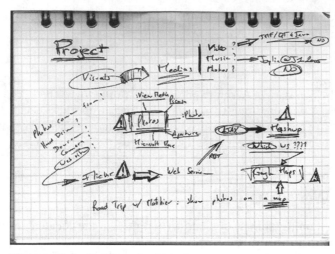

Figure 19-1   Defining Aerith's features.

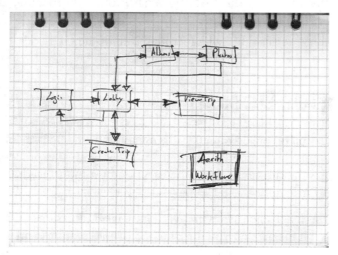

Figure 19-2   Defining Aerith's workflow.

user must go through the "Lobby," or main screen, before going anywhere else. This approach is why Aerith is a single-window application that works like a wizard.

Whenever the user goes to another screen, the new screen replaces the current one, which allows us to implement animated transitions between the screens. For instance, when you proceed from the Lobby to the Albums list, an animated cross-fade is played, as shown in Figure 19-3.

Figure 19-3 Cross-fade between two screens.

Once you have the workflow of your application on paper, you can proceed to the next step, the vision.

The Vision

Note: In this second step, you put paper and pen aside and use a graphics editing application. Adobe Photoshop is probably the one most used, but there are other options as well, some free and some not. Here is a short list of applications that I recommend you try if you do not own a license for Adobe Photoshop:

- The GIMP for Linux; free: http://www.gimp.org
- Seashore for Mac OS X; free: http://seashore.sourceforge.net
- Corel Paint Shop Pro for Windows; commercial: http://www.paintshoppro.com
- Paint.NET for Windows; free; http://www.getpaint.net
- Photoshop Elements for Windows and Mac OS X; commercial: http://www.adobe.com
- Pixel Image Editor for Windows, Linux, and Mac OS X; commercial: http://www.kanzelsberger.com/
- Inkscape for Windows, Linux, and Mac OS X; free: http://www.inkscape.org

The *vision* is a mockup of one or two screens of your application that will set the tone for further visual design. The vision is not a mockup that you will actually implement. It exists solely to give you and your team a concrete idea of the final product. As such, the vision does not need to pay too much attention to usability, ease of implementation, and other important real-world considerations.

In the Aerith project, I drew two pictures for the vision. The first one, shown in Figure 19-4, was meant to be the splash screen. Even though there is no splash screen at all in the final version of the application, this picture contains key elements of the final design: dark color theme, reflections, nice photographs, and gradients.

Figure 19-4   Aerith vision: the splash screen.

The second picture of the vision, shown in Figure 19-5, is supposed to represent the album selection screen. The final design looks nothing like this picture, but once again some key design elements are present. Compare this picture to the final result in the application, shown in Figure 19-6, and try to find the similarities.

At this point, there should be no concern about how you will implement the application, so feel free to experiment with anything you have in mind. The vision lets you express your creativity. You will worry about how to implement

Figure 19-5   Vision of the album selection screen.

Figure 19-6 Final version of the album selection screen.

the application in the next steps. For now, just make sure that your pictures convey what you have in mind and get people excited.

When your vision is ready, you can go back to paper.

Screen Paper Design

The workflow and the vision should give you enough information to start designing each screen individually. You can now start worrying about usability, layout, and implementation issues. Design each screen on paper. You do not need to choose the colors yet, nor think of every single detail.

As shown in Figure 19-7, screen paper designs should give a precise idea of what the screen will look like. However, some details are left aside. For instance, this design does not indicate that the navigation bar at the top of the screen must be painted with a gradient.

Once each screen is clearly defined on paper, you can proceed to the final step before the implementation.

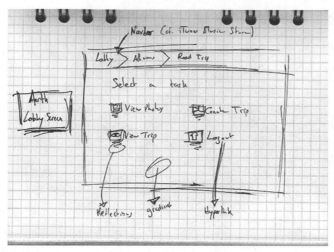

Figure 19-7   Paper design of the Lobby screen.

Mockup

For this last step, you must go back to your graphics editing application. A mockup is a picture of each screen that is supposed to be the final design. It contains all of the design elements and information required to implement the application.

Figure 19-8 shows the mockup of the Lobby screen. You can see that it is faithful to the paper design and reuses design elements from the vision. The dark color theme, the reflections, and the gradients all come from the vision pictures. But note that this mockup also adds its own design elements and details. For example, the blurry title "Select a Task" appears for the first time in this picture.

In reality, the implementation will never be 100 percent true to the mockup. Some design elements may be too hard to implement and some subtle differences will show up for various reasons. For instance, Adobe Photoshop's gradients algorithm is different from Java's, and you will never be able to produce a pixel-perfect conversion of a Photoshop gradient with Java 2D. In the final implementation, shown in Figure 19-9, the lighting effect behind the word Lobby in the navigation bar has disappeared, and the blur on the title Tasks is subtler.

Other major differences can arise after the mockup is drawn. If you look at Figure 19-9, you can see a whole new area at the bottom of the screen. This Albums selector was added late in the process without updating the mockup first. Nevertheless, the mockup gave all of the necessary information to build this screen.

Figure 19-8 Mockup of the Lobby screen, drawn in Adobe Photoshop.

Figure 19-9 The implementation is not 100 percent faithful to the mockup.

From Mockup to Code

Implementing a mockup with real code is the most difficult, and often the most frustrating, part of creating a Filthy Rich Client. Because you let your imagination run wild during the early design stages, you end up with designs that are sometimes harder to implement than your regular Java applications. One thing is certain: You will need quite a few custom components. There are, however, a few things that you can do to ease this process.

Use Layers

Any decent graphics-editing tool lets you add layers in your drawings. Layers are stacked on top of one another, allowing you to view the other layers beneath through transparent pixels.

By using layers, you can separate each design element from the others. The benefit of doing so is twofold. First, you can easily extract the element from the picture. For instance, if you draw a button, you might need to export it into an external file that will be loaded by your Java application. Second, isolating elements lets you work with multiple designs at once. If you duplicate an element and then alter its appearance, you can hide or show the layers to see how the new appearance works with the overall design.

Figure 19-10 shows one of the designs for Aerith with a black background. This background was drawn in a layer called Alternate Background that you can see in the layers palette at the bottom right of the picture. When the layer containing the black background is made invisible, another background appears. This new background, shown in Figure 19-11, is a gradient from black to blue to white, drawn in a layer called Background.

Before settling on the dark background, I was able to switch from one background to the other whenever I wanted because I kept them in separate layers.

To understand the importance of layers in the design of Aerith, go back to Figure 19-7 and try to imagine how many layers I used in Photoshop to design this screen. The correct answer is 47. I used 47 layers to create this simple picture, and they are all shown in Figure 19-12. Each design element has its own layer. For example, a task is made of four layers: one for the icon, one for the icon's reflection, one for the task's title, and one for the task's description.

Layers offer the most flexibility to design and implement a user interface. You must use them.

Figure 19-10 The black background is in the layer called Alternate Background.

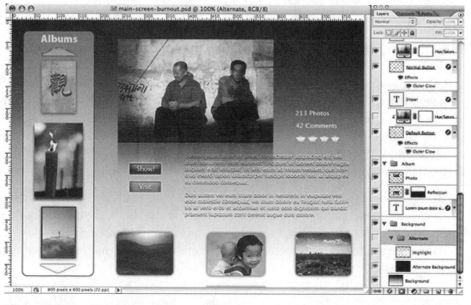

Figure 19-11 This lighter background appears when the alternate background layer is made invisible.

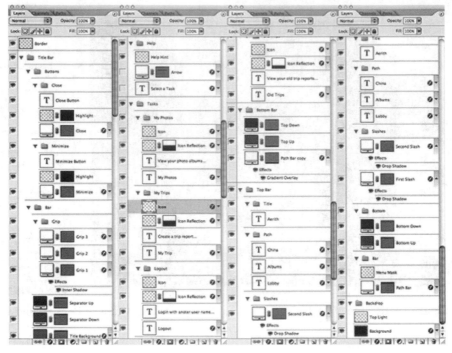

Figure 19-12   The Lobby screen's 47 layers.

Blending Modes

Graphics-editing applications with support for layers let you choose how to blend layers together. A layer's blending mode defines how its pixels are combined with those of the layers beneath it before it is displayed on the screen. In Figure 19-8, I created the lighting effect behind the word Lobby by setting the Overlay blending mode on a layer containing a white gradient. This design element was dropped from the final implementation because it was too difficult to implement at that time.

Because the Java SE platform does not offer the equivalent of most blending modes in image-editing applications,[7] try not to use them. If you cannot do without them, go back to Chapter 6, "Composites" and review the class called `BlendComposite`, which recreates 31 common blending modes in Java that can be used as a `Composite` on a `Graphics2D` object.

---

7. Rumor has it that the Java 2D team is working on implementing some of the common blending modes to make this feature much easier in JDK 7. For now, follow the advice outlined here.

Use Guides

Guides are vertical and horizontal lines that you can overlay on your drawing to help you align elements and measure distances. Figure 19-13 shows one of Aerith's design pictures with all its guides displayed. You can compare it to Figure 19-5 to see the picture only.

Guides are one of your greatest assets. First, they help you re-create a layout grid that can be duplicated with one of Java's layout managers. Also, they help you measure distances between elements. Those measurements must be precisely noted and reused when writing the user interface code in Java.

Note: Where Are the Guides? Graphics-editing applications usually hide guides in the feature called "rulers." If your application provides none of these features, you can use external applications to create guides. Mac OS X users can install xScope (http://iconfactory.com/software/xscope) to benefit from systemwide rulers, guides, and other equally useful tools. Windows users can try Screen Calipers (http://www.seoconsultants.com) or Desktop Rulers (http://www.desktopruler.com).

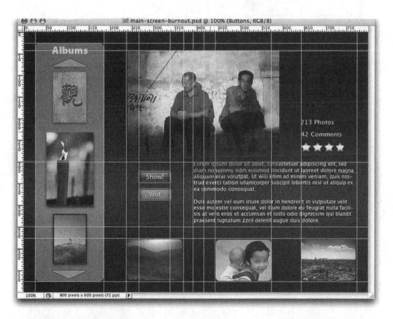

Figure 19-13 Numerous guides were used to build this picture.

But . . . I'm Not an Artist!

And neither am I. Creating good-looking applications requires neither great drawing skills nor an Arts degree. Figure 19-14 shows the best that I can do with a piece of paper and a pen.[8] You won't need to be good at drawing unless you want to draw your own icons. And even for that task, you can get away with poor drawing skills most of the time.

Figure 19-14   Lack of great art skills doesn't mean that you can't design great interfaces.

---

8. I knew that I'd learn some skill from all my time in class.

Designing good-looking applications can actually be quite easy. Here are the only rules you need to follow:

1. Steal ideas elsewhere.
2. Pay attention to the details.
3. Be consistent.

Get your inspiration from successful designs. Apple's products, most Mac OS X applications,[9] and Microsoft's latest products, such as Windows Vista and Office 2007, are great sources of inspiration.

While it is a good idea to find inspiration elsewhere, remember to be consistent. You will always have to adapt your inspirations to your own application and design to give it a coherent and solid look. Too many applications out there take one or more design elements from other applications but don't adapt them for coherence. The result can be quite bad.

Similarly, you must pay a great deal of attention to the details.[10] You must ensure that every pixel is in the right place and be ready to fight with your development team if it is not.[11]

Choosing Nice Colors

Colors are an important part of visual design, but they are very often hard to choose. Unless we are true artists, we cannot choose colors naturally. Thankfully, several tools exist to assist us in this difficult task. These tools not only offer you ready-to-use palettes of colors but also can tell you what colors work well with other colors that you would like to use.

Figure 19-15 and Figure 19-16 show examples of such tools.

---

9. If you still don't have a Mac OS X machine, please go buy one right now. You'll do yourself and your users a big favor.
10. If you have slight obsessive-compulsive disorders, you will probably be very good at that. Engineers should be very good at this task.
11. If you've ever seen the episode of the *Seinfeld* sitcom entitled "The Soup Nazi," then you can probably guess what the rest of the team called me during Aerith development.

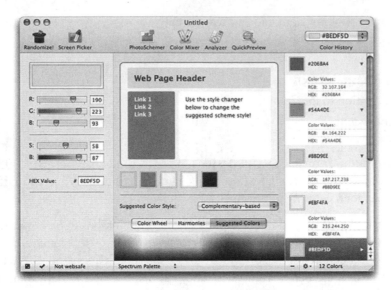

Figure 19-15   Color Schemer Studio for Mac OS X suggests a set of colors
that work with a primary color you choose.

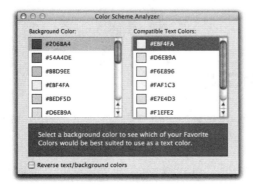

Figure 19-16   Color Schemer Studio can also tell you what text colors
are compatible with a given background color.

There are several tools that you can use to help you choose colors, but here are a
few that we recommend:

- Color Schemer Studio for Windows and Mac OS X; commercial: http://
  www.colorschemer.com
- Color Schemer Online web site; free: http://www.colorschemer.com/
  online.html

- Adobe kuler web site; free: http://kuler.adobe.com
- COLOURlovers web site; free: http://www.colourlovers.com

Adobe kuler and COLOURlovers offer hundreds of high-quality color palettes that you can use for your designs.

Tip: Too Many Colors. No matter how you decide to choose colors for your application, here is an important rule: Use as few colors as possible. Three or four is good, and up to five or six is okay.

Tip: Choosing Colors for a Gradient. In most situations, try to use colors close to one another in your gradients. Similar colors produce subtle gradients that are more aesthetically pleasing than gradients using colors that are quite different from each other.

Read Design Books

Even though the tips should help you, they cannot replace a good book about user interface design or visual design. Here is a selection of books that we highly recommend:

- *About Face 2.0: The Essentials of Interaction Design*, Alan Cooper and Robert Reimann (Wiley, 2003).
- *Designing Interfaces: Patterns for Effective Interaction Design*, Jennifer Tidwell (O'Reilly Media, 2005).
- *Designing Visual Interfaces: Communication Oriented Techniques*, Kevin Mullet and Darrell Sano (Prentice Hall, 1994).
- *GUI Bloopers: Don'ts and Do's for Software Developers and Web Designers*, Jeff Johnson (Morgan Kaufmann, 2000).
- *Paper Prototyping: The Fast and Easy Way to Design and Refine User Interfaces*, Carolyn Snyder (Morgan Kaufmann, 2003).
- *The Humane Interface: New Directions for Designing Interactive Systems*, Jef Raskin (Addison-Wesley, 2000).
- *The Non-Designer's Design Book*, 2nd ed., Robin Williams (Peachpit Press, 2003).
- *User Interface Design for Programmers*, Joel Spolsky (Apress, 2001).

If you have little money and little time to spend on such books, consider reading *Designing Visual Interfaces* by Kevin Mullet and Darrell Sano first. This small book might seem outdated,[12] since it was published in 1994, but its material is still quite valid, and it will teach you everything you need to know about user interface design in a very efficient and pleasing way.

Summary

Creating a Filthy Rich Client requires both a good preliminary design and the tools to help implement that design. Designing a good visual interface is never easy, but the information contained in this chapter should help you avoid some issues, dispel some myths, and work toward a good design. And the tools provided throughout the rest of the book should help you carry through that design to a final product that is Filthy Rich indeed.

---

12. Most pictures in the book are in grayscale because the example user interfaces really were in grayscale, not because color-prints are more expensive.

Conclusion

 $\mathbf{W}$ E hope that you have enjoyed this journey through the techniques of building Filthy Rich Clients. More importantly, we hope that you learned enough to go implement some of these techniques in your applications. We are not just software developers. We are software users, too, and we look forward to the day when more applications use these techniques to write better, more productive, and more fun applications.

Where applicable, we tried to list external resources as we went along in the book. But we thought it would be useful to provide a more comprehensive list to assist you in further exploration into Filthy Rich Client development.

Projects

Although we focused mainly in this book on APIs that are either part of the core Java class libraries or utilities that we wrote on top of those core libraries, there are plenty of other approaches and libraries in the world that are also worth looking into. We list a few of them here, but this is just a small sample. Go looking around and you will find plenty more.

Timing Framework: The book's Web site, http://filthyrichclients.org, will host the version of the Timing Framework that matches that used for the book. The Timing Framework project site, at http://timingframework.dev.java.net, may have a different version that evolves as features are added. If you want to use the Timing Framework and do not need the version that is kept static for the book content, you should check out the latest version on the java.net site.

Animated Transitions: Like the Timing Framework library, the Animated Transitions library will have a static version on the book's Web site so that the material in the book can be used with this version of the library. In the meantime, the project will also live in its own project site, probably on java.net, so that it may also evolve as necessary. The book's Web site will have a reference to the project site, so check there for more information on this library.

SwingLabs: The SwingLabs project, at http://swinglabs.dev.java.net, is known as the breeding ground for future features for the core Swing library. This project has many goodies for Swing developers, from new and exciting Swing components to utility libraries that make Swing development easier. Some of the effects and utilities in this book either come from or will probably be integrated into SwingLabs. Check out the SwingLabs project to see how it can help your Swing development.

JOGL: Java bindings for OpenGL, at http://jogl.dev.java.net, is a library that allows Java applications to use the OpenGL 3D API, including the graphics hardware acceleration that that library benefits from across most platforms. We did not have a chance to spend much quality time on JOGL, but very rich applications are possible with this library. You should check out the current state of this project and the demos on that site that show what you can do with JOGL.

Aerith: The Aerith project, at http://aerith.dev.java.net, is interesting to check out to see how various effects we discussed were incorporated into an overall application. Aerith is also a great example of integrating standard Web Services into a rich Swing application.

And So On: There are many other projects and resources available to you, in addition to the few called out in the book. Rather than try to list them all here, we will endeavor to keep a list of some of the interesting projects and sites for Filthy Rich Clients at the book's Web site at http://filthyrichclients.org. Check the site for a current list.

Java Sites

Besides projects and libraries, there are also lots of great places to find more information on all of the stuff that we described in the book. We mentioned some of these in the text when appropriate, but there is so much more available than the few items we were able to cover. In particular, the Java development community inside and outside of Sun has been very diligent in recent years about writing great blogs and articles as well as providing ongoing projects, such as some of those mentioned previously.

Rather than point to specific blogs and articles, which we did throughout the book, we just reference some general places to go searching for good content:

http://javadesktop.org: This is a great resource for all things Swing. It is a site that lists URLs to blogs, articles, forums, projects, and applications of interest to Java desktop developers.

http://java.sun.com: Most Java developers know this site, at the very least for downloads of the JDK. But there is much more to this site, including forums, articles, tech tips, and general information on Java for all developers. It's a good destination for learning about fundamental Java concepts.

http://java.net: This is a community site for Java. It is similar to javadesktop.org but with an eye on the entire developer community of Java, desktop and otherwise.

http://filthyrichclients.org: The book's Web site has all of the demos from the book as well as the versions of the Timing Framework and Animated Transitions libraries that were used in the book. There is also information on the site about any other book-related material, including pointers to more resources for Filthy Rich Client development.

Authors' Sites

If you are interested in reading more from the authors, assuming they are able to write more after their fingers grow back from the final slog to finish the manuscript, check in with their blogs:

http://curious-creature.org: This is Romain's blog, where he posts everything from cool Swing effects demos to beautiful photography.

http://weblogs.java.net/blog/chet: This is Chet's Java blog, where he posts technical blogs and articles about Desktop Java, graphics, performance, and anything in between. You might also find an occasional geeky joke there.

http://chetchat.blogspot.com: This has nothing to do with Java whatsoever. It's Chet's humor blog. If you've had enough Java for the day and are looking for something funny, you might take a peek here.

http://www.progx.org: This has something to do with Java. Sometimes. Not very often. Quite rarely, actually. It's Romain's French blog with even more photographs. If you can read French, you might find enjoyable stuff there.

(Insert Your Name)

We want to know about your projects. If you've created a beautiful, stunning, and novel application, or if you have a library that can help facilitate development of Filthy Rich Clients, please let us know and send us some screenshots. You can contact us by email:

chet.haase@filthyrichclients.org

romain.guy@filthyrichclients.org

Index